The
SELF-GIVING GOD
AND
SALVATION HISTORY

The
Self-Giving God
and
Salvation History

The Trinitarian Theology of
Johannes von Hofmann

MATTHEW L. BECKER

Foreword by B. A. Gerrish

T&T CLARK INTERNATIONAL
A Continuum imprint
NEW YORK • LONDON

T & T Clark International, Madison Square Park, 15 East 26th Street, New York, NY 10010

T & T Clark International, The Tower Building, 11 York Road, London SE1 7NX

T & T Clark International is a Continuum imprint.

Cover design: Thomas Castanzo

Library of Congress Cataloging-in-Publication Data

Becker, Matthew L.
    The self-giving God and salvation history : the Trinitarian theology of Johannes von Hofmann / by Matthew L. Becker.
       p. cm.
    Includes bibliographical references.
    ISBN 0-567-02720-1 (pbk.)
    1. Hofmann, J. Chr. K. von (Johann Christian Konrad), 1810–1877. I. Title.
BX4827.H6B43 2004
230′.044′092 – dc22

                                                   2004002537

Printed in the United States of America

04   05   06   07   08   09   10 9 8 7 6 5 4 3 2 1

For Detra and Jacob

For me it would be a canon of all research in theological history, and perhaps in all history, that one should try to present what has engaged another person, whether in a good way or a less good, as something *living*, as something that *moved* him in some way and that can and indeed does move *oneself* too; to *unfold* it in such a way that even if one finally takes some other route, the path of this other has an enticing, or, if you like, tempting attraction for oneself. Disregard of this canon, I think, can only avenge itself by rendering the attempted historical research unprofitable and tedious.

— KARL BARTH, Letters 1961–1968

Disciplinae dogmaticae forma non minus historica, quam systematica esse debet.

— JOHANNES VON HOFMANN,
De Argumento Psalmi Centesimi Decimi

Contents

Foreword

My first encounter with the theology of J. C. K. von Hofmann was indirect. It happened a very long time ago when, as a graduate student mainly interested in Martin Luther, I first read about Hofmann in a history of Christian thought well known to American Lutherans. I learned that, with his colleagues in the Erlangen school, he stood for a freer and more progressive variety of confessionalism than the "repristinators." My interest aroused, I was fascinated to discover not only that he appealed to Luther against the orthodox Protestant theory of atonement (penal substitution or vicarious satisfaction), but also that in doing theology he sought to hold together the theologian's personal experience of regeneration, the witness of scripture to God's activity in history, and the context of theological reflection in the life of the church. Hofmann's strong sense of the church, characteristic (with interesting variations) of all the Lutheran confessionalists, I found particularly striking. As a Calvinist of sorts, I had learned something like it from John Calvin and later discovered it again (to my surprise) in Friedrich Schleiermacher, for whom the church was the bearer of the redeeming life incarnate in Jesus Christ.

Although my teaching responsibilities would not permit me to overlook Hofmann, my historical and theological research led me in other directions and to other authors. Still, I never forgot my initial fascination with him, or the reasons for it, and I nursed the hope that some day he would receive his due in the English language theological literature, which included but one modest translation of Hofmann and no comprehensive study of him. In this volume, Matthew Becker has done more than bring my hope to reality. Using the whole range of Hofmann's work, including the lectures on dogmatics that Hofmann left unpublished, he has written a book that makes a significant addition as well to the extensive literature in German. *The Self-Giving God and Salvation History* ranges widely over Hofmann's theology and his intellectual world — and digs deeply, with meticulous attention to detail. Professor Becker's concern is not only to set the record straight on this often misunderstood theologian, but also to continue the critical engagement with his thoughts that began in his own day and to set them alongside the present-day theological discussion, which in some respects Hofmann

xiii

anticipated. Hence, not only Hofmann's own contemporaries, but many of the theologians and movements of our own time, too, figure in these pages — not least in Becker's intriguing, and sometimes provocative, notes.

Next to his deviation from Protestant orthodoxy on the doctrine of atonement (judiciously presented in chapter nine), the alleged subjectivism of Hofmann's theological method aroused the most vigorous criticisms from his contemporaries (chapter three). He was charged with being a "Lutheran Schleiermacher." Indeed, he seemed to outdo Schleiermacher in the famous utterance, "I the Christian am for me the theologian the unique material of my scholarly activity." Theology, he believed, was only for those who had experienced the new birth. No doubt, this attests the degree to which the piety of the religious Awakening in Germany had entered into the method of a supposedly sound theology, which was assumed to be inescapably autobiographical. It may be that Hofmann's intention was not so far from Luther's insistence that sound interpretation of the message of Scripture is impossible without experience of the subject matter, and in our own time theoreticians of hermeneutics have argued that interpretation without bringing *some* "pre-understanding" to a text is an illusion. In any case, as Becker points out, the demand for experience was not the sole requisite of the theological task, as Hofmann understood it. He directed the theologian to the salvation history (*Heilsgeschichte*) attested in Scripture, which is not a collection of infallible truths but a witness to the activity of God that, culminating in the incarnation of the Word, has brought about the reality (the *Tatbestand*) of communion between God and humanity in Christ. This reality continues in the life of the church, and the regeneration of the individual occurs only as he or she is drawn into the sphere of this new life. Another of Hofmann's sententious utterances is: "I am what I am as a Christian only in the church community."

The analysis of the theologian's Christian experience thus proceeds in correlation with historical inquiry into the evidences of divine activity, especially as delivered in the Scriptures. Of course, the problem of theological method is not entirely solved by Hofmann's correlation of the subjective and the objective moments in its execution. It remains possible that the theologian's subjectivity may control what is heard in the Scriptures, and Hofmann has been accused of not in fact dealing with biblical history by means of commonly accepted historical methods — indeed, of making an indefensible separation between *Heilsgeschichte* and the ordinary course of *Weltgeschichte,* saving history and world history. The difficulties can hardly be set aside by asserting that, for Hofmann, *Heilsgeschichte* is not isolated from *Weltsgeschichte* but determines the meaning of *all* history.

Becker's exploration of these methodological issues in Hofmann's theology is properly circumspect, inviting rather than foreclosing further discussion.

Professor Becker's thesis is that Hofmann's theological reflection is regulated, finally, by his distinctive understanding of the doctrine of the Trinity. "Far from being a 'theologian of the self,' Hofmann is among the most important Trinitarian theologians of the past two hundred years." The salvation history of which Hofmann writes is the self-emptying (*kenosis*) of God in history to bring a new humanity into existence in the human Jesus; and it is this "historicization" of God that gives rise to the doctrine of the Trinity, which it presupposes. There are echoes of speculative idealism in Hofmann's notion of the self-differentiation of God in order to be the God of love. *God* comes to fulfillment through historical development. The incarnation makes a real difference in God's being: it means that the triune life of God is completed as the new humanity in Jesus Christ is included in the being of God. In Hofmann's own words, "So that the relationship of humanity to God would become different from what it was after Adam, the Father has sent the Son, the Son has entered into Adamic humanity, and the Trinity has taken human nature as the nature of the eternal Son into its intra-divine relationship." Becker rightly comments that these ideas, relegated to a place of secondary importance through much of the nineteenth century, have come into their own again in the theology of our time.

B. A. GERRISH
John Nuveen Professor Emeritus
The University of Chicago Divinity School

Preface

Johannes Christian Konrad von Hofmann (1810–1877) has been identified as "the greatest conservative theologian" of the nineteenth century and one of that century's "most impressive figures."[1] The most important historian of modern theology calls him the chief confessional Lutheran theologian of his generation.[2] Another important historian of theology describes him thusly:

> [Hofmann] introduced the most important intellectual themes of the day into a rigorous ecclesial theology. Through his theology he was able to explode the bonds of the old dogmatism within the circles in which those bonds held the most solidly. Consequently, his great feat of intellectual activity is near the top in the history of theology. The measurement of his inner freedom toward the theological tradition was greater than that of the mediating theologians (except perhaps Rothe).[3]

According to Seeberg, Hofmann was the only contemporary theologian, other than Schleiermacher, upon whom Albrecht Ritschl (1822–1889) really depended.[4] Ritschl's most influential student, Wilhelm Herrmann (1846–1922), also judged Hofmann to be "one of Schleiermacher's greatest students" who provided "a real continuation of the work begun by

---

1. Karl Barth, *Protestant Theology in the Nineteenth Century: Its Background and History* (trans. Brian Cozens and John Bowden: Valley Forge, Pa.: Judson Press, 1973), 610, 608. Barth (1886–1968) also concludes, however, that Hofmann's theology was subjectivistic and not appropriately grounded in the word of God. See also Barth's comments on Hofmann in his essay, "Evangelical Theology in the 19th Century," in *The Humanity of God* (trans. John Newton Thomas and Thomas Wieser; Richmond, Virginia: John Knox Press, 1960), 25–26.

2. Emanuel Hirsch, *Geschichte der neueren evangelischen Theologie im Zusammenhang mit den allgemeinen Bewegungen des europäischen Denkens* (5th ed.; 5 vols.; Gütersloh: Gerd Mohn, 1975), 5:424. Hirsch (1888–1972) taught at Bonn and then Göttingen until 1945. After that time he conducted research and wrote as a private scholar.

3. Reinhold Seeberg, *Die Kirche Deutschlands im neunzehnten Jahrhundert* (2d ed.; Leipzig: Deichert, 1904), 270. Seeberg (1859–1935) studied and taught at Erlangen and then at Berlin. Richard Rothe (1799–1867) taught at Wittenberg, Heidelberg, and Bonn.

4. See, for example, the many references to Hofmann's writings in Albrecht Ritschl, *Die christliche Lehre von der Rechtfertigung und Versöhnung* (3 vols.; 3d ed.; Bonn: Adolph Marcus, 1888–1889; reprint, Hildesheim: George Olms, 1978).

Schleiermacher."[5] Numerous other historians of theology offer similar appraisals.[6]

Hofmann's influence, direct and indirect, upon the development of Protestant theology in the second half of the nineteenth century was considerable and perhaps crucial. He certainly belongs among those theologians about whom Barth was thinking when he wrote: "[I]n dealing with the theologians of the 19th century, at least with the best among them, we are faced with a type of person that merits our highest respect. This in itself is reason enough for our listening to them even today."[7]

Unfortunately, even though Hofmann's importance has been registered, he has suffered benign neglect and widespread misunderstanding, especially in the English-speaking world. Only one text of his has ever been translated into English.[8] In addition, those few works in English that do make reference to his thought often misrepresent his theology. While many attack his theological method, others have held that his understanding of the Bible narrowly separates biblical history from the rest of history and that his theology is hopelessly idealistic and naïve. Still others have concluded that Hofmann's Christology and his understanding of the atonement are incompatible with the Christian gospel. These judgments about his theology,

---

5. Wilhelm Herrmann, *Christlich-protestantische Dogmatik* in *Schriften zur Grundlegung der Theologie* (ed. Peter Fischer-Appelt; 2 vols.; Munich: C. Kaiser, 1966–1967), 1:324, 327. Hofmann attended lectures by Frederick Schleiermacher (1768–1834) on "Introduction to the New Testament" in the summer term of 1829.

6. See especially the evaluations by Franz Hermann Reinhold von Frank, *Geschichte und Kritik der neueren Theologie, insbesondere der systematischen, seit Schleiermacher* (ed. R. H. Grützmacher; 4th ed.; Leipzig: A. Deichert, 1908), 265; D. Gustav Frank, *Geschichte der Protestantischen Theologie* (4 vols.; Leipzig: Breitkopf und Härtel, 1863–1905), 4:454–60; Friedrich Mildenberger, *Geschichte der deutschen evangelischen Theologie im 19. und 20. Jahrhundert* (Stuttgart: W. Kohlhammer, 1981), 107–16; Louis Perriraz, *Historie de la theologie protestante au XIX Siecle surtout en Allemagne* (Neuchatel: Editions Henri Messeiller, 1949), 129–35; Otto Pfleiderer, *The Development of Theology in Germany since Kant, and its Progress in Great Britain since 1825* (trans. J. Frederick Smith; London: Swan Sonnenschein, 1890), 173–77; Horst Stephan and Martin Schmidt, *Geschichte der deutschen evangelischen Theologie seit dem deutschen Idealismus* (3d ed.; Berlin: Walter de Gruyter, 1973), 226–27; Helmut Thielicke, *Modern Faith and Thought* (trans. Geoffrey Bromiley; Grand Rapids: Eerdmans, 1990), 233–47; Claude Welch, *Protestant Thought in the Nineteenth Century* (2 vols.; New Haven: Yale University Press, 1972, 1985), 1:221–25; and the additional encyclopedia articles: Albert Hauck, "Hofmann, Johann Chr. K.," in *Realenzyklopädie für protestantische Theologie und Kirche* (ed. D. A. Hauck; 3d ed.; Leipzig: Hinrichs, 1908), 8:234–42; Eberhard Hübner, "Hofmann, Johann Christian Konrad v," in *Die Religion in Geschichte und Gegenwart* (ed. Kurt Galling; 3d ed.; Tübingen: J. C. B. Mohr [Paul Siebeck], 1962), 3:420–22; and Friedrich Mildenberger, "Hofmann, Johann Christian Konrad v. (1810–1877)," in *Theologische Realenzyklopädie* (ed. Gerhard Müller; Berlin: Walter de Gruyter, 1986), 15:477–79.

7. Barth, "Evangelical Theology in the 19th Century," 17.

8. Johann von Hofmann, *Interpreting the Bible* (trans. Christian Preus; Minneapolis: Augsburg, 1959). This is a good, if incomplete translation of Hofmann's lectures on biblical hermeneutics, which were published posthumously as *Biblische Hermeneutik* (ed. W. Volck; Nördlingen: C. H. Beck, 1880).

however, are not fully supportable, if one carefully examines Hofmann's own published works.

The thesis of this study is that Hofmann's Trinitarian view of God is grounded in the divine love, which is the cause of God's free decision to self-differentiate God's self in history and give God's self (divine *kenosis* or "divine self-emptying") in history in order to realize in the human Jesus a new humanity. In order to defend this thesis, I argue that the focal point of Hofmann's conception of "salvation history" (*Heilsgeschichte*) is his understanding of Trinitarian *kenosis*, that the eternal God has become historical by "emptying" God's self into Jesus in order to reconcile the whole world to God. According to Hofmann, world history can only be understood properly *within* the historical self-giving of the triune God who is love. Salvation history, therefore, is not separate from history but ultimately embraces and fulfills all history within itself. Thus salvation history (*Heilsgeschichte*) is not a part of world-history, but rather world-history is a part of salvation history.

I argue that the perspective of Hofmann's Trinitarian theology of history is properly eschatological: History is given its unity and meaning by viewing it from its end — not from its beginning — though its end appears in the midst of history and is discernible only in faith. Hofmann believed, in light of his baptismal regeneration and by faith, that God has already revealed the end or goal of history — its unity — in the event of Jesus, who is "the center of all history." In Jesus the eternal God has become temporal to give the eternal Self in love in order to restore and unite the temporal to God.

This study, then, seeks to make a contribution to the history of theological ideas. It introduces Hofmann's theological method, including his hermeneutics and his understanding of the triune God, through an analysis of his dogmatic and exegetical writings, particularly those essays and lectures which have received little attention among German-speaking scholars and none by English researchers. These works include especially Hofmann's 1842 lectures on dogmatics, his essays in *Zeitschrift für Protestantismus und Kirche* ("Journal for Protestantism and Church"), and his extended but unfinished commentary on the canon of the New Testament. A more careful reading of these texts, in the context of Hofmann's other writings, will help to correct the view that Hofmann's theological method is subjectivistic and that his theology of history is determined by a construct that completely severs "divine history" from "profane history." Despite the plethora of German studies on Hofmann's theology, none of these includes an examination of Hofmann's ideas on the *kenotic* self-giving of the triune God as these are disclosed in his 1842 lectures on dogmatics and in his massive, but unfinished, commentary on the New Testament.

But this study does more than just demonstrate Hofmann's historical importance by correcting typical misinterpretations of his theology on the basis of his neglected writings. Hofmann's thought continues to deserve our attention, and for reasons that Barth himself neglected. While this study will suggest that some of the stereotypes of Hofmann's theology need to be viewed with skepticism, one may discover in his ideas a hermeneutical move and several theological emphases that have points of contact with contemporary theological concerns. For example, his historical perspective was tempered by his concern to take seriously the inescapable pre-understanding that every interpreter brings to the text and to reckon with the hermeneutical implications that a particular religious perspective creates for the interpreter of the Bible.[9] Unlike many biblical scholars, Hofmann acknowledged that the interpreter's personal participation in his knowledge and understanding, in both its discovery and its validation, is an indispensable part of interpretation itself. In light of these concerns, his thought appears quite up-to-date next to post-Heidegger, post-Gadamer, post-Bultmann, and post-Ricoeur concerns about the historicity of language and the historicality of the biblical interpreter.[10]

Furthermore, Hofmann's hermeneutical reflections were directly related to his effort to emphasize explicitly the relational self-giving of God as triune within the world-historical process, a self-giving which he believed was related to his own personal life and his ecclesial community. Far from being a "theologian of the self" (*Ich-Theologe*), Hofmann is among the most important Trinitarian theologians of the past two hundred years. His ideas about God's historical self-giving should still matter to contemporary theology, especially in light of recent Trinitarian theologies and *kenotic* Christologies which explore, respectively, the themes of divine relationality and God's self-emptying love in Jesus. Here Hofmann's ideas show similarities to emphases in post-Barth and post-Rahner conversations about the Trinity.[11]

---

9. On the positioning of the interpreter, with reference to Hofmann's importance, see Hans Frei, *The Eclipse of the Biblical Narrative* (New Haven: Yale University Press, 1974), 180–82.

10. For Hofmann's influence on the history of biblical and philosophical hermeneutics, see especially Christoph Senft, *Wahrhaftigkeit und Wahrheit: Die Theologie des 19. Jahrhunderts zwischen Orthodoxie und Aufklärung* (Tübingen: J. C. B. Mohr [Paul Siebeck], 1956), 87–123; and Hans Georg Gadamer, *Truth and Method* (trans. Joel Weinsheimer and Donald Marshall; 2d rev. ed.; New York: Continuum, 1998), 330–41, 523–24. The latter demonstrates Hofmann's relation to the theological hermeneutics of Rudolf Bultmann (1884–1976). In chapters four, five, and six I attempt to highlight some of the ways in which Hofmann's ideas intersect with the hermeneutical reflections of Martin Heidegger (1889–1976), Hans-Georg Gadamer (1900–2003), and Paul Ricoeur (1913–).

11. For similarities between Hofmann's Trinitarian thought and that of Barth and Karl Rahner (1904–1984), see especially chapters seven and twelve below.

The structure of the work is as follows. Part one provides an overview of Hofmann's life and the principal studies of his work. Part two analyzes and evaluates Hofmann's theological method. This part is divided into four chapters. Chapter three examines Hofmann's understanding of the object of theology, the Christian *Tatbestand* ("present factual situation"). This chapter includes analysis of Hofmann's understanding of epistemology and of the distinctive task of theology, which is to develop the Christian *Tatbestand* into a cohesive and comprehensible whole. Despite the important role that religious experience plays in Hofmann's theology, this chapter argues against the view that he was solipsistic in his method. While the paradigm of subjectivity tended to guide Hofmann's Trinitarian thinking, he aimed to expand this category in order to include a communal-ecclesial-confessional, trans-individual dimension. God personally encounters the individual in community and calls the individual to receive faith, hope, and love. The individual in response to God's grace gives expression to faith and hope and seeks to act in love toward others and the world. Chapter four describes Hofmann's theological hermeneutics, which supported his particular conception of the theological task and which formed a distinct component of his theological method. Attention is given to the various fronts over against which Hofmann sought to develop his theology. These fronts included scholastic Lutheranism, rationalism, and historical criticism. This chapter explores Hofmann's understanding of Scripture and its witness to God's actions in history. Since some critics have raised the question of Hofmann's relation to the philosophical tradition of German Idealism, especially his relation to G. W. F. Hegel (1770–1831) and the later philosophy of Friedrich Schelling (1775–1854), chapter five analyzes this question. The final chapter of part two, then, offers a critical evaluation of Hofmann's theological method. The purpose of this chapter is to indicate those aspects of Hofmann's theological method that may have contemporary significance while also pointing out those features of his thought that are less persuasive.

The third part of the present study develops Hofmann's doctrine of God in relation to his understanding of the *kenosis* of the Word (*Logos*) in Jesus. Chapter seven describes Hofmann's understanding of the historicality of the triune God. Because the triune God is love, God is self-giving in history. Chapter eight extends the analysis begun in chapter seven by examining Hofmann's understanding of God's relation to the world of becoming. This chapter provides an overview of Hofmann's anthropology, his doctrine of sin and evil, and the relation of God's love for all creation to God's wrath against sin and evil. Chapter nine extends the analysis begun in chapters seven and eight by focusing on the relationship between the triune God and what this God has done in the man Jesus. This chapter explores Hofmann's unique understanding of God's *kenosis* that is oriented toward the atonement of humanity in Christ. Salvation history (*Heilsgeschichte*) centers in God's self-emptying in Jesus whereby God's active love unites all humanity to God's self. Chapters ten and eleven bring a description of Hofmann's doctrine of God to completion by examining the Trinitarian foundation of salvation history. A major aim of these chapters is to demonstrate that for Hofmann salvation history (*Heilsgeschichte*) is not separate from history but provides revelatory insight into the triune identity of God and the world as enclosed within the Trinitarian history of God. These chapters seek to relate Hofmann's eschatological theology of history with contemporary theological concerns, especially the nature and basis of Christian hope. Since Hofmann has been accused of being "a theologian of the self" (*Ich-Theologe*), these chapters further underscore the ecclesial-communal nature of Hofmann's theology. This third part of the study concludes with a critical evaluation of Hofmann's doctrine of God, his *kenotic* Christology, and his theology of history/eschatology.

Acknowledgments

This book has had a long history, too long, if you ask my wife, though its history is longer than even she imagines. I can trace its beginning to a course entitled "Old Testament Introduction," taught by Rev. E. W. Hinrichs (1901–1991), which I took as an undergraduate at Concordia College, Portland, Oregon. Professor Hinrichs first explained to me the term *Heilsgeschichte*, which he no doubt learned from his teachers at Concordia Seminary, St. Louis, who learned it from their teacher, Georg Stoeckhardt (1842–1913), who had learned it from his teacher, Johannes von Hofmann. I would like to think Prof. Hinrichs would have been pleased to learn that one of his former students went on to conduct a study of the principal *heilsgeschichtliche* theologian of the nineteenth century.

My study of Hofmann has not occurred in a vacuum. In the course of the research for this book I have come into the debt of several persons and institutions. I am beholden to a number of excellent expositions, whose interpretations support or complement my own. The studies by Behr, Breidert, Flechsenhaar, Forde, Schellbach, and Senft have been particularly helpful to me by providing insight for my own examination of Hofmann. I have benefited greatly from their analyses and erudition. While I might diverge here and there from some of the conclusions of these scholars, the present work would not have the shape that it has were it not for these earlier investigations.

At the University of Chicago, where this project took the form of a doctoral dissertation, I was blessed by the guidance, criticism, and encouragement of the members of my dissertation committee: David Tracy, Hans Dieter Betz, and Kathryn Tanner. My interest in Hofmann was sparked during Brian Gerrish's year-long dogmatics seminar, based on a close reading of Calvin's *Institutes* and Schleiermacher's *Glaubenslehre*. Dr. Gerrish served as my academic advisor from 1991–1996, and I owe much to his teaching and example. I am grateful that he has written the foreword to this book, whose theme was his suggestion. I must acknowledge my debt to him and to two other individuals who have had a significant role in my education at the University of Chicago: I appreciate very much the encouragement that Martin Marty, who also read the manuscript and offered helpful criticism, and Richard Rosengarten, the Dean of the Divinity School, have provided me along the way.

While the labor has been exacting, the load has been made easier by the help of many friends and colleagues. Among those who offered me support and assistance in order to complete this project, I must single out Hans Spalteholz. He has been my friend and mentor for over two decades. I owe a great deal of my theological development to him. I am grateful for the many conversations he and I have had about theology in general and about Hofmann's theology in particular. These conversations helped me to think more carefully about the structure and content of the book. Not only did Professor Spalteholz help to improve my translations of Hofmann's formidable German sentences, he also read the entire manuscript very carefully and offered numerous suggestions on how to strengthen and clarify my argument.

I am also thankful to my other colleagues at Concordia University, Portland, who offered comments and suggestions on earlier drafts of the book: Nolan Bremer, Dick Hill, Herb Hoefer, Norm Metzler, Richard Reinisch, Mark Ruff, and Robert Schmidt.

Several other individuals read complete drafts or portions of the manuscript and offered me helpful suggestions: Michael Aune, Carl Braaten, Terry Cooper, L. Dean Hempelmann, Stephen Krueger, Mark Mattes, Norman Nagel, Wolfhart Pannenberg, and Erhart P. Weber.

Generous financial grants from Concordia University, Portland, authorized by the provosts, John Driessner and Mark Wahlers, and my dean, Charles Kunert, allowed me to conduct research in Germany (1996 and 2003) and to take a study leave in the spring semester of 1998.

I owe special thanks to Nolan Bremer, director of Concordia University's library services, and Randy Bush, for their ceaseless work in obtaining rare books and journal articles for me. My thanks to the staff of Pritzlaff Memorial Library, Concordia Seminary, St. Louis, especially to David Berger, Director of library services, for providing me with photocopies of several of Hofmann's journal articles. My thanks to Wesley Smith, of the Office of Archives and Special Collections, Princeton Theological Seminary Library, for sending me photocopies of Hofmann's two doctoral dissertations. My thanks also to Monika Kötter, of the University Library, Erlangen, for her assistance in procuring archival data and other valuable resources.

Rainer Stahl, Michael Hübner, and Friederike Hirschmann of the Martin Luther Bund, Erlangen, were gracious hosts when I conducted research in Erlangen. Pastor Hübner made it possible for me to visit with Karlmann Beyschlag, whose appreciation and careful understanding of the Erlangen theological tradition are evident in his fine book. I am very grateful to

Dr. Beyschlag for providing me with the photograph of Hofmann that appears on the front cover of the book.

Several of the chapters have been previously published in whole or part, and all have been revised — some extensively. I would like to record my thanks to the appropriate publishers and editors for permission to reuse copyright material: Parts of chapters three, four, and six appeared as an essay in *Concordia Journal,* edited by Quentin Wesselschmidt. Parts of chapters nine and twelve appeared as a two-part essay in *Lutheran Quarterly,* edited by Paul Rorem. Parts of chapters seven and twelve appeared as an essay in *Pro Ecclesia,* edited by Carl Braaten and Robert Jenson. Information on these articles is given in the bibliography.

In addition, I am very thankful for the patient love and support, including financial support, that my parents have given me through the many years of my education. Their encouragement helped to motivate me to finish.

Finally, and most significantly, I must acknowledge the loving support that my wife, Detra, and our son, Jacob, have given me through the many years that I have worked on this project. During that time I was often separated from them, due to the requirements of my research, and yet Detra and Jacob continued to encourage me in my work. They truly went the extra mile. Without their love, patience, and ongoing encouragement, and their willingness to give of themselves, I would not have been able to complete a task of this sort. To Detra, and to Jacob, I am deeply grateful. I dedicate this book to them.

Abbreviations

AW   Friedrich Schelling. *The Ages of the World*. Translated by Jason Wirth. Albany: State University of New York Press, 2000.

BA   Johannes von Hofmann. "Begründete Abweisung eines nicht begründeten Vorwurfs." *ZPK* 31 (1856): 175–92.

BD   *Theologische Briefe der Professoren Delitzsch und v. Hofmann.* Edited by Wilhelm Volck. Leipzig: J. C. Hinrichs, 1891.

BH   Johannes von Hofmann. *Biblische Hermeneutik.* Edited by Wilhelm Volck. Nördlingen: C. H. Beck, 1880.

BS   *Briefe von Hofmann an Heinrich Schmid.* Edited by Charlotte Schmid. Leipzig: A. Deichert, 1910.

BWE   Johannes von Hofmann. "Das Buch 'Weissagung und Erfüllung im Alten und Neuen Testamente' in seinem Verhältnisse zur gegenwärtigen Aufgabe der Theologie." *Mecklenburger Kirchenblatt* 1 (1844): 54–82.

CF   Friedrich Daniel Ernst Schleiermacher. *The Christian Faith.* Edited and translated by H. R. Mackintosh and J. S. Stewart. Edinburgh: T & T Clark, 1928.

DBAE   Johannes von Hofmann. *De bellis ab Antiocho Epiphane adversus Ptolemäos gestis dissertationem auctoritate ordinis philosophorum amphissimi pro capessendis honoribus licentiati philosophiae.* Ph.D. diss., University of Erlangen, 1835.

DVL   Johannes von Hofmann. *Die Dogmatikvorlesungen 1842.* In "Aus J. Chr. K. Hofmanns Vorlesung über Dogmatik," by Christoph Luthardt. *Zeitschrift für kirchliche Wissenschaft und kirchliches Leben* 10 (1889): 39–53, 99–111.

DVW   Johannes von Hofmann. *Die Dogmatikvorlesungen 1842.* Pages 379–96 in *Johannes von Hofmann,* by Paul Wapler. Leipzig: A. Deichert, 1914.

ET   Johannes von Hofmann. *Die Encyklopädie der Theologie.*
          Edited by H. J. Bestmann. Nördlingen: C. H. Beck, 1879.

GA   Johannes von Hofmann. "Geschichtlicher Ausgangspunkt für
          die wissenschaftliche Selbstrechtfertigung des Christentums."
          ZPK 43 (1862): 259–68.

GT   Johannes von Hofmann. "Gedanken über Theologie." *ZPK* 46
          (1863): 229–38.

HS   Johannes von Hofmann. *Die heilige Schrift neuen Testaments
          zusammenhängend untersucht.* 11 vols. 2d ed. Edited by Wilhelm
          Volck. Nördlingen: C. H. Beck, 1896.

IPH   Georg Hegel. *Die Vernunft in der Geschichte: Einleitung in
          die Philosophie der Weltgeschichte.* 5th ed. Edited by Johannes
          Hoffmeister. Hamburg: Felix Meiner, 1955. ET *Introduction
          to the Philosophy of History.* Translated by Leo Rauch.
          Indianapolis: Hackett, 1988.

KG   Johannes von Hofmann. "Die Kirche und die Gnadenmittel."
          ZPK 14 (1847): 1–22.

LE   Johannes von Hofmann. "Lutherische Ethik." *ZPK* 45 (1863):
          251–56.

NKZ   *Neue kirchliche Zeitschrift* (1890–1933).

RGG   *Die Religion in Geschichte und Gegenwart.* Edited by Kurt
          Galling and others. 3d ed. Tübingen: J. C. B. Mohr, 1959.

RSW   Leopold von Ranke. *Sämmtliche Werke.* Edited by Leopold
          von Ranke, Alfred Dove, et al. 54 vols. Leipzig: Dunker and
          Humblot, 1867–1890.

SBa   Johannes von Hofmann. *Der Schriftbeweis.* 2 vols. Nördlingen:
          C. H. Beck, 1852–1855.

SBb   Johannes von Hofmann. *Der Schriftbeweis.* 2 vols. 2d ed.
          Nördlingen: C. H. Beck, 1857–1860.

SKS   Johannes von Hofmann. "Schellings kirchlicher Standpunkt."
          ZPK 12 (1846): 157–70.

SS   Johannes von Hofmann. *Die Schutzschriften für eine neue
          Weise alte Wahrheit zu lehren.* 4 parts. Nördlingen: C. H. Beck,
          1856–1859.

SW   Friedrich Schelling. *Sämmtliche Werke.* Edited by K. F. A. Schelling. 2 Parts in 14 vols. Stuttgart: Cotta, 1856–1861.

TE   Johannes von Hofmann. *Theologische Ethik.* Edited by H. Rutz. Nördlingen: C. H. Beck, 1878.

TR   *Theologische Realenzyklopädie.* 21 vols. Edited by Gerhard Müller, and others. Berlin: Walter de Gruyter, 1977–.

WE   Johannes von Hofmann. *Weissagung und Erfüllung im Alten und im Neuen Testamente.* 2 vols. Nördlingen: C. H. Beck, 1841, 1844.

WGS   Johannes von Hofmann. "Wesen und Gesetz des Schriftbeweis." ZPK 18 (1849): 195–226.

ZPK   *Zeitschrift für Protestantismus und Kirche* (1838–1876).

Part I

Situating
Johannes von Hofmann

CHAPTER ONE

Hofmann's Life and Work

Better known among late-nineteenth and early-twentieth-century German-speaking scholars than among contemporary theologians, Hofmann was born in Nuremberg on December 21, 1810,[1] and raised by his mother in an atmosphere of Württembergian Pietism and the German Religious Awakening (*die Erweckungsbewegung*).[2] The Awakening was then capturing the hearts and minds of a large number of people, both inside and outside of German regions, who had grown dissatisfied with the perceived religious sterility of a previous, rationalistic generation.[3] Many began to shift their religious focus from a rationalistic faith to one that centered on religious experience and spiritual feeling.

Central to Hofmann's early life were daily family devotions and the weekly divine services, typically two per Sunday. These spiritual experiences deeply shaped his life. From 1819 until 1827, when he was a student in the famous "Melanchthon *Gymnasium*" (classical secondary school) in Nuremberg, he was introduced to a particular synthesis of Pietism and Christian Humanism.[4] There Hofmann demonstrated a penchant for Greek and

---

1. The standard biography is Paul Wapler, *Johannes von Hofmann: Ein Beitrag zur Geschichte der theologischen Grundprobleme, der kirchlichen und der politischen Bewegungen im 19. Jahrhundert* (Leipzig: A. Deichert, 1914). See also Philipp Bachmann, "J. C. K. von Hofmann," *NKZ* 21 (1910): 909–62; Hermann Jordan, "Beiträge zur Hofmannbiographie," *Beiträge zur Bayern Kirchengeschichte* 28 (1922): 129–53; Walther von Loewenich, "Johannes Christian Konrad von Hofmann: Leben und Werk," Rede anlässlich einer akademischen Gedenkfeier des theologischen Fachbereichs zum 100. Todestag von Hofmanns am 20. Dezember 1977, *Erlanger Universitätsrede* 3,1 (Erlangen: The University of Erlangen, 1978); and Renate Wittern, ed., *Die Professoren und Dozenten der Friedrich-Alexander-Universität Erlangen 1743–1960* (5 vols.; Erlangen: Universitätsbund Erlangen-Nürnberg, 1993), 1:34–36.

2. His father, Lorenz Hofmann, died when Johannes was quite young. In 1855 Hofmann was decorated with the Knight's Cross of the Order of Civil Service of the Bavarian Crown. From that time onward he was Johannes *von* Hofmann.

3. On the *Erweckungsbewegung*, see Otto Heick, "The Lutheran Awakening," in *The Encyclopedia of the Lutheran Church* (ed. Julius Bodensieck; 3 vols.; Philadelphia: Fortress Press, 1965), 1:162–68.

4. Philip Melanchthon (1497–1560) had founded this *Gymnasium* in 1526. It was the first of its kind in Germany. Hegel served as headmaster (*Rektor*) of this school from 1812 to 1816.

Roman historians and a desire to grasp the historical nature of Holy Scripture. He also learned to call upon "the Savior" in prayer and spiritual songs and to read his Bible devotionally.

The German liberation from French hegemony in 1815 occurred when Hofmann was barely four years old. His early life thus developed within the context of the German political "restoration" and cultural Romanticism, when political liberalism within Germany was beginning to emerge and attract attention. From this time onward Prussia would become the focus of German political life, though Austria and states like Bavaria would continue to attempt to exert their own independent political identity and parliamentary structure. This turbulent period was marked by the "sense of 'groundlessness' in the European community after the decline of the aristocratic ethos."[5] The birth and transformation of ideologies in Europe contributed to the uncertainties of the period. Hofmann was especially attracted to the poems of Novalis (1772–1801) and Schiller (1759–1805), and to the depiction of human life in the *Pensées* of Pascal (1623–1662) and the plays of Shakespeare. The combination of striking political events — such as the Napoleonic wars, the year 1815, and the Restoration — with the profound intellectual currents in early-nineteenth-century German thought and literature exerted a decisive influence on many young Germans, including Hofmann. Hofmann's interest in history awakened in the *Gymnasium*, but deepened at the University of Erlangen after 1827. Here he also began the study of theology, largely because of the wishes of his mother. At that time the seventeen-year-old came under the influence of Christian Krafft (1784–1845), a Reformed pastor and associate professor of theology, and Karl von Raumer (1783–1865), professor of natural history and pedagogics. These professors had not been as influenced by Rationalism as had most of the rest of the Erlangen faculty at that time; instead they were advocates of the piety that had been emerging from the Religious Awakening. Reflecting on his first two semesters in Erlangen, Hofmann later remarked, Krafft "led me to the knowledge of our Lord and Savior, Jesus Christ" and "converted me to the living God."[6] Raumer had a particularly profound effect on Hofmann's spiritual development: "It was Raumer who taught me to know my sins."[7] He became Hofmann's mentor and spiritual advisor (*Seelsorger*). Not only did he lead Hofmann out of the nationalistic student fraternity (*Burschenschaft*) to which Hofmann then belonged, but he made sure that

---

5. Terry Pinkard, *Hegel's Phenomenology: The Sociality of Reason* (Cambridge: Cambridge University Press, 1994), 269.

6. Wapler, *Johannes v. Hofmann*, 14.

7. Hofmann, at Raumer's funeral, as quoted ibid., 17.

Hofmann was properly introduced to the best in German philosophy, literature, and theology.[8] Yet despite these significant influences, and balanced by his strong interest in history, Hofmann developed as a "personality capable of independent, self-directed study."[9]

From 1829 to 1832 Hofmann lived in Berlin and worked as a private tutor in the house of the Countess Bülow von Dennewitz (1789–1842).[10] During this time he also attended lectures in the university, though one is struck by his claim that he was generally unimpressed with both Hegel and Schleiermacher, despite the alleged dominant influences of these two Berlin giants on the budding Bavarian theologian. Hofmann remarked in a letter (1859) to his friend and one-time colleague, Franz Delitzsch (1813–1890), that he had attended Schleiermacher's lectures on "New Testament Introduction" but that he "could only endure the course through midterm and never heard him lecture again" (*BD* 37–38).[11] Apparently, Hofmann was troubled by what he considered to be Schleiermacher's inattention to historical facts and biblical details. In this same letter, though, Hofmann also stated that "as a graduate student (*Repetent*) in systematic theology I read [Schleiermacher's] *Glaubenslehre* [dogmatics], which pleased me because of its very consistent procedure though I found myself generally disagreeing with him" (ibid). In his later writings, Hofmann acknowledged the importance of Schleiermacher's conceptualization of the theological disciplines, though he also carefully distanced himself from the latter's theological method and conclusions.[12] Kantzenbach's general remark thus holds true:

---

8. V. Loewenich, "Johannes Christian Konrad von Hofmann," 2. Hofmann was a member of the *Burschenschaft Armenia* during the 1827/28 academic year. On the nature of *Burschenschaften* in early nineteenth-century Germany, see David Blackbourn, *The Long Nineteenth Century: A History of Germany, 1780–1918* (New York: Oxford University Press, 1998), 121–22. The *Burschenschaften* arose in 1815 in reaction to the War of Liberation. These fraternities were highly nationalistic.

9. Friedrich Kantzenbach, *Die Erlanger Theologie: Grundlinien ihrer Entwicklung im Rahmen der Geschichte der theologischen Fakultät, 1743–1877* (Munich: Evang. Presseverband für Bayern, 1960), 180.

10. The Countess's famous husband, Friedrich Wilhelm (1755–1816), was a Prussian general who contributed to the defeats of Napoleon at Leipzig (1813) and Waterloo (1815).

11. Schleiermacher lectured on "Introduction to the New Testament" between 1829 and 1832. These lectures were published posthumously: Friedrich Schleiermacher, *Einleitung ins neue Testament,* ed. G. Wolde, in *Friedrich Schleiermacher's sämmtliche Werke* (Berlin: G. Reimer, 1845), pt. 1, vol. 8. Hofmann most likely attended Schleiermacher's lectures in the summer semester 1829.

12. For example, Hofmann acknowledged the importance of Schleiermacher's "Brief Outline of the Study of Theology" while also stating that Schleiermacher "has only drawn out the outer and inner borderlines of theology and has defined the individual disciplines in their relationship to each other. . . . So if one does as Schleiermacher, one is doing merely a technical job. Now, however, it is still the subject matter itself which entails the scope and the division of its scientific field: So it will also have to come to representation in the examination itself. The 'integrated body' of this science itself will have to appear before us and we may not be content merely to mark the shaded outlines of its shape" (*ET* 1–2).

[E]ven though Hofmann could learn nothing from Schleiermacher's exegesis, he was influenced by Schleiermacher's systematic and methodological perspective. Hofmann as a student and assistant professor
occupied himself intensively with Schleiermacher's theology.[13]

Hofmann makes clear to Delitzsch that only later in his life did Immanuel
Kant (1724–1804), Schleiermacher, and Schelling become important for his
thinking.[14] Here, too, Hofmann states that Hegel's philosophy of history
"ruined in me all taste for his philosophy" (*BD* 38).[15] Elsewhere Hofmann
is also critical of the conservative Berlin theologian, Ernst Hengstenberg
(1802–1869), whose understanding of the Old Testament Hofmann rejected as "unhistorical." The thinkers who seem to have exercised an
early influence on Hofmann's understanding of God include Jakob Böhme
(1575–1624), Baruch Spinoza (1632–1677), and Johann Georg Hamann
(1730–1788).[16]

---

13. Kantzenbach, *Die Erlanger Theologie*, 181.

14. Schelling had taught at Erlangen during most of the 1820's, though he had just left
for Munich when Hofmann entered the university in 1827. Consequently, Hofmann had no
personal contact with him then (or later). Even so, Schelling's influence was still evident at Erlangen. He had been active in various circles of the Religious Awakening (*Erweckungsbewegung*)
and for a time had even served as president of a Bible society and a mission society. Kantzenbach remarks, "That Schelling supported these activities gave buoyancy to the religious life
of Erlangen, particularly to the youth" (Friedrich Kantzenbach, "Schelling und das bayerische
Luthertum," *Zeitschrift für bayerische Landesgeschichte* 36 [1973]:127).

15. Similar in purpose to Schleiermacher's letters to his friend, G. C. F. Lücke (1791–1855),
Hofmann's letters to Delitzsch help to correct false impressions of his theology. In particular
they help to dispel the notions that Hofmann's theological method was solipsistic and that
his theology of history was merely a version of Hegel's philosophy of history, though perhaps
Hofmann overstated his dislike of Hegel in the interests of distancing himself from German
idealism. In these same letters, Hofmann states that Hegelian-influenced Philip Marheineke's
(1780–1846) "speculative treatment of dogmas wearied and irritated me" (*BD* 37). For
Schleiermacher's letters to Lücke, see Friedrich Schleiermacher, *On the Glaubenslehre* (trans.
James Duke and Francis Fiorenza; AAR Texts and Translations 3; Atlanta: Scholars Press,
1981). Schleiermacher's two letters provide a defense and clarification of his reconfiguration of
dogmatic theology.

16. Hirsch speculates that "Jacob Böhme's system may have given [Hofmann] the most and
the best" (Hirsch, *Geschichte*, 5:420). Dependent on Hirsch's view, Roy Harrisville and Walter Sundberg conclude that "[v]on Hofmann's earliest encounter with Jacob Boehme...was
through his chief nineteenth century interpreter...Schelling" and that "[v]on Hofmann had
encountered Boehme early through his study of Schelling" (Roy Harrisville and Walter Sundberg, *The Bible in Modern Culture: Theology and Historical-Critical Method from Spinoza to
Käsemann* [Grand Rapids: Eerdmans, 1995], 147). Hofmann, however, indicates he had studied
Böhme earlier than his encounter with the ideas of Schelling. Hofmann wrote to Delitzsch that
he had carefully studied the writings of Spinoza in connection with his study of the French Revolution. Hofmann's emphasis on the freedom of God over against the world and his emphasis
on the personality of God seem to have been generated by his study of Spinoza. For speculation
on Hamann's influence on Hofmann, see Karlmann Beyschlag, *Die Erlanger Theologie* (Erlangen: Martin-Luther Verlag, 1993), 31; Kantzenbach, *Die Erlanger Theologie*, 197; Thielicke,
Modern Faith and Thought, 245; and Joachim Wach, *Das Verstehen* (3 vols.; Tübingen: Mohr
[Paul Siebeck], 1929. Repr., Hildesheim: Olms, 1966), 2:361.

Hofmann's attitude toward Schleiermacher and Hegel was most likely determined to a large degree by his favorite professor, Leopold von Ranke (1795–1886), whose lectures Hofmann called "his daily pleasure." The influence of Ranke's seminars ensured that Hofmann's theological concerns would have a largely historical focus. Indeed, for a time, due to the influence of Ranke, Hofmann thought seriously of giving up theology altogether in order to pursue only historical studies and politics as his life's vocation. Raumer, whom Hofmann questioned about this, dissuaded him from this option. Nevertheless, the stamp of Ranke is clearly evident on Hofmann's earliest works.[17]

In November 1832, after being in a lower rank among the theology students during his first years, he received the rare mark of "superior" (*vorzüglich*) on his examinations, and was given a very appreciative overall evaluation by his professors. Despite receiving such a high mark in theology, Hofmann did not become a pastor. Instead he became a teacher in the Erlangen *Gymnasium,* where he taught primarily history, but also Hebrew, Latin, and theology. During this time (1833–1841), he occasionally preached from Krafft's pulpit. Later, after becoming a salaried professor of theology at Erlangen, he also served as university preacher.

The improvement in Hofmann's financial situation allowed him to marry Charlotte La(h)meyer in 1835.[18] In July of this year he completed his doctoral examinations in philosophy, and the following month he finished his *Habilitation* dissertation on the war of Antiochus IV ("Epiphanes") against Ptolemy VI. On the basis of this work and the defense of the theses attached to it, he was allowed by the university to lecture on history in the philosophy department as a non-salaried university professor (*Privatdozent*). In this period (1835–1838) Hofmann continued to teach in the *Gymnasium,* but he also worked as a graduate student (*Repetent*) in theology and wrote his theological dissertation on Psalm 110 (*De Argumento Psalmi Centesimi Decimi*), which allowed him to lecture on theology.[19] His primary scholarly interests in this period were the history of Old Testament prophecy and Old Testament history.

Although Erlangen University promoted him to the position of associate professor (*extraordinarius*) of theology in 1841, the next year Hofmann

---

17. Hofmann's relation to the ideas of Ranke, Hegel, and Schelling is examined in chapter five below. For similarities between Schleiermacher's thought and Hofmann's, see especially chapters three and four below.

18. They had no children.

19. This dissertation, which he completed in 1838, challenged the messianic interpretation of Psalm 110, even though Hofmann also defended its Davidic authorship. He did not have to defend the theses attached to his dissertation since he already enjoyed a favorable reputation with the theology faculty. See Kantzenbach, *Die Erlanger Theologie,* 182.

accepted a call to teach theology at the University of Rostock. Here he
worked with Theodor Kliefoth (1810–1895), the most significant theological leader in the Lutheran Church of Mecklenburg-Schwerin and later one
of Hofmann's theological opponents. During this time Hofmann devoted
himself to a number of theological problems facing the Lutheran Church in
Mecklenburg. He also spoke at pastoral conferences and addressed theological issues for the *Innere Mission in Mecklenburg,* a charitable and social
work organization that he co-founded with Johann Wichern (1808–1881)
in 1843. Hofmann indicates in his letters to another of his friends, Heinrich
Schmid (then a graduate student at Erlangen), that when he began teaching at Rostock he had only two to five students present for his lectures but
that the number had risen considerably since then. (The previous year in
Erlangen he had over 100 students present at his lectures.)

At Rostock Hofmann began his custom of hosting a "theological tea"
for his students once a week in the afternoon at his home. The purpose of
these gatherings, in which Frau Hofmann also took part, was to engage in
informal theological discussion about matters that fell outside of the regular
university curriculum. He used these occasions to analyze pressing theological issues, but also to engage such classics of the spiritual life as Augustine's
Confessions and Pascal's *Pensées.*

After teaching in Rostock for three years (1842–1845), he accepted a call
back to Erlangen, where he was made full professor (*ordinarius*) of theology,
lecturing mainly on the Old and New Testaments, but also on Christian
ethics, dogmatics, and theological encyclopedia.[20] Erlangen remained the
center of his life and work until his death on December 20, 1877, just one
day before his sixty-seventh birthday. According to colleagues who were
present at his death, he died as he was reciting the Twenty-Third Psalm in
Hebrew.[21]

Hofmann taught theology at Erlangen for nearly thirty-five years (1838–
1842, 1845–1877). During this time he became the acknowledged center of
what some have called "the Erlangen School."[22] This complex theological

---

20. In 1855, the same year he was honored by the Bavarian King, Hofmann declined a call
to teach theology at the University of Leipzig.

21. Beyschlag, *Die Erlanger Theologie,* 81.

22. The literature on the so-called "Erlangen School" is extensive and varied, but in general
see Philipp Bachmann, "Die Stellung und Eigenart der sogenannten Erlanger Theologie," in
Festgabe für Theodor Zahn (Leipzig: A. Deichert, 1928), 1–17; Beyschlag, *Die Erlanger Theologie;* Hans Grass, "Erlanger Schule," *RGG* 2: 566–68; Martin Hein, *Lutherisches Bekenntnis
und Erlanger Theologie im 19. Jahrhundert* (Die Lutherische Kirche, Geschichte und Gestalten,
vol. 7; Gütersloh: Gerd Mohn, 1984); Robert Jelke, "Die Eigenart der Erlanger Theologie,"
NKZ 41 (1930): 19–63; Hermann Jordan, "Ein Beitrag zur Geschichte der Erlanger theologischen Fakultät," *Beiträge zur Bayern Kirchengeschichte* 26 (1920): 49–68; Kantzenbach,
Die Erlanger Theologie; Max Keller-Hüschemenger, *Das Problem der Heilsgewissheit in der*

tradition centered in a circle of theological professors whose ideas and actions were defined largely on the basis of the experience of baptismal regeneration, the certainty of personal faith, a critical appropriation of the Lutheran confessional writings, and an organic-historical view of the development of the Bible, the church, and the church's Confessions. In addition to Hofmann this circle included Adolph von Harless (1806–1879; at Erlangen, 1830–1845); J. W. F. Höfling (1802–1853; at Erlangen, 1833–1852); Gottfried Thomasius (1802–1875; at Erlangen, 1842–1875); Heinrich Schmid (1811–1885; at Erlangen, 1846–1885); Franz Delitzsch (1813–1890; at Erlangen, 1850–1867); Theodosius von Harnack (1817–1889; at Erlangen, 1855–1856), and Franz von Frank (1827–1894; at Erlangen, 1857–1894).

Hofmann stood out in this circle for many reasons, not least because he was its most prolific author. In addition to writing a number of articles and smaller texts, his three main writing projects were the two-volume *Weissagung und Erfüllung im Alten und im Neuen Testamente* ("Prophecy and Fulfillment in the Old and New Testaments"), the two-volume *Der Schriftbeweis* ("The Scriptural Proof"), and the unfinished, eleven-volume commentary on the whole of the New Testament.[23] Another important work from this period, Hofmann's lectures on biblical hermeneutics, is the only significant theological hermeneutics written between Schleiermacher and Joachim Wach (1898–1955) and the only text of his that has been translated into English.[24]

Erlanger Theologie im 19. und 20. Jahrhundert. Ein Beitrag zur Frage des theologischen Subjektivismus in der gegenwärtigen evangelischen Theologie (Berlin: Lutherischer Verlag, 1963); Hans Pöhlmann, "Die Erlanger Theologie: Ihre Geschichte und ihre Bedeutung," *Theologische Studien und Kritiken* 80 (1907): 390–433, 535–63; Klaus Sturm, "Die integrierende Funktion der Ekklesiologie in der lutherisch-konfessionellen Dogmatik des Erlangen Kreises" (Th.D. diss., Erlangen University, 1976); and Friedrich Wilhelm Winter, *Die Erlanger Theologie und die Lutherforschung im 19. Jahrhundert* (Gütersloh: Gerd Mohn, 1995).

23. *Prophecy and Fulfillment* is approximately 740 pages. *The Scriptural Proof* is approximately 2000 pages. The second volume of this project is divided into two books. The actual number of books that comprise his commentary on the New Testament canon is seventeen — approximately two million words on 5,910 pages! Volumes two, four, and seven of this last project were divided into three separate parts (books) each. Volume nine contains lecture notes on the nature of the New Testament as a whole. Here Hofmann was concerned to articulate the nature of the unity that binds the individual writings to each other. Volume ten contains incomplete lecture notes on the history given within the New Testament. Volume eleven contains lecture notes on the theology of the New Testament. He was nearly finished with the first part of volume eight (Gospel of Luke) when he died.

24. Hofmann's lectures were originally delivered in 1860 but published posthumously in 1880. For Hofmann's importance in the history of theological hermeneutics, see Paul Feine and Johannes Behm, *Introduction to the New Testament* (trans. A. J. Mattill, Jr.; 14th ed.; Nashville: Abingdon, 1966), 22–23. Eberhard Bethge indicates that Hofmann's hermeneutics provided stimulation to Dietrich Bonhoeffer (1906–1945), and through him, to Gerhard Ebeling (1912–2001), after the winter of 1936/37: "The term 'hermeneutics' was little used at that time; few theologians had heard of it. But Bonhoeffer had just acquired a copy of *Interpreting the Bible* [*Biblische Hermeneutik*] by J. C. K. Hofmann. . . . " (Eberhard Bethge, *Dietrich Bonhoeffer*

During his second Erlangen period (1845–1877) Hofmann entered the prime, "the *Blütezeit,*" of his career, when he also became "the acknowledged head of the entire university faculty."[25] On six separate occasions he was chosen to be vice-chancellor (*Prorektor*) of the university (1847/48, 1848/49, 1853/54, 1856/57, 1871/72, and 1875/76), a dignity that he was given more times than any other Erlangen professor in the nineteenth century.[26] According to Kolde, Hofmann's colleagues saw in him a scholarly man and strong leader who could communicate and work well with the faculty senate and make good administrative and financial decisions.[27]

As the principal figure in the Erlangen theological tradition, Hofmann's significance resides in his response to what is perhaps the premier question of modern Christian theology: What is the proper relation of Christian faith and experience to historical knowledge?[28] On the one hand, as a *post*-Enlightenment theologian, Hofmann struggled to interpret a historically-oriented faith in response to the nature of history and the critical methods used by historians when they conduct historical investigation. On the other hand, as a post-Enlightenment theologian *of faith,* Hofmann was concerned to define the nature and basis of Christian faith itself. How, if at all, are God, personal faith, and history related?

The publication of David Friedrich Strauss's (1808–1874) *Life of Jesus* (*Leben Jesu*) in 1835 heightened Hofmann's awareness of the crisis that critical-historical consciousness posed for faith in Jesus Christ.[29] As a serious student of history Hofmann knew it was impossible for the Christian scholar simply to turn a blind eye on historical scholarship and take refuge

---

[rev. ed.; trans. Eric Mosbacher et al.; Philadelphia: Fortress, 2000], 567–68). See also Gerhard Ebeling, "Hermeneutik," *RGG* 3:242–62; and Wach, *Das Verstehen,* 2:357–79.

25. Martin Schellbach, *Theologie und Philosophie bei v. Hofmann. Beiträge zur Förderung christlicher Theologie* (Gütersloh: C. Bertelsmann, 1935), 26. See also Theodor Kolde, *Die Universität Erlangen unter dem Hause Wittelsbach 1810–1910* (Erlangen: A. Deichert, 1910), 372–97.

26. The Bavarian King always served as chancellor (*Rektor*).

27. See Kolde, *Die Universität Erlangen,* 372–97.

28. "The history of theology since the middle of the nineteenth century may be seen as a series of unsuccessful salvage operations mounted to deal with this problem" (Van A. Harvey, *The Historian and the Believer: The Morality of Historical Knowledge and Christian Belief* [2d ed.; Chicago: University of Illinois Press, 1996], ix). Among the many who have addressed this problem, one thinks initially of Ernst Troeltsch (1865–1923). See Ernst Troeltsch, "Faith and History," *Religion in History* (trans. James Luther Adams and Walter Bense; Minneapolis: Augsburg Fortress, 1991), 134–45; idem, *Der Historismus und seine Probleme* (Tübingen: J. C. B. Mohr [Paul Siebeck], 1922). Troeltsch began his university studies at Erlangen (1884/85–1885/86), but became dissatisfied with the Erlangen theologians' responses to his questions about the relationship between Christianity and the modern worldview.

29. David Friedrich Strauss, *The Life of Jesus Critically Examined* (ed. Peter C. Hodgson; trans. George Eliot; 4th ed.; Philadelphia: Fortress, 1972).

in a traditional scholastic-orthodox doctrine of scriptural inspiration and infallibility, as Hengstenberg had done. For Hofmann the problem was how to interpret the basic "facts" of biblical revelation correctly without succumbing either to "unhistorical" biblicism/dogmatism or to the radical skepticism of historicism (*Historismus*).[30]

In view of these problems, Hofmann sought to understand and express his Christian faith by means of a theological method which would correlate a systematic analysis of the Christian experience of baptismal/ecclesial regeneration and personal faith with an historical investigation of the Christian scriptures. Hofmann thought that by articulating the unity between experiential faith and historical investigation he could continue "to teach the old truth but in a new way."[31] In contrast to the majority of his Lutheran colleagues especially beyond Erlangen, who continued to understand the Bible as an infallible textbook of doctrines, and in contrast to skeptics, like Strauss, whom Hofmann thought could not affirm the essential historical facts of the biblical revelation, Hofmann argued that the Bible is the record of the triune God's saving activity in history. Like his teachers, Ranke and Hegel, and like Schelling, Hofmann asserted that the Bible is "the monument of a history" (*SBb* 1:25), a history of divine redemption or salvation history (*Heilsgeschichte*).[32] Christianity, then, is not a matter of subscribing

---

30. "Historicism" (*Historismus*) has had multiple meanings in the nineteenth and twentieth centuries. For example, Johann Herder (1744–1803), Hegel, August Comte (1798–1857), and Karl Marx (1818–1883) are generally considered to have provided classic examples of *Historismus*, despite their differences from each other in their respective understandings of history. Certainly, Troeltsch's understanding of *Historismus* was quite different from Ranke's, whose own understanding of the empirical nature of "universal-world history" differed from Hegel's concept of "mind/spirit" (*Geist*). On the question of the latter relationship, see especially Ernst Simon, *Ranke und Hegel* (Munich: Oldenbourg, 1928), 54–79, 119–35. While earlier German historians, like Ranke, recognized "the historical character of all cognitions and values," they saw in "universal history" or "world history" "the expression of real value and divine will." In contrast, later German "historicists" emphasized that because all existence is an historical flux, "the historical character of all human ideas, ideals, and institutions threatens to destroy the whole world of values" (Georg Iggers, *The German Conception of History: The National Tradition of Historical Thought from Herder to the Present* [2d rev. ed.; Hanover, New Hampshire: Wesleyan University Press, 1983], 297–98; see also ibid., 29–43). In addition to Iggers, see Hans-Georg Gadamer, "Historismus," in *RGG* 3:369–71; Maurice Mandelbaum, *History, Man, & Reason: A Study in Nineteenth-Century Thought* (Baltimore: Johns Hopkins Press, 1971); and Friedrich Meinecke, *Historism* (trans. J. E. Anderson; London: Routledge and Kegan Paul, 1972).

31. See Johannes von Hofmann, *Schutzschriften für eine neue Weise alte Wahrheit zu lehren* (4 parts; Nördlingen: C. H. Beck, 1856–1859). Hofmann's "Defensive Writings for a New Way to Teach Old Truth" articulate and clarify his understanding of the atonement in light of his redefinition of theology.

32. The German word *Heilsgeschichte* is difficult to translate into English. The word *Heil* can mean "whole," "complete," "integral," "intact," "sound," "hale," or "well-being," as in "good condition," or "not broken." In a theological context, *Heil* is often translated as "redemption" or "salvation"; however these words do not capture the full sense of the word as Hofmann used it in his writings. "History of God's blessing for humanity," "history of God's

to ahistorical doctrines, nor does it seek to perpetuate "fictional myths"; rather, it is a personal experience, and at the same time a *Tatbestand*, a "given situation" or a "given subject matter" mediated to the individual Christian by Christ through the documents (Scripture) and sacramental activities of an historical community (the church).[33] Hofmann's peculiar form of "faith seeking understanding" (*fides quaerens intellectum*) led him to define theology as that discipline which is born out of the Christian theologian's own desire to understand and give expression to this *Tatbestand*, i.e., that which makes the Christian a Christian.

For Hofmann the term *Tatbestand* ("present factual situation") attempts to unite the uniquely personal experience of individual Christian faith with that which has created and established that faith. Hofmann, therefore, used the word *Tatbestand* to provide a more "objective," if also a more dynamic, grounding to his personal experience of regeneration and faith. He stressed that the experience which the theologian analyzes is not "self-generated"; rather, it is an experience of the self, grounded outside of the self. According to Hofmann, systematic theology does not provide a "description of the Christian religious-pious feeling," as in Schleiermacher's theological program, but gives "a development of the simple *Tatbestand* that makes the Christian into the Christian" (*SBb* 1:11). The *Tatbestand* of Christianity distinguishes Christianity from that which is non-Christian.

Thus, Christian theology in the post-Enlightenment period, according to Hofmann, is primarily the "self-expression" or even the "self-unfolding" of the Christian theologian's understanding of the personal-historical relationship between God and humanity in Jesus Christ. Hofmann thus shows that he was attempting to rethink Christian theology in light of the "aims of the new epoch" of modernity.[34] These "aims" centered in the desire to find an adequate synthesis of subjective freedom and natural necessity, i.e., to find a solution to the problem of uniting radical human autonomy with

---

relationship with humanity," "history of God's victory over sin and death" are possible ways of construing *Heilsgeschichte* as Hofmann used the term. In this essay the word *Heilsgeschichte* is either left untranslated or translated as "salvation history." Hofmann also uses the similar expression, *"heilige Geschichte,"* which will be translated as "holy history" or "divine history."

33. *Tatbestand* is a very important word in Hofmann's theology, though it, too, is difficult to translate. "Given situation," "subject matter," "given state of affairs," "given reality," are possible ways of translating it. For Hofmann *Tatbestand* carries a far broader meaning than "fact." In this study *Tatbestand* will either be left untranslated or translated as "given situation."

34. Charles Taylor, *Hegel* (Cambridge: Cambridge University Press, 1975), 15, 17. See also idem, *Sources of the Self: The Making of the Modern Identity* (Cambridge: Harvard University Press, 1989), 368–90. Taylor describes the growing sense of the importance of "self-expression" and "the unfolding of self" in the late-eighteenth century, but also the need for the positing of some kind of cosmic subjectivity that would provide the unity between human individuals and the natural world.

the world of nature. While Hofmann believed that the "self-expression" of his Christian faith has its origin in the trans-subjectivity of the triune God's own "self-expression," the fact that Hofmann spoke of Christianity as a matter of "self-expression" and "self-unfolding" indicates he was thinking within "the new epoch," marked by "the expressivist turn" or "the turn to the self."

In light of this new epoch, Hofmann's redefinition of the theological task led him to break with the Lutheran orthodox tradition and to formulate a revisionist understanding of God (specifically the triune God's activity in history), of the person and work of Jesus (the *kenosis* or "self-emptying" of the second person of the Trinity in Jesus), and of the authority and purpose of the Bible (i.e., as the witness to God's actions in history).

Finally, many other activities filled Hofmann's life beyond his university responsibilities. He was active in both ecclesiastical and civic/political endeavors. In union with Wichern he conducted welfare work and social ministry and was active in several missionary societies. He served on the Bavarian Central Committee for Foreign Missions, he was secretary of the Erlangen Women's Guild, and he was a co-founder of the women's shelter in Erlangen.[35] He was a regular contributor to, and later editor of, *Zeitschrift für Protestantismus und Kirche* (1846–1876), a major confessional Lutheran theological journal, and a contributor to *Wochenschrift der Fortschrittspartei in Bayern*, the magazine of the liberal political party in which he was a leading participant.[36] Wapler remarks that "Hofmann the politician was born" in the revolutionary days of 1847/48, when he was also first elected vice-chancellor of the university.[37] After this time he was active in both city and regional political life. In 1856 he was honored as "esteemed citizen of the city of Erlangen." From 1863 to 1869 he served in the Bavarian Parliament as a representative of the "Progressive Party," whose main political goals were the formation of a unified German state (a constitutional government of elected representatives), the cultivation of individual rights and freedoms, and the defense of the separation between

---

35. To give some idea of the size of the Lutheran Church in Bavaria during Hofmann's second Erlangen period, there were 1,165 pastors, 1,414 congregations, and 1,283,867 men and women who claimed membership in the Bavarian Lutheran Church. This data is from an 1862 census, cited in John Groh, *Nineteenth Century German Protestantism: The Church as Social Model* (Washington, D.C.: University Press of America, 1982), x.

36. The stated purpose of the "Journal for Protestantism and Church" was to interpret the Lutheran Confessions in a scholarly manner. In addition, the editors sought to defend the Lutheran confession of faith against perceived weaknesses and errors in other church bodies. See H. Biener, "Die 'Zeitschrift für Protestantismus und Kirche' (1838–1876) in ihrer Entwicklung," *Zeitschrift für bayerische Kirchengeschichte* 55 (1986): 113–57.

37. Wapler, *Johannes v. Hofmann*, 174.

church and state.[38] In 1863, he co-founded the Schleswig-Holstein Society, a political organization in Bavaria that sought to defend the right of self-determination of Schleswiger over against the competing aims of the major German powers of Prussia and Austria. This political group continued to level pressure against Otto von Bismarck's policies and actions, even after the annexation of Schleswig-Holstein in 1866 and the creation of the North German Federation the following year.[39] Needless to say, Hofmann's development as a political liberal (who favored a constitutional monarchy) was not in step with the majority of German theologians at this time, especially in relation to the pro-monarchical "throne and altar" position of Hengstenberg.[40]

Clearly Hofmann was "an uncommonly active and many-sided man."[41] He was "a successful teacher, a highly esteemed conversationalist, a friend of music and literature."[42] He is a good example of that "encyclopedic" theologian who is actively involved in what David Tracy calls "the three publics of theology: society, academy, and the church" and the three disciplines of theology: systematic, historical (exegesis and church history), and practical-ethical.[43] Hofmann's most famous student, Theodor Zahn (1838–1933), provides an apt concluding portrait:

> I do not remember ever being bored in one of his lectures during the three semesters of my study in Erlangen. To imitate him was never a desire on my part, and he never encouraged that kind of thing either, i.e., to collect students about himself to repeat and propagate the formulas of the master. I consider it to be one of the happiest divine providences of my life, however, that I was able to have a continuous

---

38. See Wilfried Behr, *Politischer Liberalismus und kirchliches Christentum: Studien zum Zusammenhang von Theologie und Politik bei Johann Christian Konrad von Hofmann* (Stuttgart: Calwer, 1995), 195–314. Behr's is the only extensive treatment of the relation of Hofmann's theological/ethical orientation to his political worldview and activity. Hofmann rejected the notion of a "Christian state," which he considered to be a contradiction of terms and contrary to Christian freedom and the Christian distinction between law and gospel. But while Hofmann denied that there should be such a thing as a "Christian state" or "Christian politics," he did emphasize that political responsibility develops as an ethical responsibility of one's Christian life. See also Wapler, *Johannes v. Hofmann*, 297.

39. See Behr, *Politischer Liberalismus*, 247ff.

40. Kantzenbach, *Die Erlanger Theologie*, 188. For evidence of this assessment, see Theodor Kliefoth, "Zwei politische Theologen: Dr. Daniel Schenkel in Heidelberg und Dr. J. Chr. K. von Hofmann in Erlangen," *Theologische Zeitschrift* 5 (1864): 651–778. See also Friedrich Kantzenbach, "Johannes von Hofmann und der politische Liberalismus," *Lutherische Monatschrift* 4 (1965): 587–93; and Karl Steck, "Der Erlanger Hofmann als politischer Theologe," in *Richte unsere Füsse auf den Weg des Friedens. Festschrift für Helmut Gollwitzer* (ed. A. Bandis; Munich: Kaiser, 1970), 419–31.

41. Barth, *Protestant Theology*, 602.

42. Mildenberger, "Hofmann," *TR* 15:477.

43. See David Tracy, *The Analogical Imagination* (New York: Crossroad, 1987), 3–98.

good relationship with this uncommon man from the day I met him to his death. In conversation with students he was as discreet as he was casual. He refused invitations to the parties of the academic community in principle, not only to save time and labor, but especially because he wanted to remain equally accessible to all students. If one visited him during his office hour, in order to desire advice on private study or enlightenment about a problem touched on by him in one of his lectures, he did not refuse this.[44]

44. Theodor Zahn, "Lebenserinnerungen Theodor Zahns, 1838–1868," ed. Friedrich Hauck, *Zeitschrift für bayerische Kirchengeschichte* 20 (1851): 92–93; see also idem, *Johann Chr. K. von Hofmann: Rede zur Feier seines hundertsten Geburtstages in der Aula der Friederico-Alexandrina am 16. Dezember 1910 gehalten* (Leipzig: Deichert, 1911), 16–19.

CHAPTER TWO

Basic Interpretations
of Hofmann's Theology

The difficult nature of Hofmann's writings is probably the main reason his theology has been largely avoided or dismissed with clichés.[1] Many of his "sentences" run to more than half a page. Some are even longer. His frequent use of Hebrew, Aramaic, Greek, Latin, and old German, and his penchant for neologisms (for example, *Tatbestand, Selbstbetätigung*), compound the challenge of comprehending his ideas. Another reason for his neglect is simply the scope of his theological productivity. In this regard, Hofmann's major works, including his seventeen volumes of exegetical reflections, are perhaps in the same category as Barth's *Church Dogmatics*. Very few people, on either side of the Atlantic, have been inclined to work their way carefully through such multi-volume projects.

A number of important studies of the history of nineteenth-century biblical hermeneutics and exegesis fail to mention Hofmann.[2] A few scholars, if they do recognize Hofmann's contribution, incorrectly categorize him with the confessionalists Hofmann opposed, as though he too had "reactionary tendencies" that led him "to refuse entirely to face the challenge to theology of scientific criticism."[3] One scholar confuses Hengstenberg with

---

1. Delitzsch once wrote to Hofmann, "What an unknown quantity you are and what a work of Sisyphus it is for the newer theology to assess you adequately!" (*BD* 66). Hofmann is "a difficult puzzle to solve," which is to be compared with "a picture that is veiled" (Zahn, *Johann Chr. K. von Hofmann,* 4).

2. See, for example, William Baird, *History of New Testament Research* (vol. 1; Minneapolis: Augsburg Fortress, 1992); Werner Jeanrond, *Theological Hermeneutics: Development and Significance* (New York: Crossroad, 1991); Werner Georg Kümmel, *The New Testament: The History of the Investigation of its Problems* (trans. S. Maclean Gilmour and Howard Clark Kee; Nashville: Abingdon, 1972); Robert Morgan and John Barton, *Biblical Interpretation* (Oxford: Oxford University Press, 1988); and Stephen Neill, *The Interpretation of the New Testament: 1861–1961* (Oxford: Oxford University Press, 1964). Truly surprising is the absence of any mention of Hofmann's thought in *Studies in Lutheran Hermeneutics* (ed. John Reumann; Philadelphia: Fortress, 1979).

3. Peter C. Hodgson, *The Formation of Historical Theology* (New York: Harper and Row, 1966), 85. Hodgson repeats Ferdinand Christian Baur's (1792–1860) criticism of confessional theologians, though he neglects to mention Baur's positive appraisal of Hofmann's creativity. While Baur criticized Hofmann for merely holding to the "factuality of the Church" and for

Hofmann![4] Yet labels such as "biblicist," "repristinator," or "confession-alist" do not adequately define Hofmann's theological program, nor do they account for Hofmann's strident criticisms of both Hengstenberg on the one hand and Strauss on the other. Hofmann's Trinitarian understanding of *kenosis* alone is sufficient to distinguish him from the usual categorizations of theologians between Schleiermacher and Ritschl.

Perhaps part of the confusion about Hofmann's place in the history of theology, at least within the English-speaking world, is due to the fact that only one work of Hofmann's has ever been translated into English.[5] Another factor is the dearth of studies in English on Hofmann's theology. To date, only one significant examination of Hofmann's theology has been published in English, the important dissertation by Gerhard Forde, which examines Hofmann's understanding of the atonement in the context of the German Lutheran controversy over law and gospel in the mid-nineteenth and early-twentieth centuries.[6] As the bibliography below demonstrates, the critical

---

regarding the "ecclesiastical consciousness" as the limit at which all "scientific denials" must break down, he also recognized that Hofmann displayed a kind of freedom over against ec-clesial tradition. Baur understood that the Erlangen theologians were significantly different from the other confessional Lutherans in Germany at the time. In particular, he recognized that Hofmann's *Der Schriftbeweis* represented a significant "deviation" from orthodox Lu-theran theology, particularly with regard to the person and work of Christ. "It is a strange occurrence that in such an orthodox faculty, as Erlangen certainly is, such a deviation from traditional church doctrine has come to light" (Ferdinand Christian Baur, *Kirchengeschichte des neunzehnten Jahrhunderts* [ed. Eduard Zeller; Tübingen: Fues, 1862], 403, 414).

4. S. J. De Vries, "Biblical Criticism," in *The Interpreter's Dictionary of the Bible* (ed. George A. Buttrick et al.; New York: Abingdon, 1962), 1:415.

5. Unfortunately, the translator of Hofmann's *Biblische Hermeneutik* mistranslates the word *Tatbestand* as "fact." As will become apparent, Hofmann's understanding of *Tatbe-stand* implies a richer and more dynamic meaning than mere "fact." Preus's dissertation on Hofmann's hermeneutics did help to bring Hofmann to the attention of American biblical scholars in the mid-twentieth century. See Christian Preus, "The Theology of Johan [sic] Chris-tian Konrad von Hofmann with Special Reference to His Hermeneutical Principles" (Th.D. diss., Princeton Theological Seminary, 1948).

6. Gerhard Forde, *The Law-Gospel Debate* (Minneapolis: Augsburg, 1969). In addition to Forde's and Preus's dissertations one must also note the following studies that have appeared in English: Sierd Woudstra, "Old Testament and Holy History: An Analysis and Evaluation of the Views of Joh. Chr. K. von Hofmann" (Th.D. diss., Westminster Theological Semi-nary, 1963); Paul Johnston, "An Assessment of the Educational Philosophy of Johann Michael Reu, Using the Hermeneutical Paradigms of J. F. Herbart and J. C. K. von Hofmann and the Erlangen School" (Ed.D. diss., University of Illinois — Urbana, 1989); and Samuel Mor-gan Powell, "The Doctrine of the Trinity in Nineteenth-Century German Protestant Theology: Philipp Marheineke, Isaak Dorner, Johann von Hofmann, and Alexander Schweizer" (Ph.D. diss., Claremont, 1987). Woudstra concludes that Hofmann's theological position is inadequate because of its "experiential" and "subjective" basis and because Hofmann departs from the conservative Presbyterian doctrine of "the plenary and inerrant inspiration" and infallibility of the Bible (as confessed in the 1561 Belgic Confession, no less!). According to Woudstra, Hof-mann's "most basic failure was this rejection of the Bible" (ibid., 59). The present study will show, however, that Woudstra and others have misunderstood Hofmann's theological method. Johnston merely summarizes (apparently on the basis of Preus, Forde, and Wendebourg) Hof-mann's hermeneutical principles as a prelude to his study of Reu's theological pedagogics. While

study of Hofmann's theology has been much more extensive among German-speaking scholars, though "Hofmann is difficult, even for Germans!"[7]

In general, there are three main issues in Hofmann's theology that have been important to twentieth-century Christian theology: (a) his theological method, especially the role of experience in theology, and his biblical hermeneutics; (b) his understanding of the Bible as a witness to God's redemptive activity in history (*Heilsgeschichte*); and (c) his understanding of the atonement of Christ as the central event of this divine redemptive activity in history. While a detailed review of all of the pertinent studies is beyond the scope of this chapter, the prevailing scholarly conclusions about these issues in Hofmann's thought will be addressed.

Theological Method

Many scholars accuse Hofmann of overstating the place of subjectivity in theology. In this typical interpretation, Hofmann is guilty of trying to deduce the entire content of salvation out of his personal experience of regeneration. A chief "proof-text" for this typical interpretation is Hofmann's famous statement that "I the Christian am for me the theologian the unique material of my scholarly activity" (*SBb* 1:10). Many have concluded on the basis of their reading of this one passage that the influence of speculative idealism fooled Hofmann into thinking he could begin theological reflection with his spiritual experience and develop from that experience an entire theological system. Though Kliefoth was the first to raise this charge against Hofmann, a host of others have done the same.[8] For example, Hofmann's colleague, Delitzsch, argued that

> . . . no theologian can draw out of his consciousness of faith, out of the
> life of faith as such, the whole variety of the past, present, and future of

---

Powell is to be commended for recognizing Hofmann as an important Trinitarian thinker, his study does not attend carefully to Hofmann's notion of *Tatbestand* (Powell translates this word as "fact") which leads Powell to a deficient understanding of Hofmann's concept of faith. This deficiency in turn leads Powell to conclude that Hofmann's doctrine of God is very similar to Schleiermacher's. This conclusion is untenable, however, given the Trinitarian framework of Hofmann's unique doctrine of *kenosis*. None of the above dissertations examines Hofmann's Trinitarian *kenosis* and, with the exception of Forde's work, none significantly advances the study of Hofmann's theology.

7. Karlmann Beyschlag, personal conversation with the author (May 2003). For a complete list of studies, see the bibliography.

8. Theodor Kliefoth, "Der 'Schriftbeweis' des Dr. J. Chr. K. von Hofmann," *Kirchliche Zeitschrift* 5 (1858): 635–710. This review article was reprinted with five additional parts (a total of 560 pages!) as *Der 'Schriftbeweis' des Dr. J. Chr. K. von Hofmann* (Schwerin: Otto, 1860). For a similar, if somewhat shorter critique, see K. A. Auberlen, "Besprechung von Hofmanns Schriftbeweis," *Theologische Studien und Kritiken* 26 (1853): 103–33.

salvation and develop that into an extensive doctrinal system, even if only in outline-form. If the Bible is not directly involved as the cause of its formation, such a doctrinal system at the very least needs to prove that only the Bible, as divine revelation, stands behind the doctrinal system as its normative authority. (*BD* 45)

Likewise, within American Lutheranism, Francis Pieper (1852–1931) singled out Hofmann as the main Lutheran proponent of what Pieper called *"Ich-theologie"* or "theology of the self."[9] Pieper accused Hofmann and Schleiermacher of replacing the sole, "objective authority of Scripture" with "the subjective views of 'the theologizing subject.'"[10] More recently, Paul Tillich (1886–1965) criticized Hofmann's method for similar reasons:

> [Schleiermacher] tried to derive all contents of the Christian faith from what he called the "religious consciousness of the Christian." In a similar way his followers, notably the Lutheran "School of Erlangen," which included the theologians Hofmann and Frank, tried to establish an entire system of theology by deriving the contents from the experience of the regenerated Christian. This was an illusion.... The event on which Christianity is based ([Frank] called it "Jesus of Nazareth") is not derived from experience; it is *given* in history. Experience is not the source from which the contents of systematic theology are taken but the medium through which they are existentially received.[11]

Others who have leveled similar criticism include Barth and some of his and Tillich's students.[12]

---

9. According to Pieper, Hofmann was "the father of *Ich-theologie* among the conservative Lutheran theologians of the nineteenth century..." (Francis Pieper, *Christian Dogmatics* [3 vols.; trans. Theodore Engelder; St. Louis: Concordia Publishing House, 1950–1953], 1:6). Pieper was professor of theology at Concordia Seminary, St. Louis (1878–1931), and president of the Lutheran Church — Missouri Synod (1899–1911). While he leveled his strongest criticism against Schleiermacher's theological program, he also excoriated those Lutheran theologians who had been influenced by Schleiermacher: "All are agreed that only what Christ teaches and does is Christian. And Christ definitely teaches...that the method we must employ if we would know and be sure of the truth is to continue in His Word. Now, since Christ is always right, Schleiermacher, Hofmann, Frank, and all who employ their method, all who ask the 'Christian subject' to furnish independently of the Word of Christ full assurance or, at least, half assurance, are in error. Their theological method is not Christian but unchristian" (ibid., 1:115). Wherever Schleiermacher appears in Pieper's *Dogmatik*, Hofmann is usually not far away.

10. Ibid., 1:ix.

11. Paul Tillich, *Systematic Theology* (3 vols.; Chicago: The University of Chicago Press, 1951–1963), 1:42 (emphasis is original).

12. See Barth, *Protestant Theology*, 610; Eberhard Hübner, *Schrift und Theologie* (Munich: Chr. Kaiser, 1956), and idem, "Hofmann," *RGG* 3:421–22; George Lindbeck, "Confessions as Ideology and Witness in the History of Lutheranism," *Lutheran World* 7 (1961): 393–94; Carl Braaten, "Prolegomena to Christian Dogmatics," in *Christian Dogmatics* (ed. Carl Braaten and Robert Jenson; Philadelphia: Fortress, 1984), 1:16–17; and Carl Braaten, "A

Careful consideration of Hofmann's entire literary corpus indicates, however, that this typical interpretation of Hofmann's theological method is
inaccurate. Most of those who have analyzed Hofmann's theological method
have themselves overstated the place of "subjectivity" in his thought. Perhaps part of the difficulty is that Tillich and others appear to have interpreted
Hofmann's theology through the lens of Hofmann's younger colleague,
F. H. R. Frank.[13] Frank's theology, however, was not oriented to history
or to divine revelation in history but solely to the rebirth and conversion
experience of the individual Christian, the fundamental fact of Christian
experience which, for Frank, is the origin and content of the Christian certainty.[14] In several places Hofmann asserted that the experience of baptismal
regeneration is never self-generated but is mediated by the church into which
one is incorporated through the means of grace. Christian religious experience is never merely a subjective or individual experience but an experience
of Christianity, the Christian experience. So the purpose of the doctrinal
system is not to show *how* the Christian religious experience occurs, since
clearly the experience presupposes the mediation of faith through the Spirit's
use of the church's means of grace. Hofmann emphasized, rather, that on
the basis of the Christian *Tatbestand,* through which faith is received from
outside of oneself, an independent statement of that particular and historical faith is possible. The *Tatbestand* of Christianity, the *"given* facts of the

---

Harvest of Evangelical Theology," *First Things* 63 (1996): 45, where Braaten includes Hofmann
in Lindbeck's "experiential expressivist" type, discussed in George Lindbeck, *The Nature of
Doctrine: Religion and Theology in a Postliberal Age* (Philadelphia: Westminster, 1984), 16–17,
31–32.

13. This is certainly the case with D. Erich Schaeder's analysis of Hofmann's and Frank's
theological methods. For Schaeder (1861–1936), who was a precursor to Barth's dialectical
theology, Hofmann's and Frank's methods are identical. See D. Erich Schaeder, *Theozentrische
Theologie: Eine Untersuchung zur dogmatischen Prinzipienlehre* (2d ed.; 2 vols.; Leipzig:
A. Deichert, 1914–1916), 1:24–35. Schaeder misunderstands Hofmann's notion of *Tatbestand*
when he describes it only as "an inner *Tatbestand* which lies in the conscience or experience
of the Christian as an objective, inner fact which the Christian bears in himself" (ibid., 29).
This is to confuse Hofmann for Frank. Schaeder does not account for Hofmann's explicit intention to ground the transpersonal Christian *Tatbestand* in the self-giving, triune God. In
contrast to Tillich's interpretation, Martin Schellbach correctly notes Frank's exegetical dependence on Hofmann, but also identifies Frank's methodological differences from Hofmann. See
Schellbach, *Theologie und Philosophie,* 37.

14. Frank was decidedly influenced by the post-Kantian transcendental idealism of Johann
Gottlieb Fichte (1762–1814). Through Frank's study of Fichte, Frank was led to reformulate
Fichte's "transcendental I" in terms of "the Christian I." See H. Edelmann, "Subjektivität
und Erfahrung: Der Ansatz der theologischen Systembildung von Franz Hermann Reinhold v.
Frank in Zusammenhang des 'Erlanger Kreises' " (Th.D. diss., University of Munich, 1980).
See also J. Kunze, "Frank und Hofmann," in *Festschrift zum Fünfzigjährigen Stiftungsfest
des theologischen Studentenvereins Erlangen* (ed. J. Kunze; Erlangen: Junge & Sohn, 1910),
235–72; and Gary Davis, "A Critical Exposition of F. H. von Frank's System of Christian
Certainty" (Ph.D. diss., U. of Iowa, 1972).

matter" within the ecclesial situation of the Christian, preserved Hofmann from slipping into an alleged subjectivism or solipsism.

Furthermore, contrary to the typical Barthian charge against Hofmann's theology, Hofmann was not concerned to provide "a rational proof" for his Christian faith, only to *understand* it in order to give it correct expression. What looks like "begging of the question" (*petitio principii*) is actually just another form of the well-known hermeneutical circle along which all interpreters find themselves: One has a pre-understanding of the text one is to understand which one cannot avoid bringing to the text. Through one's encounter with the text, one discovers this pre-understanding confirmed to a certain degree, yet never to the point that one's pre-understanding is simply confirmed *in toto*. For Hofmann Christian experience by its very nature leads the Christian theologian into historical exegesis in order to compare one's own experience with the experience of the historical community which precedes and conditions that experience.[15] Precisely because Christian experience is communal and ecclesial, and because Scripture belongs to the ecclesial community, the Christian has a necessary relationship to Scripture which is given through the experience. The communal and ecclesial nature of the experience dictates that the understanding of this experience be compared with and, if necessary, corrected by the understanding of the experience in Scripture and by other Christian theologians. This is one of the main points in Hofmann's defense against the charge of subjectivism.[16]

---

15. Thielicke makes this same point about Hofmann's hermeneutics. See Thielicke, *Modern Faith and Thought*, 240.

16. According to Christoph Senft, Hofmann's understanding of the relationship between the religious experience of faith and the interpretation of biblical texts makes him a nineteenth-century theologian of abiding importance to modern theology (along with Schleiermacher, Baur, and Ritschl). Senft sees the abiding significance of Hofmann in two of his hermeneutical principles: (1) the Bible is not a textbook of church doctrines, but an historical witness that is independent of the church and academy; and (2) in order to interpret the Bible as word of God the interpreter cannot be indifferent or antipathetic toward the biblical text but needs to recognize that that text calls for a living faith that will affect how the text itself is interpreted. Senft is particularly impressed that Hofmann took the historicality of revelation hermeneutically seriously. Hofmann seeks an "explanation of the Christian faith, the presupposition of which 'lies outside us' yet not outside us in a legal sense, but in such a way that what lies outside us is revealed 'experientially' as its own history" (Senft, *Wahrhaftigkeit und Wahrheit*, 105). Senft correctly shows that Hofmann came to this position as a result of grappling with the disintegration of the dogmatic unity of the Bible by historical criticism, though Senft himself is critical of Hofmann's understanding of faith. According to Senft, Hofmann should have understood faith as a radical response to the proclaimed word of God. One should note, in passing, that Senft's study has been particularly influential on Gadamer's understanding of theological hermeneutics. Gadamer concludes, following Senft, that Hofmann's response to historical criticism helped to provide a positive orientation for all later hermeneutical discussion. See Gadamer, *Truth and Method*, 330–32. While the present study supports Senft's (and Gadamer's) conclusions about the abiding significance of Hofmann's hermeneutics, it tempers Senft's criticism of Hofmann's understanding of faith since Hofmann understood his Christian

Heilsgeschichte

If the main criticism against Hofmann is that his theological method is subjectivistic, the other prevailing view is that his understanding of *Heilsgeschichte* is dependent on an idealistic notion of developmental progress that is at odds not only with traditional Christian doctrine but with history itself:

> But instead of rejecting the perspective of the philosophy of history as a whole and distinguishing faith from all world-historical conceptions, in order to base it on the eschatological "verbum incarnatum" alone, Hofmann retains his ties with Hegel and clings to his historical-philosophical point of departure.[17]

According to Wendebourg, Hofmann's theology of history is based on certain "world-historical concepts" taken from Hegel, Ranke, Schelling, and Schleiermacher, and thus Hofmann's *"Heilsgeschichte"* is "the result of two utterly contradictory conceptions of history, one aprioristic" (Hegel), the other "historical" (Ranke).[18] This interpretation of Hofmann has also been repeated by others, such as Wolfhart Pannenberg (1928–), who accuses Hofmann of "delimiting," "ghettoizing," and "severing" an "inner" redemptive

---

existence as an existence created by means of the word of God *extra nos*. For Hofmann faith is also a response to the living word of the gospel and not merely a "certain possession" in itself.

17. Ernst-Wilhelm Wendebourg, "Die heilsgeschichtliche Theologie J. Chr. K. v. Hofmanns in ihrem Verhältnis zur romantischen Weltanschauung," *Zeitschrift für Theologie und Kirche* 52 (1955): 64–104; here 82. See also Ernst-Wilhelm Wendebourg, *Die heilsgeschichtliche Theologie J. Chr. K. v. Hofmanns kritisch untersucht als Beitrag zur Klärung des Problems der "Heilsgeschichte"* (Göttingen: Vandenhoeck and Ruprecht, 1953); and the earlier study by Gustav Weth, *Die Heilsgeschichte. Ihr universeller und ihr individueller Sinn in der offenbarungsgeschichtlichen Theologie des 19. Jahrhunderts* (Munich: Chr. Kaiser, 1931). Weth's critique is like Paul Althaus's, upon whom Weth was dependent. See Paul Althaus, *Die Letzten Dinge: Entwurf einer christlichen Eschatologie* (3d ed.; Gütersloh: C. Bertelsmann, 1926), 85–96. In the first three editions of this classic study, Althaus (1888–1966) argued for an "axiological eschatology" over against a *heilsgeschichtliche* conception of eschatology as "the end of history." Althaus stressed the presence of salvation through personal faith in Jesus Christ. This "presentative eschatology" (as Jürgen Moltmann [1926–] designates it) emphasizes an individual's confrontation with eternity, with divine judgment (law) and grace (gospel), at each moment in the historical present of the individual. All points of time are contemporaneous to the eternal, as Ranke himself had asserted. In this understanding, the Church's primitive eschatological expectation was detemporalized and individualized. For a cogent critique of Althaus's eschatology, see Jürgen Moltmann, "Trends in Eschatology," in *The Future of Creation* (trans. Margaret Kohl; Philadelphia: Fortress, 1979), 18–40.

18. Wendebourg, "Die heilsgeschichtliche Theologie," 81. Forde also uncritically accepts Wendebourg's judgment that Hofmann "has a view of history borrowed from German Idealism" (Forde, *The Law-Gospel Debate*, 74). I am grateful to Paul Johnston for providing me with a copy of his translation of this essay, though my own translation differs from his at several points.

history (*Heilsgeschichte*) from an "outer," "ordinary," secular history (*Historie*).[19] Pannenberg understands Hofmann to be saying that *Heilsgeschichte* does not really belong to "history" as most historians understand and practice it, especially since Hofmann was unwilling to utilize historical criticism to its full extent and since he based his own historical investigations on a preconceived idealistic "organic-whole." Pannenberg's reading of Hofmann contends that Hofmann's theology of history is untenable due to its precritical limitations.

Pannenberg and others seem to equate Hofmann's understanding of *Heilsgeschichte* with Oscar Cullmann's (1902–1999), when they accuse Hofmann of making *Heilsgeschichte* an inner, hidden part of all history.[20] But for Hofmann, in contrast to Cullmann, *Heilsgeschichte* is a more comprehensive category than "world history" (*Weltgeschichte*), since *Heilsgeschichte* is comprehended within a Trinitarian framework. Indeed, for Hofmann, *Heilsgeschichte* is the meaning of world history, since ultimately world history will be encompassed within the self-fulfillment of the triune God. Jesus Christ is "the end of history" that has been disclosed "in the center (*Mitte*) of history" (*WE* 1:39–40; *SBb* 1:35, 54–55). Thus, Jesus Christ is the "center" or "focus" of all of history, which is itself grounded in the Trinity. For Hofmann *Heilsgeschichte* is Trinitarian and Christocentric (and thus inclusive of all reality), whereas Cullmann understood *Heilsgeschichte* as a distinct and narrow process *within* history, whose "center" is Christ.

The focal point of Hofmann's conception of "history" is his understanding of Trinitarian *kenosis,* namely, that the eternal God has become historical by "emptying" God's self into Jesus in order to reconcile the whole world to God. According to Hofmann, world history can only be understood properly *within* the historical self-giving of the triune God who is love. "Salvation history" (*Heilsgeschichte*) is, therefore, is not separate from history

19. Wolfhart Pannenberg, "Redemptive Event and History," in *Basic Questions in Theology,* vol. 1 (trans. George Kehm; Philadelphia: Westminster Press, 1970), 15–80; here 15 and 41.

20. See also especially Karl Steck, "Die Idee der Heilsgeschichte: Hofmann, Schlatter, Cullmann," *Theologische Studien und Kritiken* 56 (ed. Karl Barth and Max Geiger; Zollikon: Evangelischer Verlag, 1959); and idem, "Johann Christian Konrad von Hofmann (1810–1877)," in *Theologen des Protestantismus im 19. und 20. Jahrhundert* (ed. Martin Greschat; Berlin: W. Kohlhammer, 1978), 99–112. Not only does Steck repeat the Barthian criticism that Hofmann's theological method is subjectivistic, he does not always sufficiently distinguish Hofmann's understanding of *Heilsgeschichte* from Cullmann's, particularly with regard to the Trinitarian-*kenotic* framework within which Hofmann situates his conception. It is significant that Cullmann himself states, apparently in reference to Steck's dissertation, "I hope that it will become clear from the manner of this treatment [i.e., Cullmann's book, *Salvation in History*] that I am not at all dependent upon the systematic theologians of earlier centuries mentioned above, with whom I have been associated — even if there may be points of contact between us. I hope it will also be apparent that my own interpretation has been gained purely from my involvement with the New Testament" (Oscar Cullmann, *Salvation in History* [trans. Sidney Sowers et al.; London: SCM Press, 1967], 14).

but ultimately embraces and fulfills all history within itself. "If it is true that all things, great and small, serve to bring about the unification of the world under its head Christ, then there is nothing in world-history in which something divine does not dwell, nothing which remains necessarily alien to prophecy" (*WE* 1:7). Thus, "[t]he self-presentation of Christ in the world is the essential content of all history" (*WE* 1:40).

Therefore, like Pannenberg's own conception of history, Hofmann's conception of *Heilsgeschichte* is *inclusive* of all history, as even Bultmann recognized.[21] World history is a part of *Heilsgeschichte* because the unity and meaning of history will become apparent to all only at "the end of history." Thus, both Hofmann and Pannenberg speak of "universal history" within the context of the Trinity, of "the end of history" which has been revealed in "the middle of history." Furthermore, Hofmann, like Pannenberg, attempted to reconceptualize the nature and methodology of historical investigation in light of properly theological categories, though one must stress that Pannenberg, at least in principle, has a greater appreciation than did Hofmann for the possibilities of empirical-critical historical investigation to ascertain and evaluate historical facts.

A more favorable view of Hofmann's theology of history appeared in the same year as Schellbach's important study (1935). Günther Flechsenhaar's monograph argues that both historicism and dialectical theology are incapable of making positive theological use of history and that Hofmann's *heilsgeschichtliche* contribution to "the problem of faith and history" offers a helpful alternative.[22] In particular, Flechsenhaar appreciated Hofmann's balanced critique of historical criticism (his emphasis on the faithful perspective of the biblical interpreter and the need to be oriented to the "whole" of the Bible and history) and his desire to articulate a theology of history that is grounded independently of all philosophies of history. In contrast to Wendebourg, Flechsenhaar's study concludes that Hofmann's theology of history is a unique and independent formulation that *utilizes* categories that theology has in common with romantic and idealist philosophy (e.g.,

---

21. See Rudolf Bultmann, "Prophecy and Fulfillment," in *Essays on Old Testament Hermeneutics* (ed. Claus Westermann; trans. James Luther Mays; Richmond: John Knox Press, 1969), 55–58. Bultmann criticized Hofmann's concept of *Heilsgeschichte* ("a philosophy of history which is influenced by Hegel") because the history of Israel is "theologically irrelevant" and because Hofmann held "a philosophical idea of history as a process of development, in which tendencies originally active in whatever takes place attain their realization in the natural course of events.... According to the New Testament, Christ is the end of *Heilsgeschichte* not in the sense that he signifies the goal of historical development, but because he is its eschatological end" (ibid., 58). Bultmann, too, seems to have had Cullmann in mind, more than Hofmann, in his critique of *Heilsgeschichte*.

22. Günther Flechsenhaar, *Das Geschichtsproblem in der Theologie Johannes von Hofmanns* (Giessen: Kindt, 1935).

"organic-historical whole," "organic teleological whole") though it is not *dependent* upon them as "influences."[23] While Hofmann's standpoint shares at least formal similarity to Schelling's and Hegel's totalistic views of history and though he, like they, thought that the course of history is rational and intelligible, for Hofmann it is the eschatological gift of the Spirit at work in the life of the Christian-in-community which grants this hopeful possibility.[24] Hofmann viewed world history in light of its *eschaton,* but that *eschaton* was present to him only through the gift of faith and hope. Thus, Hofmann waited in the posture of expectant faith in the eschatological Christ, "the end of history in the midst of history," who is nonetheless present with his church.[25]

Despite these many studies, few scholars have explored the relationship between Hofmann's theological method and his understanding of the triune God's self-differentiation in history that culminates in the divine self-emptying in Jesus. In Hofmann's Trinitarian position, the being of God is understood from its temporality and historicality as united with the being of Jesus of Nazareth. Through Jesus and the divine Spirit, God seeks to unite all creation to God's self. In Hofmann's theology, the being of God is self-defined primarily in terms of love for all creation. The historical self-differentiation, self-giving, and self-fulfillment of the Trinity in creation is, we will see, the context for Hofmann's interpretation of history as *Heilsgeschichte.*

Christology

The final area of interest in Hofmann's theology concerns his creative reinterpretation of the atonement of Christ, which some have considered Hofmann's most significant achievement.[26] While nearly all studies of Hofmann's hermeneutics and theology of history also include short summaries of his understanding of the atonement, all of these ignore his emphasis on *kenosis,* namely, the self-emptying of the triune God in history for the purpose of reconciling God and all creation.[27] Only three historical surveys place

---

23. In addition to Flechsenhaar's study, see Otto Procksch, "Hofmanns Geschichts-auffassung," *Allgemeine ev.-lutherische Kirchenzeitung* 43 (4 Nov 1910): 1034–38, 1058–63.
24. Thielicke, *Modern Faith and Thought,* 244.
25. For a recent, sympathetic appraisal of Hofmann's theology of history, see Beyschlag, *Die Erlanger Theologie,* 58–82.
26. Hirsch, *Geschichte,* 5:427. See also Otto Wolf, *Die Haupttypen der neueren Lutherdeutung* (Tübinger Studien zur systematischen Theologie 7; Stuttgart: W. Kohlhammer, 1938), 57–62; and Winter, *Die Erlanger Theologie,* 114–21.
27. The concept of *kenosis* continues to be an important focus in the contemporary Buddhist-Christian dialogue, though analysis of earlier Christian discussions about *kenosis* has not been

Hofmann's general views on Christ and the atonement into the larger context of doctrinal development in the nineteenth and twentieth centuries.[28] Only two other studies, both published in 1910, provide additional analysis of Hofmann's Christology and understanding of atonement.[29] While Thomasius's ideas on *kenosis* have been summarized by Claude Welch, no such summary of Hofmann's unique view (which is different from Thomasius's) exists in English.[30]

Even Gerhard Forde's important dissertation neglects Hofmann's understanding of Trinitarian *kenosis*.[31] According to Forde, Hofmann initiated an important debate about the atonement of Christ and about Luther's

a part of this contemporary discussion. See *The Emptying God: A Buddhist-Christian-Jewish Conversation* (ed. John B. Cobb and Christopher Ives; Maryknoll, N.Y.: Orbis, 1990). None of the major *kenotic* theologians of the nineteenth century is mentioned or discussed in this volume. The notion of divine *kenosis* has also become important for several Christian thinkers who wish to clarify God's relation to the natural processes of evolutionary development. For example, see John Haught, *God After Darwin: A Theology of Evolution* (Boulder: Westview Press, 2000).

28. Martin Breidert, *Die kenotische Christologie des 19. Jahrhunderts* (Gütersloh: Gütersloher Verlagshaus Mohn, 1977), 161–84; Forde, *The Law-Gospel Debate*, 12–78; and Gunther Wenz, *Geschichte der Versöhnungslehre in der evangelischen Theologie der Neuzeit* (2 vols.; Munich: Chr. Kaiser, 1984, 1986), 2:32–62. The present study is especially dependent on Breidert's helpful analysis. His work remains the best introduction to Hofmann's Christology in relation to the other *kenosis*-theologians.

29. See Philipp Bachmann, *J. Chr. K. v. Hofmanns Versöhnungslehre und der über sie geführte Streit: Ein Beitrag zur Geschichte der neueren Theologie* (Gütersloh: C. Bertelsmann, 1910); and Bernhard Steffen, *Hofmanns und Ritschls Lehren über die Heilsbedeutung des Todes Jesu* (Gütersloh: C. Bertelsmann, 1910). Both Bachmann and Steffen minimize Hofmann's Trinitarian ideas. The polemical writings directed against Hofmann's "heterodox" understanding of the atonement include Johannes Ebrard, *Die Lehre von der Stellvertretenden Genugthuung . . . Mit besonderer Rücksicht auf Dr. v. Hofmanns Versöhnungslehre* (Königsberg: A. W. Unzer, 1857); Friedrich Philippi, *Dr. v. Hofmann gegenüber der lutherischen Versöhnungs- und Rechtfertigungslehre* (Erlangen: T. Bläsing, 1856); Heinrich Schmid, *Dr. v. Hofmanns Lehre von der Versöhnung in ihrem Verhältnis zum kirchlichen Bekenntnis und zur kirchlichen Dogmatik* (Nördlingen: C. H. Beck, 1856); and Gottfried Thomasius, *Das Bekenntnis der lutherischen Kirche von der Versöhnung und die Versöhnungslehre D. Chr. K. v. Hofmanns* (Erlangen: T. Bläsing, 1857). Analysis of the basic arguments against Hofmann's atonement doctrine is given in chapter nine below.

30. See Claude Welch, *God and Incarnation in Mid-Nineteenth Century German Theology* (New York: Oxford University Press, 1965), 3–21, 25–30. Welch treats Thomasius, Isaak Dorner (1809–1884), and Alois Biedermann (1819–1885), but does not discuss Hofmann. Unlike Thomasius, who reformulated the traditional understanding of the two natures in Christ within the legal framework of traditional Lutheran Orthodoxy, Hofmann was critical of the orthodox Lutheran formulation of the vicarious satisfaction. Unfortunately, Thomasius's Christological ideas are often treated as though they summarized Hofmann's position, which is not the case, as Welch acknowledges elsewhere: "[T]hough Hofmann's idea [of atonement] was uniformly rejected by the Lutheran confessionalists of all varieties, it was — both in its merging of the significance of the death of Christ with the whole life-career and in the 'second-Adam' theme — a point of departure for a great deal of later atonement theory among the so-called mediating theologians" (Welch, *Protestant Thought*, 1:225).

31. "A discussion of the significance of kenosis for the doctrine of the atonement . . . would take us beyond the scope of this book" (Forde, *Law-Gospel Debate*, 60).

interpretation of the atonement that extended into twentieth-century discussions and debates about Barth's theology. Forde stresses that the so-called "atonement controversy" was really about the place of "law" within Lutheran theology. He observes that Hofmann's approach to the atonement was grounded in a critique of the traditional view that God's wrath must be appeased through the vicarious satisfaction of Christ before God can be merciful toward humanity. Hofmann began with the affirmation that God is self-giving love, and this affirmation led Hofmann to reinterpret the traditional teaching about Christ's atonement. The law of God is historical and not eternal, and thus Christ is able to overcome the threat of the law through his own history.

While Forde has great respect for Hofmann's critique of the traditional scholastic Lutheran doctrine of vicarious satisfaction and its legalistic framework, he is critical of the logic of Hofmann's understanding of *Heilsgeschichte*, in which the wrath of God is really less than what Forde thinks it is: Since Jesus knew the divine plan apparently in advance, he knew its outcome, and consequently his suffering on the cross was not a radical suffering of divine wrath in himself. Since "at all times [Jesus] preserves his relationship to God he cannot suffer 'what man should have suffered' — the desolation of ultimate defeat and despair. The atonement then appears as the working out of the divine plan which was from the outset a foregone conclusion."[32] Hofmann is faulted for replacing the juridical-legalistic framework of the traditional orthodox doctrine of vicarious satisfaction with his own "scheme of *Heilsgeschichte*."[33] While Hofmann has correctly criticized the legalistic framework as being incapable of fully accounting for the divine love, he himself diminished the power of the law in the Christian's existence since he understood the divine law to be merely "a part of a historical dispensation."[34]

Forde acknowledges his indebtedness to the important study by another American scholar, Robert Schultz, which also examines the relation of law to gospel in nineteenth-century German theology, though Forde disagrees with Schultz's conclusion that Hofmann's position was destructive for Lutheran theology.[35] In contrast to Forde, who maintains that Hofmann's criticism of the traditional understanding of the atonement allowed the debate over law and gospel to begin afresh, Schultz criticizes Hofmann for neglecting the problem of the opposition of the law to the gospel in his concern for an

---

32. Ibid., 72.
33. Ibid., 76–78.
34. Ibid., 69.
35. See Robert Schultz, *Gesetz und Evangelium in der lutherischen Theologie des 19. Jahrhunderts* (Berlin: Lutherisches Verlagshaus, 1958), 110–20.

historical development of salvation. Forde, however, points out that Schultz does not seem to appreciate the untenable situation that Hofmann faced at the time. As long as Lutheran Orthodoxy remained tied to a seventeenth-century understanding of vicarious satisfaction, it would remain largely doomed to theological irrelevance. Part of Hofmann's significance resides in his critique of this traditional scheme, even if his own creative response is also problematic from a theological perspective that seeks to take seriously the proper distinction between God's law and God's gospel.

While Forde's work is very helpful for situating Hofmann's theology into a larger theological development, Forde does not sufficiently account for the Trinitarian basis of Hofmann's doctrine of *kenosis,* which is the most important feature of Hofmann's understanding of the atonement. The present study hopes to augment Forde by attending to Hofmann's Trinitarian *kenosis,* which should help to offset Forde's judgment that Hofmann's Christology tends toward Docetism. In the process of the argument, the present study will also show that Hofmann did not think the divine law was "only a part of a historical dispensation," which has no relevance or impact within the Christian's life. Hofmann explicitly stated that insofar as the Christian remains a sinner, he stands under the judgment of God's law. Nonetheless, according to Hofmann, the Christian's ultimate hope is grounded in Christ's triumph against the forces — including the historical wrath of God — that oppose God's eternal will of love. In other words, Christian hope is grounded in the atonement of Christ, who removes the historical wrath of God against sinful humanity. Hofmann opposed the concept of the historical wrath of God against human sins with the eternal will of God's love realized in the *kenotic* self-giving of Christ. Further examination of Hofmann's understanding of Trinitarian *kenosis* is needed in order to deepen an appreciation of his unique understanding of the reconciliation of humanity with God in history through Jesus Christ.

Part II

Hofmann's Theological Method

CHAPTER THREE

The Object of Theology

The issue of a proper theological method is crucial to theology because the question of how to approach an appropriate understanding of God cannot be separated from the question of who God is and how God reveals God's self to human beings. Even though one could therefore just as easily begin an investigation of Hofmann's theology directly by discussing his teaching about God and Christ, this present study will begin by first investigating Hofmann's theological method and then proceed to analyze his understanding of God and Christ.

The Problem of Theological Method in the Modern World

As a post-Enlightenment theologian, who recognized the legitimacy of David Hume's (1711–1776) and Immanuel Kant's critiques of traditional theological knowledge, Hofmann struggled against the growing suspicion that Christian theology did not properly belong in the modern university.[1] While such a suspicion had been around since at least the Renaissance, it had grown in part due to the Protestant Reformation but especially because of the scientific, historical, and philosophical challenges of the Enlightenment that began in the seventeenth century.[2] Many in Hofmann's day argued that theology had become an outdated field that was not truly a *Wissenschaft* ("scholarly discipline").[3] How does one understand the Christian faith and

---

1. See David Hume, *Dialogues Concerning Natural Religion* (ed. Richard Popkin; Indianapolis: Hackett Publishing Company, 1980); Immanuel Kant, *Critique of Pure Reason* (trans. Norman Kemp Smith; New York: St. Martin's Press, 1929); and idem, *Critique of Practical Reason* (trans. Lewis White Beck; New York: Macmillan Publishing Company, 1985).

2. For a classic treatment of this development, see especially Ernst Troeltsch, *Protestantism and Progress: The Significance of Protestantism for the Rise of the Modern World* (Philadelphia: Fortress Press, 1986).

3. *Wissenschaft* is a word that is difficult to translate into English because it has been given different nuances of meaning by different scholars in different periods of the history of German universities, and the usual English near-equivalent, *science*, tends to connote merely *natural*

theology in light of the modern critiques of theological knowledge? Have not the mass acceptance of individual autonomy within modern western cultures and the spirit of critical inquiry properly constricted the intellectual focus of human beings to matters that lie solely within "the realm of the present world and its ideal transformation"?[4] Has not historical criticism, as an outgrowth of that critical spirit, called into question traditional understandings of biblical texts and biblical authority and thereby undermined traditional theological understanding?[5]

In view of these questions, Hofmann devoted considerable attention to epistemological and methodological issues in the discipline of theology, but he did so almost entirely in relation to the interpretation of biblical texts and to questions about the nature of the biblical canon and biblical authority. In this regard, Hofmann did not want to be thought of primarily as a systematician but as a biblical theologian who sought to establish the scholarly character of theology by means of a method appropriate to its object (*BD* 13–15).[6] The fact that two-thirds of Hofmann's literary corpus is exegetical in nature, and not directly a matter of systematic theology, confirms this self-understanding. A further confirmation is the fact that Hofmann lectured explicitly on systematic theology only once in his long career, during the summer semester of 1842.[7]

---

science. "Learning," "academics," "scholarship," or "scholarly discipline" may be more accurate renditions for what Hofmann understood by the term. The word suggests thorough, comprehensive, and systematic knowledge of something. In the early nineteenth century, the word usually referred to any organized and systematic academic study, including philosophy and theology. For a discussion of the nature of *Wissenschaft* in Germany in the early and middle nineteenth century, see Herbert Schnädelbach, *Philosophy in Germany: 1831–1933* (trans. Eric Matthews; New York: Cambridge University Press, 1984), 21–32, 66–108.

4. Troeltsch, *Protestantism and Progress,* 26.

5. For the impact that historical critical investigation of the Bible has had on the development of the problem of Christian theology in the modern period, see Hans-Joachim Kraus, *Geschichte der historisch-kritischen Erforschung des Alten Testaments von der Reformation bis zur Gegenwart* (2d ed.; Neukirchen: Neukirchener Verlag, 1969); James Livingston, *Modern Christian Thought* (2d ed.; 2 vols.; Upper Saddle River, N.J.: Prentice Hall, 2000), 1:238–41; Harrisville and Sundberg, *The Bible in Modern Culture;* and Edgar Krentz, *The Historical Critical Method* (Philadelphia: Fortress Press, 1975).

6. Wach maintains that despite the importance and plethora of Hofmann's exegetical work, "[he] was a first rate systematic theologian" (Wach, *Das Verstehen,* 2:361). In Wach's assessment, Hofmann's exegetical writings were "fundamental and foundational" for "his main task" of "representing scientifically the doctrinal system of the Christian faith" (ibid.). Mildenberger qualifies Wach's assessment by stating that in Hofmann's teaching and in his writings, "the Bible occupied him much more than the systematic-theological explication of his own Christian existence" (Mildenberger, *Geschichte,* 108). Even in *Der Schriftbeweis,* which Wach treats as the centerpiece of Hofmann's systematic theology, exegesis of the Bible is Hofmann's primary task, though the doctrinal summary (*Lehrganze*) (*SBb* 1:33–57) serves as a kind of systematic summary of Hofmann's theology.

7. Hofmann lectured on dogmatics between April 21 and August 23. These lectures have been handed down in three distinct but overlapping forms. Manuscript 1998 in the library

Even though one should therefore remember Hofmann primarily as a biblical scholar, he *did* address questions of systematic theology and theological hermeneutics. Like Schleiermacher, Hofmann recognized that post-Enlightenment discussions about the nature of theology would have to focus on the issue of an adequate and responsible theological method in relation to the problem of God and one's correct knowledge of God.[8] His understanding of these questions, and his response to them, shaped his understanding of God, Christ, and his self-understanding as a Christian believer, just as his understanding of the relation of God to his Christian faith shaped and informed his theological method and defined its goals.[9] After careful consideration of the problem of theology in the modern world, Hofmann asserted that theology *is* a *Wissenschaft* since it has a unique object upon which the theologian reflects, a unique mode of knowing that object, and a unique method by which that object is expressed as a unified whole.

---

archives of Friedrich-Alexander University, Erlangen, is a 236-page notebook of a handwritten transcript of these lectures. This transcript is by a Pastor Schneider. Wapler includes a summary of part of Hofmann's lectures as an appendix to his biography (Wapler, *Johannes v. Hofmann,* 379–96). I have relied on a translation of Wapler's summary by Claudia Nolte. When citing from Wapler's summary, I will use the abbreviation *DVW.* Wapler's summary, however, is inferior to a more complete summary by Christoph Luthardt (1823–1902; Luthardt studied at Erlangen from 1841 to 1845). Luthardt's summary was published in two parts in *Zeitschrift für kirchliche Wissenschaft und kirchliches Leben* 10 (1889): 39–53; 99–111. When citing from Luthardt's notes, I will use the abbreviation *DVL.* Because Wapler's and Luthardt's summaries are more accessible and legible than Schneider's, I have generally relied more upon them. I have, however, verified the accuracy of Wapler's and Luthardt's notations by comparing them, whenever possible, with the relevant sections in Schneider's transcript. Stephan and Schmidt describe Hofmann's dogmatics lectures as having "surpassed all other systematic theologies in the middle of the nineteenth century in the historical vivacity of their interpretation" (Stephan and Schmidt, *Geschichte,* 225).

8. See Friedrich Schleiermacher, *Brief Outline on the Study of Theology* (trans. Terrence Nelson Tice; Richmond: John Knox, 1966); and Terrence Nelson Tice, *Schleiermacher's Theological Method* (Th.D. diss., Princeton: Princeton Theological Seminary, 1961). For more recent discussions on the centrality of method in theology, see Bernard Lonergan, *Method in Theology* (New York: Seabury, 1972); David Tracy, *Blessed Rage for Order: The New Pluralism in Theology* (Minneapolis: Winston, 1975); idem, "Theological Method," in *Christian Theology: An Introduction to Its Traditions and Tasks* (rev. ed.; ed. Peter Hodgson and Robert King; Philadelphia: Fortress, 1985), 35–60 (including bibliography); Edward Farley, *Ecclesial Reflection: An Anatomy of Theological Method* (Philadelphia: Fortress, 1982); and Schubert Ogden, *On Theology* (Dallas: Southern Methodist University Press, 1992).

9. One is reminded of Tillich's generalization: "Every methodological reflection is abstracted from the cognitive work in which one actually engages. Methodological awareness always follows the application of a method; it never precedes it.... Since the method is derived from a preceding understanding of the subject of theology, the Christian message, it anticipates the decisive assertions of the system. This is an unavoidable circle" (Tillich, *Systematic Theology,* 1:34).

The Object of Theology

The Christian *Tatbestand* as the Experience of the Risen Christ

For Hofmann the most comprehensive discipline in the university is Christian theology since its object embraces God (the source and goal of all that is) and the world. This object is given to the Christian theologian in "the relationship of God and humanity as it is in Christ" (*DVL* 40). Since Hofmann maintained that this relationship is *present* and *personal,* he sometimes described the object of Christian theology as "the present factual situation (*Tatbestand*) of community (*Gemeinschaft*) between God and humanity mediated in Jesus Christ" (*SBb* 1:7). Since Hofmann also emphasized that this community/communion or relationship is *trans-subjective* and *historical,* he described the object as "the historically present relationship between God and humanity in Christ" (*DVW* 381). "We therefore return to the observation that the theologian has a double truth to contend with when he addresses Christianity, a relationship of God to humanity in Christ and, as a result of that, a relationship of humanity to God in Christ, and both together are understood best when we say, 'Christian theology deals with the relationship between God and humanity as it is in Christ' " (ibid., 382). Hofmann defined the object of theology in these terms or ones like them.[10]

Each of the dimensions of this object, both the personal-experiential and trans-personal/historical, is contained within what Hofmann called the Christian *Tatbestand.* For Hofmann the Christian *Tatbestand* encompasses both "the living, personal communion between God and sinful humanity mediated presently in Christ Jesus" and also the realization of the historical and ecclesial experience of this personal communion (i.e., "what makes the Christian a Christian" [*ET* 51]). "But the development of the content of this statement is something different from Schleiermacher's description of the pious self-consciousness. It is not a Christian's comportment (*ein Sosein des Christen*) that comes to expression, but always the *Tatbestand* which

---

10. Even near the end of his life, in his final vice-chancellor speech to the university, Hofmann stated: " ... [Christianity] is the *Tatbestand* of that community with God which is created for humanity and which is essentially realized in the person of Jesus. ... This *Tatbestand* of a community of God and humanity, which did not grow out of the self-development of humanity but is realized through a history (which has established itself between God and humanity), stands, since it is a reality, with the same independence next to that of the moral order of human society or to that of nature. ... " (Hofmann, "Über die Berechtigung der theologischen Fakultäten," Rede beim Antritt des Prorektorats der königlich Bayerischen Friedrich-Alexanders-Universität Erlangen am 4. November 1875 gehalten [Erlangen: University of Erlangen, 1875], 5–6).

has realized itself objectively in me" (ibid.).[11] By using the term *Tatbestand,* Hofmann sought to identify and comprehend both the existential immediacy and the historical mediacy of the communion with God that has "its permanence and continuance [*Bestand*] in the present Christ" (*SBb* 1:10). In other words, the Christian *Tatbestand* includes both a relationship to historical knowledge as well as a personal existential relationship to the ultimate source of the *Tatbestand* as a whole, i.e., the triune God who gives God's self in Christ in order to establish personal communion with humanity. Thus the *Tatbestand* of Christianity is not merely a *past* reality, but through the living "personal and effectual working [*Selbstbetätigung*] of the Risen One himself" the *Tatbestand* is also "an effect in the present" that involves the Christian believer (ibid., 1:6; See also *ET* 7).[12] Hofmann based this fundamental understanding of the object of Christian theology on the apostle Paul's summary of his own experience of the risen Christ in Gal 1:11–2:14 (*HS* 1:59–145).

This "effective working" (*Wirkung*) of the risen Christ alone establishes the Christian in a "certain," "immediate" (existential), "personal" relationship with God (*SBb* 1:10). The faith of the individual Christian theologian, which all Christians have in common, refers therefore to "an immediately certain truth" in the present existence of the theologian (ibid., 1:11). Such faith is the self-conscious certainty of the individual's relationship with God in the risen Christ through the indwelling Spirit. "The certainty of the Christian is not grounded in himself, however, but in the relationship with God mediated by Christ and given to him in faith."[13]

> In this certainty of faith lies the communion of God and humanity. ... Therefore this relationship between God and humanity existing in Christ is available to the theologian not only in Scripture and in the church but he has it also in himself, due to his experience; and even if this experience has not ensued without the mediation of the church and Scripture, it still is therefore — insofar as it yields him a singular certainty about God — therein not dependent on Scripture and the church

---

11. Still, Schleiermacher's famous definition of Christianity is remarkably similar to Hofmann's: "Christianity is a monotheistic faith, belonging to the teleological type of religion, and is essentially distinguished from other such faiths by the fact that in it everything is related to the redemption accomplished by Jesus of Nazareth" (*CF* 52).

12. *Selbstbetätigung* is one of many neologisms that Hofmann created to convey theological meaning. It too is difficult to translate into English. "Self-activity," "personal working," "one's own effectual working," "personal actualization," and "personal mediation" are possibilities. In this study, *Selbstbetätigung* will either be left untranslated or be translated in one of these various ways.

13. Breidert, *Die kenotische Christologie,* 161.

but is the becoming aware of a closest, most immediate attestation of God himself, thus of primordial certainty. (*DVW* 383)

"The experience of the relationship mediated in Christ, although mediated through the service of Scripture and the church, still gains its independent existence in the Christian" (*DVL* 40). On the basis of this Christologically grounded immediacy, one's individual faith can now be said to exist without being tied exclusively to the trans-personal, mediating authority of a local Christian congregation or of an institutional church or to any other external authority. Indeed, Hofmann stated that this faith, which is mediated by the congregation, "lies not outside of the one who has the calling to articulate it but [exists] as his own possession [*Besitz*] in him," since now he belongs to Christ and to no one else (*SBb* 1:8).[14]

Precisely in this way, however, Hofmann's religious experience could not be the total object of his theological reflection, since that experience was itself the result of an encounter with God that transcended the religious experience. Clearly, for Hofmann, the way of the Christian "believing subject" is the way of faith that understands the triune God as the center of the universe. One might say that Hofmann's faith in the mercy and forgiveness of God in the history of Jesus and his community "de-centered" Hofmann from being the center and subject of his faith. Though Hofmann's faith was thereby *certain* and *sure*, it was not certain and sure *in itself*, but only *in God*, who nonetheless had established Hofmann in communion with God's self. In this regard, Hofmann's understanding of faith was rooted in Luther's assertion:

> God says: "I am giving My own Son into death, so that by his blood He might redeem you from sin and death." Here I cannot have any doubts, unless I want to deny God altogether. And this is the reason why our theology is certain: it snatches us away from ourselves and places us outside ourselves, so that we do not depend on our own strength, conscience, experience, person, or works but depend on that which is outside ourselves, that is, on the promise and truth of God, which cannot deceive.[15]

---

14. For other references, see Behr, *Politischer Liberalismus*, 18–20.

15. Martin Luther, "Lectures on Galatians" (1535), in *Luther's Works* (55 vols.; ed. Jaroslav Pelikan and Helmut Lehmann; St. Louis: Concordia, 1955–1976), 26:387. *Ideo nostra theologia est certa, quia ponit nos extra nos: non debeo niti in consientia mea, sensuali persona, opera, sed in promissione divina, veritate, quae non potest fallere* (*D. Martin Luthers Werke* [Weimar: Hermann Böhlaus Nachfolger, 1911], 40:1:589, lines 8–10). Luther refrains from using the notion of "security" (*Sicherheit/securitas*), which he thought was too self-centered. Such a notion leads in the direction of self-sufficiency and self-confidence over against God. Instead, Luther regularly speaks of "certainty" (*Gewissheit/certitudo*), a notion that concentrates the individual on that which is outside of oneself, namely, God or God's promises. According

According to Hofmann, the existential relationship of the risen Christ to the theologian forms the starting point of the scholarly discipline of Christian theology.

> The Christian and therefore also the theologian is immediately certain only of his being a child of God in Christ Jesus. To articulate this [relationship] in such a way that nothing is contained in the articulation that already belongs to a rational development of this most general and precisely therefore all-encompassing notion, will then be the first step in the work of theological activity, which again precisely for this reason is above all a systematic activity. The scholarly self-understanding of the Christian is the most immediate concern of the theologian. (*GT* 236)

While this starting point is distinct from but never separated from the other two points of reference, Scripture and the church, the relationship of the Christian to the theologian has its sole source and foundation in the self-authenticating self-revelation of the ascended Christ to the individual Christian, a self-revelation which expresses and actualizes the love of God for all of humanity. "The dogmatician has to express the attitude of God to the human being in Christ, as that is the same as the content of the personal experience, namely, the fact that God loves the Christian and that this includes what is presupposed by this fact and also its consequence. This fact itself is the ground, the sole reason, from which dogmatics arises" (*DVL* 42). So everything that the Christian believer holds must be clarified as rooted and comprehended in that historically established fact [the risen, living Christ]; thus "in the demonstration of that one historically established fact the whole unity of the Christian faith comes to expression" (*GA* 265).

The Christian *Tatbestand* as Mediated and Historically Conditioned

Even though Hofmann argued for the immediate, existential character of Christian faith and thought, he did not want to be understood as saying

---

to Ebeling, Luther's very concept of "faith" is "*das Sich-gründen einer Existenz ausserhalb sich selbst*," a grounding of one's existence outside of oneself, in God and God's gospel promises. Only by trust in God and God's promises is true certainty possible. "For man, even man who has received grace, is uncertain in himself. Certainty only exists when God is with man through the word, and therefore when man is with God through faith. 'Our theology is certain,' says Luther, 'because it sets us outside ourselves'" (Gerhard Ebeling, *Luther: An Introduction to His Thought* [Philadelphia: Fortress, 1970], 174. See also idem, *The Nature of Faith* (trans. Ronald Gregor Smith; Philadelphia: Fortress, 1961); Paul Althaus, *The Theology of Martin Luther* (trans. Robert Schultz; Philadelphia: Fortress, 1966), 53–63; and Keller-Hüschemenger, *Das Problem der Heilsgewissheit*, 54–56.

that Christian faith and theology are unmediated and merely matters of individual experience. While the Christian individual, in faith, stands in an existential, present relationship with the risen Christ, the one who participates in this relationship has already been mediated historically into this relationship through the service of the church, "insofar as it serves Christ's self-activity [*Selbstbetätigung*]" (*SBb* 1:7). "I am what I am as a Christian only in the church community, only because of the church's activity and service" (ibid., 1:10). Thus, the congregation is "always earlier...than its individual members" who are formed into a community of Christ (ibid., 1:7, 17).

> Above all, since we proceed from a present *Tatbestand* of Christianity, a visible presence of this *Tatbestand* is apparent to everyone: the existence of the Christian church.... The personal and effectual activities that are characteristic of this corporate existence are apparent. It testifies to itself through the word of its confession; through a baptism with water it brings [people] into its fellowship. It enacts its fellowship with a meal of bread and wine. It is ordered through an office for these personal and effectual activities, as diverse as [this office] may take form. (*ET* 52)

Hofmann could speak of his relationship with God, but "only as a result of ecclesial activity,...only through the mediating service of the congregation which has made me share in the relationship to God in Christ and continuously kept me in it" (*SBb* 1:10–11).

In this context Hofmann asserted that the object of theology is *given* in a threefold way: first, in one's personal experience of baptismal regeneration and faith; second, as the historical extension of the community of Christ in which the *Tatbestand* presents itself both in individual experience and in a corporate, ecclesial experience; and third, in the Christian Bible which witnesses to the reality of the *Tatbestand,* understood not as timeless doctrines but as the historical record of God's communion with humanity that culminates in the actions of the Redeemer (*SBb* 1:23; *DVL* 40; *ET* 26). The immediate cause of this threefold activity is the divine Spirit of the triune God, which provides the essential unity within the object of theology as well as that object's inner self-authentication in the life of the Christian (*DVL* 104). So, while Hofmann spoke of faith as a "certain" "possession" (*Besitz*) of the individual Christian (*SBb* 1:8), he certainly did not think that Christian faith is grounded in the individual. Rather, faith has its source, norm and ground in the living, risen Christ, who works mediately through his ecclesial community and the Scriptures to establish individuals in an existential relationship with the triune God. Christian theology, if it is to be Christian, starts from within this given situation (*Tatbestand*) and never leaves it.

To comprehend the historical nature of the ecclesial mediation of the *Tatbestand,* Hofmann used a related term, namely, *Tatsache* ("fact"). *Tatsachen* ("facts") are individual events that give shape to the *Tatbestand* as a whole.[16] Each individual fact (*Tatsache*) must therefore be comprehended as the realization of the relationship between God and humanity mediated in Jesus Christ.[17] For Hofmann, however, a fact (*Tatsache*) does not denote a pure facticity. Instead, "facts" (*Tatsachen*) refer to the given realities which are mediated through history, in this case the given realities that are mediated through and interpreted within the community of God. The Christian *Tatbestand,* therefore, includes such interpreted "facts" as the reality of baptismal regeneration, Holy Scripture (including the preaching and teaching of Holy Scripture), the church's liturgy and historic Confessions, and the history of Christian institutions. "Word, Baptism, Lord's Supper, and ecclesial community are thus the raw material of dogmatics" (*DVL* 104).[18]

Since all of these "facts" (*Tatsachen*) — and not merely one's own faith experience — make the Christian into a Christian (*WE* 1:51–52), *experience* (*Erfahrung*) in Hofmann's theology does not refer to general experience or common human experience (*allgemeine Erfahrung*), which the Christian shares with all other human beings, but to a specifically spiritual (*geistliche* or *pneumatische*) experience of baptismal rebirth and faith.[19] As we have

---

16. See Hans Grass, "Heilstatsachen," in *RGG* 3:193–94.

17. For a helpful description of the differences between *Tatbestand* and *Tatsache* in the theology of Hofmann, see Behr, *Politischer Liberalismus,* 33–38. See also R. Staats, "Der theologiegeschichtliche Hintergrund des Begriffes 'Tatsache,'" *Zeitschrift für Theologie und Kirche* 70 (1973): 316–45.

18. For Hofmann "the actual content" of the Christian *Tatbestand* and the "linguistic formation of that content" in the theological "system" cannot be separated from each other. "Both, in their unity, create the meaning of the facts [*Tatsachen*]. But this meaning is dependent on their necessary order within the system" (Behr, *Politischer Liberalismus,* 38). "Because the place of a sentence" in the system "gives it its meaning for the total, and if the system is an enclosed row of facts [*Reihe von Tatsachen*], then the system's individual sentences have their necessary place" (*SBb* 1:16). The understanding of a "fact" (*Tatsache*) follows from the necessary position that it occupies in the whole. See also *SBb* 1:12–13. Hofmann expressly used *Tatbestand* and *Tatsache* to distance his theological system from an idealistic system based on the term *Begriff* ("concept"), which Hofmann thought was too easily removed from concrete history. Because "concepts" (*Begriffe*) always originate from outside "the fact [*Tatsache*] of Christianity," they cannot bring their content fully into language because they have not arisen from "the one thinking inside the fact" (*SBb* 1:12). By emphasizing the "fact" (*Tatsache*) of Christianity, Hofmann hoped also to counter what he considered Strauss's reduction of Christianity to mythical imagination. See, for example, *DVW* 394–95, where Hofmann criticizes what he considers to be Strauss's fanciful speculations. Hofmann thought that Strauss's critique of "supernaturalistic" dogmatics was correct, but that Hofmann's own experiential approach avoided both the old way of doing dogmatics as well as Strauss's way.

19. See Wilfried Joest, "Erfahrung als theologisches Prinzip in der älteren Erlanger Schule," in *Glaube und Gesellschaft: Festschrift für W. F. Kasch* (ed. K. D. Wolff; Bayreuth: Fehr, 1981),

seen above, Hofmann defined the content of this experience as the love that God has for the individual and the love that the individual has for God. "The experience of the Christian is two-fold, namely the love of God for the Christian and the Christian's love for God" (*DVW* 387). Whoever lives in this special experience will now also be able to understand the entire content of his faith as a whole which is given in and through the experience.

But one might wonder, "Is there not a fundamental contradiction between speaking about the object of theology as both 'immediate' and 'mediate?' How can the object of theology have both of these characteristics?" In response to this type of criticism, Hofmann asserted that there is no contradiction between the mediation of the congregation and the Christological immediacy of the relationship of faith, just as there cannot be a contradiction between the latter and the scriptural witness to God's historical and present relationship with humanity in Jesus Christ. The relation of the Christian to God is both "realized in the person of Jesus Christ" and also exists in the present as "a visible and externally ordered community" (*ET* 53). In this way, "membership in this community of the church and participation in that relationship between God and humanity realized in Christ are one and the same" (ibid.). Hofmann made the same affirmation when he wrote, "Christianity is an entirely transcendent as well as an entirely immanent factual situation [*Tatbestand*]" (ibid., 22–23). In such a definition of Christianity, Hofmann distinguished but did not separate the transcendent origin of the community of God and humanity in the risen and present Christ from the historical, institutional reality of the church and its Scripture:

> [T]he relationship between God and the human being which is actualized in [the church] cannot be contained within her visible and external orders, but this relationship has to be . . . active through these external orders so that whoever participates in these orders of the church's corporate existence comes to experience through them the self-attestation of the relationship of God and humanity, which is [however] in and of itself independent of these external orders. The inwardness of the church's corporate existence must consist in this: A transcendent *Tatbestand* has to be active through this immanent corporate existence and evidence itself in those who belong to it. . . . But if the church is the present actuality in the world of the relationship between God and humanity given in Jesus, then she is this in her tangible actuality. And

---

165–76. Hofmann thought that by limiting the concept of *Erfahrung* to *christliche Erfahrung*, he was distinguishing himself from his teacher, Schleiermacher, who he thought was more concerned to talk about a mediation between Christian faith and general human experience of God (*Gotteserfahrung als allgemein-menschliche*).

as the latter, she is ordained to mediate the effectual working of the former in the individual. Everyone experiences for himself the actions [of this relationship] which effects participation in the tangibly perceptible reality of the church; and in no other way than this does the individual experience this. (Ibid., 9–11; see also *DVL* 40)

> Just as the certainty of our salvation does not rest for us on the witness of the Spirit to our adoption [by God], but on the fact of our baptism, to which the Spirit needs only always to give his comforting "yes," so also does the certainty, which dwells in the congregation so that it will overcome all tribulations of its communal life in the Spirit, rest not on the witness of the Spirit to its common life with Christ, but on Scripture, whose possession makes that victory certain for it in advance and to which the Holy Spirit needs only to testify in each case of tribulation. (*WE* 1:51)

Hofmann considered the Christian's present relationship with God a unity both of objective realization in Christ, within the ecclesial community, and of personal reception in one's faith:

> … [W]hen I proceed out of the unified *Tatbestand* which makes the Christian into a Christian, I do not thereby have at once something simply subjective; rather it immediately contains in it something objectively present, without which such a stance of the individual subject would not exist. (*SS* 4:17–18)

Individual Christian faith has its sole foundation in the trans-personal, present relationship with God, which itself is mediated to the believer through the "facts" (*Tatsachen*) of Christianity, including especially the orders of the church (*Ordnungen*), that is, the ecclesial means of grace.[20]

---

20. "If one might draw a line from the I-certainty of Descartes to Hofmann, one might say (somewhat boldly): 'I am baptized, and therefore I think theologically.' This does at least express the fact that in Hofmann Christian certainty arises out of the fact of present Christianity, namely, out of my being a Christian in the community as this is guaranteed by baptism" (Thielicke, *Modern Faith and Thought*, 236). Like the various efforts of many other theologians of his generation (e.g., Schleiermacher, Søren Kierkegaard [1813–1855]), Hofmann too was concerned to find "certainty" of faith within the vast uncertainty created by the discoveries of Copernicus and Galileo and the ruminations of Descartes, Kant, and Hume. "Surrounded by the immensity of infinite space, in a world apparently without God and therefore without intrinsic meaning, and left alone with his own self and his doubt, man became profoundly uncertain about himself. His thinking began to focus upon himself, as he tried in so many ways to explore and ascertain his own identity. Philosophy, accordingly, became for the most part knowledge of self" (Walter Leibrecht, *God and Man in the Thought of Hamann* [Philadelphia: Fortress, 1966], 9–10).

The Epistemology of Theology

Hofmann's conception of the theological task means that Christian theology is grounded in the theologian's personal and ecclesial faith, which itself is grounded in the risen Christ, who mediates the historical relationship between God and human beings.[21] If Christian theology does not begin from this unique relationship, it is dependent on something external and foreign to it, and therefore it will be talking about something other than the relationship between God and humanity mediated in Jesus Christ. Even though Christian theology cannot help examining the other academic disciplines, including especially metaphysics, "as soon as the theologian concerns himself with objects of these scholarly disciplines [*Wissenschaften*] other than as they concern the relationship of God and humanity and insofar as they are knowable from this relationship, he is doing something alien to the theologian" (*DVW* 380).[22] Although dimensions of the object that the theologian analyzes and expresses are also studied by scholars within the other non-theological academic disciplines, the theologian's intention must be to approach that object by a different route altogether.[23]

Hofmann thought that the experiential *tatbeständlicher* starting point of his theological method assured that his theology would be independently grounded apart from all externalities, including all other academic disciplines (especially historical criticism, but also philosophy, e.g., Kant's critiques) and even the external, heteronomous ecclesial authorities of Scripture, church doctrine and tradition, and church government.[24] If the Christian *Tatbestand* is the object of faith and accessible only by means of

---

21. See also *HS* 1:59–73, where Hofmann grounds the starting point of his analysis of the coherence of the New Testament writings in the revelation of the risen Christ to the disciples of Jesus and to Paul of Tarsus.

22. While Hofmann was conversant with the metaphysical options available to him in his day, he did not think that metaphysics provides the foundation for responsible talk of God. For Hofmann *God* establishes the conditions of his own being, not philosophy. Thus, Hofmann would disagree with those who assert that "more than anything else, theological discourse about God requires a relationship to metaphysical reflection if its claim to truth is to be valid. For talk of God is dependent on a concept of the world, which can be established only through metaphysical reflection" (Wolfhart Pannenberg, *Metaphysics and the Idea of God* [trans. Philip Clayton; Grand Rapids: Eerdmans, 1990], 6).

23. The polemical context in which Hofmann defined his theological method is very important for understanding his theological concerns. An examination of this context occurs in the next two chapters.

24. See *ET* 5, 47; *BH* 33; and *BD* 55, 71, 95. See also Beyschlag, *Die Erlanger Theologie*, 69. Beyschlag's assessment of the relation between Christian certainty of salvation and the character of the Christian *Tatbestand* is more accurate than Werner Elert's (1885–1954). In Elert's estimation of Hofmann's theological method, "The Christian of the present enters into the history of the realization of salvation and so has the opportunity to test the truth of the claims of Christianity, so to speak, in his own body, namely, to see if it really brings 'salvation' as it claims. Consequently, the answer then is not given from rational consideration but from the immediate experience. The subjective proof material secures the character of a *Tatbestand*,

faith, then a *Wissenschaft* that is independent of faith or alongside of faith is incapable of comprehending God or faith. Theology therefore "limits itself within the bounds of faith and establishes itself anew precisely only on the basis and ground of faith" (*DVW* 385).[25]

> If theology is rightly an independent discipline, then there is no other starting point for it than the Christian *Tatbestand*, immediately certain for faith, as it presents itself prior to all intellectual discussion of its content. (*DVL* 42)

Furthermore, "[t]here is no proof for that starting point, just as there is no proof for 'I think,' apart from demonstrating externally that which is the proof of what is present within" (ibid.). All understanding and interpretation of the Christian faith is possible only on the ground of Christ's living relationship with the individual, which forms the object of such faith (*GT* 265). "The foundation of truth lies already in the experience of faith, and all that is required is to uncover and expound the contents of that experience" (*DVW* 385).

Thus, Christian theology is not a *Wissenschaft* like the philosophy of religion, the discipline of history, or any other academic discipline that is grounded in the structures of human thought (*DVL* 40). Instead, theology should be understood as

> self-sufficient [*selbstständig*] and independent [*unabhängig*] knowledge of a solely unique object. In just this way, it is independent of an externally determining principle or foundation [*Bestimmungsgrund*]. For it neither has its origin in a need alien to the spirit of scientific inquiry, nor is it subservient to a heteronomous authority without thereby being simply a matter of the autonomous individual. Its ecclesiality is likewise self-evident as is its spirituality, because it is presupposed that the theologian is a living member of the given local

whose use makes all questions of method secondary" (Werner Elert, *Der Kampf um das Christentum: Geschichte der Beziehungen zwischen dem evangelischen Christentum in Deutschland und dem allgemeinen Denken seit Schleiermacher und Hegel* [Munich: C. H. Beck, 1921], 289). With his focus on "the subjective proof material," Elert minimizes the trans-personal and *extra nos* dimension of the *Tatbestand*, which includes the *Selbstbetätigung* ("personal and effective working") of the risen Christ. This *Tatbestand* grounds the personal faith of the Christian, not the other way around, as Elert puts the matter. Thus, according to Hofmann, the certainty of faith is grounded in the triune God, who also works through the personal and effectual working (*Selbstbetätigung*) of Christ, who works through the church's means of grace. (Elert and Paul Althaus were the principal Lutheran theologians at Erlangen in the twentieth century. Elert taught at Erlangen from 1923 until his death.)

25. See, for example, the first thesis of Hofmann's theological dissertation: "All theology is taken up under the knowing within regeneration" [*Notione regenerationis sublata tollitur omnis theologia*] (J. v. Hofmann, *De Argumento Psalmi Centesimi Decimi* [Erlangen: The University of Erlangen, 1838], 47).

church. But because he is a living member of it, he is also not bound to its earthly reality; rather the truth of its reality lives in him and sets him free. [This is] a freedom which he does not owe to *Wissenschaft* but to Christianity and [a freedom] to which he does not lay claim in the name of *Wissenschaft,* but rather [to which he] is obliged to guard his faith. (*GT* 232–233)[26]

Hofmann made the same point in the first section of his dogmatics lectures:

The philosopher can also come to religion from the starting point of all philosophical knowledge; but the theologian proceeds from the presupposition of a historically existing relationship between God and humanity as it is encountered in the person of Christ. If then also the philosopher comes to the historical occurrences of religion and compares them with what he has understood to be the essence of religion, that is, of course, an entirely different way and also an entirely different standard and principle. If theology is to remain an independent *Wissenschaft,* it must insist on its historical nature. (*DVL* 39)[27]

By his use of the word "historical," Hofmann meant to refer intentionally to precisely the extra-personal dimension of the *Tatbestand,* including especially the centrality of the risen Christ, who grounds the Christian in an immediate relationship with the triune God.

Clearly, for Hofmann, the personal rebirth and faith of the individual Christian have enormous consequences for how the theologian thinks and knows. The "Christian is himself conscious of a newness in his entire relationship with God, a newness that is also a newness in his entire way of thinking" (*ET* 5). Human reason is not a tool by which to find God; rather, only after people are established in a believing relationship with God or, in other words, after the *Tatbestand* is established in them, can human reason then function to understand the relationship which God has so established.[28] "It is an actual relationship, after all, that is the object of our

---

26. Hofmann's point here is reminiscent of Luther's "The Freedom of the Christian," *Luther's Works,* 31:327–77. See also Eberhard Jüngel, *The Freedom of a Christian: Luther's Significance for Contemporary Theology* (trans. Roy Harrisville; Minneapolis: Augsburg Publishing House, 1988).

27. Hofmann's conception of theology is like Eberhard Jüngel's (1934–) contemporary concern to argue that the object of theological thinking is the criterion by which that thinking is measured. John Webster writes of Jüngel's method, "An autonomous and self-justifying critical method has to be replaced by a way of approaching the [biblical] texts in which 'thinking is measured by the object of thinking': in which, that is, the critical work of the scholar reverts to its proper secondary and subsequent position vis-à-vis its object" (J. B. Webster, *Eberhard Jüngel: An Introduction to his Theology* [Cambridge: Cambridge University Press, 1986], 8).

28. This idea summarizes Hofmann's basic criticism of Kant, namely, that thinking can be pertinent to empirical reality in all of its dimensions only if thinking has God, not reason,

thinking, in which, not about which, we are doing our thinking" (*SBb* 1:12–13).[29] Hofmann often highlighted this "existential" character of theological epistemology:

> A *Wissenschaft* is all the worthier of its name the more the knower has the object of his knowing not outside of himself but in himself, indeed is it for himself. The more it is something alien or external to him, the more impenetrable it remains to him, the more external his knowing remains. In this respect only philosophy compares with theology. The difference, however, is that philosophy deals with the essential factors of human being as given through creation. And actual human existence (*Wirklichkeit*), being in the same realm [creation], stands in a contradiction with these essential factors that is irresolvable for philosophy because it cannot be resolved in this realm, whereas theology deals with actual human existence (*Wirklichkeit*) as given through the salvation-historical miracle, in which that enigma is solved. Thus it is incumbent on theology scientifically only to understand the truth of this [latter] reality (*Wirklichkeit*) which is immediately certain to faith. Only the person to whom this latter reality is alien, holds a notion of *Wissenschaft* from which theology cannot be derived. (*GT* 232)

---

as its center. To become truly reasonable, reason must maintain its proper place before God (*coram Deo*). In this regard, Hofmann's theological approach is like Hamann's. "Without God there is no genuine self-knowledge, for the self is created and sustained by God as it exists in affirmation and denial of its origin. Hamann can say that 'our self is founded in the creator of it.' The self is part of God's creation. To declare it to be divine would be unreasonable, indeed foolish. Yet neither is the self therefore an isolated and self-sufficient monad, as Leibnitz saw it. The self is historical existence — man in his wholeness — to be understood only in its relation to history, nature, its fellow man, and all the relationships in which its life exists. Defined in isolation and apart from these relationships, the self would again become a mere abstraction, whether it be defined as being, reason, feeling, or freedom" (Leibrecht, *God and Man in the Thought of Hamann*, 18). See also Isaiah Berlin, *The Magus of the North* (New York: Farrar, Straus and Giroux, 1993), 26–71. The difference between Hamann and Hofmann is that Hofmann understood God's relation to creation to be historical and temporal as well as eternal and faithful, whereas Hamann understood God's relation to creation as eternal and immutable omnipresence.

29. This statement helps to understand the meaning of Hofmann's famous statement, "I the Christian am for me the theologian the unique material of my scholarly activity" (*SBb* 1:10). See also *TE* 17 ("I the Christian am for me the theologian the object of knowing") and *ET* 17–27, where Hofmann similarly develops the independent character of Christian theology. Compare with Bultmann's statement, "We cannot talk about our existence since we cannot talk about God. And we cannot talk about God since we cannot talk about our existence. We could do the one only along with the other. If we could talk of God from *God*, then we could talk of our existence, or vice versa. In any case, talking of God, if it were possible, would necessarily be talking at the same time of ourselves. Therefore the truth holds that when the question is raised of how any speaking of God can be possible, the answer must be, it is only possible as talk of ourselves" (Rudolf Bultmann, "What Does It Mean to Speak of God?," in *Faith and Understanding* [ed. Robert Funk; trans. Louise Pettibone Smith; Philadelphia: Fortress, 1987], 60–61).

Hofmann's conception of the place of reason in theology thus reorients reason to a subservient role that is normed and guided by God's own initiative in establishing the theologian in a relationship of faith within the ecclesial community. Christian theology can thus be confident that it is able to think correctly of God only on the basis of the divine self-disclosure, i.e., as the triune God who establishes communion with humanity in and through the risen Christ.[30] In this sense, Christian theology is not "talk *about* God," but "talk *of* God" in relation to the individual and to the world. Such a relationship is not grounded in a "universal," but only in the particular, i.e., a particular history of God that has its center in the particular life of Jesus and extends to include the particular believer.

Therefore, in Hofmann's view, Christian theology does not begin from a general analysis of thought itself and then proceed to develop a view of religion or of God that correlates with this view of thought. For Hofmann there are no universal grounds for faith or Christian theology as there are for philosophy. Rather, the ground of faith and the certainty of its content are unattainable apart from faith itself. The actual encounter with God forms the starting point of Christian theology, and all other "reasonable" views of God that are "outside" of this believing relationship are to be challenged and tested to see if they accord with God's self-disclosure.[31]

> Therefore, only because that same *Tatbestand* — which makes me a Christian and the scholarly understanding of which makes me a theologian — exists outside of me just as [it exists] within me, am I in a position to demonstrate the correctness of my theological system. (*SBb* 1:17)

It was simply inconceivable for Hofmann that one's faith in God can be attained apart from being put into communion with God by God. One knows God and can think about and express God, only because God has made God's self known to the individual believer. Christian theology has its content, norm, and ground in the faith which God establishes in the believer. " ... [T]he content of the faith establishes itself as true and is not to be

---

30. Hofmann makes clear that the view that God alone establishes the conditions for knowledge of God is itself a presupposition that is grounded in faith. The encounter with God establishes the necessary precondition by which the theologian speaks of God. Thus, Hofmann would disagree that theology is "presuppositionless," though he nonetheless asserts, like Barth and Jüngel, that God's self-revelation sets the conditions by which God is known. On "presuppositionless theology," see Rolf Ahlers, *The Community of Freedom: Barth and Presuppositionless Theology* (New York: Peter Lang, 1989).

31. Mark Mattes describes Eberhard Jüngel's theological method in similar terms. See Mark Mattes, "Toward Divine Relationality: Eberhard Jüngel's New Trinitarian, Postmetaphysical Approach" (Ph.D. diss., The University of Chicago, 1995), 4, 12–16, 19–21, 40–45.

grounded in any other way" (*DVL* 40). This understanding of faith is the precondition for responsible theological *Wissenschaft*.

Thus, for Hofmann, theological reflection takes place within the *Tatbestand* and such thinking involves an "unfolding" (*Entfaltung*) or an "evolution" (*Evolution*) of the content of that relationship. All of the statements of the theologian, including those about Scripture and church history, occur "within the context of faith" (*DVW* 386). The theologian cannot "go beyond or be above faith" (ibid.).

> But now in order to let the thus articulated actuality of Christianity arrive at the exposition of its manifold content, a thinking in that actuality is required. Concepts which have emerged outside of that actuality, in whatever way, may not be allowed to have determinative influence in its self-unfolding. If, however, one allows this unfolding freely to happen, one will nowhere end up with isolated concepts which cunning reason would then first have to bring, or be permitted to bring, into relationship with one another. (*SBb* 1:12–13)

So the theologian thinks in the *Tatbestand,* not merely about it. The system then is "the development of that simple *Tatbestand* that makes the Christian a Christian and distinguishes the Christian from the non-Christian, in order to explain the manifold riches of the content of faith" (ibid., 1:11). As such, faith of itself is distinct from theological *Wissenschaft,* but theological *Wissenschaft* is the attempt to shape faith into a systematic and coherent whole (*WGS* 208–9; *ET* 27).[32] Through such an "attempt," Hofmann merely wished to demonstrate "what lies completely contained in the present *Tatbestand*" and, at the same time, "how that *Tatbestand* is realized" in himself as a theologian (*SS* 4:19–20). Thus:

> Theology is a truly free *Wissenschaft,* free in God, only when precisely that which makes a Christian to be a Christian, his own independent relationship to God, makes the theologian to be a theologian through disciplined self-knowledge and self-expression, when I the Christian am for me the theologian the unique material of my *Wissenschaft.* (*SBb* 1:10)

In other words:

---

32. Hofmann's concern to develop a "system" distinguishes him from Hamann, who thought all "systems," both of the dogmatic orthodox Lutheran variety as well as of the dogmatic rationalist variety, leave no room for the supreme reality, the reality of God, which baffles all human attempts at comprehension and systematization.

What the divine preservation of the freedom of the theologian depends upon, of course, is that the theologian finds that which he articulates not just outside of himself but within himself. By having personal experience of that which has come to voice (*Darstellung*) in Scripture and church, he is enabled to recognize the Divine in Scripture and church, namely to retrieve (*wiederzufinden*) the relationship that is willed by God. (*DVW* 384)

While Hofmann thus aligned himself with an argument for the independence of theology like that of his more famous teacher, Schleiermacher, he nonetheless differed in important respects from Schleiermacher's understanding of theology.[33] Hofmann did agree with Schleiermacher's assessment of the two conditions necessary for a particular theology to emerge in history (i.e., the degree to which a mode of faith is communicated by means of ideas rather than symbolic actions and the degree to which a mode of faith attains historical importance and autonomy), but he did not stress Schleiermacher's overarching concern to define Christian theology properly as a "practically-oriented" discipline of educating future ministers and theologians for public church service. Perhaps because of Hofmann's own intra-church disputes, he did not want to secure the place of theology in the university by means of its practical goal (though he acknowledged its place and value), but solely on the basis of its peculiar object of study, the *Tatbestand* of Christianity.

Like Schleiermacher, Hofmann recognized that for Christian faith to be presented intelligibly, the theologian may borrow certain philosophical categories or terms that receive new meaning within their distinctively Christian theological context. These terms have to do with thinking through the "independent" self-presentation of Christian faith itself and forming it into a systematic, "coherent and complete whole," or "system," and therefore they entail no specific philosophical allegiance (*ET* 17–18).[34]

---

33. See *ET* 1–2, where Hofmann acknowledges the significance of Schleiermacher's argument for the independence of theology as *Wissenschaft* for his own taxonomy of theology in his *Encyklopädie der Theologie*. See CF 52ff. (§11), 76ff. (§15), and 83ff. (§17); idem, *Brief Outline on the Study of Theology,* 19–27; and idem, *On the Glaubenslehre: Two Letters to Dr. Lücke,* 64. For a persuasive analysis of the historical and ecclesial nature of Schleiermacher's theological method, see Brian Gerrish, "Continuity and Change: Friedrich Schleiermacher on the Task of Theology," in *Tradition and the Modern World: Reformed Theology in the Nineteenth Century* (Chicago: The University of Chicago Press, 1978), 13–48.

34. See also Wapler, *Johannes v. Hofmann,* 52, 97. In light of recent discussions about foundationalism, there appear to be similarities between the theological hermeneutics of Hans Frei (1922–1988) and Hofmann's concern that philosophy cannot and should not attempt to provide a foundation or universal ground by means of philosophical criteria regarding truth and rationality in order to justify or defend the truth claims of Christian theology. Frei argued that theology is a descriptive discipline and is therefore a discipline that uses philosophical concepts only eclectically and on an *ad hoc* basis. See Frei, *The Eclipse of the Biblical Narrative;* idem, *The Identity of Jesus Christ: The Hermeneutical Bases of Dogmatic Theology* (Philadelphia:

But Christian theologians cannot avoid awareness of and dialogue with the other *Wissenschaften* in the university, since the task of Christian theology, once properly grounded, includes the responsibility to relate its way of thinking to other ways of thinking among the other *Wissenschaften* in the university and to questions that these other disciplines raise about human existence and the meaning of all contingent being. Although theology has an independent starting point, it is a "mixed *Wissenschaft*" and "not an absolute *Wissenschaft*, since it contains that which other *Wissenschaften* also pay attention to as well" (*GT* 232). "Where philosophy ends with a question, theology begins answering" (*SBb* 1:15).[35]

Consequently, despite its similarity to some aspects of a nonfoundational approach to theology, Hofmann's theological method, on the other hand, also seeks to relate the truth claims of the faith to "the world out there," which includes the other academic disciplines in the modern university and the needs of modern societies.[36] Christian theology is to be related to all of

---

Fortress Press, 1975); idem, *Types of Christian Theology* (ed. George Hunsinger and William Placher; New Haven: Yale University Press, 1992), esp. 70–91. See also Ronald Thiemann, *Revelation and Theology: The Gospel as Narrated Promise* (Notre Dame, Indiana: University of Notre Dame Press, 1985); John Thiel, *Nonfoundationalism* (Philadelphia: Fortress, 1994); and Kathryn Tanner, *Theories of Culture: A New Agenda for Theology* (Minneapolis: Augsburg Fortress, 1997).

35. "Theology fulfills its calling when it witnesses that Christianity satisfies the need for salvation; philosophy fulfills its calling when it proves that the unregenerated life bears in itself the unresolved contradiction of an unsatisfied need for salvation. Where philosophy ends with a question, theology begins answering. Together both are the expression of a present state of things, since the Christian lives in the flesh, the church lives in the world, and Christ is hidden in God. *Wissenschaft* has not been ordered to do anything more than this in the present" (*SBb* 1:15). One is struck at least by the formal similarity between Hofmann's statement here and Tillich's ideal of a "correlational" model of "answering theology" that moves between "questions" that arise from a "situation" and "answers" that are given by means of the Christian "message." See Tillich, *Systematic Theology*, 1:18–28. Hofmann shares Tillich's openness to philosophical questions that are put to theology, but Hofmann would assert, contrary to Tillich, that the believer's Christian faith has its own independent foundation in the Christian *Tatbestand*.

36. "The difference between philosophy and theology, according to Hofmann, is that philosophy proceeds from the sensual-sensible nature, that which represents or introduces the human being to himself, to his nature or his essence, and thereby enters into the difficulties of his existence (sin and death), difficulties which are overcome by the knowing theologian who is in the communion with God realized in Jesus" (Wach, *Das Verstehen*, 2:360). Compare with David Tracy's comment: "Even before the difficult question of what constitutes a genuinely public claim to truth in theology is addressed, there is one common assumption among all theologians. That assumption is the need to provide some analysis of the contemporary situation insofar as that situation expresses a genuinely 'religious' question, i.e., a fundamental question of the meaning of human existence. A public discussion within the wider theological community is entirely appropriate, therefore, on two major issues: first, whether the situation is accurately analyzed (usually this proves an extra-theological discussion); second, why this situation is said to bear a religious dimension and/or import and thereby demands a theological response" (Tracy, *The Analogical Imagination*, 61). For Hofmann Christian theology is not merely a response that is oriented to the church; the Christian theologian must take into account other "publics" beyond the church, namely, society and the academy.

reality in an effort to interpret that reality in the light of the Christian faith.[37] Because of this comprehensive orientation of Christian theology, Hofmann, not surprisingly, was especially interested in the disciplines of philology, psychology, history, and, as his dogmatics lectures demonstrate, even the philosophy of religion.[38]

The Method of Theology

The distinctive task of Christian theology is to speak faithfully to the world about the Christian *Tatbestand*, the relationship between God and humanity that God has established in Christ. This *Tatbestand* is grounded in the experience of faith, "and all that is required is to uncover and expound the

---

37. What Ingolf Dalferth says of Karl Barth's theological method could just as easily be applied to Hofmann: "Barth does not content himself with the creation of a self-sustained realm of dogmatic discourse striving towards completeness. Separatist fideism of this sort is foreign to him. Rather, he then reapplies these categories by the rule of analogy to interpret critically both traditional theological discourse and non-theological discourse alike. For example, what 'history' really means is shown by the one history of Jesus Christ which, when interpretively applied to our common understanding of history, shows this to be, at best, a preliminary, abstract, and inauthentic understanding of history" (Ingolf Dalferth, "Karl Barth's Eschatological Realism," in *Karl Barth: Centenary Essays* [ed. Stephen Sykes; Cambridge: Cambridge University Press, 1989], 38).

38. Of importance here, too, are Hofmann's vice-chancellor speeches to the university as a whole. Five of these speeches have been preserved, those given at the start of the academic terms in 1848, 1853, 1856, 1871, and 1875. A common theme in these speeches is the ethical responsibility, and not merely the *wissenschaftliche* responsibility, that scholars and students have in the university toward humanity. "Love of science, then, that is not love for humanity does not have moral value. In whatever you do here, make it bring good to humanity; let it be of service to humanity, and not for yourself" (J. Hofmann, "Die neuen Aufgaben der Universitäten in der neuen Zeit," Rede beim Antritte des Prorektorats der königlich bayerischen Friedrich-Alexanders-Universität Erlangen am 4. November 1848 gehalten [Erlangen: University of Erlangen, 1848], 4). See also idem, "Der sittliche Beruf der Universitäten," Rede beim Antritte des Prorektorats der Königlich bayrischen Friedrich-Alexanders-Universität Erlangen am 4. November 1853 gehalten (Erlangen: University of Erlangen, 1853). This *"sittlichen Beruf"* or "ethical calling" is served by *"wissenschaftliche Bildung,"* which one might translate as "the formation of character by means of scholarly work." It includes "the love for the truth" and is subservient to what Herder called "the cultivation of the human" (*Bildung zum Menschen*). The classic statement that rejects this notion that universities have an ethical responsibility to cultivate the mind and spirit through the transmission of *Bildung* is Max Weber's famous essay, delivered in 1918, "Wissenschaft als Beruf," translated as "Science as Vocation," in *From Max Weber: Essays in Sociology* (ed. and trans. H. H. Gerth and C. Wright Mills; New York: Oxford University Press, 1977), 129–56. For recent critiques of Weber's conception of *Wissenschaft,* in favor of a rehabilitation of the Humboldtian notion of *"wissenschaftliche Bildung"* that coincides with Hofmann's conception, see Mark Schwehn, *Exiles from Eden: Religion and the Academic Vocation in America* (New York: Oxford University Press, 1993), esp. 3–21; Gadamer, *Truth and Method,* 9–19; and idem, "The Idea of the University — Yesterday, Today, Tomorrow," in *Hans-Georg Gadamer on Education, Poetry, and History: Applied Hermeneutics* (ed. and trans. Lawrence Schmidt and Monica Reuss; Albany: State University of New York Press, 1992), 47–59.

contents of that experience" (*DVW* 385).[39] The only concern of Christian theology, then, is "the relationship between God and humanity in Christ" (ibid., 379–80). "The theologian's task is not to deal with God on the one side and with human beings on the other, but with God in God's relationship to human beings and with human beings in their relation to God. Whatever lies outside of this relationship, whether it be teaching about God or about human beings, does not belong to theology" (*TE* 19). "The dogmatician has to express the relation of God to human beings in Christ, as this is the content of personal experience, i.e., the fact that God loves the Christian, along with the presupposition and the consequences of this fact. That fact itself is the basis out of which dogmatics grows . . . " (*DVW* 396). Thus, the theologian "will have the further task of grasping in word and bringing to representation that relationship which exists between God and humanity in Christ also as he finds in himself" (ibid., 383). "To understand scientifically the *Tatbestand* of this actualized truth forms then the task of the theologian, a task which lies completely within the domain (*Gebiet*) of his Christian faith" (*GT* 229–230).[40] Hofmann thereby agreed with Augustine (354–430) and Anselm (1033–1109): Christian theology is always an enterprise of "faith seeking understanding" (*fides quaerens intellectum*). The goal of this enterprise, like that of all legitimate *Wissenschaften* (Hofmann thought), is to express the Christian *Tatbestand* as a unified and "organic whole." While "the same *Tatbestand* is located in each individual Christian," the theologian seeks to develop the *Tatbestand"* into a scientific whole [*wissenschaftliches Ganze*]" (*ET* 18).

Clearly, Hofmann's methodological starting point is intentionally quite different from the traditional scholastic orthodox Lutheran dogmatic starting point in Scripture (*sola Scriptura*). Hofmann viewed scriptural exegesis not as the basis or starting point of systematic theology, but only as an

---

39. See also Franz Frank's description of the task of theology, which Hofmann shared: "The task which is herewith set for Christian theology has points of contact with the apologetic endeavors of the present day; but is essentially distinguished from them by the fact, that in place of wishing to produce or maintain Christian certainty, or to restore it where it has been shaken, it presupposes the same as existing, [and] consequently, merely calls for its scientific expression about itself in the sense of Christian understanding, to the end of its rendering an account of itself, and furnishing the proof for its right of existence" (F. H. R. Frank, *System of the Christian Certainty* [2d ed.; trans. Maurice Evans; Edinburgh: T & T Clark, 1886], 18–19).

40. Compare with Bultmann's principal concern in his series of lectures *What Is Theology?* (ed. Eberhard Jüngel and Klaus Müller; trans. Roy A. Harrisville; Minneapolis: Fortress, 1997). For Bultmann, as for Hofmann, theology is a *Wissenschaft* that seeks to conceptualize "believing existence," and which requires a mode of investigation appropriate to its object, i.e., "faith." Theology cannot be undertaken "out of curiosity," but only as "a venture in which we ourselves are at risk" (ibid., 156).

activity that one entered after systematic exploration of the Christian *Tatbe-stand* that centers in the risen Christ. Since this "transcendent *Tatbestand*" is distinct from all earthly realities, including the Bible and the institutional church, Hofmann desired to hold on to the priority of the immediacy or existential and independent character of the relationship with Christ while acknowledging that the activities of the congregation mediate one into that relationship. The congregation is established so that individuals will come to faith, but within this community the individual stands in a direct and personal relationship with God in Christ.

Nonetheless, since the Christian faith is not merely a matter of the individual's relationship to the risen Christ but has itself also been mediated by a community into which the theologian is incorporated, the theologian must proceed to answer the question of how this experience of faith could be shaped the way that it is. Thus the theologian must reflect upon and seek to understand the historical nature of the presuppositions of the relationship that forms the object of the Christian's faith. These presuppositions of the theologian's religious experience, reached by means of the systematic procedure in his method (e.g., reflecting upon one's being a baptized child of God in Christ), include both historical and eternal presuppositions. Both sets of presuppositions involve those conditions which must have been the case for the relationship between God and the Christian to have developed the way that it has within the ecclesial community.

One assumption of Hofmann's theological understanding is that the past history of Christianity can only be understood on the basis of the present, Christian *Tatbestand,* which is the creation of the risen Christ, who is himself the living connection between the present and the past.[41] This present reality opens the Christian to a proper understanding of the past of Christianity and, indeed, to a proper understanding of time and history since Christ is the unity of all time, past, present, and future. As the middle of time, this present experience is the guarantee of the unity of past and future. For Hofmann time or history itself is grounded Christologically, since the center or the focus (*Mitte*) of history is the life, death, and resurrection of Jesus (*ET* 7).

> The self-representation of Christ in the world is the essential content of all history, namely, first, his pre-figuration in the life of our nature [*seine Vorausdarstellung im Leben unserer Natur*], second, his appearance in the flesh and his transfiguration of the same, and third, the

---

41. I am indebted here to Behr's analysis. See Behr, *Politischer Liberalismus,* 20. According to Wenz, "Hofmann's understanding of history disrobes the traditional dogmatic loci of their didactic nature and explains the moments of an historical course" (Wenz, *Geschichte,* 2:36).

representation of his transfigured nature in the personal life of the Christian. His appearance in the flesh serves as the antitype of his pre-figuration, his representation serves as the type or model of the life of his community. He cannot effect or fulfill the pre-figuration of himself without also giving it to his community. He cannot represent himself in the struggling community without at the same time modeling the triumph of the community. Therefore, we have in the self-representation of Christ in the world both history and prophecy: history, because it is the always progressing formation of the communion between God and humanity; prophecy, because it is the always more certain reference to the final form of the communion between God and humanity. What we are dealing with is this prophesying history and the effective working of the Spirit (which attaches itself to the word) through which this prophesying history occurs. (*WE* 1:40; see also *DVL* 53 and *BH* 36–39)[42]

"Jesus is the end but also the center of history: his incarnation in the flesh is the beginning of the end" (*WE* 1:58). Hofmann's understanding of "the present" allowed him therefore to presuppose both the unity of history and also his immediate access to this unity in the provisional fulfillment of history in the present life of the Christian.[43] But the present mode of divine activity in history is the resurrected and living Christ, not the Jesus of past history (*ET* 7).[44]

The history which the Christian theologian seeks to examine, then, is a history which reaches into the present to confirm again an experience which was also created in the past. Historical revelation is related to personal faith not as a set of teachings to a person who is to know them or to a set of timeless "concepts" (*Begriffe*) "behind the facts," but as a history which has a present dimension in the experience of the believer. It authenticates itself by happening once again to the believer in the present. "Resulting

---

42. "That which is reported as miraculous (*das Wunderbare*) is for the interpreter nothing isolated but rather a part of the developing *Heilsgeschichte* which is prophesying history about the miracle of miracles, Christ, who is the center-point of the miraculous.... The self-representation [of Christ] is at the same time history and prophecy: first, as the always progressive formation of the community between God and humanity; second, as the always certain reference to its final form" (Wach, *Das Verstehen*, 2:372).

43. Compare Hofmann's understanding that Jesus is "the end of history" with Pannenberg's similar claim that history is the locus of God's revelation and that the resurrection of Jesus Christ from the dead provides revelatory insight into the meaning and outcome of history. According to Pannenberg, the end of history is already present proleptically in the resurrection of Jesus Christ from the dead. See Pannenberg, "Redemptive Event and History," 15–80.

44. There is a clear similarity between Hofmann's view and that of Martin Kähler (1835–1912), who made a distinction between "the so-called historical Jesus" and "the historic biblical Christ."

from this [inquiry into the personal experience of rebirth and faith] there is then a system of facts, a history that has become a system" (*DVL* 42).[45] "So of necessity the activity of the theologian is to inquire into these historical objects, [i.e., to inquire into] the church's development and temporality and also into the Holy Scriptures" (*ET* 23).

The conviction of Hofmann was that theological reflection involves the mutual penetration and relation of the two dimensions of the *Tatbestand*, namely, both the present experience of the Christian individual and the history of God's relationship with humanity as it has developed in God's relationship with ancient Israel and the Christian church. The task of the theologian is to correlate the content of the faith reached through systematic analysis of the present *Tatbestand* (Hofmann's "first way") with the content of faith reached through investigation of the historical and trans-subjective dimensions of the *Tatbestand* (Hofmann's "second way"). The question is whether the results of such historical investigation are in agreement with those reached through experiential-systematic reflection. Only with the establishment of such coherence is the truth of the Christian faith established. To establish this harmony is the project of Hofmann's *Der Schriftbeweis* ("The Scriptural Proof"), wherein he first analyzes his personal Christian faith, especially his baptismal regeneration, and then proceeds to develop and express the implications of this experience as it is clarified in Scripture.[46]

Hofmann acknowledged that the results of the first way (i.e., systematic analysis of the present *Tatbestand*) are uncertain if they do not conform to the criteria that are external to the individual believer's personal relationship with the risen Christ. "Certainly, the theologian cannot unfold the content of the relationship [between God and humanity in Christ] without referring to the existing expression of this relationship in the Bible and the church"

---

45. Hofmann's approach to the formation of his systematic theology is like Schleiermacher's, who developed his systematic theology out of propositions that are presupposed within the antithesis of sin and grace. "While in general the manner in which the God-consciousness takes shape in and with the stimulated self-consciousness can be traced only to the action of the individual, the distinctive feature of Christian piety lies in the fact that whatever alienation from God there is in the phases of our experience, we are conscious of it as an action originating in ourselves, which we call sin; but whatever fellowship with God there is, we are conscious of it as resting upon a communication from the Redeemer, which we call grace" (*CF* 262).

46. Hofmann's "self-involving discourse" was quite revolutionary in his day but is more commonplace today, even among Lutherans. One thinks of Van Harvey's introduction to the 1996 edition of his great work, *The Historian and the Believer*, ix-xxiv. For other recent examples, see Mary Potter Engel and Susan Brooks Thistlethwaite, eds., *Lift Every Voice: Constructing Christian Theologies from the Underside* (San Francisco: Harper and Row, 1990); Robert Benne, *Ordinary Saints* (Minneapolis: Fortress, 1988), 40–44; Ronald Thiemann, *Constructing a Public Theology: The Church in a Pluralistic Culture* (Louisville: Westminster/John Knox, 1991); and Peter Hodgson, *Winds of the Spirit* (Louisville: Westminster/John Knox, 1994), 332–37.

(*DVL* 40). The "certainty" (*Gewissheit*) of the Christian is outside of the Christian (*extra nos*), in God and God's promises.

> … [I]f there is to be a reliable, certain exposition of the content of the personal salvific experience, we need guidance that must come from outside ourselves. The starting point of our dogmatic and ethical activity lies, to be sure, within us. But we cannot travel the path forward from that starting point reliably unless we embrace guidance that comes from outside ourselves. (*DVW* 387–88)

This external direction comes by means of historical investigation of the *Tatbestand* that is external to the Christian (i.e., Hofmann's second way). "Since all members of the Christian community are now equally capable of error, there must be a norm given, in Scripture, for all ecclesial proclamation of the truth, which is the form of the divine word for the community as a whole and for the individual according to his position within the community; and indeed this is Scripture as a whole, as this is willed by God as a total" (*DVL* 106). "The Bible offers the biblical interpreter a complete and analogous exposition of Christianity with which to compare his own understanding by means of systematic activity" (*SBb* 1:23).

> The theologian, who wants to interpret the relationship between God and humanity in Christ, as it is the content of personal experience, understands himself — to express it completely and correctly — to be dependent on continuous comparison of the same relationship as it is contained in Scripture and as it has come to formation in the church. In the experience of the individual the relationship between God and humanity is mediated through ecclesial activity. In the church, however, the relationship between God and humanity established in Christ is witnessed to through Scripture. (*DVL* 40)

"Systematic theology has its justification in that Christianity is a personal matter; but Christianity is equally a communal matter and therefore historical activity must join the ranks of systematic theology. When one does not do the latter, Christianity turns from being a personal matter into being a subjective matter" (*ET* 32–33).[47]

---

47. For a cogent critique of the Barthian charge of "subjectivism" against Hofmann, see especially Max Keller-Hüschemenger, "Das Problem der Gewissheit bei J. Chr. K. von Hofmann in Rahmen der Erlanger Schule," in *Gedenkschrift für D. Werner Elert* (ed. F. Hübner; Berlin: Lutherisches Verlagshaus, 1955), 288–95. Keller-Hüschemenger stresses that Hofmann deliberately uses the word "personal" (*persönlich*) and avoids the word "subjective" (*subjektiv*) in an effort to avoid the usual contrast between "objective" and "subjective" and to defend himself against the charge of "subjectivism." See also Kantzenbach, *Die Erlanger Theologie*, 194–95.

The personal certainty rests on God's immediate self-attestation to the human being, but it is mediated through the church. And the activity [and the affairs] of the church are then corrected when they are normed by Scripture. A one-sided emphasis on the personal experience of salvation brings either mystical or pietistic degeneration of doctrine. One-sided emphasis on the church without the necessity of a norm and without the right and the validity of the personal experience is papistic. One-sided emphasis on Scripture as the laws of God for faith and life is located in the Reformed church and its sects.... Therefore the theologian wants to express the content of the personal experience completely and correctly by means of a continual comparison with the ecclesial formulation of this relationship as well as with the content of Scripture. (*DVL* 41)[48]

This understanding of the Christian *Tatbestand* provides the context for Hofmann's response to Delitzsch's accusation that Hofmann's theological method was too subjective:

But that the *Tatbestand* which has become realized in me originates [roots] in the Word as it has become interiorized in me — well, one cannot really say that. About my Christian life this is true, but the *Tatbestand,* which has included me in itself, is the unified content of the Word. In the Word which was proclaimed to me, the one who came

---

48. Hofmann thought that this "correlational" step of his method was distinctly different from Schleiermacher's theological method. Hofmann thought that Schleiermacher did not account sufficiently for the *Tatbestand* of the Christian experience. Instead of analyzing Christianity as a modification of "the feeling of absolute dependence," Hofmann sought to analyze the historical nature of God's revelation. "The unfolding of the content of this proposition [the universal articulation of the Christian experience] is something other than Schleiermacher's description of pious self-consciousness, i.e., it is not the existence of the Christian that comes to expression, but always the *Tatbestand* which exists objectively but has realized itself in me" (*ET* 51). Also of importance is Hofmann's remark to Delitzsch: "Schleiermacher's dogmatics was epoch-making because it attempted to derive the dogmatic-doctrinal whole from pious consciousness, i.e., through the subjectivity of the content of faith which up until now has been solidified in objectivity. But how much of the inalienable has been lost to him because of this interiorization!" (*BD* 200). "For [Hofmann], therefore, the material of dogmatics is not as for Schleiermacher the condition of pious feelings, ... but the historical objectivity of the living reality created through Christ, which allows it to be deduced by each individual because of rebirth as a system of *heilsgeschichtliche* development" (Wapler, *Johannes v. Hofmann*, 93). According to Hofmann, the standpoint of the Christian (who is a Christian precisely because of the activity of God through the word of the Bible mediated through the church) places the Christian in relation to a history that calls for careful investigation and interpretation. The fact that one is a Christian is not an *isolated* fact, but one that directs one away from oneself to God, to the Bible, to the church's confessions, to the liturgy of the church, to church history, to world history. The experience of Christian rebirth is an experience which occurs by means of the divine word and the means of grace and it immediately directs one away from oneself.

down from heaven and who returned to heaven came to me and became my own so that I know him now from experience as the mediator in whom I have peace with God. I confess him to be the mediator and thus the unified content of the Word. But that content is not I nor my Christian life nor my Christian self-consciousness. Indeed it is quite beside the point that the periphery of the *Tatbestand* that includes me in itself is much wider than my inward life which is embraced by it. The point into which I enter is Christ himself. He has made me a Christian. This point [Christ] is at the same time also the circle which encloses me and the whole world, visible and invisible, present and future. (*BD* 55–56)[49]

The goal of Hofmann's historical investigation of the ecclesiality of the Christian *Tatbestand* is both to confirm and to correct the understanding of one's personal relationship to God in Christ reached through the "first way," the initial systematic investigation of that relationship.[50] Each step or procedure, the systematic and the historical, investigates the same Christian *Tatbestand*, but each procedure looks at that *Tatbestand* differently. The criterion by which Hofmann judged whether or not a theology is true is the degree to which such a theology corresponds to the Christian *Tatbestand*. The scriptural understanding of the Christian *Tatbestand* occurs in the expression of a coherent correlation between personal experience of faith and the scriptural whole (including the history of the church).[51]

We have seen that the object of faith, namely the existing relationship between God and humanity in Christ, is the content of (1) Scripture, (2) the history of the church, and (3) personal, individual experience.

---

49. In light of the above analysis, Hofmann's theological method cannot be properly understood as a form of theological Cartesianism or Hegelianism that seeks a certain foundation within the knowing subject. On this point, see Senft, *Wahrhaftigkeit und Wahrheit*, 94–97; and Schellbach, *Theologie und Philosophie*, 38.

50. Indeed, Hofmann did not claim to have provided "the definitive statement" or "proof," as he calls it, of the Christian faith, as if such a thing could ever be produced. "I name my system 'an attempt' because I am prone to mistakes which my successors will avoid more easily in the future as they attempt a solution to the task I have set forth" (*SS* 4:3). *Der Schriftbeweis* is "not about building an arsenal of biblical evidence to support the old way of making dogmatic assertions. Instead, the book is about defining the essence of Christianity as the means for providing an all-sufficient foundation for theology" (Beyschlag, *Die Erlanger Theologie*, 68).

51. "If the truth of the faith cannot (any longer) be established and guaranteed by means of the objective proof-texts of the old orthodox dogmatics, but can be established through personal experience of salvation, then the scholarly summary of Christian truth can be produced only in the following way: The present experience of faith (here the doctrinal whole) and the *heilsgeschichtliche* substance of the revelation (the biblical whole), as two independent organically structured unities, approach one another in such a way that they come together in a great dogmatic-exegetical 'equation' (Otto Procksch) into a congruence between the two" (Beyschlag, *Die Erlanger Theologie*, 70).

This object of faith is therefore to be explained and presented in a three-fold way. If this three-fold statement is, however, in harmony, then the proof of the justification of the faith will thereby be complete and finished. From the faith itself, therefore, do we extract the basis and truthfulness of that which is the content of the faith. (*DVW* 385; see also *WGS* 217)

The principles which Hofmann followed in order to explicate this object of theology are the focus of the next chapter on Hofmann's theological hermeneutics.

CHAPTER FOUR

Theological Hermeneutics

Scripture as Witness
to the Christian *Tatbestand*[1]

Hermeneutical Options:
Hofmann's Polemical Context

In order to appreciate further the uniqueness of Hofmann's theological method, one must understand the polemical context in which he defined and used it. He set himself against four fronts: Protestant Orthodoxy, rationalism, historical criticism, and German Idealism.[2]

Protestant Orthodoxy

First and foremost, Hofmann sought to distinguish himself from those who wanted to define Christianity solely on the basis of an understanding that maintains that the Bible is a divine book that contains a collection of objective, ahistorical doctrines or ideas that have, so to speak, "fallen from heaven." Here Hofmann placed himself in opposition to a view of Scripture that had been dominant in Protestantism since the end of the Sixteenth Century. Even though Luther's appeal to "Scripture alone" (*sola scriptura*) was an effort to free exegesis from captivity to dogmatic church tradition, very quickly this freedom from tradition was given up by Protestant theologians in the next generations. Within seventeenth-century Protestant Orthodoxy exegesis of the Bible was bound to established interpretations of the traditional "proof-texts," from which no one was permitted to deviate. Thus Protestant orthodox tradition predetermined for the interpreter the correct doctrinal meaning of these "proof-texts." In fact, biblical study was merely the marshalling of these proof-texts or, better, the marshalling of the established meanings of these proof-texts as they had been given in the doctrinal

---

1. The best treatment of Hofmann's hermeneutics is by Senft, whose analysis has informed the present chapter.
2. At this point I will address only three of these fronts. The fourth, German Idealism, is so significant that it will be treated on its own in the next chapter.

tradition. These texts "were explained apart from their context, with the result that the meaning of the latter was inevitably determined by the previously fixed interpretation of those proof texts. . . . Exegesis was thus again dominated by tradition . . . " (*BH* 19).

In Hofmann's day, historical criticism and the critical spirit of the Enlightenment had called into question this traditional view of the Bible. Nonetheless, some scholars, such as Hengstenberg, continued to assert that the divine inspiration and inerrancy of the Bible guarantee the indubitable verification of the timeless, eternal doctrines contained in the Bible.[3] In such a view the Bible is a textbook of divinely revealed theological propositions.

> For Hengstenberg, the inspiration of Scriptures was the foundation of all theology. To believe that Moses wrote the Pentateuch and that the messianic prophecies actually described the person and life of Jesus was a matter of religious duty (particularly against Schleiermacher, Hengstenberg zealously emphasized the validity of the Old Testament). Opposition to historical criticism was an obligation of faith. Against conservative or liberal views stressing the "organic" character of biblical truth, Hengstenberg distinctly insisted that God acted in history quite without regard to "law" or historical condition, and this arbitrary action was itself a particularly clear and even necessary sign of revelation.[4]

According to Hofmann, the main problem with this view is that the Bible is treated as an ahistorical "law-book of faith" that has priority over the past facts [*Tatsachen*] of Christianity (*SBb* 1:5). These past facts are almost incidental to the divine doctrines that the Bible contains. Like Hamann's critique of seventeenth-century Lutheran Orthodoxy, Hofmann thought Hengstenberg's view of the Christian faith was misguided because it failed to recognize the correspondence between the personal experience of faith and the Christian *Tatbestand*, and that one's Christian experience originates from a free and independent relation to God through the risen Christ within the Christian congregation. Such a relation to God cannot be reached by means of a legalistic interpretation of Christianity, its scriptures, or its history (ibid.,

---

3. For a helpful inquiry into the meaning of "inerrancy" in the history of Protestant theology, see Arthur Carl Piepkorn, "What Does 'Inerrancy' Mean?," *Concordia Theological Monthly* 36 (September 1965): 577–93.

4. Welch, *Protestant Thought*, 1:195–96. For further analysis of Hengstenberg's approach to the Bible and Christian theology, see Hirsch, *Geschichte*, 5:118–30; and James C. Taylor, "Ernst Wilhelm Hengstenberg as Old Testament Exegete" (Ph.D. diss., Yale University, 1966). Hengstenberg taught at Berlin from 1824 until his death in 1869. For forty-two years he was editor of the conservative journal, *Evangelische Kirchenzeitung*. His opposition to historical criticism is especially evident in his best known text, *Christology of the Old Testament* (2d ed.; trans. Theodore Meyer and James Martin; Grand Rapids: Kregel, 1956).

1:6; see also *WGS* 199–200). Hengstenberg's "biblicistic" view must be rejected or at least modified since it is

> not a personal relationship to and attitude towards God, such as the Christian is conscious of, but a legalistic relationship to a thing. For whether it be that which is given or the giving of it, it is always a mere something that is believed. Christianity ends up in this legalistic poverty by way of supernaturalism, because that makes out of Christianity a historical revelation the content of which must be believed simply because it is divinely revealed. (*ET* 6)

Thus, Hofmann argued that Hengstenberg misunderstood the historical nature of the divine revelation and he had failed to see how that divine revelation relates to personal, Christian experience.[5]

Rationalism

Like Hamann and Herder, Hofmann also set his understanding of Christianity and the Bible against that of the theological rationalists (e.g., especially Christian Wolff [1679–1754] and Gotthold Lessing [1729–1781]), in whom Hofmann sensed a different form of the same legalistic understanding he detected in Hengstenberg and the Protestant biblicists.[6] While Hengstenberg and other biblicists turned the Bible into a "law-book" of ahistorical doctrines, the rationalists utilized a critical consciousness that gave priority to the claims of universal, ahistorical reason which were understood to be fully consistent with the universal truths of the Christian faith.[7] Interpreters like H. E. G. Paulus (1761–1851) merely sought to demonstrate that the basic

---

5. "Since the Christian experience is self-authenticating and carries within itself its own content, one cannot approach scripture with a view to culling out authoritative doctrines which 'are to be believed.' Nor can it be the case that the teachings of scripture are to be imposed by virtue of a doctrine of infallibility. Exegesis cannot be allowed to tyrannize experience in a legalistic fashion" (Forde, *Law-Gospel Debate,* 18).

6. Christian Wolff was a professor of philosophy, natural science, and theology at the University of Halle. He had a tremendous confidence in the power of reason to discover truths. His speculative philosophy dominated German learning in the second half of the eighteenth century. Lessing and Moses Mendelssohn (1729–1786) were perhaps the most representative and influential figures in the German Enlightenment (*Aufklärung*). See Livingston, *Modern Christian Thought,* 1:31–35, and also Henry Chadwick's introduction to his translation of Lessing's theological writings in *Lessing's Theological Writings* (ed. and trans. Henry Chadwick; Stanford: Stanford University Press, 1956), 9–49. The most complete analysis of Hamann's critique of the Enlightenment is James O'Flaherty, *Hamann's Socratic Memorabilia: A Translation and Commentary* (Baltimore: The Johns Hopkins Press, 1967), 17–47.

7. On the problem of "the authority of reason" in the period between Kant's first *Kritik* and Fichte's first *Wissenschaftlehre* (1781–1794), see Frederick Beiser, *The Fate of Reason: German Philosophy from Kant to Fichte* (Cambridge, Mass.: Harvard University Press, 1987). On Wolffian rational theology, see Heinz Liebing, *Zwischen Orthodoxie und Aufklärung: Das philosophische und theologische Denken G. B. Bilfingers* (Tübingen: J. C. B. Mohr [Paul Siebeck], 1961).

meaning of the Bible is fully consonant with "reason." Critics like Paulus allowed general anthropological, philosophical and historical "laws" of reason to become the decisive criteria by which they investigated the facts of a past Christianity from a position above the faith. By doing so, according to Hofmann, they missed the personal, existential relationship to the object of faith, and thus misunderstood that object. Hofmann's primary criticisms of Lessing and Kant and other rationalists were that they reduced the form of revelation to that which agreed with their conception of what was plausible, and they reduced the content of revelation to that which agreed with their conception of reason and morality.[8] The understanding and use of "reason" by the rationalists showed that their type of reason had become a law that did not allow them to grasp the past of Christianity correctly and thereby to recognize its uniqueness.[9] Like the biblicists, the rationalists also treated the Bible as a "law-book of ahistorical doctrines," but the doctrines they found there were either teachings that agreed with "the necessary truths of reason" or which formed part of the progressive historical education of humankind.[10] The historical past of the Bible represented merely one stage in the advance from barbarity to maturity, as in Lessing,[11] or it was merely a compatible aid to the genuine moral religion of reason, as in Kant.[12] Most

---

8. See Beyschlag, *Die Erlanger Theologie*, 21–24.

9. Especially in several of his post-1860 essays in *ZPK*, Hofmann devotes serious attention to the issues of historical criticism raised by such thinkers as F. C. Baur, Strauss, Joseph Ernest Renan (1823–1892), Otto Pfleiderer (1839–1908), and Franz Overbeck (1837–1905). See also Hofmann's criticism of historical criticism in *HS* 1:1–56.

10. "If no historical truth can be demonstrated, then nothing can be demonstrated by means of historical truths. That is: accidental truths of history can never become the proof of necessary truths of reason" (Gotthold Lessing, "The Proof of the Spirit and of Power," in *Lessing's Theological Writings*, 53). This same distinction between "the necessary truths of reason" and "the contingent truths of sensory experience" was made earlier by another "rationalist," Gottfried Leibnitz (1646–1716). "Truths of reason are necessary and their opposite is impossible; those of fact are contingent and their opposite is possible" (Gottfried Leibnitz, *The Monadology and Other Philosophical Writings* [trans. Robert Latta; London: Oxford University Press, 1925], 9).

11. In fairness to Lessing's ambiguous views toward the "positive religions," including especially Christianity, one must recognize that Lessing had a greater appreciation for the positive, historical religions than did the English Deists and that other great rationalist, H. S. Reimarus (1694–1768), whose "fragments" Lessing published while he served as librarian for the Duke of Brunswick at Wolffenbüttel (See H. S. Reimarus, *Fragments* [ed. Charles Talbert; trans. Ralph Fraser; Philadelphia: Fortress, 1970]). Lessing rejected Reimarus's narrow, "static," rationalist proofs of religion and he later argued that in the history of the historical religions humanity was slowly becoming educated and perfected. See Gotthold Lessing, *The Education of the Human Race* (ed. J. D. Haney; New York: Columbia University Press, 1908).

12. Kant shared with the early Lessing an abiding distrust of history as a vehicle of truth, though Lessing's later view of the development of the religious consciousness is more truly historical than is Kant's view of religion. Kant's classic treatment of religion is *Religion within the Limits of Reason Alone* (trans. Theodore Greene and Hoyt Hudson; New York: Harper and Row, 1960). For Kant's views on Christianity, see Greene's and Hudson's introduction to the latter work (pp. ix–cxlv); Michel Despland, *Kant on History and Religion* (Montreal:

significantly, according to Hofmann, the rationalists had no personal experience of salvation, of sin and divine forgiveness, of faith in God. Thus they lacked the experience which, Hofmann thought, provides the proper conditions for understanding the Bible and the Christian *Tatbestand*.

The trouble with both the biblicists and the rationalists, according to Hofmann, is that they did not take the historical incarnation of the Word (*Logos*), the divine revelation in the form of a self-giving servant, seriously. The literalists eliminated the human witness from the Bible, but the rationalists sought to liberate the majestic form of divine truth from the lowliness of its revelation. In Hofmann's view, both the biblicists and the rationalists neglected the historical peculiarity of Christianity, and they misunderstood that the historic past of Christianity can only be properly understood on the basis of the present reality of one's living relationship with the living and freely active God given in and through the risen Christ.[13] Christianity is not simply a type of reason or moral knowledge, as in Lessing's historical-revelational scheme or in Kant's "religion within the limits of reason alone," nor is Christianity a collection of ahistorical doctrinal teachings, as in Hengstenberg's theology. Instead, Christianity is primarily "a matter of historical experience" that is truly understandable only by means of personal faith in the living God.[14] The truth of Christianity can only be understood properly because it has been experienced in the immediate, existential, and present relationship which the believer has with God through the risen Christ.

McGinn — Queen's University Press, 1973); Hirsch, *Geschichte,* 4:272–329; G. E. Michalson, *The Historical Dimensions of a Rational Faith: The Role of History in Kant's Religious Thought* (Washington: University Press of America, 1977); Allen Wood, "Rational Theology, Moral Faith, and Religion," in *The Cambridge Companion to Kant* (ed. Paul Guyer; Cambridge: Cambridge University Press, 1992), 394–416; idem, *Kant's Moral Religion* (Ithaca: Cornell University Press, 1970); and idem, *Kant's Rational Theology* (Ithaca: Cornell University Press, 1978).

13. Compare with Hamann: "The characteristic difference between Judaism and Christianity concerns therefore neither immediate nor mediate revelation in this sense in which this is taken by Jews and naturalists — nor eternal truths and dogmas — nor ceremonial and moral laws, but simply temporal historical truths which occurred at one time, and shall never return — facts, which through a confluence of causes and effects, became true at one point of time and in one place, and therefore can be conceived as true only from this point of time and space . . . " (Hamann, as quoted by James O'Flaherty, *Unity and Language: A Study in the Philosophy of Johann Georg Hamann* [Chapel Hill: The University of North Carolina, 1952], 54). Hamann, too, disdained the notion that truths could be merely "eternal."

14. "The wrong attitudes listed by Hofmann [in his history of biblical hermeneutics] can be reduced to two. The one misjudges the historicity of the Scripture: They take an 'intolerable emphasis on the individual essence of speech,' because the Scripture is a 'work of the Holy Spirit,' and thereby expect too much of the text as 'a unified witness,' or they treat the Bible as a compact ahistorical block, or they grasp the historical document of truth as ahistorical doctrine. With regard to the other, they demonstrate a 'false position with regard to the truth of salvation,' i.e., they are ignorant of the matter [*Sache*] which is witnessed to in Scripture. The first cannot understand the history of the Bible, the second cannot understand the content" (Senft, *Wahrhaftigkeit und Wahrheit,* 89–90).

The theologian must enter his exegetical activity as a Christian. He cannot cast aside his Christianity in order to become an exegete. Such alleged presuppositionlessness [*Voraussetzungslosigkeit*] would instead constitute a surrender of the essential condition by which the Scripture can be understood. (*ET* 143)[15]

In truth a complete presuppositionlessness on the part of the interpreter, as for example Rückert demanded, is something unthinkable. It is impossible for the interpreter to be neither Christian nor non-Christian, neither religious nor irreligious, but merely interpreter. He approaches Scripture as he is, not as a "tabula rasa" upon which Scripture inscribes itself. (*BH* 23)[16]

Thus, the proper examination of the Bible and its history by the theologian does not occur within a general or presuppositionless perspective but "within the perspective of one who is a regenerated Christian" (ibid., 24). Such historical investigation presupposes "the personal certainty [*Selbstgewissheit*] of Christianity in the Christian" (*ET* 116). Hofmann acknowledged that a "purely historical, non-dogmatic interpretation of the Bible is not possible"; instead, proper biblical interpretation already involves a perspective that is governed by a dogmatic outlook that is in turn informed by earlier theological study of the Bible (*BS* 66). At the same time, unlike most of his day, Hofmann sought to emphasize that the interpretation of the Bible is only possible on the basis of an inner relationship with that which is witnessed to in the Bible. Barth's criticism of Hofmann's hermeneutics, therefore, "misjudges both the necessary significance that Hofmann attributed to experience (in order to secure by means of experience an understanding of the content of Scripture) as well as the unconditioned nature (*Unabdingbarkeit*) of the experience and its certainty for the grounding of theology as a science."[17]

---

15. Compare with Rudolf Bultmann's basic argument in his essay, "Is Exegesis Without Presuppositions Possible?" in *New Testament and Mythology and Other Writings* (ed. and trans. Schubert Ogden; Philadelphia: Fortress, 1984), 145–53. Of course, Bultmann did not allow his theological faith to interfere with his rigorous use of historical criticism, whereas, for Hofmann the object of theology necessarily affects the nature and practice of one's historical methodology. Gadamer indicates Bultmann's positive relation to Hofmann on the issue of "fore-understanding." See Gadamer, *Truth and Method*, 331, 523–24.

16. Leopold Rückert (1797–1871) taught theology at the University of Jena. His dogmatics text was governed by principles of Rationalism.

17. Hein, *Lutherisches Bekenntnis und Erlanger Theologie*, 227. Contrary to Barth's reading, Hofmann's appeal to religious experience was not an effort to make "a fatal compromise" with the *Zeitgeist* of his day, but Hofmann's way of saying that presuppositionless interpretation of the Bible is not possible. Understanding and interpretation "are possible only on the ground of a living relationship to the thing: [Hofmann] does not therefore call upon experience for support, because he does not want to master the Bible on the basis of experience, but rather

The theologian does not step before the church and Scripture free of presuppositions, but as a member of the church, to be sure, as a member who has prepared himself professionally for a scholarly vocation. That is, he does not [speak] without having fallen back upon that most general knowledge of Christianity. (*GT* 237)[18]

Historical Criticism

Even though Hofmann was more critical of biblical interpreters who neglected to discern the historical character of the biblical witnesses than he was of historical critics, Hofmann also criticized those who might have a sense for biblical history but who rejected or silenced the theological message of the Bible. Though Hofmann greatly appreciated the development of history and philology as university disciplines and as ancillary disciplines to theology, he found the purely historical approach to the Bible to be deficient.[19] Long before Hans Frei or Brevard Childs (1923–), Hofmann asserted

---

because he wants to understand the Bible on the basis of experience" (Senft, *Wahrhaftigkeit und Wahrheit*, 87). Barth's "judgment overlooks that Hofmann's central concern was to make methodically clear the *assurance* of biblical faith and not merely to justify himself externally" (Uwe Swarat, "Die heilsgeschichtliche Konzeption Johannes Chr. K. von Hofmanns," in *Glaube und Geschichte: Heilsgeschichte als Thema der Theologie* [ed. Helge Stadelmann; Giessen: Brunnen, 1986], 226). For similar criticism of Barth's interpretation, see Kantzenbach, *Die Erlanger Theologie*, 201.

18. Like Schleiermacher's taxonomy of theology, Hofmann understood the study of Scripture to be the first part of the discipline of historical theology. Historical theology also includes the study of church history and the history of doctrine, but the study of the Bible is normative for theology insofar as it reflects the authentic shape and expression of the church's faith.

19. One must underscore again that Hofmann's arguments for the independence of theology in the university did not mean for him that theology has nothing to learn from the other academic disciplines or that these other disciplines are unrelated to the task of theology. Rather, since a fundamental concern of the biblical theologian is to understand the human expressions in the Bible, philology is an important presupposition for the biblical hermeneutical enterprise. (In contrast to Hengstenberg, and in agreement with historical critics, Hofmann did not think the Bible contained a special type of written language, e.g., divine language of the Holy Spirit, but that the Holy Bible is a book like any other human document from the past — as well as an inspired product of God's working in history.) Likewise, psychology and history are important toward understanding both the internal-mental conditions that gave rise to those biblical expressions as well as the external-historical contexts in which those biblical expressions were first recorded (*BH* 102). "We have to take each [statement] in the Bible in its historical position, in its historical context; and we can appeal to no scriptural expression without recalling the occasion, the intended purpose for which it occurred, so that with certainty we understand why it has just this content and why it gives itself in just this form" (*SBb* 1:25–26). Historical investigation of the biblical texts assists one in recognizing the various types of expressions in the Bible, e.g., historical narrative, prophetic speech, poetry, etc. These tools of historical criticism also help to disclose the nature of the biblical genres. For example, Hofmann acknowledged that the speeches of individuals in the Gospels and Acts of the Apostles are not meant to be understood as verbatim reports. "What had been oral tradition was molded by the historian in this manner, and his hand is clearly discernible. How much more this might be the case when speeches and conversations of the distant past have been recorded! Their present shape is due in part to oral tradition and in part to the redactor who put them down in writing" (*BH* 227).

that the underlying assumptions of modern historical criticism are not theologically neutral. While Hofmann agreed with scholars like Johann Semler (1725–1791) and Johann Ernesti (1707–1781) that on the level of general hermeneutics the Bible has to be treated "like any other book," and even though Hofmann also admitted that historical critics had often come across the right sense of a biblical text (since they were not looking for ahistorical teachings and had a better sense for the historical), they too had a "false position with regard to the Holy Scripture" (*BH* 24). Faith alone makes possible the correct understanding of the content (*Sache*) of the Bible, because faith is oriented to the humble self-giving of God as love. Thus, Hofmann held that Strauss and other interpreters like him were incapable of discerning what is unique and of lasting significance in the sources of New Testament faith.

For Hofmann the abiding skepticism of historical critics about the free and active working of God in history, especially about the central divine action to which the New Testament writings bear witness, namely the resurrection of Jesus from the dead, is their chief problem.[20] In place of faith in the living Lord Jesus, Hofmann argued, these scholars had placed their faith in a philosophical worldview that was itself a kind of rigid, dogmatic skepticism. Historical criticism does not open the interpreter to the present experience of the unique, free, and existential relationship of faith to God. Furthermore, historical critics treat the facts of history as isolated events that have no relation to each other because that which provides such a coherent view of the facts, namely, Christian faith in the humble self-giving triune God, is missing:

> The ones [the historical critics], boxed into the present world, have sense and eyes only for their own reality: they lack the ability to understand the history whose result is the life in Christ. The others, however, have, along with the new life in which they know they have been reborn, become aware also of the gist of that history, without which the life would not be. That is the situation between the Sir Critics and the Sir Apologists. And the latter err only in that they all too often make the vain effort to convince the former of the reality of such facts, who lack the organ of perception. We do the historical critics the best service

---

For this reason also it "is impossible to establish the chronological succession of all the events in Jesus' Galilean ministry" (ibid.).

20. Hofmann also recognized that historical criticism could not provide any assurance to faith, since critical historical investigation was itself an uncertain procedure. Because historians disagreed with one another about historical matters, their conclusions could only be provisional.

if we, untroubled by their contradictions, make use of our ability to understand in order to show the coherence of the history documented by the sacred Scripture, in which history our life in Christ is rooted, and then challenge them — using their method of deconstructing this coherent history into a host of separate historical narratives, [which they] assess by the criterion of their simply natural way of knowing — to produce a history from which the reality of the church of Christ is able to comprehend itself.[21]

The accord between our need of salvation and the reported salvation facts, on the one hand, and between them [these reported facts] and the yes of their confirmation which we perceive in ourselves, on the other, impart a certainty that could not be produced by any line of argumentation. Our need for salvation points back to a will of God for humanity whose realization we also can expect. The reported facts of salvation are then experiences outside of ourselves, the witness of their confirmation, an experience within us. When the unanimity of that experience with that need occurs, no doubt remains about their divinity, if one does not oneself renounce the need with which they coincide. (*WE* 1:51–52)

A more complete understanding of the content of the Bible is dependent on the interpreter's own self-understanding as one who has received that which makes the Christian a Christian and that which also then makes the Bible to be "Holy Scripture." For this reason, too, Hofmann was critical of Schleiermacher's procedure of treating biblical hermeneutics as *merely* an *application* (*Anwendung*) of general principles of interpretation.[22] While Hofmann agreed with Schleiermacher that biblical hermeneutics are related to general hermeneutics (and that biblical hermeneutics involve universal principles of interpretation and human understanding), biblical hermeneutics cannot be completely subsumed under general hermeneutics. There is still a need for specifically theological hermeneutics to provide proper access

---

21. Hofmann, "Ein organischer Fehler der Herren Apologeten," *ZPK* 54 (1867): 393–94. See also *ET* 22ff.; and Wapler, *Johannes v. Hofmann,* 356–60.

22. See Hofmann, "Die Aufgabe der biblischen Hermeneutik," *ZPK* 45 (1863): 34–36; and *ET* 137. For Schleiermacher's conception of biblical hermeneutics as a special application of general hermeneutics, see Friedrich Schleiermacher, *Hermeneutics and Criticism and Other Writings* (ed. and trans. Andrew Bowie; Cambridge: Cambridge University Press, 1998). See also Andrew Bowie, *Aesthetics and Subjectivity: From Kant to Nietzsche* (Manchester: Manchester University Press, 1993); Richard Palmer, *Hermeneutics: Interpretation Theory in Schleiermacher, Dilthey, Heidegger and Gadamer* (Evanston: Northwestern University Press, 1969), 84–97; Senft, *Wahrhaftigkeit und Wahrheit,* 1–46; Gadamer, *Truth and Method,* 184–97; and Jeanrond, *Theological Hermeneutics,* 44–54.

to the truth and reality to which the Bible bears witness.[23] This need becomes all the more acute when one realizes that the historical investigation of the scriptural texts leads to the disintegration, if not the outright abandonment, of the dogmatic unity of the biblical canon, since the biblical texts are understood as merely a collection of differing historical sources. Hence, for Hofmann, "a purely historical and undogmatic explanation of the content of the Bible is impossible" (*BS* 66). "The essential understanding of a thing does not come about by means of the historical way [i.e., by means of historical investigation]" (*ET* 26).

Hofmann's Biblical Hermeneutics

The Unity of the Scriptural Whole

For Hofmann one cannot properly understand the particular and the individual in the Bible unless one first has a rough understanding of the totality or the whole of the Bible. Thus the task of biblical hermeneutics is

> to show how the interpretation of Holy Scripture, done according to the ordinary rules of hermeneutics, is at the same time determined by the distinctive character of its object. The interpreter is in the first place confronted by the Holy Scripture as a whole, which in this capacity is the Holy Scripture of Christendom. In its totality and intrinsic unity it forms the object of biblical hermeneutics. The foremost question is how the activity of the interpreter of Holy Scripture is determined by the specific way in which he is confronted by the Bible in its totality. . . . [The Bible's] peculiarity is derived from the nature of its content which has caused it to be the Holy Scripture of Christendom. (*BH* 28)

But how does one come to this "whole"? On what basis is one able, if at all, to speak of the Bible as a "unity"? As we have seen in the previous chapter, the unity and authority of Scripture are only grounded in the theologian's personal experience of the Christian *Tatbestand,* to which the Scriptural whole also bears witness. Biblical hermeneutics must therefore begin with the fundamental assumption that Christianity is not a matter of "timeless doctrines," nor is it a matter of "ahistorical rational and ethical

---

23. "[Hofmann] is extremely conservative, but he doesn't want to avoid the problems of historical criticism, either. He sees that one cannot make do without historical-critical reflection, but his temper, his particular ecclesial orientation led him to prefer using historical criticism to rescue traditional views. . . . So his efforts offer the living drama of a conflict between his awakened sense of history and his conservative ecclesiality (*Kirchlichkeit*) about biblical hermeneutics" (Senft, *Wahrhaftigkeit und Wahrheit,* 92).

principles," nor is Christianity even a matter of doctrinal development in history; instead, Christianity should be understood primarily as a historical process of the mediation between God and humanity in and through the historical and present Christ (*SBb* 1:35). For Hofmann, the central fact of the Christian faith is not merely that God has given the world a book, but that God is seeking a relationship with humanity by means of that which witnesses to God's actions in history (*ET* 7). It is this coherence between the historicality of Scripture and the historicality of God's actions in history which makes the Bible into a unified whole.[24]

In order to express this historicality of Scripture, Hofmann defined the Bible as "the monument [*Denkmal*] of *Heilsgeschichte*" (*SBb* 1:25).[25] That is, the Bible is a single narrative that has its center or focus in Jesus and is the description of God's historical self-giving to humanity; i.e., it is the narrative history of God's establishing communion between God's self and humanity, first through the people of Israel but then in one man from that people, Jesus.[26] It is this specific content that makes the Bible as a whole the object of a special kind of interpretation (*BH* 8, 28).

Furthermore, the specific content of the Bible is *Heilsgeschichte,* a word that has both a "narrative" and a "historical" dimension.[27] (Hofmann also

---

24. The main title of Hofmann's last project is instructive: "An Investigation of the Coherence of the Holy Bible of the New Testament" (*Die heilige Schrift Neuen Testaments zusammenhängend untersucht*). In this project, Hofmann hoped to bring the origin of the individual writings of the New Testament and the interpretation of their individual parts into a unity under his concept of divine providence. According to his own plan, given at the end of his introduction (*HS* 1:55–56), he hoped to give an explication of a coherent biblical theology of the New Testament, an explanation of the doctrine of a New Testament canon, and a defense of the doctrine of the inspiration of the total New Testament canon.

25. Hofmann was not the first to emphasize the *heilsgeschichtliche* character of Scripture. He was preceded by Johannes Cocceius (1603–1669) who also abandoned the *"locus"* outline of traditional dogmatics in favor of a "covenant theology" (also called "federal theology," from the Latin, *"foedus,"* i.e., a league or covenant) which unfolded the historical relationship between God and humanity through a series of covenants. Cocceius emphasized Scripture as the record of God's covenantal-redemptive activity in history. Unlike Hofmann, Cocceius did not conceive the biblical events as an organic development within history nor did he think history itself could constitute divine revelation. Consequently, he did not relate in a conscious way the faith of the individual Christian to *Heilsgeschichte.* The other two main nineteenth-century representatives of a *heilsgeschichtlichtliche* theology were Johann Beck (1804–1878) and Karl Auberlen (1824–1864). Hofmann's main difference from these other two is his radical historicization of biblical doctrine, especially the doctrine of God. The centrality of Trinitarian *kenosis* in Hofmann's theology distinguishes Hofmann from these other main representatives.

26. Compare with Wilhelm Dilthey's (1833–1911) notion that a central "mid-point" allows the interpreter to discern "the whole" of a text. Such a "centering in a mid-point" gives "structure" to the whole. Implicit in this notion is the idea that a text must be understood in its own terms.

27. Comparison with Dilthey is instructive. Fundamental for Dilthey is the notion that all understanding is historical and temporal. The task of critical philosophy is thus to explain how historical understanding is conditioned by the structures of human life. Such historical understanding necessarily has a narrative structure. See especially Jacob Owensby, *Dilthey and*

used the German word *"Darstellung"* to convey the same thought.) God's history is a "narrative history" (*geschichtliche Darstellung*).[28] In Hofmann's theology there is a narrative quality to God's self-giving in history. Indeed, Hofmann understood the whole of biblical history, the history of Israel and the history of Jesus' whole life (and not merely his death and resurrection), including his forming of an historical, ecclesial community, as the self-revelation of God who is love. This history is the key toward understanding the Bible as a whole and, more importantly, understanding God's relationship with humanity as a whole (*SBb* 1:25).[29]

Hofmann's "salvation-historical" (*heilsgeschichtliche*) understanding of Christianity set him especially apart from the orthodox Lutherans and their understanding of the inspiration of the Bible. Although Hofmann believed in the inspiration of the Bible as a whole, he did not hold to the orthodox Protestant notion (i.e., plenary verbal inspiration), which he considered to

---

the Narrative of History (Ithaca: Cornell University Press, 1994). See also Gadamer, *Truth and Method*, 291–92.

28. Hofmann's conception of the Bible as a "narrative organic whole," an idea that was developed through Hofmann's study of Schelling and perhaps Hamann, anticipates recent and contemporary concerns to articulate a holistic biblical theology that treats the two testaments as a coherent "realistic" and "historical narrative" but which also understands that narrative whole within the unity of theology and a hermeneutical framework, i.e., the concern for a theological interpretation of the Bible. The work of Brevard Childs has some of its antecedents in Hofmann's theological hermeneutics. (Based on the numerous marginalia that Childs put in his copy of Hofmann's *Schriftbeweis*, one may conclude that Childs has studied this work very carefully.) The desire to articulate a "narrative theology" of the Old and New Testaments, as for example has occurred from within the so-called "Yale School" (especially Lindbeck and Frei, but also some of their students, notably Ronald Thiemann), also bears important resemblance to Hofmann's hermeneutical project. Both Hofmann and Lindbeck speak of the Biblical narrative as that which encompasses the world rather than the world which absorbs the text. See Lindbeck, *The Nature of Doctrine*, 117–18; Frei, *The Eclipse of the Biblical Narrative*; and Thiemann, *Revelation and Theology*, 115. See also Francis Watson, *Text and Truth: Redefining Biblical Theology* (Grand Rapids: Eerdmans, 1997). Watson articulates an interdisciplinary "biblical theology" that attempts to move beyond the criticisms of the earlier "biblical theology movement," as leveled by James Barr and others, but at the same time to avoid the unnecessary trap of "fictionalism" that earlier forms of "narrative theology" created (e.g., Frei's claim that there is a disjunction between scriptural meaning and scriptural reference and that meaning should emerge "solely as a function of the narrative itself" [Frei, *Eclipse of the Biblical Narrative*, 35]). In this respect, Hofmann differs from Frei and narrative criticism, since for Hofmann the scriptural text compels the theological interpreter of that text to take seriously the extra-textual reference to historical events that gives rise to theological truth within the biblical texts.

29. Hofmann's theological hermeneutic seems to be quite similar to Lindbeck's argument that "the Bible is to absorb the world," even though Lindbeck would probably classify Hofmann as "an experiential-expressivist." That Lindbeck misunderstood Hofmann's theological method (e.g., see Lindbeck, "The Confessions as Ideology and Witness in the History of Lutheranism," 388–401) is unfortunate given the rough parity between their understandings of the relation between Scripture and reality: "Intratextual theology redescribes reality within the scriptural framework rather than translating Scripture into extrascriptural categories. It is the text, so to speak, which absorbs the world, rather than the world the text" (Lindbeck, *The Nature of Doctrine*, 118).

be purely unhistorical. For Hofmann the doctrine of the verbal inspiration of the Bible makes an historical understanding of the Bible impossible from the start. Originally, the orthodox Protestant doctrine of the verbal inspiration of the Bible developed as a way of securing the normative independence of the Bible over against Catholic tradition, but such a view of the Bible actually led to the prioritizing of the Protestant dogmatic tradition over the historicality of the Bible. According to this old theory of the inspiration of the Bible, the event of revelation breaks into and suspends history. The point of revelation is to present inerrant truths.

In contrast to this position, Hofmann asserted, "Sacred Scripture is something better than a book without mistakes" (*BH* 82).

> In other words, Holy Scripture is not an infallible textbook of cosmology, anthropology, psychology, and so on; and the history recorded in the Bible is not to be understood as an errorless segment of a world history. This must be taken into consideration by the interpreter from the very first page of Scripture. Every interpretation of Genesis 1 which would make scientific investigation of creation unnecessary or dependent on the biblical record is erroneous. (Ibid., 75–76)

According to Hofmann, the proper presupposition for biblical interpretation is not a theoretical doctrine of inspiration or a theoretical understanding of the perfection of the Bible in all its details, but faith in Scripture as that which Christians know it to be through the experience of faith. "Holy Scripture is Holy Scripture for us only as the authoritative witness of the things which are apprehended by faith" (ibid., 75).

> The miraculous nature of Scripture, its Israelitic character, and its unity as the monument of salvation, form the theological presuppositions with which the interpreter approaches Scripture. With these in mind, the interpreter deals with the Bible as an integral whole in the sense in which it is recognized by the church as the authoritative proclamation of the saving truth. . . . Apart from these presuppositions, the interpretation of Scripture is of little avail. It may be grammatically and historically correct, but neither the language nor the content of Scripture is then understood with reference to the goal for which they are given. (Ibid., 100–101)

The experience of faith points the interpreter to divine revelation in history, a history that encompasses the biblical texts. More specifically, Scripture bears witness to God's self-giving in history, which remains "hidden" unless revealed to faith.[30] "The specific feature of Holy Scripture is precisely this: that all history is interpreted and recorded therein as transpiring between God and humanity. Its purpose is not to provide exact knowledge of the external course of events but rather to point out the significance which certain events have for the salvation realized in Christ" (*BH* 231).[31] Scripture is precisely this interpretation of history done in faith. Only in this sense was Scripture still, in its entirety, the inspired word of God for Hofmann:

> If we are nonetheless still to call Scripture as a whole the inspired word of God, then it needs to be shown that not only in the writing of each individual book but also in the collection of the books into a total, a definite, intended effect of the divine Spirit took place. Here, however, nothing else needs to be demonstrated other than a comparison between the goal toward which the Bible developed and its content as a whole and in part. (*BWE* 80)

Hofmann's understanding of inspiration emphasizes the process of the historical development of the biblical canon as the work of the Spirit. It is an aspect of the unity of divine revelation that the Spirit of God condescends to the written words of human beings — the Spirit "emptying" the Spirit of the Spirit's divine majesty — in the same way that the second Person of the Trinity humbled himself in taking the form of a slave. Thus, according to Hofmann, the process of inspiration and canonization should be understood as a corollary to the divine self-giving in history. There is a lowliness and humility to the revelation itself; the hiddenness of the divine revelation is disclosed only to faith. Although Hofmann was opposed to a simple equation of the Word of God with the words of Scripture, of the Spirit with the letter, he still regarded it as self-evident that one could perceive divine revelation only in its lowly form, in the form of a servant. Hofmann did not think it was possible to discern divine revelation by intuition apart from its appearance in the form of a humanly-conditioned servant. Thus, Hofmann's fundamental distinction-in-identity between Scripture and divine revelation is grounded in the incarnation of the Word (*Logos*), the humble

---

30. "The central certainty of faith will represent the rule or canon of understanding that itself, to speak like Hofmann, refers to the *Tatbestand* of the relationship between God and humanity mediated in Jesus. The hermeneutical task, therefore, begins with the expectation that it will correspond to this truth of the content of the Bible. (The Erlangen theologian reminds us here of the old principle of the analogy of faith.) So the scriptural variety and unity are reconciled by means of interpretation" (Wach, *Das Verstehen*, 2:373).

31. In this same section, Hofmann acknowledges that one may view "the past history of salvation from a number of different viewpoints. Thus we must always ascertain the viewpoint in *Heilsgeschichte* from which the narrative has been told, in order to be able correctly to evaluate both the arrangement of the narrative as a whole and also the significance which its details have for the whole" (ibid.).

self-giving of God in history. The scriptural witnesses serve to shed light on this fundamental self-giving of God.

In the first volume of *Die heilige Schrift neuen Testaments zusammenhängend untersucht,* Hofmann indicates that he hoped in the final volumes of this project to provide an examination of the New Testament canon from which one would be able to understand the Bible as an ecclesial document and to recognize in faith the work of the Holy Spirit in preparing this scriptural whole. The final volume was to be an examination of the relationship between the New Testament and the Old Testament. In Hofmann's understanding, the inspiration of the Bible refers to the spiritual goal or central concern of the Bible as an historical whole. In faith, the interpreter should recognize the divine character of the Bible as a witness to God's humble self-giving in history, which itself is comprehended as a totality (*BH* 35ff., 82ff., *HS* 1:55–56). The divine self-giving in history corresponds to the historical development of the biblical canon which, as a totality, witnesses to the divine self-giving. Thus, the "task arises for the theologian to establish, first, a history of Scripture itself, how it came to be in its individual books, how Scripture became a whole, how this whole came to express the intrinsic meaning it has. Thereupon the theologian finds in Scripture from beginning to end a continuous sequence of salvific acts of God" (*DVW* 382).

From the Biblical Whole to Biblical Particulars

If the first part of Hofmann's biblical hermeneutics is to treat the Bible as a unity, as a cohesive whole, the second part is devoted to the Bible's complexities and particularities in light of this whole. The two-fold process in Hofmann's biblical hermeneutics is to move from the whole to the particular and then from the particular back to the whole (*BH* 28).[32]

Hofmann's hermeneutical procedure is different from the typical modern procedure of applying general hermeneutics to the interpretation of Scripture, e.g., starting with a rigorous examination of the particulars of the

---

32. "If Hofmann wants to vindicate the biblical whole as the starting point of biblical interpretation, it will be pointed out that the hermeneutical circle is undoubtedly a given for all interpretation and that Hofmann's theological program suggested to him that a thought-out separation from this circle is impossible" (Wach, *Das Verstehen,* 2:366). Wach defends Hofmann's approach: "I don't see why an interpretation that is oriented to the general principles of interpretation should not also be able to get its bearings by means of the totality" (ibid.). Gadamer, following Dilthey and Wach, makes the same point: " ... the movement of understanding is constantly from the whole to the part and back to the whole. Our task is to expand the unity of the understood meaning centrifugally. The harmony of all the details with the whole is the criterion of correct understanding. The failure to achieve this harmony means that understanding has failed" (Gadamer, *Truth and Method,* 291).

biblical pericopes, texts, and individual books and then attempting to discern a unity among these particularities. While Hofmann recognized that biblical hermeneutics are related to general hermeneutics, his procedure of applying biblical hermeneutics is distinct from that of general hermeneutics. The "procedure of biblical hermeneutics must be the reverse of general hermeneutics" (*BH* 27). Only after one has a sense of "the biblical whole" is one able, then, to move to an understanding of the particular and the individual. One starts with a view of the biblical whole, given to the church and to personal faith, and then proceeds to the biblical particulars (words, sentences, paragraphs, pericopes, individual documents, and so on). These particulars will not be understood properly apart from the total context of the biblical "whole."

Since, for Hofmann, the biblical canon as a whole stands in organic relation to *Heilsgeschichte* as a whole and to the historical community of God as a whole, each scriptural statement must be understood in its "organic-historical relation" to the rest of *Heilsgeschichte,* including its organic relation to the historical Christian community that emerges from God's history with Israel (*WE* 1:49). This "total sense of the Bible," however, does not mean that the Bible should be understood as "a unity of doctrinal statements" but only as "a unity of salvation facts" (*DVW* 393–94). Hofmann also acknowledged that some parts of the biblical canon may be discerned which "cannot be integrated into the framework of a unified truth of salvation" (*BH* 102). This is not a major problem for the Lutheran Hofmann, since "there is no ecumenically determined canon of Holy Scripture," "nor has the Lutheran Church defined its limits in its confessions" (ibid.). The exegete must not thereby force all parts of the biblical writings into "the unity of salvation facts" or accommodate the saving truth to the whole of the Bible. Rather, an exegete "is entitled to doubt whether those parts truly belong to the Holy Scripture of Christendom" (ibid.). The interpreter has to investigate whether the intrinsic value of certain parts of the canon makes those parts fit to be part of the canon.

Thus, the task of the biblical interpreter includes the responsibility of raising out of the Bible the *right* parts of the salvation-historical (*heilsgeschichtliche*) whole and interpreting them correctly in relation to that whole.[33] Through faith each individual pericope or text or individual book

---

33. One needs to point out that many of the actual *heilsgeschichtliche* elements that Hofmann highlights, i.e., his actual exegetical assertions about *Heilsgeschichte,* are less than convincing. For example, Hofmann believed that the "necessary facts" of the *heilsgeschichtliche* whole include as real events: the origin of humanity from an archetypal human pair, the fall into sin through the deception of the original woman by the serpent, a literal millennial reign of Christ, and an eschatological return of the children of Israel to the promised land in Palestine. According to Hofmann, each one of these elements has its necessary place in the

of Scripture is to be understood — or criticized! — in relation to the historical development of the whole canon. Here Hofmann acknowledged that
the interpreter must reckon with the implicit criteria that were used to discern the relative authority of individual biblical writings, including even the
apocryphal texts. The interpreter must also reckon with such canonical issues as the distinction between the *antilegomena* (Biblical and non-Biblical
Christian writings whose authority was disputed in early Christianity) and
the *homolegoumena* (Biblical writings that were generally accepted in early
Christianity), the presence of noncanonical materials in the biblical texts
(e.g., the ending of Mark, the first verses of John 8), and the presence of
multiple sources from different historical periods within the same canonical
text (e.g., the Pentateuch, Zech. 9–11, Second and Third Isaiah, and so on).
Finally, the interpreter must also engage in textual criticism so as to establish
the canonical text.

Hofmann thought that the canon must correspond to a narrative unity
into which the various authentically canonical texts could be fit. This narrative whole became clear to Hofmann as he worked to discern a series
of successive historical stages that led up to the advent and appearance of
Christ, the further development of God's historical community of love in the
Christian church (including the development of the scriptural canon), and
the promise of eternal and perfect communion with God "on the last day"
(*eschaton*). Each new stage of history is always the development of earlier
stages that partially prefigure what is to come. Each stage of that history
contains within itself a concealed seed of future stages (*WE* 1:12–16). Thus,
history, within the *heilsgeschichtliche* context, has a dynamic character that
is only fulfilled in its future. In other words, history itself is the result of
God's working to bring history to its fulfillment and the canonical whole
then corresponds to this history.

From the Biblical Particulars to the Whole: The Example of Biblical Prophecy

In light of the canonical whole, Hofmann sought, for example, to understand
the nature of biblical prophecy. According to Hofmann, the purpose of the
biblical prophets was to disclose an historical openness in relation to both
the specific historical situation of the prophets, but also in relation to the
final goal of all history. The prophets mediated between God and humanity

---

systematic whole given in and through the relationship between God and humanity mediated
in Jesus Christ. Despite living within the intellectual world of early nineteenth-century Berlin,
a world that included Ranke, Hegel, and Hegel's students, Hofmann was incapable of fully deconstructing the biblical-symbolic world in which he lived. Nonetheless, Hofmann was aware
of the historical distance between the biblical texts and the interpreter, and thus of the need
for hermeneutics.

in their speech, and they not only looked to the future but remained rooted in the past and grounded in the present. This unique positioning gave them their insight into universal history. Indeed, according to Hofmann, the biblical prophets are the first to understand the universal character of history, which comes from God and is going toward the goal of God's eternal will (*WE* 1:253ff.). If the biblical prophets make promises, they are simply commenting on what is already present and given as promise in history through God's living, creative word (see ibid., 1:12). Therefore, according to Hofmann, *Heilsgeschichte* is not a construct, namely prophetic interpretation of history; rather, *Heilsgeschichte* is principally the history which itself demands prophetic interpretation. In other words, the facts of history regulate the course of "the prophesying history." The prophetic words are only the interpretation of the driving forces that are inherent in the facts themselves. The basis for the prophetic interpretation is the action/word of God in history (*DVL* 99; *WE* 1:14). The goal of prophecy is to bring to fulfillment the will of God. This happens as the prophetic word, grounded in the Spirit at work within the world, accomplishes what it says, and thereby history is made (*WE* 1:316).[34] One can speak meaningfully of prophecy only if one knows its fulfillment (*WE* 1:14).

> Whoever recognizes the gradual character of the revelation of God, the progress toward the fulfillment of salvation: that person will not find it strange to find the whole sacred history in all its essential progresses [*Fortschritten*] represented as prophecy or reference to the final... relationship between God and humanity. (*BWE* 57)

Each stage in the development of that historical relationship points beyond itself until it finally embraces the Christian in his or her present existence and in its movement makes the Christian a fulfillment of its prophecies.[35]

---

34. So also Pannenberg, whose study of the biblical prophets is like Hofmann's reading of the biblical prophets: "Within the reality characterized by the constantly creative work of God, history arises because God makes promises and fulfills these promises. History is event so suspended in tension between promise and fulfillment that through the promise it is irreversibly pointed toward the goal of future fulfillment. This structure is pregnantly expressed, for instance, in Deuteronomy 7:8ff.... The goal here of Yahweh's action in history is that he be known — revelation. His action comes from his love, begins with his vow, and aims at the goal that Yahweh will be revealed in his action as he fulfills his vow. What is here compressed into an especially deep and significant formulation is expressive of the structure of the Israelite consciousness of history in general.... Thus Israel not only discovered history as a particular sphere of reality; it finally drew the whole creation into history. History is reality in its totality" (Pannenberg, "Redemptive Event and History," 18–21).

35. James Robinson observes a "structural similarity" between Hofmann's understanding of *Heilsgeschichte* and Heidegger's notion of *"Lichtungsgeschichte."* *"Lichtungsgeschichte"* can either have the sense of light breaking through into a clearing in the woods, i.e., an area which has become light, or, as Heidegger seems to use it, as being emerging from the obscurity of forgetfulness into clear light within thought. The "is-ness" of things or their "being" *unveils* itself

Hofmann's understanding of prophecy and fulfillment was quite different from that of Hengstenberg. The latter taught that the historical conditions under which all prophesy occurs are purely accidental and of no inherent importance to the truth of prophesies that must be understood as merely verbal propositions. According to Hengstenberg, the doctrine of verbal inspiration means that God intervenes in human affairs by verbal propositions that have no relation to history. A biblical-prophetic statement of the past has just as much relation to the present and just as much doctrinal validity today as it did in its own time. This validity is grounded, for Hengstenberg, in the notion that all biblical prophecy is direct prediction about the Messiah. Consequently, Hengstenberg understood every Old Testament prophecy to disclose, in advance, direct and supernatural information about Jesus.

In opposition to Hengstenberg, Hofmann stressed the "nature and order" and the "interconnectedness" of historical events as essential for a proper understanding of the nature and purpose of biblical prophecy (*WE* 1:1). Just as there is in the Bible no doctrine apart from history and no mere revelation of doctrine about supposed eternal facts, so also prophecy cannot be understood as a supernatural intervention into history but only as an outgrowth of history (*SBb* 1:260–263). According to Hofmann, Hengstenberg turned God's speech into a conglomeration of doctrinal statements that were divorced from their initial historical context and put into a foreign context

---

from time to time in history. See James Robinson, "The Historicality of Biblical Language," in *The Old Testament and Christian Faith* (ed. Bernhard Anderson; New York: Harper and Row, 1963), 150–58. "According to Heidegger, language is not to be understood as arising basically from the thinking subject, man, but rather as arising from 'being' unveiling itself, speaking to us, giving rise to language which calls 'being' into thought.... Old Testament *Heilsgeschichte* as *Lichtungsgeschichte* expressed in such language as *Beracboth* and *Hodayoth* reaches its climax in the New Testament, where being is unveiled as the basic miracle of resurrection or new creation. It is the function of such language, according to Heidegger and the Bible, to call forth man's wholeness, his *Heil*.... Such wholeness Heidegger describes formally in terms of a square, in which the divine, the mortal, earth and sky touch. This concept of wholeness ... is the sense in which *Lichtungsgeschichte* is for Heidegger *Heilsgeschichte*" (ibid., 157). One should also note the similarity between Hofmann's understanding of prophecy and that of Hamann. Hamann, too, was trying to comprehend God's "speaking" in time, i.e., in history. "The 'polyhistors,' who treated history as if it were a corpse, who ignored the essential factors in their vapid recitations of historical facts, were frequently the target of Hamann's irony. Indefatigably he points out to them that which is truly historical, i.e., the happenings of the past and the future which become alive in 'our own personal present.' This vital interpretation of history as something which becomes alive for us today, is intimately connected with his belief in the omnipresence of God, which embraces the whole of the past and future. This is unthinkable without such an experience through faith. Thus prophecy is indispensable to genuine appreciation of history as it really happens. If historical science presumes to dispense with faith and the gift of prophecy, it will never penetrate to the event itself, but will mistakenly regard and publicize a dead abstraction as the event.... If this faith is eliminated and prophecy dispensed with as a clue to the interpretation of history, then 'the existential understanding of history' which remains is actually not 'existential' at all, but a hollow verbal formula instead of an inexpressible reality" (Leibrecht, *God and Man in the Thought of Hamann*, 65–66).

(i.e., Hengstenberg's own theological construct). In order to understand biblical prophecy correctly, Hofmann argued, one must pay close attention to the original historical situations that called forth such prophetic interpretation which itself was later formed into a Scriptural whole (*WE* 1:14). Hofmann insisted on the importance of attending to what was local and specific in the prophetic texts. Not all biblical prophecy is messianic. Some Old Testament prophecies have their fulfillment already in the Old Testament and some New Testament fulfillments are themselves prophecies of the end of all history (*BH* 66). But even so-called messianic prophecies must first be understood completely within their original historical situation since they do not initially nor directly point to the promised Messiah (*WE* 1:3). Instead they relate to specific *heilsgeschichtliche* facts in their original historical situation. Only from a later perspective can one see how these veiled prophecies receive their fulfillment in Christ, but in such a way that the original prophecy does not directly fit the future situation of Jesus. This difference between Hofmann and Hengstenberg resides in their respective ways in which they understood the "predictive" character of biblical prophecy. For Hofmann the biblical prophet was much more concerned with historical events that were contemporary to the prophet's life than with making predictive statements about the future. The point of prophecy is not individual, isolated proof-texts, but the movement of history itself that is discernible in the prophet's own historical situation.

Despite Hofmann's criticism of Hengstenberg, he did share with his theological adversary the view that all messianic prophecies also point ahead to the goal of God's intention for all creation. Hofmann, however, stressed that this intention is inherent within history itself and so is not something that must be added supernaturally to history. Fundamental for Hofmann was the use of typology, which he asserted should not be understood to be the same as allegory. The latter, in contrast to the former, does not require the historicity of the events to which it refers.

> This typology is indeed the most well-known element in Hofmann's understanding of history. . . . Above all, typology is the exact opposite of allegory — in this opposition the conflict between Hofmann and Hengstenberg is rooted. The type is not a mere sign, a mere symbol of the future which has no importance or value in itself; rather a type has its own unique importance.[36]

---

36. Procksch, "Hofmanns Geschichtsauffassung," 1035. Hofmann was not the first Lutheran theologian in the modern period to use typology. "In the history of hermeneutics typology has its important place. Hamann's method of exegesis derives, in spite of considerable abstruseness in detail, by no means from private eccentricity but renews an old and great tradition of theology" (Karlfried Gründer, *Figur und Geschichte: J. G. Hamanns "Biblische Betrachtungen"*

"Hofmann is an historical realist who wants to take historical types completely seriously."[37] For Hofmann "typical" persons, such as Adam and Eve, Abraham, Moses, David, the people of Israel, the prophets, and "typical" events, such as the Passover, the Exodus, Babylon as a world power, the destruction of the temple, the exile, are people and events of real historic significance which stand as types to their form of fulfillment.[38] God forgave Adam and Eve their sin by covering their nakedness, but that covering prefigures the forgiveness granted by Christ. Cain really slew Abel, but the death of the righteous at the hands of the unrighteous "is a riddle whose solution is found only in the death of the Son of God.... Thus the death of Abel, the righteous one, prefigures the death of Jesus" (*BH* 155). The one office of Moses prefigures the development of the office of prophet, priest, and king in a *Heilsgeschichte* that culminates with the Messiah, who unifies these three callings into one person again. David did not speak of the trials, tribulations, and experiences of a future individual (i.e., the Messiah), but his experiences nonetheless prefigure the experiences of the Messiah. Neither Isaiah 7:14 nor Isaiah 9:1–6 are predictions of Jesus' birth from the Virgin Mary (contrary to most conservative interpreters in the nineteenth century), but refer instead to an individual living in the original historical context of those texts, whose experience prefigures the birth of the Messiah.

Hofmann's concern was to take each Old Testament *type* seriously, and to treat it as completely oriented to its historical context, yet also show how that type fit into the whole of *Heilsgeschichte*.

> It is always necessary to interpret a single fact as part of the whole history.... By proceeding in that manner there is no danger that with this method individual features of an Old Testament event should be given a wrong interpretation as a result of isolating them.... What matters above all is that the specific significance of the total story should be recognized. By doing so its individual features will be given

---

als Ansatz einer Geschichtsphilosophie [Freiburg: K. Alber, 1958], 134). See also O'Flaherty, *Hamann's Socratic Memorabilia*, 81. For the history of the use of typology by biblical interpreters, see Leonhard Goppelt, *Typos: The Typological Interpretation of the Old Testament in the New* (trans. Donald Madvig; Grand Rapids: Eerdmans, 1982), 1–20. Goppelt understood his "salvation-historical" approach to the New Testament to be in continuity with that of Hofmann. See Leonhard Goppelt, *Theology of the New Testament* (2 vols.; trans. John Alsup; Grand Rapids: Eerdmans, 1981–1982), 1:276–81.

37. Procksch, "Hofmanns Geschichtsauffassung," 1035.

38. Through the use of typology Hofmann wanted to preserve Ranke's emphasis on the integrity and individuality of each historical epoch; nonetheless, contrary to Ranke, Hofmann asserted that the meaning of each particular event only becomes fully understandable at the end of history, i.e., "in Christ." Compare with Ranke's famous aphorism: "Each epoch is directly before God, and its value in no way depends on what it has produced, but [is] in its existence itself, in its very self" (Leopold von Ranke, *Weltgeschichte* [Leipzig: Dunker and Humblot, 1883], 9.2:14).

a typological interpretation merely inasmuch as they are related to the story as a whole." (Ibid., 163)

Only on the basis of a later development in history may those passages be understood as typological expressions about the miraculous nature by which the salvation event will occur in the future. Likewise, one must take special care in interpreting the Old Testament quotations within the New Testament, since Hofmann thinks these quotations help to identify the "antitypical" character of the New Testament as a whole (ibid., 210ff.).[39]

In order to understand the unique historical situation of Old Testament texts, as well as their potential relation to New Testament events, Hofmann developed a typological understanding of the Israelite nation/people of God and the New Testament congregation/church. Events like the Exodus from Egypt, the Passover, and the formation of Israel as a nation, are to be taken as events that have an historical integrity of their own but which nonetheless prefigure later developments in *Heilsgeschichte*. Precisely because these types occur within a divinely ordered necessary relationship in the flow of history, the meaning of each type is only fully understandable in relation to its fulfillment, which ultimately is always the goal of God's will of love established in Christ and his Kingdom (i.e., the communion between God and humanity established in Christ). The people of Israel and the Christian community represent world history in typological outline as the biblical events present the key to world history. Biblical typology links biblical prophecy with the course of world history. For example,

[i]t can also be that a future event may be outlined in an earlier event and be represented in advance. Each triumphal procession which went through the streets of Rome was a prophecy of Caesar Augustus: For what each procession constantly represented, the triumphant general did on his day of honor — the god in man — Jupiter in the Roman citizen. That Rome recognized in this military honor its victor, its future revealed itself as one in which it would master the world through its divinely revered Emperor. After the Apostle John had told how it occurred that Jesus' legs were not broken on the cross, he added, so that the prophecy might be fulfilled "no bone of the Passover lamb should be broken." Thus in the Passover lamb he sees a prototype of Jesus; and in what happens to Jesus a prophecy or intimation of the future, given in the Passover meal, fulfills itself in him. The meaning of the triumph is not fulfilled in the many recurrent triumphal processions,

---

39. See also Hofmann, "Fragen der christlichen Hoffnung," *ZPK* 38 (1859): 140–50, where Hofmann criticizes Hengstenberg's view of the history of Israel.

nor is the meaning of the Passover fulfilled in the recurring Passover meal every year; but the essential content of the one and the other, in which the truth of each consists, is not to appear until a future time, and so only then to confirm for itself the prophecy contained in it. (*WE* 1:15–16)

Included in this view of world history is Hofmann's understanding of the continuity between the people of Israel and the Christian church. The fourth thesis in his theological dissertation is characteristic of his view regarding this continuity: "There is no difference between the inspiration of the Old Testament and that of the New, because there is no difference between the Spirit of Yahweh and the Spirit of Jesus Christ."[40] The proper relation between typical figures/events and their fulfillment in Christ/church is given through the Holy Spirit, the same power that tends toward Christ and fulfills and reveals itself in Christ. Nonetheless, as stated above, Christ is only "a provisional conclusion to history in the midst of becoming, whose form is recognized in the final end . . . " (*WE* 1:33–34). So the successive development of history cannot be separated out from Jesus, since the end of all history is already disclosed in him. Typological forms and events (*Ereignisse*) in Israel are incarnations of prophecies in actual historical existence and stand in a divinely ordered, necessary connection with their fulfilled form in Christ. While all Old Testament prophecies and their fulfillment have their proper place within the *heilsgeschichtliche* whole, focusing particularly on the promise of the Messiah fulfilled in Christ, such messianic fulfillment itself has become a prophecy of the end. Since messianic prophecies are really fulfilled in Christ, who is the beginning of the end, they must also already bear within themselves the end of history, which will only be recognizable on "the last day" (ibid., 2:245).[41]

The Relation of the New Testament to the Old Testament

Hofmann's hermeneutics of proceeding from the whole to the particular is above all evident in his understanding of the relationship of the Old Testament to the New. Hofmann's emphasis on the *Israelitische* character of the Bible and Jesus put him at odds with theologians like Hengstenberg and Kliefoth, who wanted to "Christianize" the Old Testament and emphasize the differences between Jesus and "the Jewish nation."

---

40. Hofmann, *De argumento psalmi centesimi decimi*, 47.
41. See also Preus, "The Theology of Johan [sic] Christian Konrad von Hofmann," 134–35.

For them [e.g., Hengstenberg and his followers] the Israelite character of Scripture is a concealment; for us it is a revelation of the
essential relationship between God and humanity. That the history
contained in Scripture is Israelite, that makes it for us Holy Scripture,
the Word of God: for Israel is the people with the *heilsgeschichtliche*
calling/vocation. (*SBb* 1:26–27)

But Hofmann's view of the Old Testament was also different from that of
theologians like Schleiermacher, who thought that the Old Testament writings were no longer normative for Christian faith. For Hofmann the whole of
the Bible for the Christian church, both the Old and the New Testaments,
is "the completed monument of the church's prehistory" (ibid., 1:22–23;
see also *WGS* 219). Hofmann emphasized that the New Testament writings have continuity with the Old Testament precisely because both sets of
writings emerge from the Israelite community and reveal a single history of
God's relationship with humanity. For Hofmann, the New Testament as well
as the Old Testament is "Israelitic" in character (*BH* 58–74). "The presuppositions of the ecclesial present" are attached to the history of Israel (*SBb*
1:23). This history is to accompany the history of the Christian church as
a constant reminder of the church's own beginning in Israel. Because Israel
as exemplary community (*vorbildliche Gemeinde*) has its antitype (*Gegen-
bild*) in the Christian congregation, the distinction between the Old and
the New Testaments represents itself as the organic sequence of "exemplary
Heilsgeschichte" and the completion or fulfillment of *Heilsgeschichte* in the
Christian community and the final consummation of all creation in the *eschaton* (*TE* 65; *BH* 152). But the historical periods and events within this
single *Heilsgeschichte* must be properly contextualized and related to the
whole flow of *Heilsgeschichte*. Thus, for example, the laws of the nation of
Israel are peculiar to the time in which biblical Israel was a single nation.
Since the laws of a nation give a nation its distinctive structure and character,
Israel's law provided it with its order and identity. Thus, the form of Israel's
faith was necessarily a legal/legalistic one, according to Hofmann; and to
the extent that Israel neglected the *heilsgeschichtliche* character of God's relationship with Israel (e.g., God's promise that through Israel God would
provide divine blessing to all nations), Israel's legalistic faith became futile
(see *TE* 52–58). According to Hofmann, *Heilsgeschichte* means that Israel's
law merely prefigures the future of Christ and the "last day" (*eschaton*).[42]

---

42. See Forde, *The Law-Gospel Debate*, 30–32. Forde correctly notes that Hofmann re-
places the understanding of the divine law as an "eternal standard" with a *heilsgeschichtliche*
understanding of the divine law as an historical given which is itself superseded in the ministry of Jesus and of his New Testament church. Christians live in the freedom of the "new

These later *heilsgeschichtliche* events have superseded this historical Mosaic law. The legal-Israelitic stage of *Heilsgeschichte* has been surpassed by the coming of Christ whose ministry, death and resurrection, and gift of the Spirit mean the dissolution of Israel's law for the church. So, for Hofmann, the laws of Israel can only be properly understood as an outdated period within the progression of *Heilsgeschichte* that moves from type to antitype. Nonetheless, Hofmann did maintain that God's eternal will and his demand for justice and righteousness remain valid for the life of the Christian. Insofar as a Christian remains a sinner in this life, he or she stands under the judgment of the divine will.

Scripture and Church

Hofmann's understanding of the relationship between the church and the Bible also set him apart from the old Protestants who placed Scripture above the church. For Hofmann the whole of Christian truth can only be understood completely in and through the church, which also then includes the history of the church and how the Bible has been understood and appropriated by the church in its history.[43] Hofmann even went so far as to say that the individual theologian, *as an autonomous individual,* is incapable of fully appreciating Scripture as a whole: the theologian always stands in danger of taking out individual aspects of the Bible for herself and, consequently, falsifying subjectively the truth of the Bible. "There is nothing other than the presuppositions of the church's present by which the church in the present can let itself be determined. And consequently no desire could arise for the church for which the thus constituted Scripture would not be sufficient, nor can the latter contain something that the former would not desire" (*SBb* 1:23). The presupposition here is that the same Holy Spirit that created and guides the holy Christian church is the same Spirit that has created the Holy Scriptures. Church and Scripture belong together as an indivisible "whole" that is grounded in the effective working of the Holy Spirit. "Belief in the inspiration of the Bible is determined for Hofmann in the personal certainty of salvation of the Christian but in such a way that such belief is tied completely to the nature of the Bible as a monument of holy history and in its

---

humanity" given in Christ, not on the basis of the divine law. "The reborn Christian is the subject of theological ethics" (*TE* 84). Hofmann's ethics are examined in chapter ten below.

43. "For Hofmann theology is scientific knowledge of the church in its historical development, in which the church takes concrete forms in different modes: in the rebirth of the individual, in the history of its mediation of salvation, and in the documents of its independent historical origin. One can say that theology in this sense is nothing other than ecclesiology. The church is defined in principle as the continuation of the incarnation of Christ in the medium of history" (Sturm, "Die integrierende Funktion der Ekklesiologie," 310).

normative nature for the church."[44] Just as the future shape of a plant is already contained in its seed, so the future shape of the church is already represented in the Bible, and as such the Bible is in a position to serve as a norm for the faith and life of the church.

> [I]t is part of our assurance of faith that Holy Scripture, taken as a whole, has been appointed to be the rule for the Christian church. The birth of the Christian church is to be understood accordingly. To the extent that it accepts the whole Bible and considers the Bible as the purpose of its existence, the church is God's work through His Spirit. (*BH* 34)

But in order to serve as such a norm, the Bible itself must be interpreted within the history of its production, transmission, and interpretation by God's historic community: Israel and the Christian Church as a whole, all of which is guided by the same Spirit. Hofmann speaks about this mediation as the work of the Holy Spirit to create faith in the believer by means of Holy Scripture. Thus, Hofmann agrees with the reformers who taught that the Holy Spirit "was effective in the biblical interpreter himself and led him into understanding of Scripture, but this [understanding] was mediated only through the Holy Scripture itself" (ibid., 17).

The Lutheran Confessions as Witness to the Christian *Tatbestand*

While Hofmann's examination of Scripture was the principal means by which he sought to correct and confirm his systematic presentation of the object of Christian theology, the investigation of church history (including the history of the church's interpretation of Scripture) and of the Confessions of faith given in that ecclesial history formed an ancillary means of understanding and expressing the Christian faith.[45] Christian theology is therefore also *confessional* theology, since theology seeks to raise the one

---

44. Swarat, "Die heilsgeschichtliche Konzeption," 228. "The doctrine of the inspiration of the Bible is nothing other than a conclusion about the nature of the Bible on the basis of its original development. Inspiration is not first; rather the nature of the Bible is an article of faith" (*SBb* 1:677).

45. For helpful analysis of Hofmann's relationship to the Lutheran Confessions, see Hein, *Lutherische Bekenntnis*, 52–53, 113–14, 124–30, 220–32, 255–60; Friedrich Kantzenbach, "Das Bekenntnisproblem in der lutherischen Theologie des 19. Jahrhunderts," *Neue Zeitschrift für Systematische Theologie* 4 (1962): 243–317; idem, *Gestalten und Typen des Neuluthertums: Beiträge zur Erforschung des Neokonfessionalismus im 19. Jahrhundert* (Gütersloh: Gerd Mohn, 1968); Matthias Simon, "Die konfessionelle Entwicklung Bayerns im 19. Jahrhundert," *Zeitschrift für bayerische Kirchengeschichte* 28 (1959): 206–19; and Wenz, *Geschichte*, 2:50–62.

substantial confession of God's historic community out of the Bible and the "form" of the confessional writings. The theologian's encounter with the confessions of the church, therefore, includes the inquiry about the meaning these confessions have for the contemporary church, an inquiry into the origin and historical shape of the confessions (i.e., their identity and original purpose), and an inquiry into the possible relationship between the confessions and theological *Wissenschaft*.[46] While church confessions are not a *wissenschaftliches* system, they form a necessary element of the church's existence because they bring to decisive expression "the living faith" (*lebenden Glauben*) of "ecclesial communal life" (*kirchliches Gemeinleben*) (*SBb* 1:4). Thus, the "givenness" of the confessions is an essential element within the Christian *Tatbestand*.

Hofmann's concern for "the living faith" of "the ecclesial community" differentiated him still further from the scholastic orthodox confessional Lutherans who understood Christian theology to be primarily a collection of individual doctrines.[47] For Hofmann Christianity is not a summation of individual truths; rather, insofar as Christianity is truly living, the content of the faith is a living whole whose individual elements grow out from a single center, the relationship between God and humanity mediated in Christ and given to faith. While the relationship of faith in God and the content of that relationship are independent of the confessional writings (in this case, the Lutheran Confessions), the confessional theologian seeks to discover a convergence between the personal experience of salvation through Christ and the essential content of the confessional writings.[48] "Our Lutheran communion has no other right for continuation than that it is in agreement with the general confession of the church from its beginning . . ." (*DVL* 110).[49] The confessional theologian emphasizes that the personal experience of the justification of the sinner through Christ is reflected in the content of the

---

46. Hein, *Lutherische Bekenntnis*, 27.
47. This tendency can be traced back to Melanchthon's *Loci Communes* of 1521 and 1543. In the 1543 edition, the doctrinal *loci* are organized as follows: God, creation, cause of sin, human will, sin, divine law, the gospel, good works, church, sacraments, predestination, the kingdom of Christ, the resurrection of the dead, the Spirit and the Letter, calamities and the cross, prayer, civil government, human ceremonies, mortification of the flesh, offense, Christian liberty, and marriage. See Philip Melanchthon, *Loci Communes (1543)* (trans. J. A. O. Preus; St. Louis: Concordia, 1992). Martin Chemnitz (1522–1586) followed a similar pattern, as did Johann Baier (1647–1695). See Martin Chemnitz, *Loci Theologici* (2 vols.; trans. J. A. O. Preus; St. Louis: Concordia, 1989) and Johann Wilhelm Baier, *Compendium theologia positivae* (2d ed.; Jena, 1691). For the similar pattern of doctrinal *loci* in Lutheran Orthodoxy, see Heinrich Schmid, *Doctrinal Theology of the Evangelical Lutheran Church* (3d ed.; trans. Charles Hay and Henry Jacobs; Philadelphia: United Lutheran Publication House, 1899).
48. Hein, *Lutherisches Bekenntnis*, 52–53.
49. See also J. v. Hofmann, "Bekenntnisschriften der lutherischen Kirche und die theologische Wissenschaft," *ZPK* [Alte Folge] 4 (1840): 35–36.

confessions which forms an identity with the scriptural and ecclesial *Tatbe-stand* of Christianity. In this way, the theologian has a certain freedom over against the Lutheran Confessions. The latter are not an external authority *above* the theologian; rather, they witness to the internal identity between the Christian's personal experience of salvation, the Christian *Tatbestand,* and the essential content of the Confessions themselves. Because the Confessions witness to the essential content of Christian faith, they assist in providing a more concise conceptual formulation of the experience of justification. Hofmann's primary assumption here is that the same *Tatbestand* that grounds the scriptural whole has also produced the formation of ecclesial confessions in the developing life of the church. But the one confession of the church is not identical to the written Confessions, just as the scriptural whole is not identical to the biblical writings themselves.

The identification of the church's confession occurs by means of a two-fold procedure: On the one hand, one must show that a progressive realization of faith in the formulating of church confessions "is the consequence . . . of a development of the ecclesial life of faith" (*SS* 2:15). The concern here is to inquire into "the essential content of the historical development of the church" (*ET* 26). This inquiry seeks to show how the church "ever anew" has been given its formation.[50] On the other hand, one must be able to demonstrate the "scriptural content" of the church's Confessions of faith (*SS* 2:15). Confessions as statements of faith may not be understood as isolated documents, but must be analyzed as "monuments of the consequences of an ecclesial development of faith" (*ET* 14). Consequently, Hofmann recognized a common identity or convergence of content among the scriptural whole, church confessions, and his doctrinal system. Hofmann gave as the reason for the possibility of recognizing this convergence his experience of the *Tatbestand* which is the cause of both the scriptures and the historical development (including the production of Confessions of faith) of the church, a history "which is still not completed and hence her conclusive 'proof' is still in the process of becoming" (*SBb* 1:19).[51]

Now to the extent that the experiences of faith, which have become communal knowledge, recur in me, or to say the same thing, to the extent that I inwardly belong to a confessional church, that knowledge

---

50. Hofmann, like Barth, thought that there is a systematic unity between dogmatics and ethics, so that the theologian must always give the same weight to the questions of the church's historical-ethical understandings as to the questions of the church's historical-dogmatic understandings. See Hofmann's discussion of the relation between dogmatics and ethics in *DVL* 41–42 and *ET* 7–13.

51. See also Hein, *Lutherisches Bekenntnis,* 52–53.

is also my own and, if I am a theologian, that knowledge will [issue into] the components of my system. (*SBb* 1:4)

By stating this, Hofmann claimed that he was a confessional Lutheran theologian because the content of his church's confessions coincided with the *Tatbestand* of his experience of Christian rebirth and faith.

Such an understanding of the Confessions led to a renewed understanding of their importance for systematic theology: the experience of faith coheres with the content of the confessional writings, which in turn deepen the understanding of the Christian experience. Likewise, once the Christian theologian becomes conscious of the correspondence between his individual experience of faith and the ecclesial confession of that same faith in the confessional writings, the theologian becomes all the more aware of the continuity between himself and the church. Just as the Scriptures are "an organic whole" which witnesses to "an organic historical process," so also the confessional writings are "an organic whole" whose witness must be interpreted in light of that historical development of the church. "The individual statements of the church's confessions must be understood in relation to the entire corpus of the confessions" (*ET* 308).

> ... [E]ach individual confession and each sentence of the confession will only have meaning insofar as it expresses and illustrates the expression of the Christian salvific relationship in the church. Therefore, for example, the special confessions of our Confession are not a conglomeration of all sorts of arbitrarily concocted statements of dogma, but we will always be mindful of what the essential aspect of the act of God was in the Reformation. (*DVW* 394)

In this view, the confessional writings are not external authorities under which one does theology; rather, they are recognized as historical expressions that contain the content of one's own present understanding of faith which exists in organic relation to those past Confessions. A new confession of faith can only lead to the "deepening and expansion" of the simple truth of Christianity because a present confession of faith stands in organic relation to the original confession (*SS* 4:2). So, for example, on May 6, 1849, Hofmann and his colleague, Thomasius, submitted to the Erlangen faculty their "confession:"

> I hereby confess before God that I have recognized through serious examination that the facts of the Christian faith and life as witnessed to in the various confessional writings of the Lutheran Church are in

agreement with the Holy Scripture, and I vow always to live and to conduct myself accordingly in the service of the church.[52]

Despite this bold claim, in actuality, the vast majority of Hofmann's writings do not refer often to the Lutheran Confessions, even though Hofmann himself tried to defend the confessionality of his theology, especially in the wake of the atonement controversy generated by the first edition of his *Der Schriftbeweis*. In his conflict with other confessional Lutherans over the atonement of Christ (especially regarding the concept of God's wrath and the representative character of Christ's death on the cross as a penalty for human sin, two concepts that Hofmann thought were irreconcilable with the primary scriptural affirmation that God is love), Hofmann attempted to appeal to Luther and to distinguish Luther's theology (which was apparently of more significance for Hofmann than the confessional writings themselves) from expressions and ideas found in the Lutheran confessional writings that Hofmann found ambiguous (e.g., the vicarious satisfaction of Christ's death). This was especially the purpose of the second volume of the *Schutzschriften*. In the second edition of *Der Schriftbeweis*, Hofmann was more sensitive to state his doctrinal system in language that more closely approximated confessional Lutheran terminology. The controversy thus sparked a major debate not only about the doctrine of reconciliation but about the proper hermeneutics of the confessional writings themselves. As a result of this controversy, Hofmann attempted to distinguish between church dogmatic theology (i.e., his doctrinal system) and church confession, i.e., between confessional substance and confessional form. He also tried to show how his theological method and system were merely "a new way to teach the old truth" (*SS* 2:15–16). In this regard, Hofmann presented strong evidence of his independence over against the traditional confessional theology of his day. Scholarly freedom belongs as much to the task of theology as confessional orientation and ecclesial mediation (*SS* 2:2).[53] A confessional theologian cannot merely repeat past theological formulas, since the situation of the contemporary theologian is different from that of the originating context of the old formulas; true confessional theology therefore involves the creative restating of old truth in new ways because the theologian is in a new situation.

---

52. Quoted in Hein, *Lutherisches Bekenntnis*, 113. The original is located in the archives of the Erlangen theological faculty (A XIVc, number 58).
53. See Hein, *Lutherisches Bekenntnis*, 264–66; and Wenz, *Geschichte*, 2:37–41.

CHAPTER FIVE

Excursus:
Hofmann and German Idealism

Although Hofmann situated his conception of theology as a scholarly discipline (*Wissenschaft*) within an argument that asserted the independence of theology from all other university disciplines, many scholars have critiqued the degree to which his theology was dependent on external philosophical influences.[1] Already in his lifetime, colleagues, such as Delitzsch, accused Hofmann of being dependent on a speculative philosophical worldview that is alien to the Christian faith.[2] Delitzsch's consistent charge in his letters to Hofmann is that Hofmann is more "speculative" and "philosophical" in his "shaping of Christianity into a doctrinal whole" than he cared to admit. His "doctrinal system" is really a "speculative philosophical system" in disguise (see *BD* 22, 27, 33, 66). Delitzsch and others cite as evidence Hofmann's concern to formulate a "doctrinal whole" and to use language (for example, "the self-differentiation of God," "the archetypal world-goal") that seems to bear striking resemblance to certain methodological and philosophical concepts found in German Idealism.

Of particular interest are similarities between Hofmann's attempt to articulate a notion of "salvation history" (*Heilsgeschichte*) and nineteenth-century efforts to articulate an understanding of world or universal history (*Weltgeschichte*).[3] While Hegel was apparently the first to provide a

---

1. The contours of scholarship on this question have been established through the excellent studies by Wapler, which have served as useful guides for my own research.

2. Indeed the entire first section (the first sixty-six pages) of letters between Delitzsch and Hofmann concern Hofmann's apparent relation to the post-Kantian transcendental Idealist tradition, especially the ideas of Schleiermacher, Hegel, and Schelling. See *BD* 1–66. This series of letters (six each from Delitzsch and Hofmann to the other) occurred between March and October 1859.

3. For the problem of universal history in nineteenth-century German historicism, see especially Adalbert Klempt, *Die Säkularisierung der universalhistorischen Auffassung im 16. und 17. Jahrhundert: Zum Wandel des Geschichtsdenkens im 16. und 17. Jahrhundert* (Göttingen: Vandenhoeck and Ruprecht, 1960); Ernst Breisach, *Historiography: Ancient, Medieval, and Modern* (Chicago: The University of Chicago Press, 1983), 177–85; Allan Megill, " 'Grand Narrative' and the Discipline of History," in *A New Philosophy of History* (ed. Frank Ankersmit and Hans Kellner; Chicago: The University of Chicago Press, 1995), 155–60; and Gadamer,

systematic, "modern" understanding of world history, an understanding which stressed the totality of reality as a process of temporal development, other thinkers in this period — such as Herder, Hamann, and Hofmann's teacher, von Ranke — also sought to clarify the nature of history and to do so, at least in part, in relation to both philosophy and theology. The problem that confronted these thinkers was how to speak of the specific and individual "event of history" while also holding on to some sense of "the universal" or "the whole" of history. What is the point of history or even its end or goal?[4] How is one able to speak of "history" at all without some kind of larger framework or "whole" which provides a context for the individual events one seeks to understand? While "the end of world history is absolutely not an object for historical science, the question about it is decisive for our conception of history."[5]

These questions and issues captivated Hofmann's thought as well, and they gave definite shape to his understanding and articulation of theology. Like the intellectual giants of his day, Hofmann, too, sought to articulate an understanding of God in relation to "world history" (*Weltgeschichte*). He, too, stressed the historical character of God's own revelation and even of God's own Being.

Thus, before concluding the second part of this study, attention should be given to questions about Hofmann's relationship to German Idealism. In what ways were his ideas shaped by the intellectual world in which he

Truth and Method, 197–212. Although its roots can be detected already in the early church (e.g., Augustine), the notion of "universal history" first became a scholarly concern within Protestantism through Melanchthon, who regularly lectured on the subject. In the transition from a biblically-based understanding of a single history, whose unity is provided by God, to a secular understanding of history, the question arose: How is one to know "universal history," since a biblically-based account is no longer plausible? Kant's attempt to answer this question in his essay, "Idea for a Universal History from a Cosmopolitan Point of View" (1784), contributed to thought on "universal history" in nineteenth-century German philosophy and theology. See Immanuel Kant, "Idea for a Universal History from a Cosmopolitan Point of View," in *Kant on History* (ed. and trans. Lewis White Beck; Indianapolis: Bobbs-Merrill, 1963), 11–26. Kant thought that a "philosophical history" of humanity could be written. Such a history would demonstrate that the apparently chaotic, free actions of individuals, when viewed "from the perspective of the human race as a whole," could be understood as contributing to a steady and progressive betterment of human beings and their societies.

4. See also Collingwood's succinct discussion of the move toward "universal history," R. G. Collingwood, *The Idea of History* (New York: Oxford University Press, 1946), 264–66; and Gadamer, *Truth and Method*, 197–218. Commenting on Collingwood, Pannenberg writes, "... research into the particulars of history always presupposes an outline of the whole of history in relation to which the material that has been handed down by tradition is to be interrogated" (Pannenberg, "Redemptive History and History," 70). For Pannenberg, the unity of history is located in something that transcends history: "The God who by the transcendence of his freedom is the origin of contingency in the world, is also the ground of the unity which comprises the contingencies of history ... " (ibid., 74).

5. Reinhard Wittram, *Das Interesse an der Geschichte* (Göttingen: Vandenhoeck & Ruprecht, 1959), 135.

lived? In what ways are his ideas different from emphases in German Idealism? While acknowledging some affinities between his thought and German Idealism, the present chapter will demonstrate that the typical understanding of his relation to the Idealist tradition is oversimplified.

Ranke and Hofmann[6]

Leopold von Ranke had been elevated to the rank of associate professor (*extraordinarius*) just four years prior to Hofmann's matriculation to the University of Berlin in the spring of 1829 and just nineteen years after the founding of the university. Since Ranke was away from the university until the spring of 1831, Hofmann could not have had him for a teacher until the summer semester of that year.[7] That Hofmann attended seminars of Ranke is confirmed by Gunter Berg.[8] Hofmann himself remarked that Ranke's seminars "were his daily pleasure."[9] Hofmann likely participated in the following seminars that Ranke conducted between the spring of 1831 and the end of the summer term in 1832: "Modern History since the Beginning of the 16th Century" (two semesters), "On the Study of History," "On the History of the Past Fifty Years," and "World History (*Weltgeschichte*) in its Universal Coherence."[10]

Like many others of his time and later, Hofmann celebrated the achievements of Ranke. For example, Hofmann offered a critical but appreciative review of Ranke's *History of the Reformation in Germany* in which he acknowledged the preeminence of Ranke as an historian.[11] Hofmann's assessment fits with that of Lord Acton: "Ranke is the representative of the age which instituted the modern study of History. He taught it to be critical, to be colourless, and to be new. We meet him at every step, and he has done

---

6. For Hofmann's relation to Ranke, see Bachmann, "J. C. K. von Hofmann," 909–62; W. Trillhaas, "Bemerkungen zum Begriff der Geschichte bei v. Hofmann," *Theologische Blätter* 8 (1929): 54–57; Wilhelm Volck, *Zur Erinnerung an Johann Christian Konrad von Hofmann* (Erlangen: A. Deichert, 1878); and Wendebourg, *Die heilsgeschichtliche Theologie*, 113–29.

7. Ranke had been in Italy since October 1828. For an analysis of this study leave, see Theodore von Laue, *Leopold Ranke: The Formative Years* (Princeton: Princeton University Press, 1950), 33–42.

8. Gunter Berg lists Hofmann among the more important auditors of Ranke's seminars. See Gunter Berg, *Leopold von Ranke als akademischer Lehrer: Studien zu seinen Vorlesungen und seinem Geschichtsdenken* (Göttingen: Vandenhoeck & Ruprecht, 1968), 229. For a description of Ranke's seminars, see ibid., 51–56, and G. P. Gooch, *History and Historians in the Nineteenth Century* (Boston: Beacon Press, 1959), 107.

9. Wapler, *Johannes v. Hofmann*, 23.

10. Berg, *Leopold von Ranke als akademischer Lehrer*, 243.

11. Johannes Hofmann, "Deutsche Geschichte im Zeitalter der Reformation von Leopold Ranke" (1839), reprinted in *Vermischte Aufsätze von Professor von Hofmann: Eine Auswahl aus der Zeitschrift für Protestantismus und Kirche* (ed. Heinrich Schmid; Erlangen: Deichert, 1878), 272–85.

for us more than any man."[12] Likewise, Hofmann's judgment coincides with Dilthey's: "In Ranke all the forces of the nineteenth century come alive."[13]

While a detailed analysis of Ranke's approach to history is beyond the scope of this chapter, one must note several features of that approach that bear on one's understanding of Hofmann.[14] What did Hofmann learn from Ranke?

Most important for Ranke was an extensive, critical investigation of primary historical sources (especially archives, travel reports, eyewitness accounts, political documents) in order to gain an accurate understanding of "how things actually were" (*wie es eigentlich gewesen ist*), "the meaning of what things had really been like" (*RSW* 33:vii). His critical use of primary sources, particularly documents of state, set the pattern for historical research and writing in the nineteenth century. Unlike previous historians, Ranke did not rely on memoirs and personal histories, but sought verification of historical facts through intensive investigation of original sources and archive materials. "He was not the first to use the archives but the first to use them well."[15]

According to Ranke, there are four steps that comprise a proper method for investigating historical events and archival materials: (1) gaining an exact knowledge of the details of the historical event; (2) seeking to understand the personal motives behind the historical event; (3) seeking to understand the effects of the event's personalities on each other; and (4) understanding the relation of the event to its larger context, i.e., the meaning of an epoch or of a nation or a people. "But it is clear that whatever its principal impulses, the methods and results of Ranke's way as an historian were aimed straight at science: the systematizing of research, the withdrawal of ego from the presentation, the unremitting effort at objectivity, the submission of results to critical public scrutiny."[16] In this way Ranke has rightly been called "the

12. Lord Acton, "Inaugural Lecture on the Study of History," in *Essays in the Liberal Interpretation of History* (ed. William H. McNeill; Chicago: The University of Chicago Press, 1967), 335.

13. Wilhelm Dilthey, "Erinnerungen an deutsche Geschichtsschreiber," in *Vom Aufgang des geschichtlichen Bewusstseins Jugendaufsätze und Erinnerungen: Gesammelte Schriften* (12 vols.; ed. Erich Weniger; Leipzig: Teubner, 1914–1958), 9:216.

14. The literature on Ranke is extensive, but I have been assisted primarily by Breisach, *Historiography*, 232–34; Gadamer, *Truth and Method*, 204–12; G. P. Gooch, *History and Historians in the Nineteenth Century*, 72–97; Iggers, *The German Conception of History*, 63–89; Georg Iggers and James Powell, eds., *Leopold von Ranke and the Shaping of the Historical Discipline* (Syracuse: Syracuse University Press, 1990); Leonard Krieger, *Ranke: The Meaning of History* (Chicago: The University of Chicago Press, 1977); von Laue, *Leopold von Ranke*; Gerhard Masur, *Rankes Begriff der Weltgeschichte* (Munich: Oldenbourg, 1926); and Meinecke, *Historism*, 119–94.

15. Gooch, *History and Historians in the Nineteenth Century*, 97.

16. Peter Gay, *Style in History: Gibbon, Ranke, Macaulay, Burckhardt* (New York: Norton, 1974), 68.

father of historical science."[17] His critical approach sought for "strict veracity in the face of all the testimonies of human life, an unconditional demand
for the most genuine and original sources, and a distaste for all that was
dubious or distorted."[18] He once stated that he would like to efface himself
in order to see things as they were (*RSW* 15:103.).

But Ranke's method is not merely oriented to individual historical data
apart from theoretical considerations.[19] According to Ranke the historian
also has the task of attempting to understand the meaning of historical data
in relation to a larger whole. The historian cannot simply be concerned with
"how it actually was" (*"wie es eigentlich gewesen ist,"* though *"eigentlich"*
in this context means "essentially" rather than the positivistic "actually").[20]
Ranke goes so far as to say that

> truth in history is the process of life and of the spirit. Historiographical
> truth consists exclusively in describing this process which is manifested
> in the events. This description need not betray the index finger of the
> philosopher although the true historian and the philosopher meet at
> every step.[21]

Ranke thus believed that the true historian must be concerned for the meaning of history, but he or she can only arrive at this meaning by giving careful,
critical attention to the particulars that give shape to the larger historical
context. All values and meanings of history arise from within the concrete
setting of a particular, living historical situation. "Detail never seems better
than when it is seen in its relation to the whole."[22]

Like Hegel, Ranke spoke of the inner necessity of an event, its inner meaning in relation to "world history" or "universal history" (*Weltgeschichte*).
The task of the historian then is to move beyond a superficial understanding
of individual historical phenomena, i.e., merely offering an explanation of
causal forces, in order to provide a deeper analysis of history. In this view the
historian acts like a poet or artist who approaches "the particular" in order
to find "a general truth," a "significance" (*Bedeutung*), or its deeper "spirit"

17. Herbert B. Adams, "New Methods of Study in History," in *Johns Hopkins University
Studies in History and Political Science* (Baltimore: Johns Hopkins University Press, 1884),
2:65.
18. Meinecke, *Historism*, 498.
19. Iggers, *The German Conception of History*, 65.
20. Georg Iggers, "Introduction," *The Theory and Practice of History*, edited by Georg Iggers
and Konrad von Moltke (Indianapolis: Bobbs-Merrill, 1973), xix-xx.
21. Leopold v. Ranke, *Ergänzungsblätter zur Jenaischen Allgemeinen Literatur-Zeitung*
(1828), cols. 129–136. Quoted and translated by Iggers, *The German Conception of History*, 68.
22. Leopold v. Ranke, *Zur eigenen Lebensgeschichte* (Leipzig: Dunker & Humblot,
1890), 164.

(*Geist*) within the particular. The premise behind this search is that history is not a pointless or meaningless multiplicity of individual occurrences.[23] Rather, it has a discernible meaning or unity (or what Hayden White and others have called "a metahistory") that provides a means of organizing "history."[24] Ranke says:

> Let us acknowledge that history can never have the unity of a philo-sophical system; but it does have a coherence [*Zusammenhang*]. We see a range of successive events that condition one another. When I say "condition," I do not mean with absolute necessity. The great thing is, rather, that human freedom is involved everywhere. The writing of history follows from the events of freedom. This is its greatest attrac-tion. But freedom is combined with power, original power. Without the latter the former disappears, both in the events of the world and in the sphere of ideas. At every moment something new can begin, something whose entire origin is the primary and common source of all human actions. Nothing exists entirely for the sake of something else, nothing is entirely identical to the reality of something else. But there is still a deep inner unity present everywhere, of which no one is entirely independent. Freedom stands along side of necessity. Both consist in what has already been formed and can again be destroyed, which is the basis of all which progresses to new activity. What has become is related to that which is becoming. But even this continuity itself is not to be understood arbitrarily; rather, it has come into exis-tence in a unique and certain way, and not otherwise. It is, likewise, an object of knowledge. A long series of events — following one an-other and accompanying one another, tied together in a certain way — constitutes a century or an epoch. . . . [25]

Ranke was especially concerned to understand that which gave coher-ence to the modern European world, whose origins resided in the political and religious movements of the Renaissance and the Reformation. Writing a comprehensive history of the modern European world was for him tan-tamount to writing a "world history" (*Weltgeschichte*). This history would

---

23. Roger Wines, *The Secret of World History: Selected Writings on the Art and Science of History by Leopold von Ranke* (ed. and trans. Roger Wines; New York: Fordham University Press, 1981), 25.

24. Hayden White, *Metahistory: The Historical Imagination in Nineteenth-Century Europe* (Baltimore: The Johns Hopkins University Press, 1973). See also Paul Ricoeur's analysis of the problem of "historical narrative," which attends to White's criticism of Ranke: Paul Ricoeur, *Time and Narrative* (3 vols.; trans. Kathleen McLaughlin and David Pellauer; Chicago: The University of Chicago Press, 1984–1988), 1:91–225.

25. Ranke, *Weltgeschichte*, 9.2:13.

provide a broad history of "civilization" (*Kultur*), and it would thus be "no longer national, but wholly universal" (*RSW* 53.54:233–34).[26] Such a history included the papacy, the Renaissance, the Reformation, and the rise of the modern European states, especially France, England, and Prussia.

But how is it possible to write such a world history without appeal to arbitrary and subjective prejudice? Are not Ranke's prejudices painfully obvious in his Eurocentricity? Ranke's response to these questions was grounded in his own understanding of God's relation to the world. Ranke's view, shaped as it was by his Lutheran Christian faith, provided him with the means to articulate a divine order in history. A sense of the two-fold rule of God in the world kept Ranke from concluding that history is merely chaos and meaninglessness. God's right hand is at work through the gospel and his left hand is at work through all "secular," human affairs. As Ranke defined this latter aspect in one of his famous aphorisms: "Every epoch is immediate to God, and its value in no way depends on what it has produced out of itself, but in its existence itself, in its own self."[27] In other words, its intrinsic value is discerned by faith; or as he put the matter in another aphorism: "God dwells, lives, is recognized in all history. Every act witnesses to him, every moment preaches his name, but most of all, I think, the coherence of all history. It stands there as a holy hieroglyph. . . . No matter how it goes, we ought only for our part to decipher this holy hieroglyphics! In this we also serve God; we, too, are priests and also teachers" (*RSW* 53/54:89–90). For Ranke, behind the individual details of human history (particularly in its western European form) is "the hand of God."[28]

> There was thus in Ranke a combination of transcendental reverence for history and its background, and keen-eyed empirical and critical examination and artistic appreciation of the course of history. There was also a close combination of religion, not only gnosis or speculation, with a realism of outlook.[29]

While Ranke's approach to history is grounded in a theological vision of reality, he rejected Hegel's notion of the self-realization of *Geist* (e.g., *RSW* 53/54:569–70). Not only did Ranke reject such a teleology of history and other "attempts that had been made to construct history according

---

26. This word, *"Kultur,"* "comes continuously from his pen, as if it gave us the key to the general tendencies of his mind" (Antoine Guilland, *Modern Germany & Her Historians* [New York: McBride, Nast & Company, 1915], 94).

27. Ranke, *Weltgeschichte*, 8:177.

28. Laue, *Leopold Ranke*, 42.

29. Meinecke, *Historism*, 507.

to the demands of a philosophical system," he thought that Hegel's vision clouded the distinction between God and creation.[30] For Ranke, the Creator and the creation must be distinguished. This most central distinction made it possible for Ranke to utilize historical criticism while also keeping an eye out for "the hand" or at least "the finger" of God in each movement of history.[31] The hand of God might be discerned in history, but not proved.[32] Although all of reality is historical and each particular phenomenon can only be understood in terms of its history, lurking behind every ephemeral and particular phenomenon is hidden a truth to be discovered by the historian.

> World history [*Weltgeschichte*] does not present such a chaotic tumult, warring, and planless succession of states and peoples as appears at first sight. Nor is the significance of history only in the often dubious advancement of civilization. There are forces and indeed spiritual, life-giving, creative forces, even life itself, and there are moral energies, whose development we see. They cannot be defined or put into abstract terms, but one can see them and observe them. One can develop a sympathy for their existence. They unfold, capture the world, appear in manifold expressions, fight with and limit and overpower one another. In their interaction and succession, in their life, in their decline or rebirth, which then encompasses an ever greater fullness, higher significance and wider extent, lies the secret of world history [*Weltgeschichte*]. (RSW 24:39–40)[33]

Clearly Ranke was not a strict empiricist, since he rejected the view that "knowledge cannot go beyond phenomena."[34] While his methodology calls for objective, critical observation of particular historical phenomena, he did not think such critical, bare observation was the only means to historical knowledge. True historical understanding is also the result of "intuition"

---

30. Felix Gilbert, *History: Politics or Culture? Reflections on Ranke and Burckhardt* (Princeton: Princeton University Press, 1990), 23.

31. Meinecke, *Historism*, 506–7. For example, in his very first published work, Ranke analyzes the controversy between the Spanish and Portuguese governments over their competing claims to the same seas. In this context he remarked that "God...wanted something quite unexpected to arise from this controversy. What happened went far beyond human imagination" (*RSW* 33.34:45), namely, the discovery of a new continent! A few pages later he labels this discovery "a gift of God" (ibid., 47). For similar remarks in the young Ranke's writings, see Laue, *Leopold Ranke*, 29.

32. Rudolf Vierhaus, "Historiography between Science and Art," in Iggers and Powell, *Leopold von Ranke and the Shaping of the Historical Discipline*, 64.

33. This translation is based on that by von Laue, *Leopold Ranke*, 217.

34. Iggers, *The German Conception of History*, 76.

on the part of the historian.[35] Criticism and "intuitive recognition," to use Meinecke's descriptive expression, work together to form the proper understanding of history.[36] The goal of the historian is to sense the "totality" (*Totalität*), the "integrated, spiritual reality" that is behind the multiplicity of historical events and phenomena.[37] While the historian cannot aspire to the unity that is possible for the philosopher, history "does have coherence" (*Zusammenhang*). Such a coherence, according to Ranke, possesses "an objective reality fully equivalent to that of separate facts."[38] When the historian does his or her work properly, the study of individual elements in history "will always be related to a larger context."[39] The challenge for the historian, of course, is to know "how to bring the individual into harmony with the universal."[40] In other words, how does the historian "penetrate to the divine idea behind the visible world of historical phenomena?"[41]

An aspect of Ranke's solution to this problem was to assume that the institutions and movements of western civilization are true and proper expressions of the will of God. He even likened political states to "thoughts of God," another aphoristic expression, though the meaning of this expression is unclear. For example, it cannot mean that such "thoughts" are clear and distinct, since Ranke rejected all attempts to make of history a neat "system," as in the philosophy of Hegel.[42] Nonetheless, for Ranke, even state power itself is a spiritual (*geistliche*) entity that is the result of historical forces. In the words of Gooch, "The core of [Ranke's] message was the duty of states to safeguard their individuality by developing along the lines of their historic growth.... Every state possessed its individuality."[43]

The pitfalls of such a spiritualization of power are obvious: a glorification of the state, whose morality cannot be judged either by its citizens, or in relation to any outside standard, and hence a vindication

---

35. It should be pointed out that Ranke's "intuitions" were largely out of touch with many of the historical forces of the nineteenth century. This was largely due to his inability to study and appreciate historical phenomena beyond governments, politicians, and armies; he had very little understanding of the great social questions and movements of his day, and almost no sense of the growing industrialization occurring in Europe. See Krieger, *Ranke,* 138ff., and Iggers, *The German Conception of History,* 84–89.

36. Meinecke, *Historism,* 498.

37. Iggers, *The German Conception of History,* 79.

38. Trygve Tholfsen, *Historical Thinking* (New York: Harper and Row, 1967), 168.

39. Ranke, *Weltgeschichte,* 9.2:15.

40. Simon, *Ranke und Hegel,* 43.

41. Laue, *Leopold Ranke,* 16.

42. Leopold v. Ranke, "A Dialogue on Politics," in Laue, *Leopold Ranke,* 169. For a discussion of Ranke's aphorism, see Krieger, *Ranke,* 7. Krieger speaks of Ranke's "dubious legacy" with regard to understanding the power of political states.

43. Gooch, *History and Historians in the Nineteenth Century,* 80. See also Schnädelbach, *Philosophy in Germany: 1831–1933,* 44–47.

of that state's aggressions against competing states. In the end, for the historian and the citizen, might is equivalent to right.[44]

Iggers, who also criticizes Ranke's understanding of state power, notes the deep similarities between Ranke and Hegel, including also the religious dimensions of their respective attempts at writing a world history, though he acknowledges that Ranke and Hegel differed on how the historian-philosopher gets to the deeper meaning of the historical process.[45] For Ranke, that methodological route is through "love" for individual historical phenomena and the truth they hold, dedication to the sources of knowledge regarding individual phenomena, and only then through intuition of the spiritual unities lurking behind the phenomena but which relate the phenomena into an overarching universal "totality" or "whole."[46] Thus, the construction of a universal history is the result of critical historical investigation *and* spiritual intuition.[47] In a typical moment of methodological reflection, Ranke articulates this dual route:

> One sees how infinitely difficult universal history [*Universalhistorie*] is. What an unending quantity! . . . What a difficulty! I maintain it impossible to fulfill this task completely. Only God knows world history [*Weltgeschichte*]. We can only recognize the contradictions. "The harmonies," as an Indian poet put it, "are known only to the gods but unknown to people." We can only intuit, and our intuitions are only from a distance. Clearly, however, there is for us a unity, a progression, a development. Thus the path of history leads us to the task of philosophy. If philosophy were to be what it should be and history were completely clear and perfect, both disciplines would be in complete agreement.[48]

---

44. Wines, *The Secret of World History*, 11. Others have also attacked Ranke's historicism for "producing a fundamental weakness in the German political tradition which left it peculiarly susceptible to totalitarianism" (ibid., 12).

45. For Iggers's criticism of Ranke's understanding of unrestricted state power, see Iggers, *The Theory and Practice of History*, xlviii-lii. See also Iggers, "The Image of Ranke in American and German Historical Thought," *History and Theory* 2 (1962): 17–40; Meinecke, *Historism*, 505; and Simon, *Ranke und Hegel*, 156–83. See also the discussion of Ranke's epistemology in Wach, *Das Verstehen*, 3:89–133. Wach notes Ranke's criticism of *a priori* approaches to history and his desire to understand historical phenomena on their own terms. Ironically, Hegel seems to have been more capable of describing the individual characteristics of cultures and peoples than Ranke. On this point, see Iggers, *The German Conception of History*, 85.

46. One must stress, however, that Ranke himself operated with philosophical assumptions about history. "Thus the empirical orientation of the historical sciences is not without philosophical assumptions" (Gadamer, *Truth and Method*, 209).

47. On the mystical element in Ranke's process of cognition, see Laue, *Leopold Ranke*, 44–45.

48. Leopold v. Ranke, "Idee der Universalhistorie" (1831), in Eberhard Kessel, "Rankes Idee der Universalhistorie," *Historische Zeitschrift* 178 (1954): 301–2.

While Hofmann was already oriented toward an historical approach to the Bible prior to his arrival as a student in Berlin, the influence of Ranke on Hofmann's historical methodology is apparent throughout Hofmann's writings. "Von Ranke made an extraordinary impression on Hofmann," particularly in his emphasis on placing the particular in relation to the universal and vice versa.[49] The clearest example of Hofmann's dependence on Ranke's approach to history is one of his earliest writings, *Die Geschichte des Aufruhrs in den Cevennen unter Ludwig XIV nach den Quellen erzählt* (published in 1837), which Hofmann had begun in 1831. Here Hofmann paid careful, critical attention to original sources, archive materials, and eyewitness accounts, though he also tried to articulate a sense of the larger forces at work in the French Revolution. Still another example is Hofmann's two-volume textbook on world history. In this work Hofmann sought to divide history into meaningful units and to demonstrate how the larger forces of history had given rise to the major world powers.

Ranke's influence also made its way into Hofmann's theological writings. Hofmann's careful attention to "texts" and to the "facts" that such texts present betrays the influence of his teacher. Hofmann's approach to the issue of "prophecy and fulfillment," for example, discloses his lifelong effort to understand the relationships among the various biblical "facts" and their relationship to a complex, organic, "present factual situation" (*Tatbestand*) that included the history of Israel, the ministry of Jesus, the rise of the Christian church, and the Christian's own ecclesial and personal experience. A large part of this effort was placing the sources, in this case, the biblical texts, into proper relationship with each other so as to express the historical development of God's communion with humanity in Israel, Jesus, and the Christian church. The aim was to form the independent and disparate biblical texts into a unified "whole," to clarify and express the organic relationships and continuities among the various historical events that comprise salvation history (*Heilsgeschichte*), the historical dimension of the Christian *Tatbestand*. On this salvation-historical (*heilsgeschichtliche*) basis, *all* of history can be understood as a continuous series of events that have a unified origin and goal in God. Hofmann's unified conception of salvation history (*Heilsgeschichte*) thus bears important similarities to Ranke's conception of world history (*Weltgeschichte*).[50]

Despite the influence of Ranke's historical method on Hofmann, especially the demand for careful attention to historical facts, Hofmann differed

---

49. Flechsenhaar, *Das Geschichtsproblem*, 20. For Hofmann's own appreciative comments about Ranke's approach to history, see Hofmann, "Deutsche Geschichte," in *Vermischte Aufsätze*, 272–85.

50. Hofmann's conception of *Heilsgeschichte* is more fully explored in chapter eleven below.

from Ranke in important respects. While Ranke called for the historian "to extinguish his 'self'" and seek *objectivity,* Hofmann argued that such a presuppositionless approach to the Bible and to the history behind the Bible is impossible. Indeed, Hofmann argued that one's presuppositions about the historical "whole," which he believed is given in the biblical "whole," will shape one's approach to historical facts. While individual facts of history may modify one's understanding of the whole of history (including biblical history), Hofmann held that a preliminary understanding of "the biblical whole" and of the nature of historical reality informed the task of understanding history theologically. Consequently, while Ranke maintained that universal history can only be written at the end of one's extensive study of empirical history and historical sources, Hofmann began his professional career with a fundamental conception of the salvation-historical whole of world history which guided his study of historical facts.[51]

However, Hofmann did not generally use historical criticism in the same way that Ranke did, namely, to establish criteria for ascertaining the historical value of biblical texts and events. Although Hofmann was aware of historical criticism, he generally tempered it in favor of simply presupposing the historicity of certain "history-like" narratives that are not "history" in the proper sense of the term (e.g., Gen 1–11; the apocalyptic texts). In this regard, Hofmann's theology is time bound by his failure to relate his dogmatic understandings ("faith") to critical-historical investigation of the biblical texts. While Hofmann was surely correct to stress that the Bible is not a book of timeless doctrines and even though he understood the historical nature of the biblical documents, he was quite naïve regarding the doubtful historical veracity of some "history-like" material in the Bible. While Hofmann acknowledged that "Holy Scripture is not an infallible textbook of cosmology, anthropology, psychology, and so on," and that "the history recorded in the Bible is not to be understood as an errorless segment of world history" (*BH* 75–76), Hofmann still found miracle (*Wunder*) in a world which was slowly becoming more and more "disenchanted."[52] Hofmann was unable to treat language about creation, fall, election, the eschaton, and so on, as mythic or primarily symbolic, but instead interpreted such language as

---

51. Whereas Ranke wrote his world history at the very end of his long life, Hofmann's first published text was his *Lehrbuch der Weltgeschichte für Gymnasien* (2 vols.; Nördlingen: C. H. Beck, 1839, 1842; 2d ed. 1843–1844). The first volume of this textbook organizes the history of humanity as follows: the human race before the flood, the nation of Israel, the East, Greece, and Rome.

52. For a theological analysis of Max Weber's (1864–1920) famous assessment regarding "the disenchantment of the world," see Tracy, *Blessed Rage for Order,* 4–14.

literal-historical.[53] He often was quite comfortable within the then still sufficient world of "a first naiveté."[54]

There were also political differences between Ranke and Hofmann. Ranke's universal history essentially served to legitimate the centralizing reforms of the Eighteenth-Century "enlightened despots" in Prussia. He accepted the bureaucratic and military power structure of Prussia, opposed a constitution and local self-administration, opposed freedom of the press, and did not support the rights of individuals against the state. Not surprisingly, he was adamantly opposed to "pluralism" within the Prussian state, since such diverging traditions within a single "culture" would undermine the legitimacy of the state as conceived by Ranke. In contrast, Hofmann did not think that history provided a clear and unambiguous key toward political understanding. For him the ethics of the state are determined by the collective will of individuals who seek freedom. As a member of a liberal political party, Hofmann strove for all those individual freedoms and constitutional guarantees that Ranke opposed. Hofmann thus did not think that the dominant political forces were the sole ones with roots in history, nor did he think those dominant political forces were the only ones that could claim to be legitimate.

Related to their political differences were their different conceptions of how God relates to world history. While both Ranke and Hofmann understood history to be meaningful in relation to God, Ranke understood God to be somehow "immediately present" to all epochs (and thus each epoch, with its dominant political-military powers, had its own legitimacy), while Hofmann stressed that God is "immediately known" only within the community that God has established in time, i.e., Israel and the Christian church. This community alone, not the state, is called to live in the gospel freedom of God. In this freedom, the church as a community of believers is to work for positive social change and to serve human needs in society. On the basis of this freedom Hofmann argued that individual political freedom is necessary within the state, also for the sake of human good. Since the God of history is a God of love, the Christian is called to a life of faith active in love, also in the political life of the state. But it is only at the "end" (*eschaton*) that God

---

53. Here Hofmann is like Pannenberg, who also treats as literal what many history-of-religions scholars deem is mythical or symbolic. For the critique of Pannenberg's literal treatment of biblical eschatology, which applies also to Hofmann's theology, see Marc Kolden, "Pannenberg's Attempt to Base Theology on History" (Ph.D. diss., University of Chicago, 1976), 150–71.

54. Paul Ricoeur distinguishes between a precritical "first naiveté" and a post-critical "second naiveté" regarding biblical symbols and myths. See, for example, Ricoeur's conclusion ("The Symbol Gives Rise to Thought") in *The Symbolism of Evil* (trans. Emerson Buchanan; Boston: Beacon Press, 1967), 347–57.

will be "universally known," when God's community of grace and love will be consummated in perfection under the universal lordship of Christ. The unity of history is thus found in its source and goal, the communion between God and humanity in Jesus Christ, and not in God's immediate relationship to each and every historical event. In Hofmann's view all events in world history are converging on a "last day" (*eschaton*) that has already been disclosed in the resurrection of Jesus, who is "the center or focus of all history" (*WE* 1:39–40; *SBb* 1:35, 54–55). This disclosure is a central element to one's experience of faith in the risen Christ and the basic presupposition of Hofmann's historical methodology.

Hegel and Hofmann[55]

Thirty years after his matriculation to Berlin, Hofmann stated to Delitzsch that he "had attended Hegel's lectures on the proofs for the existence of God, but only out of curiosity, and they did not have a conscious effect on [him]" (*BD* 37).[56] He indicates that he had also read "at that time" (*damals*) Hegel's *Phenomenology of Spirit* (*Phänomenologie des Geistes*) and that he had studied Hegel's philosophy of history, but that the latter "ruined in me all taste for his philosophy" (*BD* 38).[57] Hofmann's use of *"damals"* ("at that

---

55. On the relation of Hofmann to the ideas of Hegel, see Bachmann, "J. C. K. von Hofmann," 916–20; Trillhaas, "Bemerkungen," 54–57; Volck, *Zur Erinnerung;* and Wendebourg, *Die heilsgeschichtliche Theologie Hofmanns,* 129–40. The literature on Hegel's philosophy of history is extensive, but I have been especially influenced by W. T. Stace, *The Philosophy of Hegel: A Systematic Exposition* (New York: Dover, 1955); J. N. Findlay, *Hegel: A Re-examination* (New York: Oxford, 1958); Charles Taylor, *Hegel,* 389–427; and Burleigh Taylor Wilkins, *Hegel's Philosophy of History* (Ithaca: Cornell University Press, 1974).

56. Hegel lectured on the philosophy of religion four times in Berlin: 1821, 1824, 1827, and 1831. Since Hofmann did not arrive in Berlin until July 1829, the lectures to which he refers must have been those given by Hegel in 1831. The English edition of the four lecture series is *Hegel: Lectures on the Philosophy of Religion* (ed. Peter Hodgson; trans. R. F. Brown et al.; 3 vols.; Berkeley: University of California Press, 1984, 1987, 1985). No actual transcripts of the 1831 lectures are extant. In 1831, Hegel lectured from a manuscript transcript of the 1827 lectures, which generally represent his mature thinking on the philosophy of religion. Strauss's excerpts from the 1831 lectures, published as appendices to each of the three volumes, provide a few significant structural changes vis-à-vis the 1827 lectures, e.g., the relation of religion to the state and the teleological proof presented in relation to Greek religion and not Roman. Strauss's excerpts are from a notebook given to him by an anonymous student who, along with Hofmann, heard the 1831 lectures. (Hegel died shortly after Strauss arrived in Berlin.) For the 1831 materials that differ significantly from the 1827 lectures, see ibid., 1:451–74; 2:703–60; 3:351–74.

57. For the critical edition of Hegel's four-part lectures on the philosophy of history, see (vol. 1) *Die Vernunft in der Geschichte: Einleitung in die Philosophie der Weltgeschichte* (ed. Johannes Hoffmeister; 5th ed.; Hamburg: Felix Meiner, 1955), (vol. 2) *Die orientalische Welt* (ed. G. Lasson; Leipzig: Felix Meiner, 1923), (vol. 3) *Die griechische und römische Welt* (ed. G. Lasson; Leipzig: Felix Meiner, 1923), and (vol. 4) *Die germanische Welt* (ed. G. Lasson; Leipzig: Felix Meiner, 1920). The English translation, based on Karl Hegel's 1840 third edition

time") could indicate he had read the second edition (1827) of this work that was originally published in 1807. In this same 1859 letter Hofmann also remarks that he had attended Marheineke's lectures on dogmatics and Schleiermacher's lectures on the introduction to the New Testament, but that he was generally dissatisfied with these teachers, too.

There is no way of knowing for sure whether Hofmann actually attended Hegel's lectures on the philosophy of history (delivered several times after 1822) or, more likely, studied student notes of these lectures. It is unlikely that he is referring here to Hegel's actual lecture notes since these were not published until 1837. A more definitive edition of these lecture notes, edited by Karl Hegel, was not published until 1840. If Hofmann had attended the actual lectures, he probably would have described his knowledge of Hegel's philosophy of history as having come from actually hearing Hegel's lectures, the way he describes his knowledge of Hegel's philosophy of religion, Marheineke's dogmatics, and Schleiermacher's "Introduction to the New Testament."

Apart from his letter to Delitzsch, Hofmann does not refer directly to his contact with Hegel in Berlin or to the writings of Hegel. Because Hofmann's immediate purpose for making these remarks to Delitzsch was to provide an explicit defense of his independence from German Idealism, Wapler is justified in asserting that one should not take these comments of Hofmann at face value.[58] Hofmann was a child of his age, his protests to the contrary notwithstanding.[59] Wapler puts the matter correctly:

> Hegel is for Hofmann the great scholarly power, whose philosophy of history had an especial attraction.... [Hofmann] learned to recognize clearly the fundamental ideas of the philosophy of history in which the new historical worldview received its classic stamp, even if he himself could not assimilate the scientific form of the master. Hofmann did this without becoming thereby a Hegelian, as Delitzsch accused him of being.[60]

---

of the lecture notes, is Georg Hegel, *The Philosophy of History* (trans. J. Sibree; Buffalo, N.Y.: Prometheus Books, 1991). Sibree's translation was originally published in 1857. A more recent and more accurate translation of the "Introduction" to these lectures is *Introduction to the Philosophy of History* (trans. Leo Rauch; Indianapolis: Hackett, 1988), hereafter abbreviated as *IPH*.

58. Wapler, *Johannes v. Hofmann*, 25.

59. In this regard Hofmann was not unique. Most of the great German historians of the nineteenth century could not admit that they were dependent, at least in part, on Hegel's idea of world history. See Gadamer, *Truth and Method*, 198–99.

60. Wapler, *Johannes v. Hofmann*, 25. On the difficulty of evaluating the complex character of Hofmann's theology, see Walter Loewenich, "Zur neueren Beurteilung der Theologie Johann Christian Konrad von Hofmanns," *Zeitschrift für bayerische Kirchengeschichte* 32 (1963): 317–19. Beyschlag is especially critical of Wendebourg's "weaving together of Ranke,

One must thus acknowledge Hegel's influence on Hofmann in the following areas:

First, both Hegel and Hofmann concern themselves with articulating clearly the relation of the individual events of history to a sense of the whole of history. The individual or the particular (what for Hegel were the nation, state, people, or political leaders) only becomes meaningful and concrete in relation to the movement of "Spirit/mind" (*Geist*) through "the whole." In other words, only in relation to the whole is the individual or particular capable of being properly comprehended and understood. While the truth is found in "the whole" and not merely in "the particular," the "whole" is immanent in every individual manifestation, and each phase of the process is an anticipation of the whole. The relation between phases is a relation between elements that collectively form the whole. Each particular is thus a partial expression of the whole.

For both thinkers, influenced as they were by the Lutheran tradition, "the finite is capable of the infinite" (*finitum capax infiniti*), though Hofmann understood this Lutheran notion differently from Hegel. For Hegel, the whole of human history is in some sense the concretization of Spirit/mind (*Geist*), whereas for Hofmann the whole of human history centers in the incarnation and atonement of the second Person of the Trinity.[61] Consequently, while *Geist* was the comprehensive category for Hegel, the triune God was the comprehensive category for Hofmann.

Second, both Hegel and Hofmann were concerned to emphasize that history is a dynamic, progressive, teleological development.[62] Such an under-

---

Schleiermacher, Schelling, and Hegel" and neglecting the originality of Hofmann's theological conception. See Beyschlag, *Die Erlanger Theologie,* 60. See also Wach's conclusion: "Hofmann's relation to philosophy and to the philosophers of his time is not easy to determine. His own remarks cannot be taken directly as correct statements" (*Das Verstehen,* 2:361). Wach concludes that Hofmann was more "a child of his time" than "a trained student of philosophy" (ibid.).

61. Both Hegel and Hofmann share the idea of *finitum capax infiniti* with Jakob Böhme. For Böhme's influence on Hofmann, see Hirsch, *Geschichte,* 5:421–22. Böhme provided Hegel and Schelling with a notion of the self-differentiation and self-determination of the Absolute. For Böhme the whole of reality is marked by an *exitus* (the self-differentiation of the whole) and a *reditus* (the return of reality into a whole). The self-differentiation of the whole is crucial for the history of the infinite or the whole. Hegel expanded this notion so as to understand the whole of reality as a process of the self-unfolding of the Absolute by which the Absolute comes to its own self-understanding in and through finite reality (including human being). For Böhme's relation to Hegel, see Cyril O'Regan, *The Heterodox Hegel* (Albany: State University of New York Press, 1994); and Mark Mattes, "Hegel's Lutheran Claim," *Lutheran Quarterly* 14 (Autumn 2000): 255–56.

62. "History is a conscious, self-mediating process — Spirit emptied out into Time; but this externalization, this kenosis, is equally an externalization of itself; this negative is the negative of itself. This Becoming presents a slow-moving succession of Spirits, a gallery of images, each of which, endowed with all the riches of Spirit, moves thus slowly just because the Self has to penetrate and digest this entire wealth of its substance. As its fulfillment consists in perfectly

standing was related to their mutual concern to understand the individual and particular in relation to the whole by means of a universal principle of interpretation. History is a process that has a *telos,* an end, a point, a purpose.[63] Like many other thinkers of their time period (especially Herder), both Hegel and Hofmann spoke of history as an organic development that reveals the identity of God but also actually contributes to the development of God's "potentiality" (*IPH* 19–21).[64] This "potentiality" is fully actualized at the end of history, an end that provides history with its meaning and becomes the normative principle for interpreting all history, though both Hegel and Hofmann stressed that the meaning of history remains unknown to the actual "bearers" or "makers" of history.[65] History is known only by means of its end, which has become comprehensible even before its arrival. This principle makes it possible to judge and comprehend all previous epochs of human history.[66] For Hegel this principle is the dialectical development

---

knowing what it is, in knowing its substance, this knowing is its withdrawal into itself in which it abandons its outer existence and gives its existential shape over to recollection.... But recollection, the inwardizing (*Er-innerung*), of that experience, has preserved it and is the inner being, and in fact the higher form of the substance" (Georg Hegel, *Phenomenology of Spirit* [trans. A. V. Miller; Oxford: Oxford University Press, 1977], 492).

63. "While the presuppositions of Hegel and Hofmann are diametrically opposed, their formal thought structures are similar: they both think of a *telos* to history" (Kantzenbach, *Die Erlanger Theologie,* 191). Likewise, Flechsenhaar stresses that Hofmann's understanding of the Christian perception of *Heilsgeschichte* is fundamentally different from Hegel's perception of history's *telos.* See Flechsenhaar, *Das Geschichtsproblem,* 52–53, contra Wendebourg, who writes, "What for Hegel is 'conceptualized history,' is for Hofmann *Heilsgeschichte"* (Wendebourg, "Die heilsgeschichtliche Theologie," 80).

64. On Herder's theology of history, see Marcia Bunge, ed., *Against Pure Reason* (Minneapolis: Fortress, 1993), 12–19.

65. For example, Hofmann indicates that the participants mentioned in Matthew 27:9ff. do not think of connecting the purchase of the potter's field with Jeremiah 32:6ff., as the writer of Matthew does (along with the exegete). See *WE* 2:127ff. Likewise, already in his theological dissertation, Hofmann argues for Davidic authorship of Psalm 110 while simultaneously rejecting the usual Christological interpretation. According to Hofmann, David was quite unconscious of the typological interpretation of his psalm by early Christians, but both David and the early Christians were inspired by the same Holy Spirit. See Hofmann, *De Argumento Psalmi Centesimi Decimi,* 38–46. According to Hegel, the goal of history "is not necessarily seen by history's participants. What Hegel calls the 'Cunning of Reason' can make use of even irrational drives in history's players in order to achieve history's rational goal. The major actors on the stage of history, the 'world-historical individuals' (e.g., Napoleon), are not in the least aware that the World-Spirit is using them for purposes of its own, not theirs. And when history has finished with them, it discards them" (Rauch, *IPH,* ix).

66. It is misleading to identify these principles as "a priori," as Wendebourg does, since both Hegel and Hofmann argue at length that their respective interpretive principle is the result of an empirical orientation and sensitivity. See Wendebourg, *Die heilsgeschichtliche Theologie,* 131ff. Wendebourg does not acknowledge that both Hofmann and Hegel attempted to be empirically oriented, though they acknowledged openly that all interpreters of history have a pre-understanding of that which they interpret based on a prior (more limited) familiarity with the events they seek to understand more profoundly. Wendebourg does not appreciate Hofmann's insistence that all historical investigation involves presuppositions which are entangled in the investigation from the very start. These "pre-understandings" are either confirmed or

and growth of "world Spirit/mind" (*Weltgeist*) toward the point of attaining the historical consciousness of its freedom (*IPH* 22).[67] The truth of this principle is given with the philosophical "system," which is a coherent, scholarly (*wissenschaftliche*) rendering of the growth and development of Spirit/mind (*Geist*). For Hofmann the principle by which all epochs are judged is the growth of the community of love between God and humanity established in and through "the new human being," Jesus Christ. Whereas Hegel interpreted the end or goal (*telos*) of history as the growth of intellectual/spiritual (*geistliche*) freedom, Hofmann subordinated freedom in the service of the realization of divine love. More specifically, the "end" (*eschaton*) of Christ is the consummation and complete fulfillment of the community of love between God and humanity.[68] One is not far off to suggest, then, that Hegel's concept of "the State" functions roughly similar to Hofmann's understanding of "the community of God" wherein the love between God and humanity is actualized in Jesus and the Spirit (cf. *IPH* 42).

Third, both Hegel and Hofmann emphasized the historicality of all human experience, including hermeneutical experience. Contrary to Ranke, Hegel and Hofmann underscored that there is no such thing as a "presuppositionless understanding." All understandings are mediated understandings that involve the historicality of the interpreter's own understanding.[69] But whereas Hegel's hermeneutical point of departure is his rationality,

---

criticized/modified as one interprets. In contrast to Hofmann, Wendebourg maintains that "objective" historical investigation is possible, when in fact many historians today recognize that all historical investigations necessarily involve pre-understandings that undergo modification during the hermeneutical process. Hofmann was not "un-empirical," as Wendebourg claims. Hofmann was an "historical realist," whose historical investigations nevertheless were undertaken in full cognizance and disclosure of his basic standpoint as an interpreter. He does not pretend to be "objective," as if this were even possible.

67. The *Phänomenologie* is the account of Spirit/mind (*Geist*) growing and developing toward self-fulfillment and self-expression, its own self-understanding. Included in this development is the "speculative Good Friday," "the Calvary of Absolute Spirit," the experience of "the negative," whereby *Geist* incorporates death and negation as a moment of the whole.

68. Of course, Hegel did not believe in a literal *eschaton*, as did Hofmann. For Hegel, there is an important distinction between an *eschaton* (mythical-religious) and a *telos* (conceptual-philosophical). A consistent eschatology suggests that history has no meaning, i.e., that meaning is beyond history, and Hegel's main point is that history has meaning because it has a goal or purpose. "What Hegel is asserting, therefore, is that the process of world history is the persistent striving of human communities for the attainment of a goal, which is human freedom. This does not entail that, even if and when that goal is achieved, history will come to an end (in the sense of termination)" (Errol E. Harris, *The Spirit of Hegel* [New Jersey: Humanities Press, 1993], 213).

69. In this regard, both Hegel and Hofmann anticipated Gustav Droysen's (1838–1908) reflections on the historicality of the historian. This aspect of Droysen's hermeneutics has been highlighted by Gadamer. See Hans-Georg Gadamer, "On the Problem of Self-understanding," *Philosophical Hermeneutics* (ed. and trans. David Linge; Berkeley: University of California Press, 1976), 48. See also idem, "Heidegger and the Marburger Theology," in *Philosophical Hermeneutics*, 198–212.

which coincides with the Reason of the world-historical process (or, in other terms, the capacity of world-spirit, as absolute spirit, to encompass the entire historical reality and to recollect that history rationally), Hofmann's point of departure is faith in Jesus Christ as the one who has reconciled human beings to God and in whom one receives one's proper relation to God. Hofmann believed, in light of his baptismal regeneration through the Holy Spirit and in light of the preaching of the word of God, that God has revealed the goal of history in the death and resurrection of Jesus. In Jesus Christ "history, the history which occurs between God and humanity, has come to a provisional conclusion" (*WE* 1:33). Christ is thus the "focal point" (*Mitte*) of history, the one who determines the final outcome of human history, and the one who enables the Christian to understand the meaning of history. Since one must first have "a measure" before one can "measure all historical events," Christ provides the Christian with that "measure" (ibid.). "All individual historical facts stand in relation to the final end, which provides them with their value and meaning" (ibid.). It is in this context that Hofmann speaks of Christ as "the provisional end of history," the one who anticipates ahead of time "the end" of all history. See also *SBb* 1:11–12, where Hofmann defines faith in Christ as "the essential consequence in which all history has found its end."

Hofmann never stated that the Christian actually sees the end of history, only that on the basis of one's living faith in Christ one anticipates and hopes for the end of history in Christ. The Christian remains open to the future. In this regard, both Hofmann and Hegel struggled against charges that they were merely "reading into" the individual events of history a meaning that the events could not bear.[70] For Hofmann isolated events on the stage of world history have their proper meaning only within the perspective of faith. This perspective led Hofmann to distinguish between that which is essential and that which is inessential in world history.

Hofmann's basis for understanding world history is different from that in Hegel's system. While both Hegel and Hofmann thought the course of history is intelligible, Hegel argued that the proper perspective on history is only given by Reason (*Vernunft*), which alone is capable of discerning "the self-development of freedom" (*IPH* 68). Hofmann, on the other hand, stressed that only the historical-eschatological gift of the Holy Spirit at work

---

70. Hegel appears to be more sensitive to the "negatives" of world history, which Hegel also calls a "slaughter-bench" (*IPH* 24), than Hofmann. Hofmann's conception of *Heilsgeschichte* is much less dialectical than Hegel's, though Hofmann's understanding of the "suffering servant," the suffering of Israel, and the suffering and crucifixion of Christ attempted to embrace the radical separations and divisions between God and humanity (and within human existence itself, e.g., the experience of sin and death) that are the divine ground for that event.

in the life of the individual believer grants the possibility of discerning the whole. The Spirit, who is active in and through the church's means of grace, enables the regenerated Christian to see the course of history as an expression of the living and present God in the world and in the inner-life of the Christian. Hofmann held that the content of faith cannot be translated into philosophical categories, as in Hegel's system. "Absolute knowledge" is not possible, according to Hofmann.

One might say that in Hofmann's system the counterparts to Hegel's Reason (*Vernunft*) and Spirit/mind (*Geist*) are the Christian's faith and the historical actions of the triune God. Just as Hegel thought his project disclosed "the cunning of Reason" (*die List der Vernunft*) in history, so also Hofmann thought his "system" disclosed the divine activity in history toward which creation is brought to its consummation in, with, and under Christ. Hofmann believed he could perceive and comprehend this divine activity, but only within the perspective of his faith in Christ. For Hofmann everything in history is to be understood and comprehended in relation to this goal of history, the new human community in Christ.

Finally, one must stress that it is a misreading of both Hegel's and Hofmann's respective projects to conclude that each functions in an *a priori* and non-empirical manner or in a manner that is highly or even totally arbitrary with historical details. For example, Wendebourg misunderstands both Hegel and Hofmann when he asserts that each was guided by an *a priori* construct that was non-empirical and that each sought to fit the facts to their ahistorical construct.[71] While the following passage contains much ambiguity (though the reference is undoubtedly to Ranke), at least Hegel's intentions are clear:

> We must take history as it is, and proceed historically, i.e., empirically. Among other things, we must not be misled by the professional historians, particularly the Germans, who possess great authority, and do precisely what they accuse philosophers of doing, namely creating a priori fabrications in history.... Let us leave all such a priori constructions to the clever professionals, for whom (in Germany) such constructions are not uncommon. As the first condition to be observed, we could therefore declare that we must apprehend the historical faithfully. But with such general terms as "apprehend" and "faithfully"

---

71. Wendebourg, "Die heilsgeschichtliche Theologie," 76. Wendebourg's conclusion has also influenced Steck. See Steck, "Die Idee der Heilsgeschichte," 31–32. For an extended defense of Hegel's empirical orientation, see Errol Harris, *The Spirit of Hegel*, 108–09, 208–22; and H. S. Harris, "The Hegelian Organon of Interpretation," in *Hegel, History, and Interpretation* (ed. Shaun Gallagher; Albany: State University of New York Press, 1997), 19–31.

there lies an ambiguity. Even the ordinary, average historian, who believes and says that he is merely receptive to his data, is not passive in his thinking; he brings his categories along with him, and sees his data through them. In every treatise that is to be scientific, Reason must not slumber, and reflection must be actively applied. To him who looks at the world rationally, the world looks rational in return. The relation is mutual. (IPH 13–14)

So also one must assert that Hofmann did not "cling to a philosophical point of departure."[72] His point of departure was his faith in Jesus Christ as the one who has reconciled all human beings to God and in whom one receives one's proper relation to God. Experiential and historically-mediated faith provided Hofmann with his perspective on the course of history, just as Reason provided Hegel with his perspective. Hofmann claimed that he was what he was because of a history, and his interpretation of Christianity sought merely to interpret that history which had made him what he was. But even this interpretation was provisional. He was aware of the "not yet" character of Christian existence.

Both Hegel and Hofmann thus undertook their empirical investigations in full cognizance and full disclosure of their basic standpoints as interpreters seeking historical understanding. Neither thinker pretended to be purely objective, as if this were even possible, nor did each thinker exclude differing interpretations of history from his own interpretations. For example, Hofmann acknowledged that he could make mistakes and that therefore the theologian must be open to comparing his method and historical exegesis with interpretations put forward by other historians and theologians. In point of fact, Hofmann's assumptions about many of the history-like details in the Bible *are* unconvincing. In this regard, he was much more naïve about historical realities than Hegel was. Neither Hegel nor Hofmann interpreted world history with the idea of "closing off all opposing discussion." Rather, like Hegel's own efforts at "comprehending history," Hofmann's interpretive efforts sought genuinely to be the beginning of self-understanding.

That Hofmann felt the need to reject Hegel's philosophy of history may have been due to his own (perhaps false) judgment that Hegel's system did not sufficiently stress the "givenness" and "factualities" of history and that it was improperly grounded in "Reason." More to his liking was the later philosophy of Schelling, which Hofmann held was less "ideal" and thus more realistic than Hegel's philosophy of history. In Hofmann's judgment

---

72. In Wendebourg's reading, Hofmann's *Heilsgeschichte* is "the product of two utterly contradictory conceptions of history, one a prioristic, the other historical" (Wendebourg, "Die heilsgeschichtliche Theologie," 76).

Schelling's philosophical reflections on history provided a more solid, transcendental foundation for the reality of history. Schelling took seriously the *thatness* of history, especially the historical *thatness* of Christianity.

Schelling and Hofmann[73]

That Hofmann was familiar with the ideas of Schelling's lectures from the 1820s and later is beyond doubt, but there are some questions as to when he first examined them and to what extent they influenced the formation of his theological understanding.[74] Wapler and Schellbach conclude that Hofmann's relation to Schelling was accurately described by Hofmann himself, i.e., he was less dependent on Schelling than Delitzsch had charged (cf. *BD* 22, 27, 33, 66). In contrast to Wapler and Schellbach, Wendebourg thinks that Delitzsch was essentially correct in his basic assumption.[75] All three studies of this question, however, conclude that Hofmann's originality and his eclecticism prohibit one from making an easy correlation between Schelling and Hofmann. This is an accurate conclusion, though the present essay finds the analyses of Wapler and Schellbach to be more accurate than Wendebourg's.

The similarities between Hofmann and Schelling could be the result of their mutual dependency on the Christian *Tatbestand* itself, or they could be due to their common background in Pietism and/or their common interest

---

73. The influence of Schelling on Roman Catholic philosophers and theologians (e.g., Johann Joseph von Görres [1776–1848] and Franz von Baader [1765–1841] at Munich in the nineteenth century and Walter Kasper in the twentieth) is generally better known than his influence on the Erlangen theological tradition, including Hofmann. The most extensive study of Schelling's influence on contemporary Roman Catholic thought is Thomas O'Meara, *Romantic Idealism and Roman Catholicism: Schelling and the Theologians* (Notre Dame, Ind.: University of Notre Dame Press, 1982). For Schelling's influence on Tillich, see Robert Scharlemann, "Schelling's Impact on Protestant Theology," in *Inscriptions and Reflections: Essays in Philosophical Theology* (Charlottesville: University Press of Virginia, 1989), 92–105. For Schelling's influence on Protestant theology in Germany, see Hirsch, *Geschichte*, 4:407–32.

74. For Schelling's relation to the Erlangen theological tradition as a whole, see Kantzenbach, "Schelling und das bayerische Luthertum," 115–45; Holsten Fagerberg, *Bekenntnis, Kirche und Amt in der deutschen konfessionellen Theologie des 19. Jahrhunderts* (Wiesbaden: Otto Harrassowitz, 1952), 52–57; and Hein, *Lutherisches Bekenntnis*, 46–48. For studies that concentrate on the relation of Hofmann to the later Schelling's positive philosophy of revelation and mythology, see Adolf von Harless, "Briefe an Höfling 1833–1852," ed. E. Dorn, in *Beiträge zur Bayrischen Kirchengeschichte* 22 (1915): 195–203; Wapler, "Die Theologie Hofmanns," 699–718; Schellbach, *Theologie und Philosophie*, 97–113; and Wendebourg, *Die heilsgeschichtliche Theologie*, 140–59. See also Seeberg, *Die Kirche Deutschlands*, 270 and 278.

75. Wendebourg, *Die heilsgeschichtliche Theologie*, 112ff.

in the theosophical ideas of Böhme.[76] Schelling had studied Böhme's writings carefully in the years after 1804, and Hofmann indicates that he had studied the *Aurora* as a student (perhaps as early as 1827). Hofmann's friend and colleague, Heinrich Schmid, confirms that Hofmann studied Böhme prior to and independent of his reception of Schelling's ideas.[77] This connection between Hofmann and Böhme must be kept in mind as one explores the similarities between Hofmann and Schelling.[78]

Hofmann's study of — or, perhaps more accurately, his acquaintance with — the ideas of Schelling seems not to have been primarily by means of Schelling's published materials but through written and oral reports of Schelling's unpublished lectures.[79] (The last substantial work of Schelling's to be published in his lifetime was his 1809 treatise, *On the Essence of Human Freedom*.) In the same 1859 letter to Delitzsch, referred to earlier, Hofmann lists a number of major contemporary philosophers and thinkers whose influence upon himself he wishes to discount or de-emphasize, including Schelling's. About the latter Hofmann writes, "Kant and Schelling I have known — until very recently — only from written and oral reports [about him, not from his own writings]" (*BD* 38). Hofmann continues:

> The impression that Schelling has had on me, in light of the recent preface to the posthumous writings edited by Steffens, you can view in my

---

76. "Tracing the impact of a thinker by way of direct influences is, at best, an uncertain undertaking. For, in the first place, a similarity of ideas between two thinkers is not necessarily evidence of direct influence, since some ideas seem to present themselves almost as a matter of course at a certain time to those who are thinking through the positions of their predecessors; and, in the second place, the direct influence of one thinker on another may not appear at all in a similarity between the ideas of the two of them" (Scharlemann, *Inscriptions and Reflections,* 92). Both possibilities appear to be true for Hofmann's relation to Schelling. It is also possible that Hofmann in his powerful originality and creativity as an independent thinker, finds in Schelling corroboration for his own insights and his terminology to express them, and affirms thereby also the interdependence of the academic disciplines of philosophy and theology.

77. Heinrich Schmid, *Vermischte Aufsätze,* vi. See also Wapler, *Johannes v. Hofmann,* 39.

78. For Böhme's influence on Schelling, see especially Robert F. Brown, *The Later Philosophy of Schelling: The Influence of Böhme on the Works of 1809–1815* (Lewisburg, Pa.: Bucknell University Press, 1977).

79. The most important works of this "late" period include *System der Weltalter* (1827–1828) (ed. S. Peetz; Frankfurt: Klostermann, 1990); *Grundlegung der positiven Philosophie* (1832–1833) (ed. Horst Fuhrmans; Turin: Bottega d'Erasmo, 1972); *On the History of Modern Philosophy* (1833–1834) (trans. Andrew Bowie; Cambridge: Cambridge University Press, 1994); *Philosophie der Mythologie* (1841–1842) (ed. Manfred Frank; 2 vols.; Frankfurt: Suhrkamp, 1985); and *Philosophie der Offenbarung* (1841–1842) (ed. Manfred Frank; 2 vols.; Frankfurt: Suhrkamp, 1977). Parts of these 1841–1842 lectures have been translated in *Schelling's Philosophy of Mythology and Revelation* (ed. and trans. Victor Hayes; Armidale, Australia: The Australian Association for the Study of Religions, 1995). While none of these writings of Schelling were published with Schelling's permission during his lifetime, Hofmann indicates he was familiar with his friends' notes and summaries of Schelling's lectures given in the late 1820's and early 1830's. He also had read Paulus's "pirated" edition of Schelling's 1841–1842 lectures on the philosophy of mythology and revelation.

comments about Schelling's ecclesial standpoint in *ZPK* 12. However, the manner in which my blessed friend [Emil von] Schaden carried on about Schelling and what came to my hands through [Franz von] Baader, spoke far less to me than [did] Jakob Böhme's *Aurora*. (Ibid.)[80]

Hofmann's statement here minimizes the direct influence of Schelling on his thinking. While Hofmann had been familiar with Schelling's ideas for some time prior to this statement, he only knew of them through second-hand reports.

The reports to which Hofmann refers had been coming to him already in the late 1820's and early 1830's, and later the ideas of Schelling would have filtered through Hofmann's reading of works of his elder colleague, Gottfried Thomasius, who had also studied Schelling.[81] One of Hofmann's closest friends, Emil August von Schaden (1814–1852), had been a student of Schelling's and had heard Schelling's first lectures on "the philosophy of religion" in Munich in 1830.[82] Wapler calls Schaden "a prophet of Schelling."[83] Schaden's father-in-law, Friedrich W. Thiersch (1784–1860), a classical philologist and the so-called "tutor of Bavaria," worked closely with Schelling to organize the Bavarian educational reforms. When Schaden died in 1852, Schelling sent a consoling letter to his mother. Wapler indicates that Schaden and Franz von Baader were Schelling's most important students.[84] That Hofmann knew Baader through Schaden is verified by Hofmann in his 1859 letter to Delitzsch. The Erlangen philosopher and friend of Hofmann, Karl Heyder, had also attended these lectures, as had another of Hofmann's friends, Heinrich Schmid.[85] Since Schelling did not publish his post-1809 lectures until much later, it is not unreasonable to think that each of these close friends of Hofmann had discussed the main ideas of Schelling's lectures with their friend.

Surely Hofmann and his friends would have discussed Schelling's critiques of Friedrich Jacobi (1743–1819), the irrational elements in the German Spiritual Awakening (*Erweckungsbewegung*), the ideas of Hegel, and the ideas

---

80. See also *SKS* 157–70.

81. See Wapler, "Die Theologie Hofmanns," 701–2.

82. Schaden joined the Erlangen philosophy faculty as a non-salaried lecturer [*Privatdozent*] at the same time that Hofmann joined the Erlangen theology faculty (1838/1839).

83. Wapler, *Johannes v. Hofmann*, 80.

84. Wapler, "Die Theologie Hofmanns," 703.

85. *BS* 7, 16. In this letter, Hofmann tells Schmid to give greetings to Schaden, whose book on the church Hofmann had recently seen reviewed. In an Oct. 1840 letter from Erlangen, Hofmann tells Schmid that he often visits with Schaden. In a Feb. 1844 letter, Hofmann indicates he was familiar with "Krabbe's dissertation on the essence of revelation in reference to Schelling" (ibid., 57). For Hofmann's personal remarks about his friendship with Schaden, see also ibid., 15–16, 20–21, 28, 55–56, 76, 94, 177. Even while Hofmann was in Rostock, he and Schaden maintained their friendship.

of Spinoza. They also would have discussed Schelling's positive treatment of Böhme's statements. Hofmann himself acknowledged the importance of Schelling's positive philosophy, especially its affirmation of Christianity as a *Tatbestand,* as a "reality" (*Wirklichkeit*) (*SKS* 161–62). Indeed, Hofmann asserted that Schelling was "the one living master today" (ibid., 157), very likely because Schelling had, in Hofmann's judgment, correctly understood Christianity as a "fact" (*Tatsache*) and not as a collection of "doctrines" (ibid., 164–65). Hofmann was convinced that Schelling was able to speak about the proof for the possibility (*Möglichkeit*) of Christianity only because that possibility had been *given* with the historical actuality (*Wirklichkeit*) of Christianity. He thus acknowledged Schelling's philosophy as an aid for making clear and plausible the relationships that have actually given rise to the reality and actuality of Christianity. "The science of possibility is philosophy. Theology therefore is to be assisted by philosophy in the realization of its task and thereby to help the church toward its fulfillment. But where is such a philosophy which is capable of providing this service? [The answer is given in] . . . the system of Schelling's positive philosophy" (ibid., 159–60).

What did Hofmann find valuable about Schelling's philosophy?

First, Hofmann appreciated Schelling's concern to recognize and interpret Christianity as a *Tatbestand,* as a living factual situation that is an organic whole of the historical revelation of God.[86] If Hofmann desired to understand Christianity as grounded in an historical *Tatbestand,* the later Schelling desired to articulate a truly historical philosophy.[87] For Schelling, as for Hofmann, Christianity is "a given which simply cannot be done away with. It exists, and it must be made comprehensible, and indeed, comprehensible as historical fact" (*SW* II, 4:234). Jesus, too, is treated as an historical fact and not as an "appearance" or "representation" (as in Hegel) nor as a "mythological" construct, as Strauss thought. Jesus is "an historical fact" (ibid., II, 4:230). The concern for "fact" is rooted in the concern to avoid illusion.

---

86. For Schelling's concept of "organism," see especially Bernd-Olaf Köppers, *Natur als Organismus: Schellings frühe Naturphilosophie und ihre Bedeutung für moderne Biologie* (Frankfurt am Main: Klostermann, 1992); Wilhelm Mauer, "Der Organismusgedanke bei Schelling und in der Theologie der katholischen Tübinger Schule," *Kerygma und Dogma* 8 (1962): 202–16; and idem, "Das Prinzip des Organischen in der evangelischen Kirchengeschichtsschreibung des 19. Jahrhunderts," *Kerygma und Dogma* 8 (1962): 265–92. Schelling was not the first to speak of nature (or later, reality, *Wirklichkeit*) as a "dynamic" or "historical" "organic whole." Hofmann and the Erlangen theologians were also influenced by Herder's and Johann v. Goethe's (1749–1832) reflections on the dynamic organization of nature and their criticism of the Enlightenment's "mechanical dismembering of things" (Beyschlag, *Die Erlanger Theologie,* 67). See also Hirsch, *Geschichte,* 4:207–47.

87. This notion was the standard by which Schelling criticized previous philosophical systems. See Schelling, *On the History of Modern Philosophy,* 134–63.

A philosophy which takes no interest in, and has no place for, reality as such eventually arrives at the point of making up for itself a history as it should be, which then has only a negative, hostile relation to the real history. (Ibid., II, 4:22)

Like the central historical concern in Hofmann's theology, the emphasis on the historical "givenness" of the world is the significant feature of Schelling's "late" philosophy. This emphasis is already implicit in the *Ages of the World* (1811–1815), but Schelling really began to develop it in the 1820s, while he was still lecturing at Erlangen. Schelling's interest in the "concrete being" (*Dasein*) of the world is similar to Hofmann's interest in the historical *Tatbestand* of Christianity. Even as early as 1795, Schelling had stated his fundamental, lifelong concern: "The main function of all philosophy is the solution of the problem of the being (*Dasein*) of the world" (ibid., I, 1:313). At this time, however, Schelling thought that the best solution to this question was by following Fichte's unified science. It was not until later that Schelling came to concentrate on the dynamic organization that organically developed from the inanimate to the animate, from necessity to freedom. This focus is similar to Hofmann's central and abiding historical concern.

Schelling's later philosophy thus attempted to establish what he called a "positive philosophy" in contrast to Hegel's "negative philosophy," exemplified in the latter's *Wissenschaft der Logik* (1812–1816), which explicated the forms of pure thought that determine *what* things are.[88] In Schelling's later view, all previous attempts at developing a philosophical system were unsatisfactory because they were basically unhistorical and did not do justice to the basic contingency of the world as grounded in the given fact of its "createdness." According to Schelling, a true philosophy is historical, and such a philosophy accepts that God belongs at the beginning and not at the end. Indeed, "God is the oldest of beings" (*AW* 5). "From now on begins the history of the actualization, or of the real revelations, of God" (ibid., 78). The goal of "positive philosophy" is to come to terms both with the fact *that* things are and with the contingencies of the historical emergence and development of thinking. But in order to do this, in Schelling's view as well as in Hofmann's, religious language is necessary because the philosophical problem of the meaning of being finds its answer in what lies beyond human experience. "For it is not because there is thinking that there is being, but rather, because there is being, there is thinking" (*SW* II, 3:161). The ultimate aim of positive philosophy is "to derive a philosophically viable

---

88. Georg Hegel, *Science of Logic* (ed. H. D. Lewis; trans. A. V. Miller; Amherst, N.Y.: Prometheus Books, 1999).

religion from a reinterpretation of the historical development of Christianity."[89] That aim is congruent with Hofmann's overall project to reinterpret the Christian faith for his day.

Second, Hofmann began his system with the same starting point as Schelling's, namely, the free self-determination of the Trinitarian God to be and to become "love" (*DVL* 43–45). For Schelling, beginning already in his 1820 treatises, but especially after *Ages of the World,* the self-determination of God as love means that God in freedom proceeds out of God's *aseity* ("God's being in and of itself") to seek that which is not God. This idea, for Schelling, can only be expressed mythologically, while for Hofmann the idea is an actual historical process of events. According to the latter, God's Trinitarian essence as "will of love" provides God's free relationship to creation and the redemption of humanity. The Trinitarian relationship in God has transformed itself "into an historical process of self-fulfillment" and has even become "a relationship of inequality" wherein God has "emptied himself" (*kenosis*) into time (*SBb* 1:36–37). Christ is the "revelation of the meaning that God is love" (*DVL* 45). So Hofmann shared with Schelling a similar understanding of God's relation to the world and to temporality: history is the realization or self-fulfillment of an inequality in God.[90] History is the history of the Trinitarian God. "Because God is triune, he wills also to become it for the people of God" (*SBb* 1:36). Salvation history (*Heilsgeschichte*) is the "immanent" historical realization of the "intra-divine relationships" (ibid., 1:36–37). A complete historicization of God is the result of God's self-emptying into time, yet God remains independent of the world.[91]

A third similarity between Hofmann and Schelling (which both share with Hegel, though Schelling and Hofmann thought they were paying closer attention to the historical *Tatbestand* that is external to the one knowing it than Hegel did) is their mutual concern to emphasize the existential correspondence between external truth and the internal recognition and recollection of that truth. For Hofmann the ideational "systematic total" is given through the individual's ecclesial experience of baptismal rebirth, which establishes the individual in a relationship to the "historical whole."[92] This experience forms the starting point for the proper recognition of the truth of the organic whole of history. The later Schelling was ideally suited

---

89. Andrew Bowie, *Schelling and Modern European Philosophy: An Introduction* (London: Routledge, 1993), 14.

90. See, for example, Hofmann's third thesis from his 1838 theological dissertation: "The Trinity is twofold, eternal and temporal" (Hofmann, *De Argumento Psalmi Centesimi decimi,* 47).

91. On this point in Schelling, see Paul Collins Hayner, *Reason and Existence: Schelling's Philosophy of History* (Leiden: Brill, 1967), 80, 107–24.

92. See Kantzenbach, "Schelling und das bayerische Luthertum," 139.

to provide philosophical categories that supported the "positivity" or factuality of the historical essence of the Christian *Tatbestand,* but he did so in such a manner that one is not forced to reject the notion that the facts of the historical process can be encompassed within a mental concept of "the whole." Thus Schelling said that the positive philosophy does not start *from* experience but proceeds *to* experience, i.e., the supra-historical stands for the intelligibility of nature and history. Empirical history is treated by Schelling as the *a posteriori* demonstration of that realm of eternal truth (namely, the supra-historical) that actually underlies and gives rise to the meaningfulness of empirical history. The supra-historical is the principle of the intelligibility of empirical history. In that he found that empirical history is a fulfillment of his rational deduction from the immediate notion of existence, he claimed that he had found the organic unity of reason and existence behind the epistemological division of subject and object.

Here Hofmann distinguished himself from Schelling's procedure, since for Hofmann the experience of rebirth (which has a fundamental priority in Hofmann's theology, though the experience is itself mediated through the church's means of grace) leads the theologian to reflect on the historical and eternal presuppositions necessary for that ecclesial experience. The movement is from Christian experience to the presuppositions for that experience. Empirical history provides the demonstration and fulfillment of eternal truth, without which history as a whole remains meaningless and unintelligible. For the Erlangen theologians in general, and for Hofmann in particular, the present *Tatbestand* of personal faith and the Christian church stand in a living, organic relationship to the past. Consequently the present *Tatbestand* is comprehensible only on the basis of its continuity with its past, but that past is itself comprehensible because it has become an inner truth in the individual believer.[93]

Hofmann thus was sympathetic to Schelling's valuation of the organic relation between past tradition and present confession of faith, between external reality and the inner comprehension of that reality. For Schelling and the Erlangen theologians, including especially Hofmann, Christianity is not a sum of doctrinal teachings but is essentially history, the history of God with the world. This history not only discloses who God is, but it also provides the only proper way to understand Christianity. The entire history of the world is therefore a progressive revelation of God, but what is important are the eternal presuppositions that condition the possibility of such a divine process. As Schelling put the matter:

---

93. For the relation of Schelling to this aspect of the Erlangen theology as a general whole, see especially Hein, *Lutherisches Bekenntnis,* 54–55.

Everything, absolutely everything, even that which by nature is eternal, must have already become internal to us before we can present it externally or objectively. If the writer of history does not awaken in himself or herself the past age whose image they want to project to us, then they will never present it truly, nor vividly, nor in a lively fashion. What would all history be if an inner sense did not come to assist it? It would be what it is for so many who indeed know most all that has happened, but who know not the least thing about actual history. Not only human events but the history of nature has its monuments and one can surely say that they do not abandon on their wide path of creation any stages without leaving behind something to indicate them. These monuments of nature, for the most part, lie there in the open, and are explored in manifold ways and are, in part, actually deciphered. Yet they do not speak to us but remain dead unless this succession of actions and productions has become internal to human beings. Hence, everything remains incomprehensible to human beings until it has become internal to them, that is, until it has been led back to that which is innermost in their being and to that which to them is, so to speak, the living witness of all truth. (*AW* xxxvii)

One cannot help but conclude that Schelling's "monuments of nature" stand in close proximity to Hofmann's "organic" understanding of Scripture as "a monument of *Heilsgeschichte*" (*SBb* 1:25). The existential relation of the individual to that "monument" is the key to understanding that "monument" properly.

A fourth similarity between Hofmann and Schelling, related to the second, is their mutual concern to systematize thought, to create an "organic system," an idea which was widespread in the German humanities (*Geisteswissenschaften*) at the beginning of the nineteenth century.[94] Here Hofmann and Schelling were distinct from such thinkers as Hamann and Kierkegaard, for whom "systems" were antithetical to authentic Christian faith. Not only did Hofmann understand the Bible as a document that was a part of the organic root of the church and its development, but he also interpreted the Lutheran confessional writings as a visible expression of the church's organic growth. Unlike Schelling, however, Hofmann continued to believe that the Lutheran Confessions in their entirety contained a "living" confession of the true faith.[95] The result of the theologian's work is a complete doctrinal

---

94. On the philosophical concept of "system" in Schelling, see Martin Heidegger, *Schelling's Treatise on the Essence of Human Freedom* (trans. Joan Stambaugh; Athens: Ohio University Press, 1985), 22–61.

95. See also Wapler, "Die Theologie Hofmanns," 717–19.

whole or system (*Lehrganze*) which seeks to express Christianity as an historical development that is on the way to an eschatological fulfillment. Such an understanding involves expounding the content of the Bible as a series of facts, placed in proper relationship to each other, which forms a totality or whole that corresponds to the systematic whole (*SBb* 1:32). In this regard, but for different purposes, both Hofmann and Schelling sought to ground their systems in the historicality and particularity of Christianity.

> For the true system will only be one which embraces all the particular suggestions or utterances of the Scriptures without excluding one of them and explains them precisely through this union. In addition, one must try to stay as closely as possible to the simplicity of these [biblical] statements and not, as most mystics have done, put into Christianity a pretentious wordiness which is totally alien to it.... Also with Christianity one should not inquire: How am I to interpret it so as to bring it into agreement with a particular philosophy? One should instead ask: Of what kind must philosophy be in order also to comprehend and take up Christianity into itself...? I want for the moment to consider Christianity in just the same way that I have also considered mythology, namely, as a phenomenon which I want to make intelligible as much as possible out of its own premises. Hence, strictly speaking, I want only to let it explain itself. (*SW* II, 4:33–34)

This quotation directly conforms *mutatis mutandis* to Hofmann's understanding of the theological task.

The goal of Hofmann's theology was to allow his method to be shaped by the Christian *Tatbestand* and not the other way around. The goal of theology is to allow the Christian *Tatbestand* to unfold itself in the thinking and acting of the theologian. Schelling's philosophical method thus provided Hofmann with an important confirmation of the correctness of his own approach to theology.

Concluding Appraisal

While there are similarities between Hofmann's theology and the philosophies and worldviews of certain key figures in what came to be called German Idealism, and even though there are certain idealistic traits in his dogmatic assertions, Hofmann's principal intention was not to be a speculative theologian or philosopher. His explicit intention was to be a faithful interpreter of the Bible. He understood such interpretation to be of service toward expressing the factuality and truth of the Christian *Tatbestand*. Even though his theology is clearly marked by the idealistic spirit of his age, "he was not a speculative thinker" (*"er war kein spekulativer Kopf"*).[96] As he himself admitted in his letters to Delitzsch, he had no formal education in philosophy and his mind was not oriented toward the "pure objectivity" of "strict speculation" that he found in such thinkers as Hegel and Schelling. With the exception of the latter, Hofmann thought that most philosophers (and not a few theologians) of his day paid scant attention to the historical "facts" of the biblical texts. For Hofmann the meaning of these "facts" resides in their literal historicality, to which the written sources refer. Nonetheless, while he tried to live in the literal, historical world of the Bible, and to relate that world to his own, he also breathed the air of Ranke, Hegel, and Schelling. This combination of the biblical world and the world of the mid-nineteenth century led Hofmann to seek to make the biblical world understandable to his generation, even though he evidently did not realize just how close some of his theological conceptions were to the reigning *Zeitgeist*. "So it is understandable how his desire to be scientific led him to seek a certain completion in philosophy."[97] To put the matter differently, elements in Hofmann's theology (e.g., his understanding of God's relation to the world) were given conceptual voice and meaning by ideas from Ranke, Hegel, and Schelling.

That Hofmann engaged the philosophical ideas of his era and even utilized such ideas to explicate the content of his biblical faith marks him as similar to other creative, classic theologians who did the same thing in their era. But his engagement with these ideas also ought to make him important for contemporary theology since the issues he found important are still with us today: questions about theological method (including hermeneutics), questions about the historicality of the Christian *Tatbestand,* and the question of God's being in relation to the world of becoming. Perhaps Hofmann's contemporaneity may, in part, be attributed to the influence of German Idealist thinkers both on his world and on our own.

---

96. Wapler, "Die Theologie Hofmanns," 705.

97. Ibid. Senft makes the point that Hofmann's appeal to experience is not, as Barth thought, the concession of a biblicist to the *Zeitgeist;* rather, "the important insight is expressed by Hofmann, namely, that all understanding and interpretation is possible only on the ground of a living relationship to the thing: He does not therefore call upon experience for support, because he does not want to master the Bible on the basis of experience, but rather because he wants to understand the Bible on the basis of experience" (Senft, *Wahrhaftigkeit und Wahrheit,* 87).

CHAPTER SIX

Evaluation and Criticism of Hofmann's Method

Before proceeding to a description of Hofmann's doctrine of God, I will offer a preliminary evaluation of Hofmann's theological methodology. A more complete evaluation will be offered in the final chapter, in conjunction with my analysis and final evaluation of his understanding of God.

Positive Features of Hofmann's Theological Method

The Christian *Tatbestand* Is Experiential and Historical

Certainly the most significant aspect of Hofmann's theological method is its axiomatic assumption that Christianity is a communal-historical-experiential "present factual situation" (*Tatbestand*). The methodology by which one investigates this *Tatbestand* of necessity must include both an accounting of personal experience of the Christian *Tatbestand* as well as an accounting of its historical nature (including also the historical nature of one's personal experience). Gadamer is correct to point out Hofmann's significance for the rise of modern theological hermeneutics: Hofmann understood that Christian experience is itself historical in nature.[1] It is as such both personal and trans-personal/ecclesial.

For Hofmann Christian experience by its very nature leads the Christian theologian into historical exegesis in order to compare one's own experience with the experience of the historical community which precedes and conditions that experience.[2] Thus one could argue that the uniqueness of

---

1. Gadamer, *Truth and Method*, 523–25.
2. Compare with Gadamer's central assertion that "[u]*nderstanding is to be thought of less as a subjective act than as participating in an event of tradition*, a process of transmission in which past and present are constantly mediated. This is what must be validated by hermeneutic

Hofmann's theological method resides in his attempt to steer a middle course between an uncritical and untheological use of historical criticism, which he thought was incapable of truly understanding the unique object of theology, and an uncritical and ahistorical use of traditional dogmatic proof-texting. The goal of Hofmann's method is to understand one's personal experience of salvation in light of the events of salvation that are external to one's own life and which have been mediated to the individual by the risen Christ through the Christian Scriptures and the Christian community. Hofmann's hermeneutical move here guided his intentional effort to overcome the false alternatives of "subjectivism" and "objectivism" in theology. This effort, unfortunately, also opened him to misunderstandings, whether by Delitzsch or Pieper or others, since Hofmann's creatively fresh approach to the theological task led him to formulate new concepts and new language (neologisms).

Hofmann's personal faith is enclosed in the events that form the transpersonal Christian *Tatbestand*, including also the external and historical word of the living Christ and his revelation of the triune God. The triune God is that which encompasses the entire Christian *Tatbestand*. Hofmann's thought begins and ends with the triune God, and in this train of thought he took into account his own finite creatureliness, his historicality, his sinfulness, and his rebirth. By stating the matter this way, Hofmann hoped to counter the charge that his systematic procedure is merely a theological form of speculative Idealism and mere solipsism.[3] One could argue that the permanent value of Hofmann's theology is his seeing the "community as a whole as the method of God's authority in the world, that the community is the actual bearer and object of the divine power of salvation, that being a Christian and being a theologian only occur within the Christian

---

theory, which is far too dominated by the idea of a procedure, a method" (Gadamer, *Truth and Method*, 290 [emphasis in original]). "Real experience is that whereby man becomes aware of his finiteness" (ibid., 357). For Gadamer, understanding is an experience of "the fusion of horizons" (*Horizontverschmelzung*) which is conditioned by the history of the effects or influences (*Wirkungsgeschichte*) of the work in question. For a similar hermeneutical attempt to move beyond the false alternatives of "subjectivism" and "objectivism," see Richard Bernstein, *Beyond Objectivism and Relativism: Science, Hermeneutics, and Praxis* (Philadelphia: University of Pennsylvania Press, 1983).

3. Hofmann and Delitzsch seem to have been talking past one another. Delitzsch's concern was to emphasize the objective and external nature of that which grounds faith. For Delitzsch, faith is certain and sure only because it is grounded outside of the individual Christian in the "objective" Word of God. For Hofmann personal and existential faith is certain and sure because it corresponds to and coheres with the *Tatbestand* that can be viewed as both internal to the believing Christian as well as external to the Christian. But Hofmann, too, acknowledged that personal faith is only certain "outside of oneself" (*extra nos*), in God, in God's word, in God's action.

community, and that Scripture as a whole corresponds to the history of this community, since Scripture is a witness to this history."[4]

This understanding of the Christian *Tatbestand*, which is both personal/present as well as external/historical to the individual Christian, provides the context for Hofmann's response to Delitzsch's accusation that Hofmann's theological method was too subjective: " ... the periphery of the *Tatbestand* that includes me in itself is much wider than my inward life which is embraced by it. The point into which I enter is Christ himself. He has made me a Christian. This point [Christ] is at the same time also the circle which encloses me and the whole world, visible and invisible, present and future" (*BD* 56).[5] Hofmann made a similar point in the course of his debate with G. Thomasius and T. Harnack about the atonement.

> But is there not also an erring conscience? Should we define according to our easily misunderstood needs what God must have done, or serve ourselves with our own ideas about what he has done? For one must take care here that one does not impose one's own thoughts on what God is saying in the conscience. We should not measure God's righteousness by what we call human righteousness nor bargain with him when he is wrathful nor prescribe how he may be gracious. "What is presumed about God according to law, measure, and goal, does not hit the mark," says Luther. (*SS* 2:91)

Here Hofmann argued that theology could err if it imposes or interjects its thoughts on the conscience as it speaks God's truth (e.g., God's law always accuses the sinner [*lex semper accusat*]). Moreover, each systematic representation of Christian faith can be regarded as a valid scholarly representation only if it correlates with that dimension of the *Tatbestand* which lies outside of the believing theologian — that which is given in Scripture as a historical whole and which is still in the process of developing in the history of the church.

The Hermeneutical Circle

Hofmann was among the earliest of nineteenth-century theologians to acknowledge that all interpreters have certain presuppositions that shape and inform their theological understanding. In this, he anticipated a common

---

4. Schellbach, *Theologie und Philosophie*, 88.
5. In Hofmann's theology, "it is entirely clear that the subjective first has its possibility and truth because the objective is absolutely effective" (Schellbach, *Theologie und Philosophie*, 38).

assumption of biblical hermeneutics in the twentieth century.[6] Like Rudolf Bultmann, who was drawing upon his teacher, Adolf Schlatter (1852–1938), who was also quite familiar with Hofmann's theology, Hofmann articulated the necessity for an existential, personal relationship to the content (*Sache*) of the Christian *Tatbestand* (including Scripture and the history of the interpretation of Scripture). Hofmann's personal "faith" experiences during his student years, through the influence of Krafft and Raumer, seem to have given Hofmann this insight. The interpreter cannot avoid a personal relationship with that which is interpreted, if one wishes to gain a fuller understanding of that "other."

The question, then, is: which are the most appropriate hermeneutical presuppositions that are the conditions for proper theological understanding? Those who think they interpret without presuppositions have merely replaced ecclesial dogmatic presuppositions with some other kind of dogmatic presupposition. While Ranke sought "the death of the self" in the quest for "objective" historical knowledge, Hofmann recognized that the self is part of understanding. The interpreter is not a *tabula rasa,* a blank slate, on which the Bible can paint itself, but he or she enters into the process of interpretation as the one he or she is. Indeed, the process of interpretation is both a seeking to understand that which is other than oneself but also a seeking of self-understanding. In other words, Hofmann's concern was to interpret the Christian *Tatbestand* that is both internal ("personal") and external ("trans-personal") to himself, though "certainty" is grounded outside of the self.[7] Thus Hofmann was constantly aware that in response to God's self-giving revelation, the theologian is expressing himself or herself and

---

6. Compare with Bultmann: "The question whether exegesis without presuppositions is possible must be answered affirmatively if 'without presuppositions' means 'without presupposing the results of exegesis.' In this sense, exegesis without presuppositions is not only possible but imperative. In another sense, however, no exegesis is without presuppositions, because the exegete is not a *tabula rasa* but approaches the text with specific questions or with a specific way of asking questions and thus has a certain idea of the subject matter with which the text is concerned" (Bultmann, "Is Exegesis Without Presuppositions Possible?" 145). See also Jeanrond, *Theological Hermeneutics,* 137–48; and Gadamer, *Truth and Method,* 331–41.

7. Hofmann's concern to articulate an adequate theological-biblical hermeneutic that takes seriously the presuppositions of the interpreter, especially the historicity and faith commitment of the interpreter, as well as the need to understand the history of the effects of the scriptural events/texts in shaping Christian self-understanding, is similar to concerns voiced in recent discussions of hermeneutics by and about Gadamer and Ricoeur. For a cogent critique of Gadamer and Ricoeur that takes seriously the positive contributions of each thinker, see Werner Jeanrond, *Text and Interpretation as Categories of Theological Thinking* (New York: Crossroad, 1991), 64–72. See also Tanner, *Theories of Culture,* 131–35. Tanner is particularly critical of Gadamer's false assumption that "tradition" is an "object," i.e., that "traditional materials . . . are found, discovered, or received, and not constructed in a significant sense. Postmodern cultural theory makes the important claim that traditions are invented, meaning by that not merely that traditional materials are often new rather than old and borrowed rather than indigenous, but that they are always products of human decision in a significant sense"

God's self-giving simultaneously. In other words, Hofmann could not speak of God theologically without being caught up in this speech with his whole being. "The knowledge and expression of Christianity must be above all the self-knowledge and self-expression of the Christian" (*SBb* 1:10). Theological speech is conceivable only as a confession or witness to the communion that God has established between God and humanity in Christ.[8] Indeed, everything that Hofmann wanted to say about God, the world, humanity, and himself, was consonant with the experience of his own communion with God in the risen Christ, to which his theological language sought to bear witness.

But is not this central element of Hofmann's hermeneutical procedure problematic? Bultmann, for example, asked what possible relevance Hofmann's union of experiential analysis and historical investigation can have for the theologian. For Bultmann, such a union cannot "prove" the certainty of Christ, since Hofmann is caught in a vicious circle: Christ has to be known as the goal of history before the significance of Israel's history can be viewed in the light of Christ.[9] Barth levels a similar accusation:

> [T]here is no mistaking the peculiarity in Hofmann's proof from Scripture: that what is supposedly to provide the proof, Scripture, is in reality what is also to be proved. Or, to put it the other way around, what is supposed to be proved, the content of Christian experience, has also to provide the proof in the form of a scriptural proof which is in effect no more than a further expansion of the circle of Christian experience. His scriptural proof suffers from the fact that it is only an extended proof from experience and his proof from experience from the fact that it is itself already a proof from Scripture.... In view of this inner vitiation of Hofmann's theology one can only point out yet again that his interest in the two factors, knowledge of experience and knowledge of Scripture, was an unequal one. He pursued it with the instruments and interests of an extreme Schleiermacherian

---

(ibid., 133). Gadamer and Hofmann acknowledge, however, that construals of "tradition" encompass an open-ended process of human decision-making that is always in need of revision. Furthermore, while "traditions" are the product of individual decisions, they are certainly also "trans-individual" and formative of individuals.

8. Hofmann's emphasis on the relation of radical self-knowledge to the knowledge of God who gives God's self to be known in the present seems to be very close to central assertions in the respective theologies of Augustine, Kierkegaard, and Pascal. See also the first chapter of Book 1 of Calvin's *Institutes* (I.1.1–2). "Without knowledge of self there is no knowledge of God.... Without knowledge of God there is no knowledge of self" (John Calvin, *Institutes of the Christian Religion* [ed. John T. McNeill; trans. Ford Lewis Battles; Philadelphia: Westminster Press, 1960], 1:35–37.

9. Bultmann, "Prophecy and Fulfillment," 58.

and thought that as a Schleiermacherian he could establish its character as a scholarly discipline (*Wissenschaft*).[10]

Unfortunately, Bultmann's and Barth's criticisms of Hofmann's theological method demonstrate a basic misunderstanding of Hofmann's method. Hofmann was not concerned to "prove" his Christianity, only "understand" it. "The unity and completeness of *Heilsgeschichte* will give a witness for the reality of *Heilsgeschichte,* which will have validity and power for everyone who through the personal experience of salvation is in a position to understand it" (*BWE* 55–56). What looks like "begging of the question" or a vicious circle is actually just another form of the well-known hermeneutical circle along which all interpreters find themselves. One has a preunderstanding or expectation of the text one is to understand that one cannot avoid bringing to the text.[11] Through one's encounter with the text, one discovers this pre-understanding confirmed to a certain degree, yet never to the point that one's pre-understanding is simply confirmed *in toto.*[12] While Hofmann admitted that "[i]n truth, the whole order [of the system] depends on a dogmatic view [of the Bible] which itself is already an outcome of a general study of the Bible," scriptural texts, like all classic texts, have a way of surpassing and correcting the interpreter's pre-understanding, of "de-centering" the interpreter (*BS* 66). Thielicke is correct when he criticizes Barth and Bultmann for not recognizing in Hofmann's theological method the well-known hermeneutical circle:

> That which Hofmann calls the experience of being a Christian (i.e., regeneration) constitutes the preunderstanding of the biblical text, or

---

10. Barth, *Protestant Theology,* 614–15 (translation altered).

11. For a discussion of hermeneutical "pre-understanding," see Gadamer, *Truth and Method,* 265–307; Jeanrond, *Text and Interpretation,* 12–22; and David Tracy, *Plurality and Ambiguity: Hermeneutics, Religion, and Hope* (New York: Harper and Row, 1987), 16–27. "A person who is trying to understand a text is always projecting. He projects a meaning for the text as a whole as soon as some initial meaning emerges in the text. Again, the initial meaning emerges only because he is reading the text with particular expectations in regard to a certain meaning. Working out this fore-projection, which is constantly revised in terms of what emerges as he penetrates into the meaning, is understanding what is there" (Gadamer, *Truth and Method,* 267). Of course, the challenge is: "How can a text be protected against misunderstanding from the start?" (ibid., 268).

12. See Paul Ricoeur, "Explanation and Understanding," in *Interpretation Theory: Discourse and the Surplus of Meaning* (Fort Worth: The Texas Christian University Press, 1976), 71–88, especially Ricoeur's discussion of the circular process of interpretation that moves from "guessing" to "validation," and from "explanation" of the other to "self-understanding" by means of the encounter with a text that is other than one's self. More recently, Ricoeur has shown how all understanding follows an "arc" that begins with an initial pre-understanding of reality that we bring to the text (mimesis 1), the restructuring and reconfiguring of this initial understanding of reality by the text (mimesis 2), and the final intersection between the text and the world of the interpreter (mimesis 3). See idem, *Time and Narrative,* 1:52–87.

of the text of salvation history. It rests on first and relatively naive encounters with it, especially by way of the proclamation of the community in which Christians find themselves. The contact with the text that comes to light in the preunderstanding effects a relationship of analogy and coordination with it which makes possible . . . a divinatory understanding. Christians who engage in theological reflection then lay claim to this.[13]

Clearly the goal of Hofmann's theological method is "understanding" and not some form of "rational proof" or "internal security." Precisely because Christian experience is communal and ecclesial, and because Scripture belongs to the ecclesial community, the Christian has an historical and necessary relationship to Scripture which is given through the experience. The communal and ecclesial nature of the experience dictates that the understanding of this experience be compared with and, if necessary, corrected by the understanding of the experience as presented in Scripture and the history of the church (*ET* 26–27).[14] While the development of the content of experience is an independent task, one must recognize that one can make mistakes. The interpreter may be blind to prejudices and assumptions and ideological illusions that need to be properly criticized. Thus Hofmann emphasized that one's method and exegesis must be open to comparison with the understandings of the Christian experience put forth by other theologians. Likewise, Christian theology is not merely a scholarly discipline in and for the believing community but as such also belongs in the university. Hence, Hofmann's theological method does not trivialize or marginalize the other academic disciplines of the university but seeks to relate the truth of the Christian faith to these other disciplines and vice versa. At least that was his intent, even if Hofmann could not bring himself to acknowledge

---

13. Thielicke, *Modern Faith and Thought,* 240. See also Wach, *Das Verstehen,* 2:365–67. Wach maintains that Hofmann saw, correctly, that each interpreter is incapable of freeing himself or herself from "the hermeneutical circle," i.e., that such a circle "is undoubtedly a given for all interpretation."

14. See also Forde, *The Law-Gospel Debate,* 18. Compare with Jeanrond's concept of "interpretation," which "encompasses understanding and its methodical revisions. Accordingly the concept of interpretation — in Gadamer's sense also — does not represent a falling back into an objectivist methodologism but rather encompasses the open-ended process of understanding together with its methodical and, by the same token, finite, efforts at achieving certitude" (Jeanrond, *Text and Interpretation,* 36). Barth at least in principle acknowledged that Hofmann's theology was open to correction from Scripture and other biblical interpreters. " . . . [T]he discipline [Hofmann] was engaged in was scriptural. And since he pursued this discipline with great acuteness (his exegesis is well worth studying, even now) in a sphere that he shared with others, he in practice heightened the unrest in this sphere, the un-Schleiermacherian opposition of subject and object, the remembrance that man, even reborn man, is not alone, but has in God a powerful and ultimately unavoidable point of encounter" (Barth, *Protestant Theology,* 615).

that the biblical texts themselves, and their explicit and implicit ideological assumptions, may be in need of criticism.

Negative Features of Hofmann's Theological Method

The Relation of Faith to History

Wapler is correct to observe that Hofmann had "a very sharp mind, but it was at the same time a naïve mind."[15] Hofmann surely was aware of historical-critical questions relating to the historicality of biblical events, particularly within the primeval narratives of Genesis 1–11, the eschatological visions of the prophets (including the apocalypse of John), and the Gospels, but he himself stressed that a proper theological hermeneutic must comprehend individual pericopes and biblical events in relation to the content of the faith, which coincides with the whole of the biblical salvation history (*Heilsgeschichte*). Hofmann seems to have been untroubled by the problems that historical and literary criticism created for a theological conception that asserted that "Adam" and "Noah," for example, were historical figures (like Moses and David). Contemporary biblical scholarship recognizes that such literary figures belong to a genre that is "primal history," and thus different from what we usually call "history." Hofmann often was quite comfortable within the then sufficient world of a first naiveté.

Following Bultmann's and Barth's critique of Hofmann's hermeneutics, some have wondered why there was a need to study the trans-subjective history of the Christian "present factual situation" (*Tatbestand*) if Hofmann's faith was an "independent existence within himself."[16] In other words, if Hofmann knew the faith, what need was there for him to know the history that confirms that faith? Could he really even know this history? If history is only a presupposition of his experience of faith, then a more objective and critical understanding of history was not really possible for Hofmann. His understanding of faith did not allow him to undertake what would now count as a rigorous historical-literary contemplation of the texts. Instead, since faith is certain of its object, the Christian *Tatbestand*, all historical investigation occurs within the parameters of that certainty. Such an understanding of faith and history both justified and hindered his reflection on the history to which the Bible gives witness. Like many biblical interpreters after him, including Kähler, who was deeply influenced by Hofmann, Hofmann

---

15. Wapler, *Johannes v. Hofmann*, 25.
16. Senft, *Wahrhaftigkeit und Wahrheit*, 105–6.

seems to have been uninterested in combining rigorous historical criticism with theological interpretation of the biblical texts.

Understandably, Hofmann's hermeneutical procedure did put him at odds with his most esteemed teacher, Ranke, and most other nineteenth-century historians. Ranke's critical spirit, his skepticism about the past, and his desire for "objectivity" did not seem to have taken a hold in Hofmann's hermeneutical approach to the biblical texts and their narration of divine acts in the past. Hofmann merely sought to comprehend matters whose historical veracity was already assumed. The question about the historical value of the biblical events, their facticity or the nature of the historicity to which they supposedly witness, is simply not perceived by Hofmann to be a serious problem. Thus, Hofmann did not devote much time and energy to the problem of establishing criteria by which to judge the historical veracity of the particularities within the biblical texts. While Hofmann on occasion asserted that in principle an historian's approach to the Bible is to be no different from his approach to any other ancient text, this Rankean principle was never executed in a rigorous manner. Hofmann's faith in the acts (*Wunderwerke*) of God and his sense of a divine *Heilsgeschichte* in the narrative whole of the Bible kept him from approaching the Bible with the historical criticism as practiced by those Protestant scholars in the turn-of-the-century "History-of-Religions School" (*Religionsgeschichteschule*), e.g., Wilhelm Bousset (1865–1920), Herman Gunkel (1862–1932), Adolf Deissmann (1866–1937), Albert Eichhorn (1856–1926), Johannes Weiss (1863–1914), Wilhelm Wrede (1859–1906), and Troeltsch.[17] In this important sense, Hofmann remained a precritical interpreter of the Bible, even though he utilized the philological and historical-critical work of Wilhelm Gesenius (1786–1842), Georg Ewald (1803–1875), Johann Winer (1789–1860), Semler, Baur, and others.

Faith as Human Projection

Hofmann's method is also open to attack on the basis of Ludwig Feuerbach's (1804–1872) critique of Christianity. Such an attack would charge that Hofmann had projected theological meaning onto reality (whether that reality is the biblical texts or extra-biblical historical events) and then had utilized his conception of the historical task to confirm that preconceived theological meaning. Delitzsch highlighted precisely this concern: "No theologian can

---

17. For the history of this school, see Kümmel, *The New Testament*, 206–25; and Kraus, *Geschichte der historisch-kritischen Erforschung des Alten Testaments*.

produce out of his consciousness of faith...the whole multiplicity of past, present, and future of salvation" (*BD* 45).

While Hofmann's writings present no direct evidence that he was familiar with Feuerbach's atheistic-materialist and anthropological interpretation of Christianity and his reinterpretation of the nature of Christian faith, Hofmann's writings do contain a line of argumentation that he could have used to counter the claim that Christian faith is mere "projection" or "illusion." Hofmann, like Luther and Schleiermacher, asserted that God cannot be spoken of *in God's self*, but only on the basis of God's giving of God's self to faithful human beings, though Hofmann would not agree with the main point of Feuerbach's view, that God is nothing but the result of human projection and that theology is really anthropology in disguise.[18]

The criticism that Hofmann leveled against Strauss's mixing of philosophy and theology — as well as Strauss's inability to comprehend the certainty of faith which is independent of history, philology, and philosophy, — even if not entirely persuasive, could also have been leveled against Feuerbach, though Hofmann never referred directly to him. The refutation of Feuerbach would, no doubt, imply the possibility of a proof for God's existence outside of faith, something Hofmann thought was not possible. According to Hofmann, the kind of existential certainty that faith has cannot be proved from the outside. God is only knowable in faith, which corresponds to God's self-revelation. In this understanding, faith is a divine gift and not the result of human projection.

Excessive Individualism

Related to criticism about Hofmann's tendency to project a subjective meaning onto the Bible and extra-biblical history is the critical question of

---

18. See especially Ludwig Feuerbach, *The Essence of Christianity* (trans. George Eliot: New York: Harper and Row, 1957). In the introduction to this edition, Barth refers to Hofmann as "an associate of Schleiermacher" who was blind to Feuerbach's charge that "theology has become anthropology" (ibid., xxi). Despite the lack of direct evidence, it is likely that Hofmann at least knew of Feuerbach's basic materialist view. Feuerbach and Hofmann were in Erlangen at the same time for two years. Feuerbach transferred to Erlangen from Berlin in 1827, the same year seventeen-year old Hofmann matriculated at Erlangen. In 1828 Feuerbach received his degree from Erlangen, and afterward he became a *Privatdozent* in the philosophy department there. This position lasted until 1830, at which time Feuerbach was forced to leave Erlangen due to controversy about his atheism. Wapler hints that Hofmann surely would have been aware of Feuerbach's presence in the philosophical faculty, whose lecture hall was right next to that of the theological faculty. In 1827, the Erlangen philosophical faculty (which also included the discipline of history) was Hofmann's second home. Two of Hofmann's closest friends on the faculty were the Erlangen philosophers, Schaden and Heyder, who also likely discussed Feuerbach's ideas with Hofmann (though there is no firm evidence to support this supposition).

whether such a focus on individual religious experience or personality betrays an illusory individualism that reflects much of Western individual
possessiveness. In recent years, poststructualism and deconstructionism have
raised questions about the nature of *the self* and the lack of transparency of
the self.[19] Deconstruction of the self by psychoanalysis and deconstructive
philosophical analysis have led many to set forth persuasive arguments that
the modern self is a fiction resulting from people's pretensions to autonomy
and their desire to control and manipulate reality. In view of this criticism,
Hofmann's theological method would need to be modified to stress what
Hofmann himself also often acknowledged, namely, that his personal experience of faith is an aspect of the interpretive experience of his religious
community (including Scripture and ecclesial confessions) and not "an independent existence" within the theologian. Personal religious experience
is always historically conditioned experience that is informed by the history of one's religious community and its confessional tradition. Such a
tradition, Hofmann argued, is in principle open to revision to accord more
closely with the *sine qua non* of the Christian faith, communion between
God and humanity mediated in and through Jesus Christ and received by
faith. Christian theology seeks to articulate an experience of a community's
"community tradition" which itself receives its life and vibrancy by being
established and reformed by "the external word of God," the living voice of
the gospel. In this communal hermeneutic, faith-shaping events are not outside the community but within the community's interpretive and on-going
life. Likewise one's Christian identity is not grounded in the past or the
present personal experience but in the present communal experience, i.e.,
evangelical proclamation and the ecclesial means of grace.

Hofmann's Conception of *Heilsgeschichte*

While I will return to criticize Hofmann's conception of salvation history
(*Heilsgeschichte*) in the final chapter of my study, I need to offer a preliminary critique at this point. In view of Friedrich Nietzsche's (1844–1900)
criticism of historicism and in light of the cultural crises that have developed
in western civilization since at least the end of the First World War, Hofmann's conception of *Heilsgeschichte* is problematic in its original form. In
recent years, all such "meta-narratives," both theological and secular, have

---

19. See, for example, "The Disappearing Self," in William Barrett, *Death of the Soul* (New
York: Anchor, 1986), 119–41.

been criticized, especially by so-called post-structuralists.[20] As Walter Benjamin (1892–1940) observed, such constructions result in a history of the victors.[21] Is it not the case, however, that "the center" of *Heilsgeschichte* (i.e., a Christian understanding of world history on the basis of the ministry, death, and resurrection of Jesus) is no longer as sure and certain as Hofmann thought? Nietzsche's questioning of all such narratives clearly articulated the crisis of consciousness about time and reality that many have experienced since the late-nineteenth and early-twentieth centuries. Many today still agree with Yeats that "the center cannot hold."[22]

Despite this strong criticism of Hofmann's notion of *Heilsgeschichte*, one could respond on his behalf that his understanding of biblical *Heilsgeschichte* also involves the presence of disruption and incompleteness in the contingencies of history. His conception of *Heilsgeschichte* is not a simple and progressive development; rather, it is a development that is also marked by conflict and opposition between God and fallen creation and between church and world. Just as Schelling left room for the irrational, evil, and the judgment of God in the unfolding drama of history, so too did Hofmann. Furthermore, one could point out that even Nietzsche and post-structuralist historians involve themselves in "totalizing" discourse and the formation of meta-narratives like Hofmann's own. Recent criticism of so-called "new historicism" is like Hofmann's criticism of old historicism: the historian or biblical interpreter always operates out of an inescapable, totalizing framework that is constantly in need of revision.[23] Though Hofmann wanted to address history's fundamental questions, he did not claim to have comprehended and explained an "end" that has already been reached, as Hegel did, and upon which he could then only look backwards. Hofmann was aware that history runs in all sorts of directions and creates confusion. Precisely for this reason there is the need for a focal point, a "center," the *Mitte*, which in faith provides a perspective on the whole of reality. For Hofmann this "center" is the risen Christ, "the end" of history that has been given "in the middle." Hofmann's theological method is thus ultimately grounded in the concrete form of the triune God's self-giving, saving love in Jesus, which is the focus of part three of my study.

---

20. See, for example, White, *Metahistory*; Megill, " 'Grand Narrative' and the Discipline of History," 151–73; and the essays in *The New Historicism* (ed. H. Aram Veeser; New York: Routledge, 1989).

21. Walter Benjamin, "Theses on the Philosophy of History," in *Illuminations* (trans. Harry Zohn; New York: Schocken, 1969), 256.

22. W. B. Yeats, "The Second Coming" (1921), reprinted in *The Humanistic Tradition* (ed. Gloria Fiero; 6 vols.; 4th ed.; New York: McGraw Hill, 2002), 6:52.

23. "In the tendency to profess an empiricism free from all metaphysical presuppositions, we see only the curious attempt to jump over one's own shadow" (Troeltsch, *Der Historismus und seine Probleme*, 670).

Part III

Hofmann's Doctrine of God

CHAPTER SEVEN

Trinitarian Historicality: The Self-Determining God

The typical interpretation of nineteenth-century theology suggests that the doctrine of the Trinity fell into disuse in Protestantism from the time of Schleiermacher, who seemingly relegated it to an appendix in his dogmatics (*Glaubenslehre*), until its renewal in the theology of Karl Barth.[1] Apart from Hegel, who used Trinitarian symbols for the explication of his philosophical system, and apart from those theologians who were influenced by Hegel (e.g., Marheineke), most Protestant theologians in this period either "ignored" Trinitarian dogma or "relegated [it] to a relatively unimportant place in the theological structure."[2] From Schleiermacher until Barth the Trinity was "a doctrine of the second-rate."[3]

The work of Hofmann, however, stands out as an important exception to this trend in the nineteenth and early twentieth centuries. That Hofmann's Trinitarian theology has been neglected is unfortunate.[4] Not only was he "one of the first, after the period of rationalism, to carry through the task of the restoration of this doctrine to its rightful place as the ultimate ground of the assurance of faith," but his thought also anticipates the renewal in Trinitarian thought that began in the last century.[5]

---

1. "Finally, in Barth himself the theological incorporation of all these dynamics is a decisively Trinitarian theology, after centuries in which Trinitarianism was in Western reflection a problem rather than a resource. It can fairly be said that the chief ecumenical enterprise of current theology is rediscovery and development of the doctrine of Trinity. It can also fairly be said that Barth initiated the enterprise" (Robert Jenson, "Karl Barth," in *The Modern Theologians* [ed. David Ford; 2 vols.; New York: Basil Blackwell, 1989], 1:46–47).

2. Claude Welch, *The Trinity in Contemporary Theology* (London: SCM Press, 1953), vii. To be sure, the doctrine of the Trinity was a standard *locus* in the Orthodox Lutheran dogmatics texts, but its place and treatment in the dogmatic structure tended to minimize its importance and to ignore post-Enlightenment critiques of dogma. Both Protestant and Roman Catholic theologians in this period tended merely to repeat the traditional Trinitarian dogmatic phraseology. They saw no need for a creative renewal of Trinitarian theology.

3. Ibid., 3.

4. Most standard surveys of nineteenth-century theology, if they do refer to Hofmann's theology, neglect this aspect of his work.

5. Preus, "The Theology of Hofmann," 141. Welch refers briefly to the Erlangen School (cf. *The Trinity in Contemporary Theology*, 35–36), but only treats Thomasius, Hofmann's

After giving a brief summary of this renewal, the present chapter sets forth Hofmann's own understanding of the triune God's self-giving in history. The purpose of this chapter is to explicate the properly Trinitarian character of Hofmann's theological work and to highlight his efforts at making the doctrine of the Trinity a living, central element in Christian theology.

The Renewal of Trinitarian Theology

At the heart of recent Christian thought has been the renewal of Trinitarian theology which has occurred largely as a result of the works of Barth and Rahner.[6] In general those theologians who have participated in this renewal stress that if God is to be understood as gracious love ("God is love," "God-for-us"), then God's being must be both relational and temporal.[7] In other words, to use Eberhard Jüngel's descriptive phrase for Barth's mature doctrine of God, "God's being is in becoming."[8]

This understanding of God differs from the traditional understanding of God within mainstream Christian tradition. The dominant view in the tradition has been that if God is the ground of cosmic order and stability then God as such cannot change. In this major Western metaphysical tradition God is understood as Pure Being. This tradition asserts that God's actions follow from God's being (*operatio sequitur esse*), but God's being does not change per se.[9] God is separate from and unaffected by relational change and temporality. Such an *apathetic* view of God, influenced especially by Greek metaphysical reflection, subverts the notion of divine relationality that is inherent within the witness to the incarnation of the Word (*Logos*) in Jesus.

---

colleague. Hofmann's 1842 dogmatic lectures were delivered earlier than Thomasius's *Christi Person und Werk* (1853) and likely influenced the latter's conception of both the *kenosis* of Christ and the Trinity.

6. As representative examples, see thinkers as diverse as Wolfhart Pannenberg, *Systematic Theology* (trans. Geoffrey Bromiley; 3 vols.; Grand Rapids: Eerdmans, 1991–1998); Jürgen Moltmann, *The Trinity and the Kingdom* (trans. Margaret Kohl; London: SCM Press, 1981); idem, *History and the Triune God* (trans. John Bowden; New York: Crossroad, 1992); Eberhard Jüngel, *God as the Mystery of the World* (trans. Darrell Guder; Grand Rapids: Eerdmans, 1983); Robert Jenson, *The Triune Identity* (Philadelphia: Fortress, 1982); Joseph Bracken and Marjorie Hewitt Suchocki, eds., *Trinity in Process* (New York: Continuum, 1997); Christoph Schwöbel, ed., *Trinitarian Theology Today: Essays on Divine Being and Act* (Edinburgh: T & T Clark, 1995); and John Zizioulas, *Being as Communion* (Crestwood, N.Y.: St. Vladimir's Press, 1985).

7. See Catharine LaCugna, *God for Us* (New York: HarperCollins, 1991). See also Ted Peters, *God as Trinity: Relationality and Temporality in Divine Life* (Louisville: Westminster, 1993).

8. Eberhard Jüngel, *The Doctrine of the Trinity: God's Being Is in Becoming* (trans. Horton Harris; Grand Rapids: Eerdmans, 1976).

9. See Emil Fackenheim, *Metaphysics and Historicity* (Milwaukee: Marquette University Press, 1961), esp. 29–30.

In contrast to the dominant tradition, especially in its Augustinian and Thomistic expressions, new Trinitarian theologies emphasize God's temporality and relationality on the basis of God's complete identification with *the* human being, Jesus of Nazareth. Whereas the ancient and medieval theological tradition understood the triune God as a divine *substance,* early modern Christian thinkers began to emphasize God as a divine *Subject.* Whereas the scholastic theological tradition (in both its Catholic and Protestant forms) separated the treatment of God into two sequential treatises, "On the One God" (*De Deo Uno*) and "On the Triune God" (*De Deo Trino*), the new Trinitarian theologies correlate the divine economy of salvation (*oikonomia*) with the mystery of God's being-as-such (*theologia*).

According to Barth and Rahner, God's being is best understood in terms of a specific history, namely, the history of God's self-giving in Jesus and his community. God is said to have a history, and this *Heilsgeschichte,* or the historical economy of salvation, is definitive of who God is as a self-revealing Subject.[10] The economic Trinity thus reveals the continual self-communication of God under the conditions of time and history, hence in the missions of Christ and the Spirit.[11] " ... [I]t is a fact of *Heilsgeschichte* that we know about the Trinity because the Father's Word has entered our history and has given us his Spirit.... We shall start by showing that the economic Trinity is also already the immanent Trinity, and not merely presuppose this tacitly or add it as an afterthought."[12] "The 'economic' Trinity is the 'immanent' Trinity and the 'immanent' Trinity is the 'economic' Trinity."[13] God's self-giving in the economy of God's salvation *is* God.

Similarly, if the Trinity is truly the mystery of human redemption, then there must be a fundamental connection or relation between the Trinity and human beings. The Trinity cannot be absolutely unrelated to human

---

10. Karl Barth, *Church Dogmatics* (trans. G. W. Bromiley and T. F. Torrance; 13 vols.; Edinburgh: T & T Clark, 1956–1969), 1.1:371–383. See also Mattes, "Toward Divine Relationality," 75–85.

11. Contrary to Augustine's notion of "appropriations," which holds that any one of the three "persons" of the Trinity could have been sent into the world to redeem the world but that that mission was only "appropriated to the Son," Rahner develops the idea that the mission of the Son is proper only to the Son. Only the second person of the Trinity became a human being and thus his "mission" is unique to the *Logos,* to his particular history.

12. Karl Rahner, *The Trinity* (trans. Joseph Donceel; New York: Crossroad, 1997), 48. The original edition of this work is "Der dreifaltige Gott als transzendeter Urgrund der Heilsgeschichte," in *Die Heilsgeschichte vor Christus* (vol. 2 of *Mysterium Salutis: Grundriss heilsgeschichtlicher Dogmatik;* ed. Hans-Urs von Balthasar et al.; Einsiedeln: Benziger, 1967). See also Karl Rahner, *Foundations of Christian Faith* (trans. William Dych; New York: Crossroad, 1992), 117–37; and idem, "Remarks on the Dogmatic Treatise, 'De Trinitate,' " in *Theological Investigations* (trans. Kevin Smith; Baltimore: Helicon, 1966), 4:77–102.

13. Rahner, *The Trinity,* 23.

beings in any way.[14] God's being-for-self (*pro se*) is to be expressed always as God's being-for-us (*pro nobis*), God's being-for-you. By proceeding in this fashion, the theologians influenced by Barth and Rahner conclude that through God's actions God remains true to God's self and promises to be faithful to humanity through time.[15]

Behind the new Trinitarian theologies stand the figures of Hegel and Schelling, and behind them the figures of Böhme and Hamann. Both Hegel and Schelling understood God as a Subject (over against Spinoza's view of God as Substance), though they articulated this understanding differently from each other. In this "minor" Western metaphysical tradition, "God is understood as Pure Freedom who, in creating *ex nihilo*, Himself passes *ex nihilo in aliquid*."[16] For Hegel the Trinitarian relations present ultimate reality as a concrete identity, grounded in lively plurality, self-differentiation, self-emptying, and self-giving.[17] The idea of God "develops" (for the consummate religion, at least) in history in terms of the three "moments" of the Trinity — in representational language: the "persons" of the Father, the Son, and the Spirit; in conceptual language: the moments of divine self-identity, self-differentiation/self-emptying, and self-return. God comes to be God by means of God's movement through history.

---

14. "How can the contemplation of any reality, even of the loftiest reality, beatify us intrinsically if it is absolutely unrelated to us in any way?" (Rahner, *The Trinity*, 15).

15. See Robert Jenson, *God after God: The God of the Past and the God of the Future, Seen in the Works of Karl Barth* (Indianapolis and New York: Bobbs-Merrill, 1969), 110–13, 125–28. "By acting in this way, God reveals Godself to humanity. God shows us at the same time both *how* God acts and *what* God does. This activity has a name: Jesus Christ. The foundation of theology is God's act of making Godself present in Jesus Christ. This act at the same time involves God's self-revelation in God's Word. For this reason, the *history of Jesus Christ is the focus of all history*. In Christ the relation of all events to God is perceptible, which allows a glimpse of the *universal perspective*" (Gerhard Sauter, *What Dare We Hope?* [Harrisburg, Pa.: Trinity Press, 1999], 75; emphasis in original).

16. Fackenheim, *Metaphysics and Historicity*, 30. Fackenheim calls this minor tradition "meontological." "The God of meontological metaphysics would have to be described as a process which (a) because it is pure *making* proceeds from the indifference of sheer possibility of nothingness (μη ον) into the differentiation of actuality — *ex nihilo in aliquid*; (b) because it is *self*-making establishes its own identity throughout this process by returning upon itself; or, otherwise put, proceeds into otherness, yet cancels this otherness and in so doing establishes itself; (c) because it is *absolute* self-making, actualizes *ex nihilo* the totality of possibilities" (ibid., 31–32; emphasis original).

17. See Emil Fackenheim, *The Religious Dimension of Hegel's Thought* (Bloomington: Indiana University Press, 1967); Quentin Lauer, *Hegel's Concept of God* (Albany: State University of New York Press, 1982), 145–61, 305–8; and Taylor, *Hegel*, 389–427. See also Walter Jäschke, *Reason in Religion: The Foundations of Hegel's Philosophy of Religion* (trans. J. Michael Steward and Peter C. Hodgson; Berkeley: University of California Press, 1990); Hans Küng, *The Incarnation of God* (trans. John R. Stephenson; New York: Crossroad, 1987); Dale Schlitt, *Hegel's Trinitarian Claim* (Leiden: E. J. Brill, 1984); and Edgar Thaidigsmann, *Identitätsverlangen und Widerspruch: Kreuztheologie bei Luther, Hegel, und Barth* (Munich: Kaiser, 1983).

Because the connection of God with the world is a determination in Himself, so the being [of] another from the one, the duality, the negative, the distinction, the self-determination in general, is essentially to be thought of as a moment in Him, or God reveals Himself in Himself, and therefore establishes distinct determinations in Himself. This distinction in Himself, His concrete nature, is the point where the absolute comes into connection with man, with the world, and is reconciled with the same. We say God has created man and the world, this is His determination in Himself, and at the same time the point of commencement, the root of the finite in God Himself.[18]

According to one of the most important contemporary interpreters of Hegel, "God in the moment of self-differentiation is not simply identical with the world.... Rather the divine differentiation *ad intra* is the ground for the possibility of creating a world of nature and finite spirit whose vocation is also to be the otherness of God."[19] God and God's Other have an intimate relationship that mutually conditions each other on the way to God's self-actualization as Spirit/Mind (*Geist*). God is the "identity of identity and difference." God is *Geist*-in-history. At the center of this history is the philosophical concept of "the speculative Good Friday," whereby the process of intellectual/spiritual (*geistliche*) self-fulfillment includes finitude, "self-emptying" (*Entäussung*), death, and "the negative."[20]

Likewise Schelling also understood God's self-differentiation in terms of an historical positing of God's "Self" as "other" in creation; however, unlike Hegel (whose Trinity is constructed according to the goal [*telos*] of divine self-actualization), Schelling's view of the Trinity is understood on the basis of the starting point (*arche*) of divine self-actualization.[21] "History as a whole is a progressive, gradually self-disclosing revelation of the absolute."[22] The later Schelling, however, addressed more completely, and on the

---

18. Georg Hegel, *Lectures on the History of Philosophy* (trans. E. S. Haldane and Frances H. Simson; 3 vols.; Lincoln, Neb.: University of Nebraska Press, 1995), 2:385–86. See also idem, *Lectures on the Philosophy of Religion*, 3:189–206, 290–94.

19. Peter Hodgson, "Editor's Introduction," in Hegel, *Lectures on the Philosophy of Religion*, 3:87.

20. Hegel, *Phenomenology of Spirit*, 453.

21. Rowland Gray-Smith, "God in the Philosophy of Schelling" (Ph.D. diss., University of Pennsylvania, 1933), 75–98. See also Emil Fackenheim, "Schelling's Conception of Positive Philosophy," *Review of Metaphysics* 7 (1953/54): 563–82; Horst Fuhrmans, *Schellings letzte Philosophie: Die negative und positive Philosophie im Einsatz des Spätidealismus* (Berlin: Junker und Dünnhaupt, 1940); idem, *Schellings Philosophie der Weltalter* (Düsseldorf: Schwann, 1954); and Klaus Hemmerle, *Gott und das Denken nach Schellings Spätphilosophie* (Freiburg im Breisgau: Herder, 1971).

22. Friedrich Schelling, *System of Transcendental Idealism [1800]* (trans. Peter Heath; Charlottesville: University of Virginia Press, 1978), 211. Hamann's understanding of the Trinity, which led him to his view of the wholeness of the universe and the unity of nature and history,

basis of his philosophy of revelation and mythology, why the absolute identity becomes differentiated in time and, further, why differentiation is the
ground of the divine self-revelation in historical existence. The major question for the later Schelling was, "Why is there anything and not nothing?"
Schelling's response to this question was a kind of theism that is grounded in
the dynamics of nature and history, but which accounts for the free creation
of the world in time, whereby the sequence of "potencies" in God's nature
becomes a sequence of "principles" of real being of increasing potency. In
contrast to Hegel, for whom the Absolute is "essentially a result" and which
is "only at the end what it is in truth," Schelling asserted that philosophy
can only begin with the Absolute.

> The "essence of the absolute identity" is the God that is posited as
> Alpha, but, as Alpha, he is only Deus implicitus or the unevolved God;
> or rather since the name of God is used less exactly when designating
> an unconscious intelligence, Schelling now says it is that which is not
> as yet, but which comes to transfigure itself into, the personal God.
> This "one original essence" that stands prior to the unfolding into
> opposition is, therefore, called simply "the Absolute."[23]

Thus a free act is at the basis of finite existence, and yet the character of
finite existence is governed by the same necessary dialectic between the potencies in God's nature. In other words the dialectic of the essence of things,
their *whatness,* is asserted to be made subject to existence, to the fact that
they are. Finite existence, an intelligible world of reality, depends upon, and
is indeed the compound of, an initial free act and a necessary process (i.e.,
reason cannot explain the fact of its own existence and thus cannot encompass itself and its other within a system of philosophy, contra Hegel); but it
is a process that also includes an intrinsic freedom, an irrational principle,
and evil. The all-encompassing rationality of reality and the divine optimism,
two cardinal elements in the thought of Lessing and Herder, are severely re-
stricted by Schelling. So the cosmogony/theogony of Schelling, based on his
philosophical reading of the first three chapters of Genesis, provides a philo-
sophical/theosophical analysis of the union between idealism and realism
and demonstrates the necessity of an intelligible, existential world.[24]

---

was an influence on Schelling and Hegel, as well as Hofmann. For Hamann's understanding
of the Trinity, see especially Ronald Gregor Smith, "The Living and Speaking God: A Study
of Hamann's Doctrine of 'the Word,'" *Hibbert Journal* 42 (April 1944): 198–203; James
O'Flaherty, "Some Major Emphases in Hamann's Theology," *Harvard Theological Review* 51
(January 1948): 39–50; and Leibrecht, *God and Man in the Thought of Hamann,* 56–79.

   23. Gray-Smith, "God in the Philosophy of Schelling," 65.

   24. See also Frederick de Wolfe Bolman, Jr., "Introduction," in Friedrich Schelling, *The Ages
of the World* (New York: AMS Press, 1967), 75–76. Bolman speaks of the later Schelling's

For Schelling the history of humanity is the process that returns to "the Absolute Subject." Conceived negatively, the absolute Subject is "indefinable, incomprehensible, infinite" (*SW* 1, 9:219). Conceived positively, the absolute Subject "is nothing other than the eternal Freedom" (ibid., 220). The end of human history and the final goal at which the process of God's revelation aims coincide with the complete actualization of God, the distant future time when "God will be all in all." God as final goal is "absolute personality," the identity of perfect Will and perfect Love.[25]

The affinity of the great philosophical thinkers of nineteenth-century German Idealism for Trinitarian reflection in terms of historical process points to the place and importance of Hofmann's Trinitarian thinking. He saw the need to rethink the Trinity in its relation to human history in a way that avoided sterile Lutheran orthodox repristination, on the one hand, and sterile Liberal Protestant non-Trinitarianism, on the other. Because of his achievement his work is not only a significant and creative nineteenth-century rethinking of the Trinity but it also identifies critical issues in Trinitarian theology that continue to deserve our attention today.

Hofmann's Way to Knowledge of God

The Christian *Tatbestand* as the Basis for Christian Reflection on God

Like Hegel's and Schelling's thought, Hofmann's thought was also informed by the distinctively modern concerns of history, personhood, subjectivity, and relationality.[26] He stressed that God is a Subject which is in the process of historical self-determination by means of divine self-differentiation in the world for the sake of the salvation of human beings.

Hofmann's perspective on the doctrine of God derived from his understanding of God's relation to human beings in Jesus as given in what Hofmann termed "the Christian *Tatbestand*" ("present factual situation"). As we have already seen, the Christian *Tatbestand* encompasses both "the living, personal communion between God and sinful humanity mediated

---

positive philosophy as "metaphysical empiricism." See also Andrew Bowie, "Introduction," in Schelling, *On the History of Modern Philosophy*, 3–35; and Edward Allen Beach, *The Potencies of God(s): Schelling's Philosophy of Mythology* (Albany: State University of New York Press, 1994), 47–109.

25. Gray-Smith, "God in the Philosophy of Schelling," 64.

26. See Schellbach, *Theologie und Philosophie*, 93–106. Schellbach's study has the merit of clarifying Hofmann's relation to the Trinitarian ideas of Schelling.

presently in Christ Jesus" and also the realization of the historical and ecclesial experience of this personal communion (i.e., "what makes the Christian a Christian;" *ET* 51). By using the term *Tatbestand,* Hofmann sought to identify and comprehend both the existential immediacy and the historical mediacy of the communion with God that has "its permanence and continuance [*Bestand*] in the present Christ" (*SBb* 1:10). In other words, as we have already seen, the Christian *Tatbestand* includes both a relationship to historical knowledge as well as a personal existential relationship to the ultimate source of the *Tatbestand* as a whole, i.e., the triune God who gives God's self in Christ in order to establish personal communion with humanity. Thus the *Tatbestand* of Christianity is not merely a *past* reality, but through the living "personal and effectual working [*Selbstbetätigung*] of the Risen One himself" the *Tatbestand* is also "an effect in the present" that involves the Christian believer (ibid., 1:6; *ET* 7). All Christian reflection on God develops from the presently experienced reality of the relationship between God and humanity mediated in Jesus, who reveals the identity of God in history: The crucified and risen Jesus is the center (*Mitte*) and the fulfillment of the triune God's history with humanity.

Thus for Hofmann there is no speculative way to a developed doctrine of God. Human beings cannot ascend to God through their own efforts. The theologian has no sure way to knowledge of any supposed pretemporal divine attributes on the basis of any preconceived idea or concept of "God." If the Christian is to speak truthfully of God, he or she cannot start from a speculative idea of God but must proceed only on the basis of God's own condescension and self-revelation in history as given to the Christian in the Christian *Tatbestand.* "God is understandable as he gives himself to be understood, comprehensible by means of that in which he wants to be comprehended" (*SBb* 1:68). The Christian doctrine of God is not thinkable apart from its historical realization in Christ and through the community in which he mediates himself to human beings. "Only in Christ will God be our God. Apart from Christ we are 'without God,' ἄθεοι [atheists]. Indeed, God has us and not we him. God gives himself to us" (*DVL* 42). Accordingly, Hofmann asserted that the existence of God cannot be "proved" or "deduced" outside of Christian faith, but only "presupposed" in Christian faith (*SBb* 1:61).

As a rule one begins dogmatics by first teaching God's existence, while biblical theology generally begins with a discussion of the biblical names of God. This difference about how each discipline begins is not random but has its basis in that Scripture speaks only to those who know of God, that he is, whereas dogmatics believes that it must first state that God is. It needs only to be recalled that in proceeding this way dogmatics is not being scriptural. (Ibid., 1:62)

"That fact of the experience of salvation is the proof of God's existence or, rather, as with all the others, not a proof of God but an assertion about God brought into the form of a proof, but in which the already presupposed is what is to be proved" (*DVL* 43). "We know about God in no way other than through [the fact] that we have come to be because of his will of love" (ibid., 44). Thus, the Christian believes in God because God reveals God to faith. God's self-giving as love is the ground of the individual's knowledge of God. God's existence as a matter of faith means that the individual should allow God's self-giving to establish God as a Subject in relation to the individual. God is self-objectifying for human beings only in God's gracious self-giving. It would not help the individual to know *that* God exists; rather, to create and sustain Christian faith, a person needs to know *who* God is in relation to oneself, to the world, and to all human beings (*SBb* 1:63). This identity of God is itself given in the Christian *Tatbestand* through God's own self-giving.[27]

The Theological Presuppositions of the Christian *Tatbestand*

Who, then, is God? For Hofmann the answer to this question surfaces through reflection on Jesus and the historical relationship that he mediates between God and humanity. Since the identity of God is given through God's history with humanity, that identity becomes clear only through reflection

---

27. Hofmann did not often speak of Luther's contrast between the hidden God and the revealed God. For Luther, God is a terror to sinners, apart from the crucified Christ. Here the concern of Luther is how to find a merciful God. For Hofmann the issues are: "Who is God?" and "How do human beings know God?" To answer these questions, Hofmann developed his Christocentric Trinitarian understanding of God. Barth's position at this point is also obviously similar to Hofmann's. For Barth, God is self-revealing in the manner that God freely wills. This self-giving of God alone establishes God's relationship with human beings. Barth understands God's being to be one with God's being-for-humanity. Since human beings have no claim on God, nor does humanity deserve relationship with God, God's self-giving is identical with God's grace. The triune God who is love seeks a relationship of love with humanity that is outside of God. Barth thus states that God is truly known only as grace, contrary to Luther's distinction between "God hidden" and "God revealed." "The reality of God in His revelation is not to be bracketed with an 'only,' as though somewhere behind His revelation there stood another reality of God, but the reality of God which meets us in revelation is His reality in all the depths of eternity" (Barth, *Church Dogmatics*, 1.1:548). The later Barth, starting with the first part of volume four of his *Church Dogmatics*, develops this revelational understanding of God in terms of God's specific narrative history. The Trinity is a concrete history for the salvation of all human beings. This Barthian understanding of the Trinity has its antecedents in the world of thought that Hofmann inhabited and helped to develop.

on that historical relationship. The identity of God is disclosed for Christians only in the experience of the risen Christ who establishes communion between God and humanity. There is no true knowledge of God which is not the effect of an encounter with Jesus Christ and that does not see Jesus Christ as its central focus and content.

> But because we know Christ and the salvation of the world that has been brought about in him and through him, we also know a history which has been occurring, is occurring, and will be occurring between God and humanity from the beginning of time to its end. We therefore know of a history of the present interchange and mutual relation between God and humanity, of a historicality of God which is no less certain than his eternal self-identity. While we should indeed not forget that the expressions for these historical acts in which God himself appears historical are taken from analogous processes in human life, we are not thereby prevented from recognizing the historical character of these expressed facts of God's life. (*BH* 57–58)

This concrete historicization of God, centering in Jesus, gives rise to the doctrine that God is triune. The Christian systematic investigation of the relationship between God and humanity starts with "the man Jesus Christ" and proceeds backwards to that which must be the presuppositions of the historical appearance of Jesus as mediator between God and humanity (*SBb* 1:13). That relationship is itself understood as the historical realization of an intra-divine relationship of the three persons of the Trinity. "The Trinity is only to be recognized from the fact of revelation" that occurs within the present and historical Christian *Tatbestand* (*DVL* 51). "The divine Trinity is for the Christian not a mere doctrinal proposition, but a salvific *Tatbestand* which encloses and surrounds him and gives shape and form to his religious life" (*TE* 130). On the basis of this *Tatbestand*, Hofmann described God as

> that community of the Father and the Son in the Spirit, as it represents itself in *Heilsgeschichte*, i.e., the Father is the one [who is] always prior, the Son is the one [who is] always coming, the Spirit is the one [who is] always present. In other words, the Father is the one [who is] always acting upon the world, the Spirit is the one [who is] always acting in the world, the Son is the one [who is] letting himself act in the world. (*DVL* 51)

The eternal relationship becomes an historical "community of the love of God:" God the creator who is transcendent to the world, "God the immanent ground of life, and God the archetypal goal of the world (*das urbildliche Weltziel*)" (*SBb* 1:37).

Therefore we have found this [intra-divine] relationship in Scripture as historical only in the context of the history occurring between God and humankind, and have learned that this relationship is eternal only through its historicality. Consequently, the relationship stands as eternal in the same relationship to God's eternal will which fulfills itself in the history occurring between God and humanity, just as it stands as historical in the same relationship to this history itself. (Ibid., 1:177–78)

Even the Bible does not witness directly to "the Trinitarian relationship in and for God himself," nor does it witness to the eternal-immanent Trinity (God *in se*), but only to the historical-economic Trinity (God *pro nobis*).[28] "The Bible only teaches the eternal Trinitarian relationship in God as historical, and ... the Bible does not designate this relationship as an eternal relationship but as an historical relationship ... " (*SBb* 1:206).[29] "The Bible has only to do with the eternal insofar as the eternal has given itself into time" (*WE* 2:8). The Scriptures do not even offer "a doctrine of the self-differentiation in God" (*SBb* 1:141). "Not otherwise and not earlier than through these salvation-historical [*heilsgeschichtlichen*] facts has the truth of the divine Trinity come to revelation and to knowledge ... " (*HS* 11:79).[30]

Through reflection on the Christian *Tatbestand*, the theologian is led to formulate three kinds of presuppositions about God that disclose God's triune identity in history.[31] First, since the relationship mediated to the Christian is a relationship with the eternal God, there are some *eternal* presuppositions. In other words, the present experience of the risen Christ, mediated also historically, gives rise to certain eternal presuppositions which are the self-determining conditions that God must have established in order to relate God's self to human beings in history. The recognition of the eternal as the presupposition of the historical represents the beginning point of

---

28. See Breidert, *Die kenotische Christologie*, 164–66, where Breidert makes this same point about Hofmann's Trinitarian thought.

29. But Hofmann is quick to add that "apart from [this historical relationship] a person does not have the right to turn the representations of the [historical] *directly* into representations of the [eternal]" (*SBb* 1:206). Here Hofmann is different from Rahner's strict identification of the economic Trinity with the eternal Trinity. Elsewhere, Hofmann also states that "the Bible does not teach natures and attributes [of God]. ... The Bible teaches the nature of God when it says that God is Spirit, that God is love" (ibid., 68).

30. Hofmann here is clearly attempting to distance the process by which he receives understanding of God from that of Hegel. See also *SBb* 2.2:18, where Hofmann states that he rejects Hegel's "speculative doctrine of the Trinity."

31. Forde sees a similarity between Hofmann's three kinds of presuppositions and Schleiermacher's three forms of dogmatic propositions. See Forde, *The Law-Gospel Debate*, 24–25.

Hofmann's system (but one must stress that this starting point is not identical to the experience of Christian faith).[32] Second, since the relationship of God with the individual Christian is established in and through history, there must be some *historical* presuppositions. These presuppositions involve God's history with humanity in the world, how God has acted in history to create and establish the relationship that God has with humanity. Finally, since the historical experience of Christianity is not yet perfected, one must presuppose that the relationship with God mediated in Jesus Christ will be perfected in the future. Hence, reflection on Christian faith also leads to the positing of *eschatological* presuppositions about the hope that Christians have toward the future.

The development of these three types of presuppositions and their consequences forms the substance of Hofmann's system, which he outlines in his dogmatics lectures, develops through the eight doctrinal parts (*Lehrstücke*) of his "Scriptural Proof" (*Der Schriftbeweis*), and repeats in various sections of his New Testament commentaries.

The Eternal Trinity
Is the Historical Trinity

God's Self-Revelation through God's Historical Self-Differentiation

According to Hofmann, on the basis of one's experience of the risen Christ, one must presuppose that God has willed an historical process of self-realization (*Selbstvollziehung*), moving from eternal identity to historical differentiation (*Ungleichheit*). "The eternal as the presupposition of the historical is thus the first thing to which the historical present leads" (*SBb* 1:13). On the basis of the Christian *Tatbestand*, the Christian must presuppose that God's "eternal Self" is a Self that undergoes self-differentiation and change: "Now we distinguish within the divine nature, God as the originator of what is becoming and what has become, God the archetype which sets the goal of what is becoming and what has become, and God the indwelling ground of life that guides what is becoming and what has become" (*TE* 28). "The eternal intra-divine relationship proceeds from its eternal equality into an historical dissimilarity" (ibid.).[33]

---

32. "It is the peculiarity of Hofmann that he begins his dogmatic system with the eternal, after he has explicated the way of the historical to the eternal" (Breidert, *Die kenotische Christologie*, 162).

33. Hofmann's use of the expression "historical dissimilarity" in reference to the Trinity indicates affinities between Hofmann's understanding of the historicality of the Trinity and

But how the intra-divine relationship has moved into this dissimilarity comes to expression in our doctrinal whole only as the presupposition of the beginning of history. So also the beginning of that dissimilarity is nowhere specifically stated in Scripture, but the history of that dissimilarity is that which points back to its origin. (*SBa* 1:237; cf. *SBb* 1:270–71)

We see Scripture lay hold of the Trinitarian relationship constituted in God in historical reality but [we see it] as eternal as soon as it leads back to its pre-existence, [i.e.], as the eternal presupposition of its historical reality. But it does this in such a way that it does not express what the relationship is in its eternity but only that it is eternal. (*SBa* 1:176)

Hofmann's theological system begins with the eternal God, not because the eternal claims interest in itself, but because the eternal gives itself to be understood as the eternal *in* history. Accordingly, God's eternal being as such must be comprehended as a self-differentiated being-in-becoming. " . . . [W]e have discovered this intra-divine relationship in the Bible as an historical one that has given itself only in the context of the given history between God and humankind, and have learned that this relationship is an eternal one only because of its historicality" (*SBb* 1:178).

Not as the absolute Being, neither as the unchanging, nor as the unchangeable faithful one is Jehovah herewith designated by means of this name [as] interpreted by himself; not as the one who is but as the historical one, but also not as the one who will be or as the one who is becoming but as the one [who is in the process of] becoming, [the one who is] being himself in history. (*SBa* 1:82)[34]

Thus, Hofmann affirmed: *"Trinitas duplex est, aeterna et temporalis"* [The Trinity is two-fold: eternal and temporal].[35] While he did not make the strict identification of the immanent Trinity with the economic Trinity that Rahner and Walter Kasper (1933–) do, Hofmann did assert that there is a fundamental relationship between God's self-giving in history and the eternal ground of that self-giving within the intra-divine life of God. Through God's self-giving in history, the eternal God becomes God in a new way.

Schelling's understanding of God's "Self" "becoming dissimilar" through God's self-mediation in the gradual process of history.

34. See Behr, *Politischer Liberalismus*, 82ff. See also *DVL* 43 and *SBb* 1:86–87.

35. Hofmann, *De Argumento Psalmi Centesimi Decimi*, 47.

The Freedom of God

The beginning of "the self-realization of the eternal will of God" is "the intra-divine relationship that has committed itself to a historical self-completion" (*SBb* 1:37). The "self-translation of the Trinitarian relationship from eternity into historicality" may therefore be described as a transition from potentiality to actuality (*ET* 62).[36] This "self-translation" (*Selbst-begebung*), this "transition of God from himself into time whereby he nonetheless remains the one [who is] self-identical and complete in himself," can only be thought of as "a purely free act of God" (*DVL* 44). Indeed, because God is eternal, God is the totally free origin of the self-differentiation of God for the sake of human redemption. Thus God's dominion over the world is revealed not in God's otherworldly transcendence but in God's humility to give God's self freely into creation. God's free self-emptying in creation is the revelation of God's identity.

Hofmann wanted to maintain that the eternity of God is not undone by means of God's self-differentiation in history. "This Trinitarian relationship of God is as independently eternal as God himself" (ibid., 51). The freedom of God is the precondition of God's historical self-differentiation, which is itself the means by which the eternal God fulfills the divine will in history. The biblical view of God centers upon the creative freedom of God to fulfill God's eternal will of love in history. God is truly and creatively free in relation to the world and history, and thus God is free to shape the ultimate outcome of history. For Hofmann the transcendent freedom of God is operative through all of the individual facts of salvation history (*heils-geschichtliche Tatsachen*), but especially in raising Jesus from the dead and making him Lord over all things. Thus, the freedom of God to do new things is the precondition for viewing reality as historical and as oriented toward the divine future.

Hofmann affirmed that God is under no internal or external compulsion to be the God of love for the sake of humanity. The triune God is not dependent upon humanity in any sense. God is freely self-giving to human beings since this is a precondition of the assertion that God is love.[37] The condescension of God is a free decision of God that is grounded in God's

---

36. Here, too, Hofmann stood in proximity to Schelling, who analyzed the free activity of God as "the transition from potency to act."

37. Hofmann would not agree with those theologians who argue that God "needs" the world in order to be God. Contrary to Forde's claim that "Hofmann did not seem to be concerned about an abstract idea of freedom as such" (Forde, *The Law-Gospel Debate*, 61), Hofmann was concerned to understand the freedom of God as a corollary to the affirmation that God is love. In this regard, Hofmann's doctrine of God is distinct from Hegel's idealist formulation wherein God necessarily needs the world to be God. Hofmann argued that God does not "need" the world precisely because God's love for the world, as authentic *love*, is freely given.

love. God's decision to reveal God's self came out of the purest freedom. Hofmann's affirmation of this idea clearly sets forth his essential difference from the idealists. In Hofmann's theology there is no room for the idealist thesis that God *must* enter into this world and into history in order to realize or fulfill God, in order to return to God's self.

God Is Love

Hofmann's understanding of the freedom of God is grounded in the vision of St. John and St. Augustine: God is love. Salvation, Hofmann believed, is grounded in God's pretemporal decision to be the God of love for the sake of humanity. The relationship that Jesus establishes between God and humanity is grounded in God's own self-determination to be the living God "who is love" (*SS* 3:3). This relationship fulfills itself in a reciprocal relationship of love that must be understood as a "community of love" (*Liebesgemeinschaft*) (*SBb* 1:35). The content of Christian experience is precisely "the love that God has for the individual and the individual's love of God" (*DVW* 387). "[T]he attitude of God in Christ to the human being . . . is the content of the personal experience, namely, the fact that God loves the Christian" (*DVL* 42). This content "implies both the forgiveness of sins which God grants me in Christ and my love of God which is rooted in Christ" (*BH* 33). "Through [the self-giving love of God] we are fulfilled, and thereby we have peace" (*DVL* 42). Hofmann believed that the future of *Heilsgeschichte* will confirm this view of God.

> The triune God has given himself into a succession (*in ein Nacheinander*), and with his eternity has entered into historicality; his eternal be-ing [*Verhalten*] that is one with his eternal will of love has become historical. . . . Since, however, the triune God does not merely establish a historicality but gives himself into it, the Trinitarian relationship moves necessarily into a dissimilarity from itself. (*ET* 61)

The word "necessarily" must here be understood to be conditioned on the divine freedom and love. Because God is love, God is necessarily triune. God is triune in order to be "love," i.e., "in order to be the God of humanity" (*DVL* 42). "The immanent relationship is for the relationship of God to humanity; in other words, God is triune in order to be the God of human beings" (*SBb* 1:177). God's self-determination to be "love" is the ground for God's self-determination in history: God wills to be triune in order to be the God who is love for humankind (*DVL* 51). This will of love is identical with God's being triune (*SBb* 1:36). This will of love is thus the basis for God's humble self-giving in history. "For God, of course, first creates for himself that one to whom he wants to give himself, and he creates him in such a way that he can give himself to him" (*DVL* 43). "God gives himself to us. This self-giving is love" (ibid., 42). Every act of God, be it creation, redemption, or eschatological fulfillment, is grounded in the divine humility with which God condescends to God's creatures. This in turn means that the unity of divine action consists in the love by which God condescended to enter into communion with humanity. This unity of the total work of divine love was revealed and clarified through the incarnation and ministry of Jesus Christ. In Christ the ultimate reason for creation and the establishment of a new creation is revealed. But Christ also reveals the inner heart of God:

> The mediatorship of Jesus Christ that unites God and humanity into personal communion, which is mediated in him, made the intra-divine relationship of the Trinity into the intra-divine relationship of the Trinity for humanity; in other words, to understand God's will of love and the relationship of the former to the latter. I was able to recognize the intra-divine as the eternal and the historical as the fulfillment of the intra-divine. (*BD* 25–26)

"That God is love becomes a matter of knowledge only when the intra-divine relationship of the Trinity is its presupposition" (*ET* 59). "For God is love insofar as he loves the world, to be sure, in Christ" (*DVL* 51). "The Trinity has been deduced from love. But [that] love is asserted about God, not about the Father; its object is thus outside of God. [God's] love is not self-love. Its object is humanity" (ibid., 43).[38] "God, who is a Self and not a thing, wants to satisfy the human being (who is both a self and a thing) with himself through his self-giving to him" (ibid., 43). Thus, "the intra-divine relationship is for the relationship of God to humanity.... God is triune in order to be the God of humanity" (*SBb* 1:177–78). Hofmann believed that the life of Jesus is definitive for the life of God-for-humanity. The Gospels' witness to Jesus' life and ministry is the narrative witness of God's love for humanity. "God is as much the one who completes himself in himself as he is the one who completes himself for the world and for humanity — his εὐδοκία [good pleasure], his love — both are equally eternal" (*DVL* 43). Hofmann believed that we have grounds to claim that God is relational toward human

---

38. See also *DVL* 102. Hofmann's "subject model" of the Trinity is distinct from those that are more properly described as "social" or "communal" models. A communal model of the Trinity posits an otherness within God, namely, a "beloved" from all eternity. Hofmann argues that God is love and that this love for the world is the free cause of God's self-differentiation, i.e., for the sake of God's love for humanity. Hofmann's "subject model," thus, has affinities with Hegel's notion of absolute subjectivity, Barth's understanding of the humanity of God, Rahner's understanding of the Trinity as triune Subject, and Jüngel's understanding of God as the self-othering Subject. For "communal" models, see the references to Pannenberg, Moltmann, LaCugna, and Zizioulas in the footnotes at the beginning of this chapter.

beings because of the Christian certainty that God is indeed present in the life and ministry of Jesus, "whom God raised from the dead." The event of Jesus' resurrection is the key to the Christian affirmation that God is love, that God is triune.

Hofmann never tired of expressing God's condescension to God's creation and the complete dependence of all created things on the triune action of God. Here too it is in the incarnation of the second Person of the Trinity that the true relationship of God to creation is made manifest. This manifestation or revelation of the divine love is not so much through Jesus' preaching of God's love as it is that in his own Person he is the revelation of that love and thus he is the revelation of the triune God.

The unity or equality of the Trinitarian relationship in God is God's eternal will of love for humanity which remains constant through the process of historical self-differentiation.[39] Thus, the eternal ground of God's love does not disappear in the process of moving into historicality; rather, God's eternal will of love is the constant presupposition of God's historical self-realization. "[T]he interpretation of the eternal decision of love" can only be understood "at the same time that one understands . . . the historical self-completion" of that will of love (*SBb* 1:75).

> God's eternal will of love fulfills itself in the history which occurs between God and humanity. God's will of love enters into historicality for this reason, namely, to become historical itself and consequently to enclose time and history within the Trinity of God. God accomplishes his will, however, through his self-activity, his eternal and historical Trinitarian ways. (*SS* 3:3–4)

The eternal will of love provides the necessary presupposition of God's free decision to enter into history for the sake of God's love for human beings. "God's eternal will of love has begun to fulfill itself" by God "resigning himself to a process of becoming through the mediation . . . of the created world" (*DVL* 45). For Hofmann the freedom of God and the love of God are inseparable.

While Hofmann held that the eternal relationship among the Father, the Son, and the Holy Spirit "appears as a relationship of dissimilarity because it is a historical relationship," he also asserted that "the relationship of

---

39. Schellbach notes that Hofmann's new way of conceiving the Trinity avoided speculation by "translating the idea of the Trinity out of the circle of being and into the circle of becoming" (Schellbach, *Theologie und Philosophie*, 75). Because Hofmann understood God as "Being-in-Becoming," Dorner's criticism that Hofmann only teaches the mutability of God is not accurate. See Isaak Dorner, *Divine Immutability: A Critical Reconsideration* (trans. Robert Williams and Claude Welch; Minneapolis: Fortress, 1994), 61–62.

threeness has not begun with the transition from eternity into time. . . . The Christian experience demands both equally strongly: God's unity and simultaneously the eternity of those three" (ibid., 51). Without affirming the eternity of God *in* history, Hofmann would have had to give up the ground and reason for God's historical fulfillment. Thus,

> the relationship of the eternal, who is the Father of Jesus, and of the eternal, who is the Son of God, and of the eternal, who is the Spirit of God, and of the human Jesus, demonstrates itself both as an eternal relationship of similarity as well as a relationship of dissimilarity in time and consequently joins itself together in the unity of that which he the eternal is. (Ibid.)

So simultaneously in the Trinity there is the immanent and the transcendent, the historical dissimilarity and the fact that "each moment of that historical dissimilarity is sustained by the eternal equality of the Trinitarian relationship in God" (*TE* 28). Thus it would be incorrect to think that Hofmann's view of God was one that is wholly developed on the basis of a subject paradigm in which the subjectivity of the eternal Father generates the Son and the Spirit. Instead, Hofmann appears to have been seeking a truly relational/social model of the Trinity which affirms that each of the eternal Persons reciprocally gives and receives from the other two Persons — for the sake of God's love of the world, though he did not develop this idea further. According to Hofmann, then, the divine eternal will of love is the ultimate foundation for God's self-differentiation in history, but such self-differentiation cannot be understood to call into question the unity of God.

God Is Personal

Since the relationship with God that is mediated and disclosed in Jesus is a personal one, one must also presuppose that the eternal God has a self-determining personal dimension and is accessible as person. God has essentially "brought us to peace through his self-giving, insofar as we are a person, and insofar as we are something (*Etwas*) is essentially still to bring us to peace. He is person and not something. He is God" (*DVL* 42). We can infer from this quotation (and many others) that for Hofmann God is not a metaphysical *Etwas*, a "something," which human beings can view and consider from afar. God is a "Thou" that seeks relationship with God's creation. Since God is personal and relational in Jesus, the being of God must be oriented to and indeed defined by God's revelation of God's self in history. As one scholar puts it, "Because God is personal and only wants to be thought of in relation to human beings, he must proceed out of his eternal self-similarity into the contrast of the three persons of the Trinity."[40] The personal character of God therefore cannot refer to a metaphysical *aseity* ("being totally in itself") of God; God's personal character only becomes clear in the process of God's becoming in and through history, specifically in the history of Israel that culminates in Jesus and his community.

> Our reflection on Christianity as a present *Tatbestand* with a view toward its underlying eternal ground has led us to a three-fold outcome: the personality [*Persönlichkeit*] of God, the inner relationship of the Trinity, and the predestination of humankind. As personal God he is the one who is self-determining, his Trinity is his inward self-determination, and the predestination of humankind is his outward self-determination. (*ET* 60)

Because God is personally mediated to human beings in Jesus, God is an "eternal Self" whose self-constituting being-in-becoming is personal and relational. "God is a self (a Thou), a person (*Er*), and not a something; from himself, in himself, to himself, absolute personality" (*DVL* 43). In contrast to all things belonging to the world (which can, in principle, be manipulated and controlled), God as "absolute personality" invites people to trust in God's self. God is the ground or cause of God's self and as such is alone "absolute personality," who as "eternal Self" can move in freedom and power over against creation, including human beings (*SBb* 1:74).[41] Thus, as was stated above, Hofmann did not think that God is dependent on the world for God's identity and being, but through God's free and loving relationship with the world, God enters history and becomes historical. By entering history, God actualizes and expresses God's free and pretemporal will of love for humanity.

Hofmann's understanding of the "personality" of God is grounded in the relational character of God's unified *self*-giving. Hofmann thereby did not think of the three "persons" of the Trinity as three distinct consciousnesses or three centers of spiritual activity. Such a notion would transform the

---

40. Flechsenhaar, *Das Geschichtsproblem*, 25–26. Elsewhere, however, Flechsenhaar is incorrect to suggest that Hofmann thought of an intra-divine Trinity "next to" or "alongside of" an economic Trinity. The historical Trinity *is* the self-fulfillment of the eternal Trinity, though the eternal will of love remains constant through that historical fulfillment. When Hofmann spoke of "the eternal in history," he was emphasizing the constancy of God's eternal will of love that actualizes itself in history.

41. Lurking behind Hofmann's argument may have been a concern to criticize Spinoza and Fichte for their criticism of the idea of God as "person." See *BD* 38 and 43 for Hofmann's acknowledgment that he had carefully studied Fichte and Spinoza. Like Pannenberg, Hofmann argued that the "personality" of God is grounded in the freedom of God to be the God of love who gives himself to human beings. See Wolfhart Pannenberg, "The Question of God," in *Basic Questions in Theology* (trans. George Kehm; Philadelphia: Fortress, 1971), 2:231ff.

doctrine of God into a kind of modalism, in which the three "persons" multiply the divine essence and subjectivity. For Hofmann the unified self-giving of the one God manifests itself in the missions of Jesus and the Holy Spirit from the Father. This self-giving actualizes the one will of God.

The Eternal Relation between God the Creator and God the Archetypal World-Goal

Since Jesus Christ is the one who mediates the divine-human relationship, one must also presuppose that Christ himself is in a relationship to God which itself is in no need of mediation; hence, Christ is in a relationship internal to the divine life itself. Thus a further eternal presupposition of the Christian *Tatbestand* is the eternal relationship of God the creator to God "the archetypal world-goal" (*urbildliche Weltziel*), which can only be presupposed on the basis of the historical self-determination of Jesus. "The mediator of the loving community between God and humanity is not merely a temporal person, but one who stands in an intra-divine relationship to God" (*SBb* 1:36). The self-determination of the man Jesus must be immediate to God and have its origin in God himself" (*ET* 59). "A relation of God to the man Jesus has arisen historically out of a relation of God to God" (*SBb* 1:73).

Nonetheless, while Hofmann affirmed the permanent identity of the two Trinitarian persons — since for Hofmann there is an identity of "Selfhood," grounded in the divine will of love, which unites the two Persons — he did reject the teaching of the eternal generation of the Son from the Father. For Hofmann the generation of the Son from the Father can only be understood as "an historical process" (*SBb* 1:203). "It is precisely the human being Jesus who, on the basis of the relationship with God established with the beginning of his life, calls himself God's Son and calls God his Father, and who by his own [followers] is called the Son of God in that same exclusive sense" (*SBb* 1:121). Hofmann was particularly concerned to interpret the Scriptural passages in which Jesus speaks of God as "Father" and those in which Jesus is called "the Son of God" in light of the meaning that these expressions would have had *for Jesus* in a first-century Jewish context.[42]

---

42. See similarly Rahner, *The Trinity*, 61–66. "Jesus knew that his relation to God, whom he called his 'Father,' distinguished his sonship from that of other men. Nonetheless it remains methodically dangerous, even if ultimately correct, to understand at once and from the very start this unique sonship, which the Synoptics show us to have been known by Jesus, as referring only, in Jesus' own understanding of himself, to the eternal generation of the Logos. Jesus knew himself first as the concrete One, who stands before the Father and meets us as the Son (as such). Hence it would be dangerous to separate, at the very beginning, various aspects of this concrete reality (his human, created 'nature') from the whole which he himself calls 'Son.' His concept may be much more complex" (ibid., 62).

For example, the Old Testament calls Israel "the son of the LORD" (e.g., Ex 4:22) since Israel owed its origin to the redemptive act of God which placed the children of Israel in a special relationship to God. Thus, on the basis of analysis of these biblical expressions, Hofmann concluded that one can only say that Jesus has an eternal relation with the Father, not that he was eternally begotten of the Father.

Furthermore, while Hofmann spoke of a relationship between Jesus and the Old Testament witness to God's revelation in the history of Israel, he did not think Christ and the LORD are identical. Christ's incarnation necessitates a distinction between the two. "Jehovah is not Christ and Christ is not Jehovah, but the appearance of Christ in the world has taught us to differentiate in God, who in the Old Testament is called Jehovah without differentiation, [between] him who is God — ὁ θεός — and him who is God — θεός — with God" (*SBb* 1:170).[43] The relationship of God, the Father of Jesus Christ, is an eternal, intra-divine relationship with Jesus the man, but in the time of the Old Testament that relationship had not yet been historically revealed as such.

> Here it now needs to be demonstrated above all that this intra-divine relationship is not taught in Scripture . . . immediately and to begin with as eternal; but it is taught in its historical revelation and as the eternal presupposition of this historical revelation. The Old Testament teaches just as little that God is plural in himself any more than it teaches the unity with reference to a plurality in him. The classic proof-text for the latter, Deuteronomy 6:4, says neither that Jehovah is a singular one nor that he is a completely unique Jehovah but should rather be translated: "Jehovah is our God, Jehovah alone." Thus it expresses only affirmatively that which is often expressed negatively, that none other except he is God. (*SBb* 1:90)

As is clear from the above quotation, Hofmann also rejected the traditional Trinitarian interpretation of such passages as Genesis 1:26 and Isaiah 6:3. He argued that the plural form of Elohim in the former passage is not a scriptural proof of God's plurality, since it is used with a singular verb. Likewise, Hofmann interpreted the three-fold "holy" in Isaiah 6:3 (as well as other parallels, e.g., Jer 7:4) as Hebrew crescendo, that is, for emphasis. So, in contrast to Hengstenberg, Hofmann found in the Old Testament "not the preparation for a New Testament ontological doctrine of the Trinity, but the Old Testament foreshadowing of the historically revealed relationship of the Trinity in the New Testament" (*SBa* 1:111). According to Hofmann, we

---

43. See also Breidert, *Die kenotische Christologie*, 169.

must avoid the misunderstanding that the one who acts in the Old Testament is the fully revealed triune God.

Only on the basis of God's historical self-giving through the events of the New Testament may one speak of the Trinitarian intra-divine relationship. Since no explicit doctrine of the Trinity is located in the Old Testament (or in the New Testament, for that matter), it is only on the basis of reflection about the appearance of Jesus in the world that the church has been led to a deeper understanding of how the eternal Trinity has entered an historical relationship of dissimilarity to establish a community of love that seeks to embrace all creation. The New Testament witness gives rise to the affirmation that "the archetypal world-goal" (*urbildliche Weltziel*) wills to be the man Jesus in the incarnation. The God of the old covenant — ὁ θεός, as such, who is already known by revelation to Israel — sends the Word (*Logos*) and the Spirit to fulfill God's will of love. Jesus is the realization and perfect embodiment of God's eternal will of love towards humankind. For Hofmann this will of love for humankind is confirmed by his resurrection and exaltation, and by the fulfillment of his promise that he would send the Spirit of God, his Father, upon his disciples.

The Eternal Spirit

Hofmann's reflections on the Spirit of God were also oriented to the historical actualization of God's eternal will of love through Jesus. With God's entrance into history,

> the intra-divine relationship, even as historical, is eternal, and its eternal self-equality is completed in an historical differentiation. It is now a relationship of God and his Spirit, the One who sends and the One that is sent, the One governing the world and the One who accomplishes that transcendent will in the world, and therefore, as we have expressed it, God the transcendent Creator and God the immanently effective ground of life. (*SBa* 1:235)

While God's Spirit has been active in the world from the beginning of creation and has been implicit in the actions of the LORD in the history of Israel (e.g., "the Spirit of the LORD," Isaiah 40:13), the Spirit is only recognized as "the Holy Spirit," "as a Self," by means of the incarnation of Jesus, the baptism of Jesus, and the outpouring of the Spirit at Pentecost (*SBb* 1:90). The Spirit mediates the generation of the Son from the Father in history, reveals the Son's identity to the Son in his baptism, and empowers the disciples of Jesus in his outpouring following the latter's resurrection (ibid., 1:170). These three events, to which the New Testament bears witness, reveal that it is not possible to think of the inner relationship between the Father and the

Son apart from the relationship of God and the Spirit of God. But the Spirit's mode of existence in the time prior to the incarnation of Jesus was different from that after Pentecost. "What the conception is to the Son, the outpouring is to the Spirit" (ibid., 1:196). Each event is a further transformation of the eternal in the historical.

Hofmann concluded that that same Spirit which supports the life of Jesus must also support all human life. The God of Israel has sent his Spirit into the world as the basis of all life. God as Spirit is this ground of all life, "the immanent life-force," which is also internal to the divine life, since that which God intends for humanity must be perfect and eternal in God. The same Spirit that is the ground of all life is also inherent within the community mediated between the Father and the Son (*DVL* 50–51). So the same Spirit that dwelt within the man Jesus dwells now within the community established by Jesus. Indeed, the Spirit defines itself solely on the basis of the historical perfection of the community established by Jesus.

> The immanent presence of the Holy Spirit, initiated with his outpouring, has taught [us] to distinguish the Spirit as divine 'Self' from the transcendent Father and from the Son who has returned to the Father, in that the believer knows the Spirit with equally personal effect and as immediately close to himself (indwelling his own) in the place of Christ who has returned to the Father. The out-pouring of the Spirit therefore is the factual proof for the personal character of the Spirit. (*SBb* 1:197)

Hofmann concluded that just as the relationship of Jesus to God is defined solely on the basis of the historicality of Jesus, so also the procession of the Holy Spirit is defined only as an historical process (ibid., 1:203). Indeed, Christians would not know that God is triune except for the historical outpouring of the Spirit at Pentecost. Only on the basis of the eschatological gift of the Spirit may Christians speak of the Trinitarian self-fulfillment in history.[44]

Nonetheless, just as the historical relationship of Jesus to God is at the same time an intra-divine relationship, so also the historical Spirit must be "at the same time eternal with Christ" (*SBb* 1:35–36). Christ is eternal, as is the Spirit through whom the eternal God has established the historical life of the man Jesus. Likewise, it is through the Spirit that Jesus himself has defined his human nature. On the basis of the eternal and historical self-determination of Jesus, the Spirit is also to be thought of as an eternal,

---

44. See, for example, *WE* 1:128, where Hofmann criticizes Hengstenberg's misguided attempt to find "the Trinity of Jehovah" in the Old Testament.

personal, intra-divine Self like the Father and the Son, and not merely as a "divine Something" (ibid., 1:192). But this assertion is only the result of reflection on the Spirit's historical self-determination in the human Jesus and in the community established by Christ. The Spirit too is an eternal self in the process of becoming the fulfillment of God's will of love for all creation. In this perspective, the Spirit has agency as Spirit and is not merely the relation of the Father to the Son (as in the theology of Augustine). Thus, Hofmann's doctrine of God moves ever so slightly in the direction of a social model of the Trinity, despite Hofmann's predominant subject model.

Because the names of the Father, the Son, and the Holy Spirit occur in the same biblical statements (e.g., Matt 28:19; 2 Cor 13:13), an apprehension of God has occurred that corresponds to that particular moment of development in *Heilsgeschichte*. As with the Son, so also with the Spirit: The Scriptural doctrine of the Trinity is the defining expression of a particular moment in the development of salvation history (*Heilsgeschichte*), which always points back to the eternal presupposition behind the historical event. Preus rightly notes, "The descriptions of the inner relationship pertain to the historical event, not to its presupposition, so that whenever the historical reality is described, its pre-existence is presupposed."[45] The historical reality that is described is the fulfillment of the eternal will of divine love in history whereby God unites humanity to God's self through Jesus Christ.

Clearly Hofmann's Trinitarian reflections anticipate theological emphases that became more popular some ninety years after Hofmann delivered his dogmatic lectures. Similar to the respective theological projects of Barth and Rahner, Hofmann's theological reflections are the outcome of his attempt to take seriously God's self-revelation in Jesus Christ through the Holy Spirit. The divine self-revelation is the all-encompassing circle that surrounds the Christian *Tatbestand*. Thus his theology cannot properly be understood to be focused merely on individual religious experience and subjectivity. Instead, his theology sought to express the divine self-revelation as the fulfillment of the divine love for all creation. Hofmann's understanding of God's relation to creation and its need for redemption is the focus of the next chapter.

---

45. Preus, "The Theology of Johann von Hofmann," 135–36.

CHAPTER EIGHT

Trinitarian Historicality and the World of Becoming

The Beginning of Creation and the Beginning of History

For Hofmann creation and history are not "from nothing" (*creatio ex nihilo*) through the fiat of God; instead, creation and history are the means for Trinitarian fulfillment of the eternal God and God's will to be united in loving union with humanity, even sinful humanity. In order to establish a community of love for all creation, the eternal relationship enters into historical-Trinitarian dissimilarity and thereby establishes the historical process itself wherein such a community of love could develop. God's eternal will of love is thus the ultimate ground for creation and history, which together serve the goal of the creation and redemption of humanity.[1] Thus Hofmann could not speak of creation without at the same time speaking of redemption, for creation is only properly understood when God's will of love is revealed to be the reason or ground for creation. Although the historical revelation of God led Hofmann to make assertions about the eternal being of God who has established time and history as the means of God's own coming to fulfillment, the goal and content of the history of God is the developing historical community of love between God and humanity. So the same *Tatbestand* that gave rise to Hofmann's reflections on the eternal presuppositions led him to reflect also on the historical presuppositions of that *Tatbestand*. These presuppositions, too, contributed to Hofmann's understanding of Trinitarian historicality.

The "self-realization of the eternal will of God" takes place only in history, whose center is the "historical appearance of Jesus Christ" (*SBb* 1:36).

---

1. According to Hofmann, "[t]he purpose of the whole creation is the human being; without the human being, creation would be pointless" (Flechsenhaar, *Das Geschichtsproblem*, 30). See also the analysis of "person" and "nature" in Behr, *Politischer Liberalismus*, 77–82. My own analysis generally follows that of Behr's, though he does not take into account important material from Hofmann's dogmatic lectures.

Since this "center" established and inaugurated history's promised "fulfillment," this fulfillment or "new beginning" points back to the original beginning of history. The Trinity goes into history and thereby time and historicality are themselves established by God. "This self-translation of the Trinitarian relationship from eternity into historicality is the precondition of all becoming" (*ET* 61).[2] "Not that the beginning of the world is one and the same with the dissimilarity of the intra-divine relationship, but it is the beginning of the self-activity of the developing dissimilarity" (*SBb* 1:237). As the eternal, God is himself "the ground (*Grund*) of . . . what he is," but also at the same time he is the ground of the world of becoming (*ET* 24, 58). Thus, by starting with the triune God, Hofmann saw an all-inclusive relatedness between God and creation, so that the unity of the world of becoming is ultimately grounded in the triune God, but Hofmann also attempted to maintain a strict distinction between God and creation. The world itself is drawn into the divine love through the action of God, which establishes and preserves the world.

Since all "becoming" culminates in the development of human beings, Hofmann asserted that God "as the Trinity can give himself historically into the opposition which completes itself with human beings" (*SS* 3:3).

> The biblical account of the origin of things thus testifies that the creation of the world essentially was the creation of the human being, and that the rest of the world was made before the human being and was intended for him. (*SBb* 1:283)

While Hofmann acknowledged that a relation exists in God's eternal being between God and the world, the world is nevertheless actually created through the second Person of the Trinity, who is called God's Son only after his appearance in the world. "That the human being Jesus Christ was with God when the world and time began is self-evident, [that] before he became a human being [he] was God, and [that] as the world came into being he mediated through himself [both] its becoming and God's creation [of it]" (ibid., 1:147). As "the eternal archetypal world-goal" (*urbildliche Weltziel*), the incarnate Christ is both "the center of creation," through whom all things are made (e.g., Col 1:16–17; Jn 1:1–3; Heb 1:2), and also the goal of creation that has been disclosed in "the center of history" (*SBa* 1:247). But

---

2. Compare with John O'Donnell, "It is not time that makes possible God's self-communication but it is God's being as self-communicating love that makes time and history possible" (John O'Donnell, *Trinity and Temporality: The Christian Doctrine of God in the Light of Process Theology and the Theology of Hope* [Oxford: Oxford University Press, 1983], 199).

both affirmations can only be asserted as presuppositions of the historical-economical revelation of God's self in Jesus and the giving of God's Spirit in history. The world finds its uniform completion in the creation of the human being and in him creation has its goal (*ET* 62). For Hofmann the creation of Eve represents in the biblical narrative God's intention to enable the continuation of the history of the one human being in the history of humanity. "The creation story must be understood from its goal, which is humanity. Its purpose is to show that the world was created for humanity and has reached its climax in humanity. The thought expressed in the creation story ... stands in close relationship to the saving truth to which the Scriptures bear witness, namely, to the purpose of God as ultimately realized in Christ" (*BH* 76). So creation and redemption can only be understood in their unity when viewed in their relationship to the eschatological goal of God's will of love. Hofmann thought that the biblical account of the Sabbath day underscores this divine intention toward the human being:

> Not merely has God created further after the seventh day, but [he] has brought his work to rest in that goal to which he has led it. Thereby the creation is severed from the history of the created (about which paganism did not know); and against the mixing of the one with the other, the Sabbath is established, to which an incomparable importance is attached because it was the monument and sign of this knowledge which sharply distinguishes between mythology and holy history. The goal, however, in which the creator has completed his work, is the human being, and what begins on this side of this conclusion is that history itself which occurs between God and the human being. (*SBb* 1:206)

Although Hofmann made a distinction between "creation" and "history" and although he sometimes spoke of "the creation of the world," he usually preferred to speak of "the becoming" of the world and of human beings: *das Werden des Menschens* ("the becoming of the human being," e.g., *TE* 44, 65; *SBb* 1:218; *ET* 62), *gewordene Menschen* ("the developing human being," e.g., *SBb* 1:41), *die Entfaltung des Anfangs* ("the unfolding of the beginning," e.g., *WE* 1:66), and similar expressions. While history is understood as a process of development, creation itself is also understood as a process that initiates the "start" of history.[3] Accordingly, Hofmann identified the purpose of history as a process that is both the movement of the Trinity into historicality but also "the coming-into-being of the world," which is

---

3. Compare with Barth's distinction between creation and history, *Church Dogmatics,* 3.1:42ff.

the same as "the coming-into-being of the human being" (*TE* 28).[4] "The content of the eternal will of God is not a something, not a law of God . . . , but God wills God's human being" (*DVL* 43). Consequently, Hofmann did not use the language of "creation from nothing" (*creatio ex nihilo*) or even "continuing creation" (*creatio continua*). Instead, he preferred to speak of history as a process that is distinct from creation, which is understood to be the "beginning" of history.

The Coming-into-Being of the Human Being

While Hofmann understood the beginning of the world to be the beginning of the realization of God's will of love, this will of love is oriented to the coming-into-being (*Werden*) of the human being (*DVL* 44–45).[5] In this perspective, the creation of the world is understood as the essential starting point of God's own self-fulfillment through an historical self-differentiation, but this self-differentiation is itself oriented to the coming-into-being of *the* human being, Jesus of Nazareth. All human beings are called to find their fulfillment as human beings in Jesus. It is not surprising that "the new creation" in Christ was the object toward which Hofmann's thinking was directed.

The process of becoming that defines human beings in relation to the triune God, who is completing God's Self in history, means that human beings

---

4. Hofmann's ideas on creation bear important similarities to emphases in Schelling's understanding of the relation of nature to God and creation. "In demanding a Philosophy of Nature as a basis for Theology Schelling has prescribed a requirement that could also be prescribed for a Philosophy of History. This requirement he satisfies in his own way by first making man the goal of nature. If the 'potencies' of God are looked upon as successive stages of his revelation, God must be regarded as first actually existing as Mind in the human intellect's perception of itself as the absolute identity of the 'real' and 'ideal' sides of 'Will.' 'The process of creation stands still only where, out of this consciousless, out of matter, which is nothing other than the unconscious part of God, consciousness is awakened and produced, that is, in man. In man God first rests; in him his main end is reached.' Man is the 'first bond between nature and the spiritual world'; on him the whole universe hinges. . . . With man, or with Man's misuse of his freedom, history began. Man's goal is expressed in the same terms as the initial unity" (Gray-Smith, *God in the Philosophy of Schelling,* 72–73).

5. Compare with Taylor's comment about Hegel's concept of *Geist* in relation to human development: " . . . the full realization of absolute Spirit presupposes a certain development of man in history. Man starts off as an immediate being, sunk in his particular needs and drives, with only the haziest, most primitive sense of the universal. This is another way of putting the point that Spirit is initially divided from itself, and has yet to return to itself. If man is to rise to the point where he can be the vehicle of his return, he has to be transformed, to undergo a long cultivation or formation (*Bildung*). But this cannot just be an alteration of his outlook. Since following the principle of embodiment, any spiritual reality must be externally realized in time and space, we know that any spiritual change requires a change of the relevant bodily expression. In this case, Spirit can only return to itself through the transformation of man's form of life in history" (Taylor, *Hegel,* 366).

are created in "the image of the intra-divine relationship, which has become dissimilar" (*SBb* 1:285). Since God can only be understood in God's historical self-revelation, human beings are only understandable as beings in the process of becoming. This "being created in the image of God" (*Gottesebenbildlichkeit*) means, for Hofmann, that human beings are constituted as "personalities" or "selves" over against "creation," understood as "the world of nature." "We speak therefore scripturally about the image of God in the human being, that it consists in the personality of his bodily existence" (ibid., 1:290). Embodiment and personality condition each other in a reciprocal relationship. Just as God has freedom over against the world, so also human beings have freedom over against the world, through the exercise of their embodied personality or self (ibid., 1:37). Human beings are "selves" in the process of becoming; they are "self-defining" persons who stand in personal relationship with God their Creator, a relationship mediated through the working of God's Spirit in the world of becoming (*TE* 63). So human beings are not merely free "persons"; they are also participants in the world of becoming, participants in "nature." "Humankind is both personal and something, person and nature" (*DVL* 42). In this sense, human beings are subject to God's working in the world, especially through the immanent actions of the Holy Spirit.

As "nature," human beings stand under the power of the Holy Spirit, and consequently they stand in relation to "God, the immanently effective ground of life" (*SBb* 1:37). The Spirit is the ground of human self-determination, since the Spirit is the dominant and decisive force at work within human nature. The indwelling of the divine Spirit allows and enables the self-determination of human beings, but seeks to align that same self-determination with the divine self-determination in history (ibid.). As "persons," however, human beings are moving toward their self-fulfillment in their participation in the community of God's love, realized in the person of Jesus.

Only because of the rebirth in Christ does the human being learn correctly to recognize himself not only as an individual, but also as what a human being really is: (1) that he is a person, as a free, self-determining personality, and that what he has in himself, his nature, is a presupposition for his being a person and what he is as a person; and (2) that the condition of his life as a person and in nature is the presence of that power of God which he recognizes as creative [presence], from which he knows just as well that it is powerful in the world as he knows that his personal life rests upon it and its presence. The human being as a bodily creature is the completion of the bodily creation. Thus, after the creation of the human being, the world is a completed house of God and the human being is the door and key to it. (*DVL* 44–45)

Evil and Sin

Because Christians are aware that the relationship to God is mediated by Christ, they are aware that the original relationship between God and humanity has become distorted and broken (*DVL* 47). "That God loves me in Christ has the following presupposition: Since it is only in Christ that I have become an object of God's love, the human being simply as he is born, though creation of God, is still not [yet] an object of God's love" (*DVW* 387). Humanity is now determined in a manner contrary to the original divine will. In keeping with his theological method, Hofmann stressed that the theologian is only able to form a concept of sin on the basis of his own knowledge of sin in the Christian *Tatbestand*. This knowledge includes the awareness that the theologian is self-determined in a way that is contrary to the will of God. "The human being comes to the concept of sin only from himself, from out of his sin. One must therefore above all be fully acquainted with the sin of human beings before one can speak of sin at all" (*DVL* 45).

According to Hofmann, this determination against God could not have come from God, nor from humanity itself, nor from nature, but only from the realm of spirit, though he also affirms that "through the corporality of his life the possibility of opposition between person and nature was given for the human being" (*SS* 3:4), and this possibility provides the precondition for the advent of sin.[6] Hofmann's detailed and complicated doctrine of spirit included the notion that the Holy Spirit is the immanent life-ground of the world, but in the created and natural world this life-force is divided into a plurality of spirits, including evil spirits that are opposed to the will of God (which will be discussed below), which account for variety and plurality in the world.

> The distinction between "self" and "something" leads to a differentiated relationship of the eternal to one and to the other, in the sense that the eternal Person and the temporal Person tolerate nothing [to be] between them; but the eternal Person and the temporal thing render necessary a multiplicity of temporal spirits between themselves, through which the former mediates himself to the latter and to the willed multiplicity of things that appear in the world.... This pre-

---

6. See also *DVL* 45–46. Compare Hofmann's point here with Paul Ricoeur, *Fallible Man* (trans. Charles Kelbley; New York: Fordham University Press, 1986).

supposition of good and evil spirits is a presupposition both for the continued existence as well as for the origin of the creaturely world. (*DVL* 44)[7]

In other words, the divine Spirit itself undergoes self-differentiation in history. This is the result of the nature of the world itself and its process of becoming. The Spirit is "the power of life uniquely originating through him (God), which is established outside of himself as the ground of the developing and becoming life of the world" (*SBb* 1:189). While God's one Spirit is active in the multiplicity of individual appearances of life, the Spirit cannot be directly equated with this multiplicity in the world (*TE* 30). Its immanent effectiveness must be mediated by a "multiplicity of spirits" (*Geistervielheit*), which themselves cannot be directly equated with the finite world (*SBb* 1:38). In fact, these spirits are distinct from the physical world over which they have power. Nevertheless, the spirits form the invisible background of the physical world and are in very close proximity to it.[8] "We are justified in maintaining that whenever *Heilsgeschichte* reports appearances of God it means that God has made his active presence physically perceptible in such a way that the spirits mediate this manifestation of God" (*BH* 50).

Nowhere in Scripture do we read anything about the creation of the spirits. They do not belong to the world that was created with humanity in mind. Yet all of Scripture presupposes that there is a world of spirits. But what is a mere supposition in other religions is here an established fact because it is connected with Holy history. The miracle of divine participation which alone makes *Heilsgeschichte* possible rests upon the fact that there is a world of spirits. Otherwise history would move altogether within the unchangeable context of nature and its given laws. (*BH* 83–84)

By stressing God's direct actions in the world through these spirits, Hofmann hoped to avoid identifying God with nature while also affirming God's

---

7. Here again, Hofmann's thought bears important similarity to that of Schelling. For Schelling's ideas on the multiplicity of finite spirits, see *AW* 23–53, 64–72; Beach, *The Potencies of God(s)*, 136–42; and Robert Brown, "The Transcendental Fall in Kant and Schelling," *Idealistic Studies* 14 (1984): 49–66. See also Schellbach, *Theologie und Philosophie*, 104ff.; Wapler, "Die Theologie Hofmanns," 716–18; and Wendebourg, "Die heilsgeschichtliche Theologie Hofmanns," 84–98. Hofmann acknowledged in his *Schriftbeweis* that his ideas on *die Geister* were problematic from a scriptural perspective. In his *Schriftbeweis*, Hofmann tends only to speak of the Spirit as God's indwelling (*Einwohnung*) in the human being and that through this indwelling the Spirit is not a "part" of the human being as such. See *SBb* 1:300–315.

8. See also Hofmann's discussion of "the elemental spirits of the universe" (στοιχεῖα τοῦ κόσμου) in Gal 4:3–9 and Col 2:8–20 in *HS* 2.1:110–12, 127–29; See also *HS* 4.2:17–18, 64–65, 97–98.

intimate relation to the finite world. In such an affirmation, Hofmann hoped to preserve the free activity of God vis-à-vis the necessary laws of nature. For his understanding of *Heilsgeschichte* he needed to defend the plausibility of God's free activity in the world and in history. Since the spirits are always and directly subordinated to God's power in their effectiveness, God's activity in the world can neither be determined through a relation with nature nor by a certain, necessary relationship to history (*SBb* 1:314–315). On the basis of this view of God's activity in the world, Hofmann concluded that the entire process of history, centered in Christ, was a process of God's activity in history (*BH* 38–39). This conclusion becomes important for gaining a clearer understanding of the relation of salvation history to world history. For Hofmann the latter is included *within* the former, not vice versa. The activity of the spirits is oriented to all historical events and not merely to an isolated stream of biblical events. In this context, according to Hofmann, the world of human beings is not possible apart from the activity of the multiplicity of spirits.

Since God in the world works through a multiplicity of spirits, God's will can no longer be unambiguously perceived nor can his activity in the world be so easily recognized (*SBb* 1:37). For Hofmann everything that happens in the world must lead back to the activity of these spirits, but their activity leads back to the will of God. Despite the fact that evil things happen in the world, and that some spirits attempt to frustrate the will of God, even the evil spirits must ultimately serve God's one will of love that will triumph in the end. All spirits are subordinate to the effective power of the one will of God. The multiplicity of spirits carry out the rule of God in the world and are one with the Holy Spirit insofar as they are dedicated to the goal and completion of the world in "the humanity of God" (i.e., Jesus) (ibid., 1:55). Consequently, when the multiplicity of spirits is directed toward this goal, creation is in harmony with God. When this is not so, creation threatens to collapse into a chaos of competing spirits (ibid., 1:354–66).

If humanity is now determined otherwise than was intended by God in the original creation, this determination must have happened because as part of the created world humanity is open to activity which stems from the multiplicity of spirits. The contradiction of God's will did not originate in humankind or in the world created by God (because then the "temptation to sin would originate in God" and Hofmann wanted to avoid this conclusion) but within certain spirits opposed to God (*BD* 56). According to Hofmann, a revolt in the spirit realm, which is distinct from God's creation, must have overcome humanity in an effort to defeat the divine purpose (*TE* 33). In the fact of the first sin there must have been spirits at work in contradiction to God's will.[9] This rebellion must have been directed to deceive humanity about the divine plan for a human community of love. Thus, human sin entered the world in the form of deception stemming from spirits in revolt against the divine plan (*DVL* 45). Apart from the activity of these spirits, "human sins are incomprehensible" (*TE* 33).

Humankind was deceived into thinking they could take the place of God ruling over the entire world. Humanity has now exchanged its relationship to God and the world for one of personal dependence on that which is not God. While sin originates in human nature, it also now affects the human person, specifically the human community of love that is God's intention for all human beings.[10] Humankind now stands "in a dependence on that anti-godly nature of spirit mediated in their nature" (*SBb* 1:39–40). Human beings have lost their independence within their personal relationship to God and instead have put themselves into a relationship of dependence on that which is not God. For Hofmann, therefore, "sin" is the self-determination of the human being in opposition to the will of God (ibid., 1:482).[11] And this sinful self-determination is, for Hofmann, *historical*; i.e., the advent of sin must be sharply delineated from the creation of the world by God.

Thus sin, in Hofmann's view, is all-embracing. It destroys not only an individual's relationship to God and therewith the individual's own life, but also an individual's relationships to other people, to society, and to the whole

---

9. Hofmann believed that the unity of these antigodly spirits "under Satan" only became clear through Jesus Christ and his victory over Satan and the evil spirits; see *SBb* 1:441–51. But Hofmann detected in the early Genesis narratives, especially the story of Noah, indications of the influence of antigodly spirits on human beings, e.g., Gen 6:1–4. He understood the story of the Tower of Babel to be a further indication of the disintegration of an original human unity into multinational plurality. Hofmann's understanding of "Satan" is similar to Schelling's. On this point, see Wapler, "Theologie Hofmanns," 715–16.

10. Although Hofmann acknowledged that "Holy Scripture is not an infallible textbook of cosmology and anthropology" (*BH* 75ff.) and that one should not "reinterpret natural science according to Genesis" (e.g., "one will not attempt to learn from Holy Scripture how much time it took to create the world...since the creation story is not concerned with this question"), he held to a fairly naïve understanding of Genesis 1–11. While Hofmann's naiveté regarding the genre of Gen 1–11 often gets in the way of contemporary understanding, his theological insights into the meaning of Gen 1–11 are often profound. For example, Hofmann understood Gen 2:4ff. to focus on the need for human community and on the tragic breakdown of human community.

11. Forde offers a very good summary: "What happened — and this can be taken as [Hofmann's] definition of sin — was that because man succumbed to a desire and activity which went contrary to the divine order, he exchanged, as far as was possible for him, his relationship to God and the world established by creation for one in which he is in his personal dependence to the contra-divine spirit, becoming an object of God's wrath instead of his love. Sin has two sides. In the relationship to the world, man has become subject to the spirit which wills its dissolution; this means that he finds himself in a world captive to dissolution (death) rather than one which has its unified telos in himself as God's. In relationship to God, man is aware that God excludes him, that he has become a stranger and an enemy. This means that he is aware of sin, guilt, and death" (Forde, *The Law-Gospel Debate*, 26).

created order. Sin, understood (following Luther) as a radical "curving in on oneself" (*curvatus in se*), thus marks the depths of human misery. It is the condition of humanity, a prison into which human beings have put themselves but from which they cannot escape by their own power. Sin thus breaks asunder the perfect communion of God and God's creation. Through their rejection of dependency on God, human beings have alienated themselves from God, from nature, from history, from each other, and finally even from their true selves.

The Unity of History in the New Human Being: Christ as Beginning, Center, and End of History

According to Hofmann, with the advent of sin and the disintegration of the original unity of humanity, God chose or elected one human being, Abraham, whose family would be the representatives of God's intended relationship with all human beings. Through the family of Abraham, Isaac, and Jacob/Israel, God would ultimately bless all of creation (Gen. 12:1–3). Accordingly, it is God's will to reveal God's salvation for all the nations in the history of Israel (*SBb* 1:22).[12]

> Through participation in this blessing, all the generations on earth will eventually be saved. The whole subsequent history is concerned with the realization of this promise. Its ultimate fulfillment as shown in the New Testament still lies in the future. (*BH* 67)

The realization of the divine promise to Abraham centers in Jesus, "Israel reduced to one man," who is understood to be the fulfillment of the history of Israel and thus the fulfillment of human history. "Israel is the realm of history which has its goal in Jesus," yet "Israel's hope aims at the fulfillment of the promise given to them. Its fulfillment will imply that Israel's God will eventually be recognized as the only God" (ibid., 67–68).

Since Jesus is the fulfillment of the historical process of human development, he must be both its beginning and end. In him, therefore, the world must have been created and in him it will be perfected. *The* human being, Jesus, is therefore not merely an individual human being in history; rather, in him history has its focus and continuity: Christ is both the archetype and

---

12. While Hofmann stressed that God's will of love is to bless all nations through Abraham and his descendents, Hofmann did not teach that God has necessarily elected each human being for salvation. Hofmann acknowledged the biblical emphasis on the universality of God's grace while also acknowledging those biblical statements that speak of an eternal judgment/separation of unbelievers from God at the eschaton.

the *telos* of the world historical process. Because all human beings are created in the image of the "person" of Christ, they are created in image of "the archetypal world-goal" (*urbildliche Weltziel*) and are oriented toward him (*SBb* 1:37). For Hofmann humanity in Jesus is the apex or the *telos* of creation, and thus humanity in Christ gives creation its unity and purpose (ibid., 1:218). "One is humankind in the goal of humankind's history; all namely [are] one in Christ: could humankind's history end thus if it had not also begun with One? Why, is not all humankind's history nothing other than the unfolding of humankind's origin or likewise the restoration of the same in a second, and final, completion!" (*WE* 1:66).[13]

The assumption here is that history centers in "the process of becoming of the human being" toward which "the self-realization of the eternal will of God" aims (*ET* 62). The historical realization of the divine will can only be accomplished in relation to the self-realization of the human being, which occurs in the human Jesus. God's self-realization can only be fulfilled in unity with the self-realization of the human being (God's being is analogous to the coming-into-being of human being).

> The tri-personal God gives himself into this history, which he will live with humanity in such a way that his Trinity envelopes sinful humanity as such, as he has entered into historicality, to encompass the process of becoming and that which is coming into existence within its tri-personality. (*TE* 44)

God's Eternal Will of Love and God's Historical Wrath

While Hofmann believed in a literal, historical "first sin," namely, Adam's (whose sin did not originate in himself but was evoked only through an effect on his nature), the correspondence between the outer effect of nature and selfish self-determination is inescapable for each subsequent human being. A dependence on evil is mediated through nature which is inherited by all subsequent human beings (*TE* 42–43). The selfish will of human beings also has a negative effect on the world. Chief among these is the loss of the unity among God, human beings, and the world (including also nature). Since human community is conditioned by human nature, human beings are incapable of freeing themselves from a necessary dependence on sinful human nature (ibid., 67). Therefore, each human being is as guilty as the

---

13. For Hofmann the beginning of this history is the creation of the first human being, "Adam," but the end of this history in the "second Adam" is more important than its beginning. See *SBb* 1:404–10.

first human being. Humanity is therefore aware of sin, guilt, and death, the world has become for human beings a source of evil, and human beings themselves have widened the gulf between their "person" and their "nature" (*SBb* 1:482). Human beings are divided within themselves (*SS* 3:4).[14] In their relationship to the world, human beings have now become subject to the spirits which seek their dissolution, the death of each individual personality, and the loss of relationship with God and with one another (*SBb* 1:487–89). As sinners before God, human beings are now aware that God rejects humanity, that humanity has become a stranger and enemy of God. Now "God is against humankind" and human beings are exposed to the wrath of God (*TE* 35, 69).

Since, however, the Christian understands "that God has made provision for the ultimate realization of his will" through Christ, the Christian "must presuppose that God must have foreordained the possibility of a fall" into sin whose eventuality could not frustrate his will of love.[15] It is only because God is triune that the possibility of salvation remains open. In this regard, God's wrath is only directed against human sins; the divine wrath is not rooted in the divine essence itself. God's relation to human beings does not originate from his wrath (*DVL* 48–49). Instead, even in view of sin, God's relation to human beings is grounded in God's love. "It is not merely in the creation that God is the one loving the human being and the world in relation to him, but he also remains that where sin enters the world; and if God's love expresses itself in the former as goodness, then here it is expressed as grace" (ibid., 48). Thus, God's historical wrath is subordinate to God's eternal love. " ... God blocks the path of what is alien to him with the omnipotences of his eternal nature" (ibid., 49). Only God's love has an eternal foundation:

> It is inaccurate to say that God's wrath is an activity of his love; but in the way that God operates his wrath toward human beings, a wrath that is not an eternal but an historical relation of God, God proves his love, which is the eternal presupposition of his historical relations, even against sinful human beings. (*TE* 35)[16]

---

14. Flechsenhaar identifies a four-fold historical shape of "sin" in Hofmann's theology: (1) the original sin of Adam, (2) the sinfulness of the whole human race that is descended from Adam, (3) the sins of each individual human being, and (4) the sin of Satan.

15. Forde, *The Law-Gospel Debate*, 26–27.

16. "For Hofmann the wrath of God virtually receives the character of a form of revelation from God" (Flechsenhaar, 40). Compare Barth's assertion that "the very fact of God's speaking with us is in itself under all circumstances grace" (Karl Barth, "Gospel and Law," in *God, Grace and Gospel* [trans. James Strathearn McNab; Edinburgh: Oliver and Boyd, 1959], 4).

Flechsenhaar has correctly pointed out that by putting the matter this way, Hofmann attempted to avoid two extremes.[17] On the one hand, God's wrath cannot be equated with God's love. The eternal nature of God vis-à-vis human beings is love. It is therefore the most proper expression of God's eternal will which has proceeded out of an eternal Trinitarian similarity into an historical dissimilarity. God's wrath is therefore only historical.[18] On the other hand, God's wrath is not merely an historical activity of God's love, nor is God's wrath merely the result of the subjective imagination of a guilty and frightened human conscience. God's wrath is truly real. So the whole of *Heilsgeschichte* always reveals God's love and wrath at the same time, but the wrath is subservient to the eternal will which seeks its ultimate fulfillment in the community of love between God and humanity mediated in Christ. "God's wrath against sin placed Israel under the law of commandments and prohibitions...," but with the coming of Christ in history the standard by which God ultimately judges the world has changed. Human righteousness is not measured any longer by means of the divine law, but only through faith in the righteousness of Christ (*SS* 2:95). Ultimately, this righteousness alone will constitute the perfect communion between God and humanity. Thus, according to Hofmann, Scripture only teaches one divine will of love for all, not a double will (e.g., one toward the saved and one toward the damned), though Hofmann also acknowledged that Scripture teaches that those who persist in unbelief will be excluded from this perfect communion. While Hofmann stressed Paul's universal grace (e.g., Rom 5:12–18), he did not dismiss or gloss over the apocalyptic texts that speak of God's triumph over the forces arrayed against God and Israel and the church.

But the end of history, the stage of which will be Israel according to God's election, will bring to non-Israelitic humanity both blessing and judgment. The Gentile world will be judged on account of its enmity against the people of the true God, but all those will be blessed who were willing to be led to the knowledge of God (cf. Ps. 22:27). The promise given to Abraham stated that no generation on earth will receive a blessing except through him and his descendents. The

---

17. See Flechsenhaar, *Das Geschichtsproblem*, 41–42.

18. "How does God know whether and when sin occurs? The only crucial point to make here...is that this knowledge of the existence of sin is not a *condition* of God's forming God's very complicated intentions with respect to the world. God's knowledge of sin is dependent upon, and is logically subsequent to, God's creative intention for the world. It is therefore part of what could be called God's *practical* knowledge, or knowledge of what the created world is like in God's will for it. God does not directly will sin but sin (insofar as it is a defect) presupposes God's will for the world in which it occurs" (Kathryn Tanner, "Human Freedom, Human Sin, and God the Creator," in *The God Who Acts* [ed. Thomas Tracy; University Park: Penn State University Press, 1994], 134).

psalmist knows that enmity against Israel can have no other end than the destruction of her enemies. (*BH* 91–92)

The goal of the Trinitarian will to love is the restoration of human beings who now are determined in a way that is contrary to that will of love and thus in need of redemption from sin and evil. According to Hofmann, humanity needs saving most from death and sin, which mark the loss of true relationship with God and with the world. Sin and death create the conditions by which true human goodness and life, including life's relationships, are perverted and destroyed. Sin, the result of a lack of trust in God, frustrates the goodness of humans and intensifies human insecurity in an uncertain world of change. Such uncertainty, in turn, further fuels the forces of sin at work in human lives. These forces finally cut people off from relating to one another and to God. Death, the judgment of God for human sin, spells the end of all human relationships. There is, therefore, the need for the restoration of all these relationships in the world. The next chapter examines Hofmann's understanding of the Trinitarian restoration of the world of becoming.

CHAPTER NINE

A New Way to Teach Old Truth:
Trinitarian *Kenosis*

In Hofmann's theology God is a Subject who has determined God's self in God's historical self-giving and self-differentiation in the world for the sake of the salvation of human beings. Because God is love, and because God loves the world, God is triune. This means that God is both personal and relational and thus also historical. Because God has self-determined God's self to be triune, God can enter into history as a human being in order to establish the beginning of a perfected communion between God and humanity. The second person of the Trinity has become a human being in order to restore human beings to perfect fellowship with the triune God.

For Hofmann, Jesus is "the center" or "focal point" (*Mitte*) from which both God and humanity are to be truly understood. Jesus' human life is definitive for who God is as personal Subject, as self-determining, self-giving love for all humankind. Jesus' human life is also definitive for who human beings are as creatures of God, loved by God. As such, Jesus is the mediator between God and humanity; he is the one who develops within himself "the renewal of the human race" (*DVL* 49). The purpose of this chapter, then, is to clarify Hofmann's conception of *kenosis* and atonement as grounded in his understanding of the Trinity. Before examining this conception, however, it is necessary to situate Hofmann's kenotic Christology within its larger theological context.

The Theological Context
for Hofmann's Trinitarian *Kenosis*[1]

Hofmann's articulation of Trinitarian *kenosis* was part of a broader movement in the early and middle nineteenth century that sought to overcome

---

1. The best studies of Hofmann's Christology in relation to other Christologies of his day are by Bachmann, *Hofmanns Versöhnungslehre*; Breidert, *Die kenotische Christologie,*

the difficulties associated with the traditional two-natures doctrine, particularly with regard to affirming the full humanity of Jesus and his truly human personality. In addition to Hofmann, the main representatives of this new *kenosis*-Christology included Ernst Sartorius (1797–1859), Karl Liebner (1806–1871), Wolfgang F. Gess (1819–1891), and Hofmann's Erlangen colleagues, Thomasius, Johannes H. A. Ebrard (1818–1888), and Frank.[2] For these thinkers, the *kenosis* is not merely a state of humiliation that the incarnate Son of God endures, as in the traditional doctrinal *loci,* but it is itself the self-limitation of the second *person* of the Trinity who "emptied himself" into Jesus.[3] The subject of the *kenosis* ("emptying," "divesting") is therefore not the incarnate man but the second person of the Trinity who becomes a man. Such a reinterpretation, which attempted to avoid the apparent Docetism in the traditional two-natures doctrine, led to a new way of speaking about the incarnation of God in the man Jesus.[4]

While this new movement should itself be situated within the context of Hamann's ideas of the "condescension of God" and the "humility of God,"[5]

161–84; and Paul Wapler, "Die Genesis der Versöhnungslehre Johannes von Hofmanns," *Neue kirchliche Zeitschrift* 25 (1914): 167–205. These works have laid the foundation for my own analysis. Breidert demonstrates that the representatives of *kenosis* in the nineteenth century "come from very different directions and connect very different theological interests to [*kenosis*]" (Breidert, *Die kenotische Christologie,* 18). See also Wenz, *Geschichte der Versöhnungslehre,* 2:453–67; and Hirsch, *Geschichte,* 5:379–92.

2. See Beyschlag, *Die Erlanger Theologie,* 83–111. Thomasius became a professor at Erlangen in 1842 and spent his entire teaching career there until he died in 1875. He and Hofmann formed the core theological faculty during the zenith of the Erlangen School. See especially Gottfried Thomasius, *Christi Person und Werk. Darstellung der evangelisch-lutherischen Dogmatik vom Mittelpunkte der Christologie* (3 vols.; Erlangen: Bläsing, 1853–1861). Hofmann was a major conversation partner with Thomasius, who frequently cites the former's *Schriftbeweis* in his own theological writings. Ebrard joined the Erlangen faculty in 1847, and Frank a decade later. For the kenotic ideas of these later thinkers, see also Oscar Bensow, *Die Lehre von der Kenose* (Gütersloh: Deichert, 1904), 79–153. A similar kind of kenotic-Christology was also articulated outside of German Lutheran circles, especially in the work of Charles Gore (1853–1932), Peter Taylor Forsyth (1848–1921), and among several nineteenth- and twentieth-century Russian theologians.

3. "...but he emptied himself, taking the form of a slave" ("...ἀλλὰ ἑαυτὸν ἐκένωσεν μορφὴν δούλου λαβών..." [Phil. 2:7]). On the verb "Κενόω," see Walter Bauer, Frederick Danker, et al., *A Greek-English Lexicon of the New Testament and Other Early Christian Literature* (3d ed.; Chicago: The University of Chicago Press, 2000), 539 (including bibliography); and Albrecht Oepke, "Κενός," *Theological Dictionary of the New Testament* (ed. Gerhard Kittel; trans. Geoffrey Bromiley; Grand Rapids: Eerdmans, 1965), 3:659–62. Oepke himself takes a view similar to Thomasius: "What is meant is that the heavenly Christ did not selfishly exploit His divine form and mode of being, but by His own decision emptied Himself of it or laid it by, taking the form of a servant by becoming a man. The subject of ἐκένωσεν is not the incarnate but the pre-existent Lord. There is a strong sense of the unity of His person. The essence remains, the mode of being changes — a genuine sacrifice. Docetism is excluded" (ibid., 661).

4. See Welch, "General Introduction," in *God and Incarnation,* 3–18.

5. See especially Helmuth Schreiner, *Die Menschwerdung Gottes in der Theologie Johann Georg Hamanns* (2d ed.; Tübingen: Katzmann, 1950).

and Hegel's[6] and Schelling's[7] appropriations of the ideas of *kenosis* and incarnation for the development of their respective philosophies, its origins can already be detected in the doctrine of the communication of attributes (*communicatio idiomatum*), including the *genus maiestaticum* (communication of the majesty of the divine nature to the human nature), especially as articulated by other Lutheran theologians in the course of the Reformation. The doctrine of the *communicatio idiomatum* stresses the real communication of the specifically divine attributes or properties to the human nature in Christ's person and activity. This communication between the two natures in Christ means that there is a genuine condescension of God into the depths of human existence and a genuine communication of the full majesty of God into the man Jesus. So Lutheran theologians generally affirm that "the finite is capable of the infinite" (*finitum capax infiniti*). By God's condescension into the finite, which God creates, preserves, and redeems, God makes the finite capable of receiving God, so that God is revealed in the form of a humble servant.

This traditional Lutheran understanding of the *communicatio idiomatum*, however, is consistent with the wider Catholic tradition in affirming that the permeation of attributes in the person of Jesus did not involve any change to the divine nature. In order to secure the divine majesty and the traditional divine attributes of immutability, omnipotence, and omniscience, the divine is said to be "hidden" in Jesus, especially in his humiliation, sufferings, and death.[8] In this view, the *genus maiestaticum* is still in force, even in Christ's state of humiliation. So the traditional dogmatic theologians in Lutheranism continued to operate within the traditional Chalcedonian definition of the person of Christ, even as they attempted to elucidate that

---

6. For an overview of Hegel's Christology, see Wenz, *Geschichte*, 1:296–316; James Yerkes, *The Christology of Hegel* (Albany: State University of New York Press, 1983); and Mattes, "Hegel's Lutheran Claim," 249–79. Interest in *kenosis* was reawakened in the 1960s through a renewed appreciation for Hegel's reflections on "the death of God." See, for example, Thomas Altizer, "Kenosis," in *The Gospel of Christian Atheism* (Philadelphia: Westminster Press, 1966), 62–69; Dorothy Sölle, *Christ the Representative: An Essay in Theology after the "Death of God"* (trans. David Lewis; London: SCM Press, 1967); and Jürgen Moltmann, *The Crucified God* (trans. R. A. Wilson and John Bowden; 2d ed.; New York: Harper and Row, 1973), 205–7. Interest in *kenosis* has also been motivated by recent Christian-Buddhist conversations.

7. Walter Kasper has attempted to bring the ideas of the later Schelling into theological discussion about the person of Christ. See Walter Kasper, *Jesus the Christ* (trans. V. Green; New York: Paulist Press, 1976); idem, "Krise und Neuanfang der Christologie im Denken Schellings," *Evangelische Theologie* 33 (1973): 366–84; idem, *Das Absolute in der Geschichte: Philosophie und Theologie der Geschichte in der Spätphilosophie Schellings* (Mainz: Matthias-Grünewald, 1965). See also Robert Brown, "Resources in Schelling for New Directions in Theology," *Idealistic Studies* 20 (1990): 1–17.

8. Theodosius Harnack's discussion of Luther's understanding of the "hidden God" in his classic work on Luther's theology was written directly against Hofmann's qualified rejection of that distinction. See Theodosius Harnack, *Luthers Theologie* (2 vols.; Erlangen: Bläsing, 1862; Repr., Munich: C. Kaiser Verlag, 1927), 1:91–149.

definition in terms of the *communicatio idiomatum*. As such, they did not question the classical attributes of the divine nature in the person of Jesus.

By the beginning of the nineteenth century, however, this traditional Chalcedonian definition of the two-natures doctrine was being criticized by some theologians. The classical definition, "one Christ in two natures, without confusion, without change, without division, without separation," was deemed inadequate since it defined Christ on the basis of ontological categories that did not fit well with modern notions of psychological growth and personality development. The publication of Strauss's *Life of Jesus* not only heightened dissatisfaction with this traditional two-natures doctrine, it actually created a major theological crisis for those who sought to defend the notion that "God was in Christ reconciling the world to himself." Claude Welch has nicely summarized the key problem:

> [The issue was] the question of the being of God in the historical per-son Jesus Christ, or in the language of the classical doctrine, of the union of God and man in the God-man. Thus the matter is first of all that of the "person" rather than the "work. . . . " Whether in relation to the new biblical criticism and the "quest for the historical Jesus," or to rationalism's earlier demand for the human figure instead of the attributes of divinity, or to romanticism's taste for individuality, or to other factors — the humanity of Jesus has become the pivot of recon-struction. The question could no longer be, as it had been for so long: Given the fullness of deity in Christ, how can the genuineness of the humanity be maintained? Now it is rather: Given the integrity of the human existence, how is it possible to speak of the presence of the divine?[9]

Traditional Reformation Lutheranism had tended to understand the *com-munio idiomatum* as a nonreciprocal imparting of the divine to the human and not as a genuine and mutual exchange of attributes. Thus the tradition had failed to resolve a question that had risen to the center of theological discussion due to the development of critical historical consciousness: How can the divine attributes of omnipotence, omniscience, and omnipresence be imparted to the human nature of Jesus without thereby annulling his real humanity? How can the true humanity of Jesus, which is finite and subject to the temporal process of development, be reconciled with the divine Word (*Logos*), which had been understood to be infinite, eternal, and immutable?

---

9. Welch, *God and Incarnation*, 7–8. One should note that Hofmann himself rarely used the expression "God-man" (*Gott-mensch*).

One major response to this new situation was offered by Isaak Dorner, who articulated the idea of the gradual formation of the divine Word into the human nature of Jesus, but not in such a way that the Word underwent any change. Dorner's Christology is important for understanding Hofmann's theological context since Dorner developed a kenotic Christology that was like Hofmann's, though Dorner later rejected such a Christology and was critical of Hofmann's. Dorner's early kenotic Christology, which affirmed a "progressive" or "developing" view of the incarnation, maintained that the incarnation

> is not to be conceived as finished at one moment, but as continuing, even as growing, since God as *Logos* constantly grasps and appropriates each of the new facets that are formed out of the true human unfolding, just as, conversely, the growing actual receptivity of the humanity joins consciously and willingly with ever new facets of the *Logos*.[10]

Dorner held that despite the development within the personal union,

> the *Logos* is from the beginning united with Jesus in the deepest ground of being, and Jesus' life was always a divine-human one since an existent receptivity for deity never remained without its fulfillment. Human development and the immutability of deity are congruous in that God as *Logos* can enter history without loss of self, for the purpose of a progressive self-revelation in humanity, and humanity is capable of being set increasingly in immutability, again without alteration of its essence.[11]

Since the personality and self-consciousness of Jesus were not fully formed at his birth but underwent development as he grew older, the divine *Logos* gradually unites with the person of Jesus as Jesus gradually awakens to his self-consciousness. This process of unification is only fully completed in the resurrection and ascension of Jesus. However, in his state of humility (i.e., in his state of self-emptying) the personal union realizes itself in the gradually developing process of the *communicatio idiomatum*.

Dorner connected this understanding of the *communicatio idiomatum* to a Christology that was very much influenced by Schleiermacher's "ideal Christology" (*Urbildchristologie*), namely, that Jesus is the second Adam, the ideal human being.[12] Like Schleiermacher's view of Jesus, Dorner

---

10. Isaak Dorner, *System der christlichen Glaubenslehre* (2 vols.; Berlin: W. Hertz, 1879–1881), 2:431, sec. 104. My translation here is dependent on Welch's.

11. Ibid.

12. See CF 371–417. According to Schleiermacher, "the redemption accomplished by Jesus of Nazareth" consists in the elevation of human consciousness of God through "the living influence of Christ," who has "an absolutely powerful God-consciousness" which has the power of affecting the redemption of humanity. People are drawn into and assimilated in the powerful

understood Jesus to be "the central-individual," the perfect human being. Because he realized in himself the perfect human being, he is at the same time both the crown of creation, the head of humanity, as well as the mediator between the Creator and the creature. The self-emptying of Phil. 2:7 does not refer therefore to a divine self-limitation or de-intensification of the divine in Jesus, but to the initially dormant but later developing self-communication of the *Logos* to the man Jesus.[13]

Dorner himself, however, later realized that his Christology was also fraught with difficulties since it, too, seemed to demand the impossible, namely, that two persons, the divine person of the *Logos* and the human person of Jesus, should gradually develop together into one person. Consequently, Dorner modified his Christology by attempting to ground it in the doctrine of the Trinity. In his later view, Dorner held that the divine persons of the Trinity should be understood as ways of being one absolute personality. Accordingly, Jesus Christ is not the product of the gradual development of the union between the *Logos* and a human being but a unification of the divine and human natures out of which the divine-human personality develops itself. "So Dorner tries to get around the *Anhypostasis* of the human nature by going directly to the *Anhypostasis* of the Logos."[14]

God-consciousness of Christ who continues to have an effect on people through his historical community, the church. To further explain how Christ is able to draw people into his God-consciousness, Schleiermacher employs the words *Urbildlichkeit* and *Vorbildlichkeit*. According to Schleiermacher, Christ has both "the quality of being an ideal" (*Urbildlichkeit*) and "the quality of being able to evoke an ideal in others" (*Vorbildlichkeit*). Schleiermacher attempted to get beyond the problems of the classic two-natures doctrine by maintaining the notion that Christ is both the one ideal type of a perfect human consciousness of God and the one who alone is able to evoke or arouse this perfect consciousness of God in others. See B. A. Gerrish, "Friedrich Schleiermacher," in *Nineteenth Century Religious Thought in the West* (ed. Ninian Smart et al.; 3 vols.; Cambridge: Cambridge University Press, 1985), 1:143. Like Hofmann's theological method, Schleiermacher argued back from observed effect to its sufficient cause. Jesus must have a unique identity since his dignity must be commensurate with and grounded in his work or activity to create this perfect consciousness of God in others. Thus, in keeping with Melanchthon's dictum, Schleiermacher affirmed that to know Christ is to know his benefits. To speak of Christ's benefits is to speak of his identity and to speak of Christ's identity is to speak of his benefits. Both Schleiermacher's and Hofmann's respective Christologies are continuous with ideas of Irenaeus (ca. 130–200), particularly the latter's stress on Christ as the recapitulator and perfector of humanity.

13. "This seems to be what Philippians 2:5ff. means, not that Christ has ceased to be in the form of deity, or has given up his equality with God, but only that he, standing in this fullness and glory, has not shirked this alienation and humiliation. The subject of the sentence is Jesus, not the *Logos*, as Lutheran theologians have irrefutably demonstrated..." (Dorner, 66).

14. Breidert, *Die kenotische Christologie*, 28. In the Christological disputes of the sixth century, Leontius of Byzantium established the distinction between the *enhypostasis* (personal union) and *anhypostasis* (impersonal union). The unity of the man Jesus with the second person of the Trinity was expressed in post-Chalcedonian Christology with the formula of the *enhypostasis* of Jesus in the *Logos*. Human nature is *enhypostasized* by the *Logos* because it is possessed, used, and manifested by the *Logos*. "In his concrete reality the man Jesus has the ground of his existence (his hypostasis) not in himself as man but 'in' the *Logos*" (Wolfhart

The *kenosis* theologians, influenced as was Dorner by Schleiermacher's basic principle that everything in Christian theology must be directly related to the redemption accomplished in Jesus of Nazareth, also offered a creative response to the new situation in Christology. Like Dorner, the *kenosis* theologians found in the biblical expression of *kenosis* the means for integrating new ideas about personhood into the traditional understanding that the personalizing center of the human being Jesus is the second person of the Trinity. This new idea of *kenosis* meant that God limited God's self so that the presence of the divine in Jesus did not destroy the full humanity of Jesus. This self-limitation implies that the second person of the Trinity underwent modification or change as a necessary condition of the personal entrance of the *Logos* of God into human history and human experience. If the incarnation occurred, it could only happen through a free self-limitation of the eternal *Logos* under the conditions of temporality and finitude. "At the incarnation, the Son gave up the *relative* attributes of divinity, that is, those which characterize the *relation* of God to the world: omnipotence, omniscience, omnipresence. He retained only the *immanent* perfections proper to God, independent of his relation to the world: holiness, power, truth, and love."[15] For the *kenosis* theologians the self-determination of God is the key to understanding how God has changed in the incarnation of Jesus so as to fulfill God's eternal will of love for humankind. The self-emptying that occurred in the incarnation implies a real change in God that is at odds with the classical theistic notions of God's immutability and impassibility. Thus, the *kenosis* theologians retrieved elements of Luther's Christology that had been lost in Lutheran Orthodoxy, especially Luther's realism regarding the communication of attributes and the suffering of God in Jesus.[16]

The Self-giving God:
Trinitarian *Kenosis* and Atonement

Like the later Dorner, Hofmann grounded the divine *kenosis* in the love of the triune God for the world. Hofmann's concept of *kenosis* rests on his

---

Pannenberg, *Jesus: God and Man* [trans. Lewis L. Wilkins and Duane Priebe; Philadelphia: Westminster, 1977], 338). See also Aloys Grillmeier, *Christ in Christian Tradition* (trans. John Bowden; 2d ed.: Atlanta: John Knox Press, 1975), 1:437–39.

15. Pannenberg, *Jesus,* 310.

16. For the *genus tapeinoticum* in Luther's theology, see Marc Lienhard, *Luther: Witness to Jesus Christ* (trans. Edwin Robertson; Minneapolis: Augsburg, 1982), 339–46. "... Luther goes further than the communication of attributes from nature to person. There is for him the idea of a real communication of attributes between the two natures themselves ... " (ibid., 339).

understanding of the incarnation of the *Logos* as the fulfillment of the historical realization of the eternal Trinity.[17] Already in his 1842 lectures on dogmatics, which were not published in his lifetime, Hofmann developed the Trinitarian foundation for the person and work of Jesus the Christ. The whole life of Jesus, culminating in his death and resurrection, is best understood as the actualization of the triune God's self-giving, self-emptying love for humanity. The eternal Trinitarian relationship completes itself in time in the incarnation and life of Jesus for the sake of restoring communion between God and humanity. "The intra-divine relationship (whose eternal manner is a relationship of self-equality and self-similarity) has given itself over into historical dissimilarity. Out of the relationship between God the transcendent Creator and God the archetypal world-goal there has developed a relationship of the man Jesus to God, his God and Father" (*SBb* 2.1:19). With the incarnation, the pretemporal relationship of the three persons is no longer defined as the relationship of God the creator to the archetype-like world-goal, but now, in the incarnation, that relationship has become one of God the creator to the man Jesus in the divine Spirit. The intra-divine relationship has changed to become "the relationship of God the Father in the Spirit with his Son, the man Jesus Christ" (*DVL* 103).[18]

Although the beginning of Trinitarian historical self-fulfillment already occurs with the creation of the world, "the historical formation of the intra-divine relationship" finds its provisional conclusion in the incarnation of Christ (*ET* 81). The historical dissimilarity of the Trinity, established with the creation of the world, assumes a new form in the incarnation of Christ.

> God has established himself in a human beginning of life as the archetype-like world-goal in relation to God the transcendent Creator through God the immanently effective ground of life, and thereby the intra-divine relationship has become the community of the Father of Jesus with Jesus the Son of God in the Spirit of both. (*SBa* 1:45)

---

17. Breidert correctly observes that Hofmann's kenotic interpretation of the Trinity is quite different from Thomasius's understanding of *kenosis*. Thomasius, unlike Hofmann, still attempted to maintain the traditional doctrine of the vicarious atonement. "With Hofmann, *kenosis* has the function of mediating the eternal Trinity to the historical so that history itself turns into the *heilsgeschichtliche*-Trinitarian process and realizes in the incarnation of Christ God's will of salvation which is demonstrated up to the death of Jesus" (Breidert, *Die kenotische Christologie*, 181).

18. Hofmann's dogmatics lectures were delivered a decade prior to Thomasius's classic work, *Christi Person und Werk*, that started the debate about *kenosis*. Breidert is correct to suggest that Hofmann was a creative influence on the development of Thomasius's notion of *kenosis*, contra Pannenberg's statement that "through Thomasius the kenosis doctrine became a part of the neo-Lutheran Erlangen theology" (Pannenberg, *Jesus*, 310). See Breidert, *Die kenotische Christologie*, 174.

"We can . . . say that Christ has emptied himself of the divine glory, omnipotence, omnipresence and that out of a God has become a human being" (*SBb* 2.1:212). By means of the incarnation God's static being is transformed into a dynamic becoming, a "coming-to" or "coming-into" the temporal world. Thus, the incarnation of Christ makes a real difference in God. The being of Jesus makes a difference in the being of God. Through the incarnation Christ has

> exchanged the predicate of θεός [God] for that of ἄνθρωπος [human being] or σάρξ [flesh], in the sense that he has ceased to be God in order to become a human being. . . . So in this sense John names Christ θεός [God] prior to the incarnation, as Paul says of him, that he had been ἐν μορφῆ θεοῦ [in the form of God] when he became a human being. John therefore is not talking about the eternal nature of Christ but about the historical being of Christ, as he was first transcendent, then immanent; first God, then a human being. (Ibid., 1:166)

In the incarnation

> the dissimilarity of the intra-divine relationship became as great in its historical configuration as it could become without the self-negation of God. Nevertheless, even in its most extreme dissimilarity, it remained itself. Not partially but completely and without reservation, Christ gave up every aspect of his transcendent existence when he became incarnate, without ceasing to be the eternal God. Christ has put himself into human finitude without thereby becoming a finite creature. (Ibid., 2.1:23)

While Hofmann struggled to deny that the incarnation means that Christ became "a finite creature," perhaps against Hegel's notion of the self-negation of God but also to avoid Arianism, the implication of his understanding of *kenosis* is that indeed the second person of the Trinity has become a finite, human being.[19] Despite Hofmann's reservations to the contrary, he wanted to affirm that the second person of the Trinity has completely entered into human finitude — without ceasing in some way to be "the eternal God." But to say this, Hofmann had to divest "God" of God's usual attributes (omnipotence, omniscience, and so on). The only attribute Hofmann sought to hold on to was that of "eternal love," which forms the bond between the Father and the Son in their historical relationship. Apart

---

19. Arius (d. 336) stressed the subordination of Christ to the Father and denied that Jesus was fully divine. Arius held that the Son of God was not eternal but was created from nothing. Arianism was rejected at the first Ecumenical Council in Nicaea in 325. The Nicene Creed affirms the eternal nature of the Son of God.

from this "eternal love," the second person of the Trinity has completely exchanged his divine existence for a human existence. "Because he was with
God before he became a human being, he is the incarnate υἱος θεοῦ [son
of God] in a special sense and thus also θεός [God], but θεός in the world
as a human being, after he had been it before transcendently with God"
(ibid., 2.1:23). Hofmann thus presupposed an eternal relationship between
the Father and the Son, but this is only the consequence of reflection on
Jesus' lack of divine mediation (i.e., as mediator, Jesus himself has no need
for mediation). " . . . [A]n intra-divine relationship exists between God, the
Father of Jesus Christ, and Jesus, the Son of God, which did not come into
existence but is eternal; however, a relationship of God to the man Jesus has
developed historically out of a relationship of God to God" (*SBa* 1:154).
Only in view of God's historical self-determination and self-fulfillment may
one speak of God the Father, God the Son, and God the Holy Spirit. "The
name of the historical form of the eternal triune God is now Father, Son
and Spirit and hereby *Heilsgeschichte* as type has reached its fulfillment as
antitype" (*TE* 56).

According to Hofmann, then, the New Testament statements about Jesus
were never intended to be developed into propositional dogmatic statements
about Jesus' nature or essence, but are instead affirmations of the unique
relationship of Jesus to God. This relationship is only disclosed in the life of
Jesus, which reveals that there is an intra-divine relationship between God
the Father and Jesus, the Son of God, a relationship that only indirectly can
be called a relationship of God to God but which has developed historically
into a relationship of God to the human being Jesus. "God" is "the Father
who raised Jesus in the power of the Holy Spirit." "Therefore in an eternal
way Jesus Christ is God, but in an historical way he is a human being; the
human nature has enveloped his eternal divine nature" (*SBb* 2.1:21).

Only after carefully stating in what ways Jesus Christ may not be said
to be "God" or "divine" did Hofmann turn his attention to the one way
in which Jesus may be said to be "God." The fulfilled relationship between
God and humanity, prefigured in the history leading up to Jesus Christ,
but which has now become an historical reality in Jesus Christ, means that
Jesus may be called "God" (e.g., as the apostles John and Paul do), but only
because he stands as a human being within the Trinitarian community of
God that fulfills itself in history. For Hofmann the divinity of Jesus is not
an assertion about a supposed metaphysical, ahistorical *nature,* but about
Jesus' historical *relation* to God the Father, who has sent him into the world
to bring the world into communion with God. Hofmann maintained that
any statements about the preexistence or divinity of Christ must be limited

to God's eternal self-determination toward human beings that fulfills itself historically in Jesus (*DVL* 49). The preexistence of Jesus is nothing else than God's eternal will to be the God of love for humanity, i.e., to be God for humanity in Christ from all eternity.

While some of Hofmann's statements above might lead one to conclude that Hofmann had not moved beyond the traditional two-natures doctrine (e.g., his language about Christ as both human being and God), a closer analysis of Hofmann's language discloses that he in fact had moved to a creative position which he thought addressed the criticisms against the classic Christological dogma, especially the criticisms articulated by Strauss.[20] The key for Hofmann is the distinction between "person" and "nature" in Jesus.[21] Insofar as Jesus belongs to creation and the world of finite nature, Jesus is "nature." Insofar as Jesus freely determines himself in the course of his personal history, he is "person." Since his history, however, is the center (*Mitte*) of the history of the triune God, he participates as "person" in the Trinitarian process. Indeed, the specific life, death, and resurrection of Jesus is the basis for affirming that God is "personal" and "relational."

More specifically, Jesus is "person" in the Trinitarian process through the indwelling of God's Spirit in Jesus as the ground of his self-determination (*DVL* 50). The Spirit which dwells within Jesus the human being is both divine and creature-like since it has "proceeded from God." But as such the Spirit must be distinguished from the human nature of Jesus. Because creation itself is directed toward the development of the perfect human being, Jesus, he is to be regarded as the incarnation of the perfect image of God, "the archetypal world-goal" (*das urbildliche Weltziel*). The "eternal Person" enters human life, through the working of the Spirit through Mary, and thus joins himself to human nature. Because the incarnation of Jesus is not an isolated event but the conclusion of a history between God and human beings, the human being as such must be a participant in the incarnation as an historical process, but at the direction of the divine activity of the Spirit (*WE* 2:18). By putting the matter of Christ's "person" in this way, Hofmann attempted to provide a positive interpretation of the *anhypostasis* of the human nature of Jesus. The person of Christ does not unite the divine nature and the human nature in himself, as the Chalcedonian definition

---

20. Hofmann's principal criticisms of Strauss are that Strauss's skepticism makes him incapable of sensing and understanding God's activity in history and that the certainty of faith cannot be dependent on critical historical investigations. Strauss lacks the experiential faith that is both independent of history but which is also a necessary prerequisite for sensing and understanding God's actions in history on the basis of Christ, who is the unifying goal of all history and "the end of history."

21. Here I am following Behr's analysis. See Behr, *Politischer Liberalismus*, 77–80.

states; rather, Christ is the union of the divine person and human nature. Christ as "person" is "God"; Christ as "nature" is "human being."[22]

What distinguishes Jesus from the rest of humanity is his "person," but the person of Jesus cannot be separated from his work, since in Jesus God's love for all humankind has been actualized. God did not become a human being in order to unite God's self with a single human nature, but in order to have communion with all humankind and thus redeem humanity as a whole. Thus, as "person," Jesus stands in an eternal relationship to God and so he was already grounded in the communion of the Spirit with God when he became a human being. Indeed, even then he is eternal God and his spiritual communion with God is an eternal one, not something that began in time.

For Hofmann the *enhypostasis* of the human being of Jesus is the eternal decision on God's part to enter human history *as Jesus*. The self-determination of the man Jesus occurs as the historical "self-fulfillment of an intra-divine relationship," which is grounded in eternity (*SBb* 1:36–37). It is God's desire from all eternity to establish a relationship between God's self and that which is other than God but which God creates, namely, all human beings. God does this in the person of Jesus, who might be described as "humanity reduced to one." The *enhypostasis* of Jesus' being made Jesus' *anhypostatic* actions possible. God's decision to be the God-for-humanity was temporalized in Jesus, enabling Jesus to live his life on behalf of the well-being and salvation of humankind. The *enhypostasis* means that God, from all eternity, is oriented toward the well-being of humankind, both by God's eternal will of love to establish a relationship between God's self and humankind but also by God's will to overcome death in Jesus' resurrection.

> The history of Jesus is at the same time the self-demonstration and development of that which is given in and with his person, an explication of the act of the divine Trinity in the incarnation. For the incarnation — including already in itself its future — is the beginning of that great act of the divine Trinity, through which has come into being the one who begins a new humanity but thereby also brings to an end the old humanity. (Ibid., 53)

Clearly, Hofmann's Christology is a "Christology from above," though he wanted also to take seriously the free determination and development of Jesus' full and complete human life. So Hofmann affirmed that in the incarnation the historical activity of the eternal God is no longer simply

---

22. Breidert, *Die kenotische Christologie*, 175.

divine action but also the human action of Jesus. Yet Hofmann also affirmed that divine self-determination and personal self-determination cannot be separated in the man Jesus. His self-determination in relation to God, the Creator, and his personal self-determination that develops in him as a human being through the effective working of the Holy Spirit have in Jesus a unity that cannot be undone. This unity is already established at the beginning of Jesus' life, through Mary's conception, since Christ himself "has been established in a human origin by God the transcendent Creator through God the immanently effective ground of life" (ibid., 1:46). Thus, according to Hofmann, the self-giving of the Son of God, far from undermining his freedom and the reality of his humanity, is constitutive of him as a human person. This divine self-giving is the ground of Jesus' human being and is that which makes him into "the new human being," the mediator of the new "humanity of God" (*die Menschheit Gottes*), the one who restores humanity as a whole (ibid., 1:55).[23] The "completion" of the triune life of God is thus the inclusion of renewed humanity in Christ in God.[24]

Since Hofmann defined the human being as "self" or as "person," the personal relationship between God and humanity is defined as a relationship between an "eternal Self," which is in the process of "becoming," and a "developing humanity," which is the object of the eternal Self (ibid., 1:37). The eternal object of the divine will of love is Jesus as true human being. In Jesus, all of humanity is also the object of God's eternal will of love. God's will is that humanity should be God's own in Jesus Christ. Correspondingly, all human beings are called to define themselves in relation to this God that is

---

23. Barth was thus not the first modern Christian theologian to speak of "the humanity of God." See Karl Barth, "The Humanity of God" in *The Humanity of God*, 37–65. "In Jesus Christ there is no isolation of man from God or of God from man. Rather, in Him we encounter the history, the dialogue, in which God and man meet together and are together, the reality of the covenant mutually contracted, preserved, and fulfilled by them. Jesus Christ is in His one Person, as true God, man's loyal partner, and as true man, God's. He is the Lord humbled for communion with man and likewise the Servant exalted to communion with God" (ibid., 46).

24. Hofmann appears to have been not always consistent regarding the nature of "Trinitarian self-fulfillment" through the incarnation. On the one hand, he sometimes referred to God's free decision to self-determine God's self in history as the means to God's self-fulfillment as the God of love. When speaking this way, "the beginning of history" is a decision of God to allow God's self to self-differentiate God's self in history. In this way of thinking, the incarnation is the outcome of God's self-differentiation in history to be the God who is love. Here Hofmann sounds quite similar to Hegel. On the other hand, Hofmann (less frequently) spoke of the incarnation as God's free decision to redeem sinful humanity. When speaking this way, Hofmann wanted especially to differentiate himself from the Hegelian concept of the necessity of God's positing God's self in an Other for the sake of fulfilling God's self. For example, Hofmann states that "if sin had not occurred, the incarnation of the Son would not have been needed in order to realize the eternal will of the triune [God] through an historical self-fulfillment of the intra-divine relationship" (*SBb* 2.1:20). This comment does not fit easily with the more dominant view in Hofmann's theology that from eternity the triune God has freely elected humanity in Jesus Christ. The incarnation is the free decision of God to be the God of love for humanity.

"eternal being in the process of becoming," this God that determines God's self in history for the sake of humanity (ibid., 1:35).[25] So God has decided to define God's self eternally as the historical man Jesus in order to establish the beginning of the perfection of God's will of love for all humanity. Through "the man Jesus," redeemed "human nature has been accepted into the relationship of the three in God" (*DVL* 52). For Hofmann Christology is not about the "being" of the person of Christ, but about the historical relationship/communion between the man Jesus and God, his Father, that seeks to embrace all human beings in the divine love. Through the divine self-emptying or "self-renunciation" God realizes God's love for humanity. "God . . . accomplishes his will temporally in relation to humankind, that is through self-renunciation in history" (ibid., 44).

> This history is the work of Jesus. In every respect the import lies upon the concrete historical character of the work of Jesus: It is not, as in the orthodox theory, a factual achievement, the fulfillment of an abstract demand according to the scheme of forensic justice, but an historical new creation. It does not consist of a row of deeds which produce an abstract metaphysical effect, the condition for God's graciousness, but it is an interrelationship of life which indeed possesses the highest metaphysical significance, but it possesses this as the immediately living eternal religious power in its concrete historicality. Or dogmatically expressed: Christ's work is not the forensic production of the condition for grace but the historical realization of the divine will of grace itself.[26]

This passage clearly shows Hofmann's basic difference from the classic Lutheran orthodox view of vicarious satisfaction.[27] The dominant understanding of Christ's atonement in Lutheran theology had been heavily influenced by Anselm's (1033–1109) theory of "vicarious satisfaction."[28]

---

25. Compare with Jüngel: "From all eternity, God is in and of himself in such a way that he is for man. As the Eternal he is for the perishable man, whose perishability has its ground in the Pro-Being of God, a ground which prevents the process of perishing from ending in nothingness" (Jüngel, *God as the Mystery of the World,* 221).

26. Johannes v. Hofmann, as quoted from lecture notes by Wapler, "Die Genesis der Versöhnungslehre," 172. My translation differs slightly from that of Forde, *The Law-Gospel Debate,* 39.

27. On the understanding of "vicarious satisfaction" in the history of Christian theology, see Bengt Hägglund, *History of Theology* (trans. Gene Lund; St. Louis: Concordia Publishing House, 1968), 171–74; and Jaroslav Pelikan, *The Christian Tradition* (5 vols.; Chicago: The University of Chicago, 1971–1989), 4:23–25, 156–57, 161–63, 324–25, 359–61.

28. On Anselm's theology, see *St. Anselm's Basic Writings: Proslogium, Monologium, Cur Deus Homo, Gaunilo's In Behalf of the Fool* (trans. S. N. Deane; 2d ed.; intro. to 2d. ed. by Charles Hartshorne; La Salle, Ill.: Open Court Publishing, 1962), 3–46; and *A Scholastic Miscellany: Anselm to Ockham* (ed. and trans. Eugene Fairweather; Philadelphia: Westminster Press, 1956), 17–68.

This view of Christ's work maintains that God's wrath must first be appeased before God is merciful and gracious:

> If God, therefore, under the impulse of his love to men, is still to assume once more a gracious relation to them, something must first occur that can enable him to do this without derogating from his justice and holiness; the guilt that men have brought upon themselves by their sins must be removed, a ransom must be paid, an equivalent must be rendered for the offense that has been committed against God, or, what amounts to the same thing, satisfaction must be rendered. Now, as it is impossible for us men to render this, we must extol it as a special act of divine mercy that God has made it possible through Christ, and that he for this end determined upon the incarnation of Christ, so that he might render this satisfaction in our stead.[29]

For Hofmann, the mission or the work of Jesus was not to appease the wrath of an angry God; his mission was to actualize God's loving grace for all of creation and in the process remove the obstacles (e.g., sin, death, the power of the devil) that separated God from human beings.[30] In the "relation of God to the eternal Christ" the eternal will of God is directed to humanity in Christ since it is the eternal will of God "that the human being comes to be God's," that is, enters into a love-relationship with God (*SBb* 1:36).

Indeed, the "historical object" of the divine will of love is entirely contingent on the "eternal object within the intra-divine relationship" (ibid.). The historical man Jesus stands for humanity as a whole within the intra-divine relationship (*DVL* 52). God's eternal will is directed only to "humanity in Jesus Christ," which in Christ is "redeemed humanity" (*SBb* 1:221). "In the person of Jesus Christ the unity of humanity is produced once and for all in order to receive individuals now into itself" (ibid.). This is only possible on the basis of the perfect union between the man Jesus and the eternal will of the God the Father.

Since the union of Jesus with the will of God is grounded in the eternal unity of the Trinity, Christ's self-determination in obedience to God cannot

---

29. Schmid, *Doctrinal Theology of the Evangelical Lutheran Church*, 343. That this Anselmic understanding of vicarious satisfaction has been dominant within the Lutheran tradition is evident from Schmid's citations from the Lutheran Orthodox theologians. See ibid., 344–70. "The term *vicarious satisfaction* reproduces the teaching of Scripture that through Christ's substitutional obedience and death God's wrath against men was appeased, in other words, his judgment of condemnation was set aside.... It was God who laid his anger by on account of the ransom brought by Christ.... But the wrath of God struck Christ in our stead, and expending itself on him, it is changed into grace" (Pieper, *Christian Dogmatics*, 2:346–52).

30. As we will see below, for Hofmann the "wrath of God" is nothing other than the alienation from God that human beings experience as a result of their sins. The ministry of Christ is to overcome this alienation between God and human beings.

be frustrated by any historical event. The course of history between God and humanity is unequivocally certain from the beginning of creation to its fulfillment in the eschaton. This is not only true in relation to God's eternal self-determination but also in view of the object of God's love, humanity as a whole in Christ. The eternal will of God will not be frustrated, even by evil powers or through human sins. Because "the incarnate eternal God could not negate himself, Jesus the man could not sin, his humanly historical will could not contradict his immanent eternally divine will. The eternal God has become a human being precisely because this was the way to certain victory over sin" (ibid., 2.1:46).

If God's relation of love to humanity is already certain from eternity, then "the determination of the membership in the community of God is also not dependent on something human, but is only a matter of God's free will" (ibid., 1:240). God's eternal self-determination vis-à-vis humanity is grounded in God alone because God's eternal election is a decision of God's freedom. "As the personal God, he is decisive of himself, his Trinity is his self-determination internally, the predestination of humanity his self-determination externally. These three parts stand in a necessary relation to each other; each demands the other" (*ET* 60). Elsewhere, Hofmann states that it is "scriptural to teach that the intra-divine relationship is for God's relationship to people, or God is triune in order to be the God of humanity" (*SBb* 1:204). Consequently, when Hofmann spoke of "election" or "God's elect" or "divine predestination," he is referring to the redeemed community of people (Israel and the church) and to individuals only insofar as they are members of this community (i.e., ultimately included within the body of Christ). The divine election also means that God has never rejected Israel or taken away the calling which distinguished it from all other nations, namely, to be the people of *Heilsgeschichte*.[31]

The divine election of humanity in Christ serves as the basis for Hofmann's understanding of God's actions in history. According to Hofmann, God had to establish a "new beginning to history" in order to bring to an end the old history marked by evil, sin, and death. To establish such a "new beginning" God needed to break into the sinful situation of humanity. Such an "in-breaking" was necessary in order to complete God's eternal will of love for humanity and all creation, since humanity for Hofmann is the culmination of creation. This "new beginning" would re-establish God's eternal will of love for humanity (*SBb* 1:40–42).

---

31. See also J. v. Hofmann, "Zur neutestamentlichen Lehre von der Erwählung," *ZPK* 41 (1861): 326–27, where Hofmann criticizes Philippi's notion of an "election" based on God's "wrath."

The goal of the history of Jesus lies in the final realization of its initial form which was the unconditioned assumption of human nature through the divine Self. By becoming a human being, Jesus has made human nature his own. With this determination of human nature, however, humanity has already become one with God. This has originally occurred in that here for the first time this human being has become a "human being of God," and the whole further history of humanity lies enclosed in this beginning since the glorification of human nature is the beginning of the completely restored relationship between God and humankind.[32] "[S]o that the relationship of humanity to God would become different from what it was after Adam, the Father has sent the Son, the Son has entered into Adamic humanity, and the Trinity has taken human nature as the nature of the eternal Son into its intra-divine relationship" (*SS* 2:101).

Whereas Jesus' own nature is innocent in itself because it is determined from the beginning in itself through the divine Self, nonetheless Christ puts himself under "the consequences of sin" (*SBb* 2.1:35) and places himself within a life conditioned by those consequences (*DVL* 52). He thereby makes himself one with the fate of humankind (*BWE* 60–61). But such an identification with humanity brings Jesus into conflict with sin, evil, death, and even his heavenly Father. Hofmann stressed the Son's complete identification with sinful humanity. Such an identification is the concrete result of the divine self-giving, the goal of which includes the removal of the divine wrath from sinful humanity (*SS* 3:27).

> The triune God — because humanity permitted itself to be determined unto sin through the doing of Satan (which made humanity the object of God's wrath), in order to bring to completion the relationship between himself and humanity established at creation (in the perfect communion of love) — placed himself into the worst possible opposition between the Father and the Son without the self-negation of God — namely, the opposition between the Father who was wrathful because of human sin and the sinless Son, a member of this sinful humanity who proved himself faithful in all the consequences of its sin (even to the death of a criminal that befell him through Satan's doing), so that after Satan did the worst he could do to the sinless One because of sin, without achieving anything other than the final proving faithful, therein now the relationship of the Father to the Son was the

---

32. Breidert is correct to state that for Hofmann the atonement is "realized in principle with the event of the incarnation of God" (Breidert, *Die kenotische Christologie,* 181). See also Sturm, "Die integrierende Funktion der Ekklesiologie," 145. One needs to add, however, that the atonement is actualized through the entire life, death, and resurrection of Jesus, though the incarnation is the necessary condition for that realization.

relationship of God to the humanity that has begun anew in the Son, which was no longer determined by the sin of the lineage of Adam but through the righteousness of the Son. (*BA* 179–80)

The initial level of conflict is between Jesus as "the righteous Son of Adam" and the antagonism of the unrighteous sons of Adam.[33] The typology of this conflict is found already in *Heilsgeschichte,* starting with the slaying of Abel by Cain and continuing through the suffering of the "Servant of the LORD" (cf. Isa 42:1ff.) and Israel that is caused by the "unrighteous" nations. The suffering of this Servant and of the faithful in Israel came as a result of their faithfulness and obedience to God, which in turn created opposition among the unrighteous, who were held captive to the power of sin and thus experienced the historical wrath of God.[34] Yet the goal of such an experience of divine wrath was to cause the oppressors to repent of the suffering they had caused so that they might be transformed.[35] So, too, with Jesus: by remaining obedient in his calling, even to the point of death at the hands of the unrighteous, Jesus fulfills his prophetic office to bear witness to God's eternal will of love for humanity. This obedience of Jesus is the most profound meaning of the *kenosis* of God, who willingly went the way of suffering love for the sake of humanity. In other words, for Hofmann, the *tapeinosis* ("humiliation") of the Son is the consequence of the *kenosis* in the life of the incarnate Word (*Logos*) in Jesus. The *kenosis,* through which the historical Trinity has assumed a new form of dissimilarity, refers to Christ's relationship to God the transcendent Creator. The humiliation (*tapeinosis*) of the Son, through which the archetypal world-goal had to endure the limitations and conditions placed on human beings as a result of sin, refers to Christ's relationship to all other human beings. The humiliation (*tapeinosis*) of Christ places Christ in opposition to God, insofar as Christ shares in the sufferings and death that all people experience.

So Hofmann admitted that Jesus also suffered under the wrath of God. For the sake of his sinless nature Jesus is the object of "the eternal will of love" since the love of God is not directed toward human beings as sinners but toward Christ in his self-determination, toward him as "the human being that is becoming." As sinner, the human being stands under the "wrath of God" and Jesus as human being also stands under the effects of this wrath. Consequently, in this way the Son gets into a conflict with the Father and

---

33. See *SBa* 2.1:115–139, where Hofmann traces this conflict through various biblical stories.

34. See *SS* 3:14–15, where Hofmann describes sin as a satanic power that hands people over to death.

35. So Forde, *The Law-Gospel Debate,* 40–41.

the historical "dissimilarity" of the eternal divine relationship reaches its greatest dissimilarity (*DVL* 52).[36] Against Schleiermacher, Hofmann stated:

> The history that has commenced with the incarnation arises...in part from the form into which the intra-divine relationship has thereby entered and in part from the purpose for which it entered into it. Since the opposition of God the Father and his Son, who was subjected to the consequences of sin, had its ground in the contradiction which needed to be resolved between the eternal divine will of love and the sin of humanity crying out for the wrath of God, it will therefore have been executed to the point where the Son's personal relationship with the Father under the full consequence of sin, even into death, was proven [preserved] to the end and thereby that contradiction was resolved in his person. (*SBb* 1:47)

Although the Son of God preserved his obedient and loving relationship with God the Father to the very end of his earthly life in death, the suffering and death of Jesus brought him to a situation wherein he experienced the ultimate separation from God, his Father. By going to that point that was most separated from God, the situation of sinful humanity, the Son of God removed the opposition between God's eternal love and God's historical wrath in his own person. This is how the Son of God is to be affirmed as the mediator between God and humanity. "Jesus endured to the end in that he suffered in the most extreme manner the full force of the opposition focused on him because of sin (the activity of the contra-divine forces acting through man)."[37]

Clearly, the historical "contradiction" between God and Christ could be overcome because the "eternal identity of the Trinitarian relationship" serves as its fundamental cause (*TE* 28). The preexistent archetypal world-goal has determined to proceed out from its transcendent way of being eternal into the temporal way of being a human being in order to establish the divine will of love for temporal human beings. So the obedience of Jesus is not merely "passive," i.e., receiving suffering in himself; it is also "active." According to Hofmann, the active obedience of Jesus must be understood as Jesus' free decision to sacrifice himself, to empty himself of his human life, in his struggle against all that is arrayed against God. While the "personal communion" between the Word and the Father remains constant, even within the experience of this contradiction (due to human finitude, suffering, and

---

36. See also *TE* 59, where Hofmann discusses "the solution of the contradiction in the person of Jesus" (*Die Lösung des Widerspruchs in der Person Jesu*). Here Hofmann sounds very similar to Hegel, even if Hofmann could not admit to the similarity.

37. Forde, *The Law-Gospel Debate*, 28.

death), the Son of God is obediently self-sacrificial even unto death — the reality that spells a break in the human-divine relationship — so that God the Father might establish by grace a renewed relationship of life between God and humanity. Thus, the biblical type of "sacrifice" also receives its historical fulfillment in the person of Jesus. The free decision of Jesus to give his life "as a sacrifice for many" (Mk 10:45) is Jesus' active struggle against the powers of sin arrayed against God and humanity.

In view of his understanding of Trinitarian *kenosis,* Hofmann offered a creative reinterpretation of the passive obedience of Christ to the divine will of love, which leads to Christ's suffering and death at the hands of sinful people, and Christ's active obedience to the divine will of love by which Christ sacrifices himself freely in order to overcome the alienation and antagonism between God and sinful humanity.[38] Jesus' obedience to the Father proves itself "under all the consequences of sin...even in death," so that "this contradiction" in the "person" of Jesus Christ is "overcome." By means of the "righteousness of the Son of God that proves itself all the way to the end," both passively (suffering the sin of the people) and actively (removing the consequences of sin from the people), reconciliation between God and humanity has occurred and the new communion between God and humanity has been established.

In Jesus' obedience the relationship between God and humankind experiences now "its determination," "no longer on the basis of the sins which are being propagated by humanity," but on the basis of Jesus' will of love (*SBb* 1:48). Since "death as a consequence of sin" has lost its effect in the new relationship between God and humankind established in Jesus, it follows, according to Hofmann, that Jesus the man could "not remain in death" (ibid.). In this transition from death to life the personal communion between the Father and the Son fulfills itself, and this is why the resurrection of Jesus is understood to be both an act of the personal self-determination of the Son as well as the work of God the Father. The resurrection of Jesus means that Jesus lives as Messiah and Lord from the power of God. Christ's resurrection from the dead is the assurance that God has won the ultimate victory over the creaturely forces arrayed against God. Sin and evil spent themselves in their attack on the eternal archetypal world-goal, the historical Son of God, and in the process they were overcome.

Just as the first Adam marked the beginning of humanity, so now Christ, "the second Adam," marks the beginning of "a new human nature" (*DVL* 103; BWE 57). Indeed, Christ is "the new human being" (*DVL* 102). Hofmann called this new human existence the transfigured (*verklärte*) existence,

---

38. Ibid., 44.

the existence of the risen Christ. He is no longer merely a human being, but he has entered

> into a new kind of human life in which he now possessed his nature as the unconditioned means of participation in his eternally and historically completed communion with God the Father, so that in him an unconditioned communion of God with humanity was realized and his participation in the same in relation to the Father and to humanity was from now on the mediation of the relationship of God and humanity. (*SBb* 1:48)

Still, although the exalted Jesus becomes God again in his exaltation, he does not give up his humanity but remains a human being. Only his relationship to God the Father becomes different. In this exalted position he has now become the mediator who has overcome the actions of God against humanity and the actions of humanity against God. Thus, atonement is not merely the incarnation of the *Logos* in the man Jesus, nor is it merely the death of Jesus on the cross; for Hofmann the atonement is the whole life, death, and resurrection of Jesus. The whole movement of atonement is the Trinitarian, kenotic process by which the new relationship between God and humanity is realized.

Although the Son now exists in the communion of the transcendent Lordship of the Father, he exercises his self-giving power through his earthly, historical community that is even now being extended through the world. Thus, it is clear that the historical dissimilarity of the Trinity has not ended with the exaltation of Christ, since this history has continued even after the ascension of Christ. This reality means that Christ is only "the beginning of the end" of history that has begun "in the middle of history" (*BWE* 55–57). In other words, a new historical process, analogous to the beginning of creation, was begun by Christ. Only with the conclusion of all history is the historical self-fulfillment of the Trinity complete, and thereby the historical Trinity of dissimilarity comes back into the eternal intra-divine self-equality.

The effective power at work within this new historical-Trinitarian process is the Spirit. On the way to the fulfillment of the Trinity, "the physically living man, Jesus Christ, sets his Spirit, that is, the Spirit of his physical life, as nothing less than the indwelling ground of life of a world, namely, the one that needs to be, and has been, restored, just as God the creator [gives] his [Spirit] as the indwelling ground of life for the creating and created world" (*SBb* 2.1:540). The Spirit which Jesus gives to the world is the "Spirit of the living Christ in his glorified human nature" (*ET* 95). With the resurrection, therefore, Jesus' relationship to the Spirit has become different. Jesus' human nature has been penetrated by the Spirit in such a way that its finitude is transformed. "But in order for [Jesus] to impart the life of his Spirit to his members, he had to leave the world and go to the Father, and thereby exchange the limits of the immanent life for the communion of the transcendent life of his Father: the outpouring of the Spirit was the expansion of the transcendence which he had entered" (*SBa* 1:169). The event of Pentecost, therefore, is like the event of the incarnation in that both historical events have contributed to a new form of the historical Trinity. With the pouring out of the Holy Spirit, the Spirit has been changed since it is now both transcendent in the risen Christ and also immanent in the church.

Through this Spirit people participate in the glorified nature of Christ and the beginning of a renewed world has been inaugurated (*WE* 2:299). To be a Christian is to be aware that one participates in the transfigured or glorified nature of Christ, to be included in his body, the church.[39] Kliefoth was therefore correct to note that according to Hofmann "the glorified human nature" of the risen Christ is "the new substance of life, which he mediates to the world; through this mediation, he renews and glorifies the world."[40] Yet Christ's presence is not ubiquitous: His Lordship over the world is only gradually spreading through the immanent Spirit through the church, i.e., only to the degree that humanity becomes the humanity of God (*SBb* 2.1:534; *SBb* 1:55).[41] The fulfillment of that Lordship will only occur at the eschaton, when God will be "all in all."

The Atonement Controversy[42]

Hofmann knew that his teaching on the atonement would generate controversy with his fellow Lutheran theologians in Germany, so he was prepared for the theological attacks that soon followed the publication of the first edition of his *Schriftbeweis*. The course of the debate suggests that he was also prepared to expend considerable time and energy in defending his theological views.

---

39. Ibid., 29.

40. Kliefoth, *Der Schriftbeweis*, 503.

41. See also *WE* 1:39–40, where Hofmann describes the church as "the body of Christ" in the world. "The body of Christ" is both an earthly, imperfect community and an historical institution that points ahead to the perfect communion with God in the *eschaton*. The entire life of the congregation is "the self-representation of Christ in the world" and thus a prophecy of the final form of the communion between God and humanity (ibid., 40).

42. On the controversy over Hofmann's doctrine of the atonement, see especially Bachmann, *Hofmanns Versöhnungslehre*, 36–61; Hein, *Lutherisches Bekenntnis*, 254–71; Forde, *The Law-Gospel Debate*, 12–78; Wolff, *Die Haupttypen der neueren Lutherdeutung*; and Wenz, 2:46–62. Hein demonstrates that both Hofmann and his opponents attempted to appeal to the Lutheran Confessions in order to settle their disagreements. Wolff demonstrates Hofmann's importance for the renewal of the modern study of Luther's theology.

Among the first to attack Hofmann's teaching on the atonement was Friedrich Philippi (1809–1882), professor of theology at Dorpat and Rostock, and one who was deeply influenced by Hengstenberg. In the preface to the second edition of his commentary on Romans, Philippi accused Hofmann of transposing "the objective biblical and ecclesial doctrine of reconciliation and the doctrine of justification" into a subjective key that separates God's love and God's holiness.[43] Philippi attempted to defend the traditional understanding of vicarious satisfaction which maintained a juridical framework. Most important for Philippi was defending the ideas that God's law is eternal and that God's wrath is grounded in the very justice of God, which is also eternal.

Philippi's initial attack on Hofmann's teaching and the tone of his accusations, led Hofmann to write a critical response (*BA* 175–82).[44] While Hofmann admitted that there were differences between his understanding of the atonement and that of Philippi, he stated in this article that one must make a distinction between the actual faith of the church and the form which conveys or expresses that faith. Hofmann thought, however, that the form of the traditional understanding needed to be improved and that his formulation did so. The problem with the traditional view that Philippi defended is that it does not deal adequately with the theological significance of Christ's suffering. The juridical framework of the traditional understanding does not account sufficiently for Christ's patient endurance in his prophetic calling under "the consequences of sin" in order to establish a new humanity in his death and resurrection. Likewise, Hofmann argued, the juridical framework is deficient since it implies that the atonement was the result of a transaction or payment and not as the result of a free gift grounded in God's eternal will of love. The traditional understanding of the vicarious satisfaction is also conceptually weak in that it does not indicate how the work of Christ has actually changed the relationship between humanity and God. Furthermore, in the old scheme of vicarious satisfaction, Christian faith is directed to a past event. This orientation of faith, however, is incapable of conceptualizing how this faith is mediated in the present through the risen Christ, who establishes individuals in a new relationship with God. In the old system, faith merely accepts the knowledge of past events and thus is conceptually removed from active participation in the benefits of those events in the present. According to Hofmann, only in the present "factual situation" (*Tatbestand*) are past, present, and future brought into an organic unity in the risen Christ. Most problematic of all, for Hofmann, was the

---

43. Friedrich Philippi, *Commentar über den Brief Pauli an die Römer* (2d ed.; Erlangen: Heyder & Zimmer, 1856), x–xi.

44. See also Forde's analysis, *The Law-Gospel Debate*, 50–51.

traditional view that God's righteousness must first be appeased or satisfied before God can be loving and merciful toward humanity, but Hofmann also found unpersuasive the idea that the atonement involved Christ suffering as "another" alongside of humanity, that is, as one who died "in the place of humanity." Hofmann rejected this idea since it did not truly reflect the biblical relationship between God and humanity in Christ, at least as he understood that relationship.

> How I grasp the mystery of our reconciliation results from an understanding of the incarnation of our Redeemer. What else is the history, the result of which is our reconciliation, other than the fulfillment of that relationship with God the Father into which the Son has entered through his incarnation? In contrast, [the notion] that the punishment of our sin was put upon him instead of on us is a self-generated mysterium which also therefore does not follow from his incarnation. This idea has its origin in the fact that one devises one's own thoughts about how God must have worked to expiate sin instead of learning from holy history how he has expiated our sin. (*SS* 2:106)

Philippi was so disturbed by Hofmann's response that he wrote in the same year a separate treatise that further attacked Hofmann's theological assertions.[45] In this treatise Philippi set forth a detailed defense of the traditional doctrine of the vicarious satisfaction of Christ. Philippi maintained that the justification of sinners through faith is entirely dependent on the objectivity of the salvific events (ibid., 7–8). The righteousness of Christ is entirely objective, outside of the individual (*extra nos*), and is merely imputed to the sinner forensically. An individual sinner receives such imputation solely by faith. Justification, in other words, is entirely a matter of forensic imputation and not the participation of the individual believer in the new humanity in Christ. For Philippi, the imputation of grace *extra nos* is distinct from the Thomistic notion of infused grace (*gratia infusa*), which Philippi accused Hofmann of holding (ibid., 28). Philippi also defended the traditional understanding that the love and wrath of God are "antithetical determinations in the divine nature" (ibid., 33). Humankind's sin is understood as the infinite injury to the majesty of God's holiness that can only be undone by means of an infinitely valuable satisfaction. In this satisfaction the God-man expiates the infinite blame of human sin by taking it onto himself. Christ has endured the pains of hell for us which exist "essentially and chiefly in his abandonment by God and in his positive expulsion and

---

45. Friedrich Philippi, *Herr Dr. von Hofmann gegenüber der lutherischen Versöhnungs- und Rechtfertigungslehre* (Erlangen: T. Bläsing, 1856).

exclusion from communion with God" (ibid., 39). According to Philippi, the atonement of Christ resolves the tension between God's holiness and love. The Christian receives the resolution of the contradiction between God's holiness and God's love by faith in the death of the God-man. Only the sure knowledge that the God-man has suffered God's wrath will bring peace to a guilty conscience. While Philippi held out that indeed in principle God's atonement is grounded in God's love, God cannot be loving toward sinners at the expense of his holiness (ibid., 35). God's love cannot be given until God's holiness is satisfied vis-à-vis human sin. Thus, according to Philippi, the main problem with Hofmann's theology is its inability to understand the death of Christ as the satisfaction of God's wrath against human sin. Hofmann's doctrine of atonement only speaks of a change in the attitude of human beings toward God, while God's love toward human beings remains constant even in view of human sin (ibid., 44). Philippi concluded that Hofmann's understanding of the atonement led Hofmann to a view which must admit that there is no objective necessity for the atonement (ibid., 36).[46]

Philippi's second attack led Hofmann to counter-attack in the first of his four "defensive writings" (*Schutzschriften*), which clarifies that Hofmann's theological methodology necessitated the reformulation of church teaching about the atonement.[47] Hofmann accused Philippi of completely misunderstanding his reformulation of "the old truth" regarding the atonement. For example, Hofmann indicated that he did not teach that reconciliation was the result of a subjective change (e.g., repentance and faith) in human beings, but the result of what God had done in the incarnation, ministry, the death, and the resurrection of Jesus to change God's relationship with humanity. Hofmann stressed that Philippi had not seen clearly the inseparable unity of God's love and holiness. According to Hofmann, the "love" of God cannot be viewed as an "attribute" of God, but only as God's basic orientation toward the world. Therefore the love of God and the holiness of God cannot be viewed as in conflict with each other (*SS* 1:12). The love of God is God's self-determination, the essential self-activity of the divine Self, while God's holiness is the expression of the same self-determining identity of the triune God. As the Holy One, God is the uniquely existing one whose being is self-determined (ibid., 1:13ff.; see also *SBb* 1:83). The love and holiness

---

46. " . . . [W]hen the rational framework demanded by the orthodox system has been denied, atonement is divested of the necessity which the framework gave it. Philippi can no longer make sense of the atonement when the system based on law is removed" (Forde, *The Law-Gospel Debate*, 53).

47. This first *Schutzschrift* appeared in 1856, the year before the second edition of the *Schriftbeweis*. In the second edition of his *Schriftbeweis*, Hofmann included references to the traditional language concerning the "wrath of God," but he reinterpreted the wrath to coincide with his understanding of *kenosis*. See also Wapler, "Die Theologie Hofmanns, 714.

of God therefore stand for the uniform self-fulfillment of the triune God. God enters history on the basis of God's eternal will of love. In view of the reality of sin, however, God's love is turned into "wrath against sinful humanity" (*TE* 58). Nevertheless, God remains as such self-determining and self-realizing in history. Jesus, through his incarnation, enters into the opposition between the love of God and the wrath of God. But his entrance into this opposition is only an "apparent contradiction," since the personal communion between the Father and the Son remains constant, grounded in the eternal self-determination of God toward humankind (*DVL* 103). The historical wrath of God is unequivocally subordinate to the eternally and historically fulfilled divine will of love, which cannot be frustrated even by sin and evil. Because the love of God is directed to the creation of the "newly begun humanity" in Christ, this new beginning must develop at the same time that the divine wrath is vented against sins (*SS* 1:7). This means that the new relationship between God and humanity could not be established without bringing the old creation, marked by sin and death, to an end. Such an end, Hofmann argued, has occurred in Jesus, who has accomplished the expiation (*Sühnung*) of sin in his own suffering, death, and resurrection (ibid., 1:17). The eternal will of love of the triune God has realized itself in the life of Jesus, even as "the anger of the holy God against sins is necessary," but the love overcomes the wrath (ibid., 1:7). So the atonement of Christ is not an accident, according to Hofmann, but the necessary action of the self-giving God to inaugurate a new creation and bring the old one to an end. Such a necessity is grounded in the historical development of God's eternal will of love for creation.

Following Philippi's attack on Hofmann's teaching and Hofmann's response, other theologians also joined the discussion. For example, Dorner criticized Hofmann's understanding of *kenosis* because it does not allow Christ

> to develop to independence over and against God, as reconciliation requires. The substitutionary atonement would necessarily become a mere empty game, if the Son of Man were only a disguised God and not a genuine human being with a soul. Instead of atonement (accomplished to be sure through the power of the Logos) there would be left for this developing deity only the exhibition of obedience, through which communion with God is supposed to be achieved. The defects in Hofmann's doctrine of reconciliation are closely related to those in his Christology.[48]

---

48. Dorner, *Divine Immutability*, 63.

For Dorner, Hofmann's kenotic Christology came at too high a cost. Dorner accused Hofmann of Docetism, since Jesus is not a genuine human being but God who has changed into a human being, and he accused Hofmann of denying a human soul to Jesus.[49]

Closer to home, Hofmann's Erlangen colleagues Thomasius and Harnack sided with Philippi's argument, if not with his tone, and criticized Hofmann for departing from the Lutheran confessional understanding of vicarious satisfaction.[50] Thomasius and Harnack held that the traditional, confessional understanding of vicarious satisfaction is the only proper presupposition of the doctrine of justification and not a dispensable theory, as Hofmann maintained.[51] Thomasius appealed to Luther for assistance in defending the necessity of the theory of vicarious satisfaction (ibid., 22). Like Philippi, Thomasius was especially disturbed by Hofmann's understanding of the relation of divine wrath to God's love. If Christ was fully conscious of the divine will of love which is the ground of his incarnation, ministry, and death, then Christ did not truly suffer the divine judgment and wrath in himself (ibid., 100). By denying that Jesus suffered the wrath of God in the place of humanity, Hofmann was accused by Thomasius of rejecting an essential element in the Christian gospel. For if Christ has not suffered the wrath of God in the place of humanity, then his suffering is no different from the sufferings of other righteous people. If this is true, according to Thomasius, then there is no real relationship between God's wrath and Christ's suffering, as Hofmann himself maintained. If the divine will of love is the foundation for Christ's suffering and death, then Christ has not truly suffered to the degree he must in order to expiate all that is truly against human beings. According to Thomasius, the persistence of Jesus' consciousness of his eternal origin in the divine will of love throughout his earthly life and death minimizes the qualitatively different degree that is essential to the calling of the mediator between God and humanity. A true mediator between God and humanity

---

49. Contrary to Dorner's criticism, Hofmann expressly stated that in the incarnation "the archetypal world-goal" had become a complete human being. Likewise, "Christ has a mental life that is no different from that which is born of every other woman" (*SBb* 2.1:43). According to Hofmann, Jesus participated in a human development that did not differ from any other human being.

50. Thomasius, *Das Bekenntnis der lutherischen Kirche*. More recently, Robert Schultz has attacked Hofmann's theology for reasons similar to Thomasius's. See Schultz, *Gesetz und Evangelium*, 110–20. Contrary to Kantzenbach, Schultz emphasizes the differences among the Erlangen theologians, especially the contrast between Harless and Hofmann, and argues that Hofmann's theology was generally destructive of Lutheran theology, since it rejected the vicarious atonement.

51. Thomasius, *Das Bekenntnis*, 21.

must satisfy the divine wrath.[52] Thus, Thomasius and Harnack stressed that Christ has taken the divine judgment against human sin onto himself in his death and by thus suffering God's wrath has reconciled the world to God.

Hofmann responded to his Erlangen colleagues in the second and third "defensive writings" (*Schutzschriften*).[53] He continued to deny that the traditional understanding of vicarious satisfaction belongs to the essential content of the gospel and to affirm that such an understanding was merely an historical form of doctrine that could be changed without loss to the substance of the faith. To prove his point, Hofmann conducted his own study of Luther's writings to try to demonstrate that Luther's understanding of justification did not need to be tied to the traditional Lutheran formulation of vicarious satisfaction and that Luther himself had often spoken of Christ's death and resurrection as a victory over Satan's attack upon Christ (*SS* 2:23–83). The eternal Son of God has become a human being in order to do battle against Satan and the tyrannical powers of sin, death, and evil, in order to win the victory for all humanity.[54] Luther's doctrine of justification does not require a theory of vicarious satisfaction (*SS* 2:35–39).[55]

---

52. Harnack's "afterword" to Thomasius's response to Hofmann stresses the same point. Like Philippi, Harnack asserted that the juridical framework is essential to a proper understanding of the atonement. See ibid., 138.

53. The second *Schutzschrift* appeared in 1857 and the third in 1859.

54. Compare Hofmann's reading of Luther's theology at this point with that of Gustaf Aulèn, *Christus Victor* (trans. A. G. Hebert; New York: Macmillan, 1951), 101–22. "It may be roundly stated that no side of Luther's theology has been more summarily treated or more grossly misinterpreted than his teaching on the Atonement. The fundamental mistake has been the assumption that his teaching on this subject belongs to the Anselmian type.... Luther's interpretation of Christ's work has all the typical characteristics of the classic Idea of Atonement.... First, there is here a continuity of Divine operation. Time after time Luther returns to this theme and emphasizes it with all his might: the one power which is able to overcome the tyrants [sin, death, power of the devil] is God's omnipotence. If the tyrants were victorious, then were God Himself overcome. But now almighty God Himself steps in and carries His work to victory. Second, the Atonement is once again closely connected with the Incarnation.... Third, the whole view is dualistic and dramatic. The description is of a stupendous conflict, a *mirabile duellum*, in which Christ prevails" (ibid., 101, 107–8). Aulèn (1879–1977) did not even mention Hofmann's atonement theory, even though the "fact that Hofmann set Luther against orthodoxy on the question of atonement was in itself vitally important not only for the subsequent history of the debate but for the history of modern theology as well. It meant that the argument about the atonement would become inextricably involved with the argument about Luther's theology" (Forde, *The Law-Gospel Debate*, 64). See also Hirsch, *Geschichte*, 5:427.

55. Hofmann's retrieval of the classic "victory motif" in Luther's understanding of the atonement was embarrassing to most nineteenth-century Lutheran theologians, who really didn't know what to do with it since it conflicted with the orthodox view of vicarious satisfaction. "Despite all the criticism and further correction which took place in Hofmann's doctrine of the atonement, one may not lessen the deep achievement of Hofmann in going back to Luther.... Hofmann, the interpreter of the Bible, rediscovered the reformer, who called himself Doktor biblicus. Hofmann was the most significant Erlanger theologian and the most important student of Martin Luther in the 19th Century" (Kantzenbach, *Die Erlanger Theologie*, 208).

Hofmann was particularly attracted to Luther's first congregational hymn, "Dear Christians, One and All Rejoice" (*Nun freut euch, lieben Christen gemein*), the ten verses of which recount "how God's right arm the vict'ry won."[56]

One must point out, however, that Hofmann *did* admit in the course of his argument that he could have accepted a reinterpretation of the vicarious nature of Christ's reconciling work. In the third *Schutzschrift,* Hofmann acknowledged that in a certain sense Christ put himself "in the place of humanity."

> The Son has done over against the Father what was possible only for the eternal holiness and has suffered the wrath of the Father against humanity, as the eternally beloved alone could suffer it. Herein he took humanity's place and has accomplished that which was impossible for humanity to accomplish for itself over against the triune [God]. In this sense, but only in this sense, can his work be called vicarious. (*SS* 3:28)[57]

A very interesting and important ambiguity lies in the phrase, *"ist er für die Menschheit eingetreten...."* It can mean "take or fill (someone's) place" or "take (someone's) part, champion (someone's) cause, stick up for (someone)." As "the new human being," Christ suffered "as a human being," but not in the sense that his death is to be equated with the penalty which humanity deserved. Rather, the confessional expression, *"Christus, quia sine peccato subiit poenam peccati et victima pro nobis factus est...,"* means that Christ, through his complete identification with sinful humanity, has suffered in himself all of the consequences of sin, even death, which is the most extreme consequence of sin (*SS* 3:27–28).[58] In death, the kenotic Christ came to that situation that put him most at odds with God the Father. But this separation between the Father and the Son was not the work of the Father or Son, but the work of Satan against the Son. Hofmann could never say that God the Father put Jesus, God's Son, to death on the cross.

> The Son is not the object of God's wrath, even if only in a representative manner, but humanity is. And the punishment which would have

---

56. A translation of this hymn is printed as Hymn 299 in *Lutheran Book of Worship* (Minneapolis: Augsburg, 1978).

57. Forde mistranslates this passage by omitting the important reference to the Trinity. See Forde, *The Law-Gospel Debate,* 67.

58. "Christ, because he was without sin, was made to suffer the penalty of sins and was made a victim for us" (Apology 4:179). See also *HS* 2.3:158–65, where Hofmann offers a similar understanding for how God "made him who knew no sin to be sin for us" (2 Cor. 5:21). That God made Christ "to be sin" means that Christ, by making himself completely one with sinful humanity, suffered in himself all the effects of sin, including death.

been visited upon unredeemed humanity for eternity was not executed
on the Son, but his vocation as Savior was the reason for all of his sufferings, which his vocation brought along with itself as a consequence
of his entering Adamic humanity. (*SS* 2:103)

Partly as a result of the controversy over the atonement, Hofmann further
defined the meaning of Jesus' suffering and death in the second edition of
his *Schriftbeweis*. The suffering and death of Jesus mean

first, that Jesus died the death of a criminal through [the actions of]
his people; second, that he became subject to this death only because
he wanted to maintain himself over against this most extreme effect
of the antigodly will; and third, that through this fulfillment and this
result of his life's work he has established a relationship between God
and humanity realized in his person which was no more conditioned
by sin. (*SBb* 2.1:115)

In view of this reconstruction, Hofmann could even admit that he accepted
a modified understanding of vicarious satisfaction. But clearly, the death
of Jesus is not a "penalty" for sin (as in Anselm), but the triune God's
identification with sinners and their experience on the basis of the triune
eternal will of love.

The Triune One has completed his work for which he stepped into
the opposition between the Father, who was wrathful against sinful
humanity, and the Son, who entered that humanity (though he did not
share in its sin as something he did, but indeed bore it in his suffering,
doing so by means of the resolution of this opposition). And this Triune
God has bestowed historically an eternal righteousness upon humanity
(i.e., within the history of humanity itself) as it was as a result of sin,
i.e., under the plight and conditions which God's wrath brought with
itself, but which eternal righteousness came to be historically by virtue
of the eternal divinity of the Son. This now is a righteousness that
belongs to everyone who lets it be given to him. (*SS* 2:104)

Because of Trinitarian *kenosis*, the eternal Son of God has suffered as a
human being, as the true human being, for the sake of all human beings.
Only in this sense would Hofmann have been willing to continue to use the
expression "vicarious atonement."

Despite Hofmann's best efforts over the better part of a decade to per-
suade his opponents that his view grappled seriously with the necessity of
Christ's kenotic-tapeinotic death on the cross, they were never reconciled to

Hofmann's "new way to teach the old truth."[59] After a decade of sometimes bitter argument, general exhaustion finally led the principals to give up on each other. "The opponents had exhausted their respective arguments and new problems crowded into their field of vision...."[60] Hofmann turned to his last great work, a commentary on the individual parts of the New Testament canon.

59. See Wenz, Geschichte, 2:59–62. More irenic in tone, but just as critical of Hofmann's understanding of "sacrifice" was his friend, Franz Delitzsch, whose commentary on the book of Hebrews was written partly to refute Hofmann's rejection of the orthodox understanding of vicarious satisfaction. See Franz Delitzsch, Commentar zum Briefe an die Hebräer: Mit archäologischen und dogmatischen Excursen über das Opfer und die Versöhnung (Leipzig: 1857); ET: Commentary on the Epistle to the Hebrews (trans. Thomas Kingsbury; Edinburgh: T & T Clark, 1868). See also idem, "Prolegomena über den bisherigen Entwicklungsgang der Grundbegriffe der Versöhnungslehre," in Vom Zorne Gottes: Ein biblisch-theologischer Versuch (ed. Ferdinand Weber; Erlangen: Bläsing, 1862), 5–46. For Delitzsch's friendship with Hofmann, see Siegfried Wagner, Franz Delitzsch: Leben und Werk (2d ed.; Giessen: Brunnen, 1991), 110–23 and 183–98.

60. Wenz, Geschichte, 2:60. As a result of the controversy, Hofmann did revise several sections of his Schriftbeweis, in order to account more fully for the concept of human guilt and the experience of God as wrathful. See SBb 1:45–47; 2.1:473ff. See also Bachmann, Hofmanns Versöhnungslehre, 53.

CHAPTER TEN

The Future of Humanity:
The Church in the World

According to Hofmann, the meaning of salvation history (*Heilsgeschichte*) is the "self-emptying" (*kenosis*) of the triune God, understood as the process of divine self-differentiation in history that culminates in the incarnation of the Word (*Logos*) of God in Jesus and the eschatological gift of the Spirit. The history and future of humanity can therefore only be understood properly within the context of the historical self-giving of the triune God who is love. The eternal will of God is directed toward the perfection of the communion of love between God and all human beings. "[T]he content of all history is the completion of the divine will of love" (*DVL* 49). While the human community has disintegrated into fragmentary and divisive groups (e.g., Hofmann's interpretation of Gen 4–11), it is God's will that humanity become unified as "the new humanity in Christ" (e.g., Hofmann's interpretation of the biblical story of Pentecost). This new humanity is already prefigured in the call of Abram (Gen 12:1–3) and the history of his family, including the promise to David (2 Sm 7:16), that culminates in the coming of Jesus, "a son of David, a son of Abraham" (Matt 1:1), and the divine blessing of all the nations of the world. The advent of Christ marks the beginning of the new creation. In the new creation "the church which originated in Abraham and was brought to its completion in Christ" will become "the fulfilled humanity of God" (*BH* 256). While the whole of humanity does not stand within this new relationship to God, the new humanity has begun in Christ, who continues to act through his church to bring others into communion with God. The church as the "humanity of Christ" participates in this new communion with God through the mediation of the risen Christ. He is "the beginner of a new human community," which is not merely a collection of individuals related to the risen Christ, but truly is a "community" (*Gemeinschaft*) of God (*DVL* 104).

While Christ continues to work in and through the church to extend his community throughout all creation, the historical development of the extension of this community of the triune God has its eschatological fulfillment only in the end of history (*ET* 90). Only with the conclusion of all history is the historical self-fulfillment of the Trinity complete.[1] Thereby the historical Trinity of dissimilarity comes back into the eternal intra-divine self-equality. Consequently, the historical self-fulfillment of the Trinity necessarily includes the historical development and eschatological perfection of the Christian church. With the perfection of the church, which stands already under the Lordship of the risen Christ, the rest of creation will reach its divinely-intended goal of "Sabbath rest" in God. Thus, for Hofmann, eschatology is a subcategory of ecclesiology. The relationship of ecclesiology to eschatology, including the implications of Hofmann's doctrine of God for his doctrine of the church and for his understanding of universal history, completes Hofmann's doctrine of God.

The Mediation of Faith, Hope, and Love

"Because Christianity does not consist of a number of doctrinal propositions, nor of a number of chief teachings and subordinate teachings, but is the community between God and humanity which is given in Christ," the Christian community should be understood as the effective domain of the risen Christ wherein the mediation between God and humanity occurs (*SKS* 164). "Theology finds the relationship between God and humanity in Christ expressed also in the church, in the totality of the participants in this relationship" (*DVW* 383). Christ "establishes the congregation through whose service he places individuals into his community" (*WE* 1:47). The risen Christ accomplishes this placement through the effective working of his Spirit, the "Spirit of the transformed human life of Jesus," which transforms the human nature of sinful human beings into the nature of "the humanity of God" (*ET* 89; *SBb* 1:55). Through the pouring out of the Holy Spirit "individual believers are formed into a unique community" (ibid., 1:49). This Holy Spirit, the Spirit of the risen Christ, is thus also the common Spirit of the church in whom the church has its unity. Consequently, the congregation of transformed individuals is not the result of the free self-determination of individuals to form themselves into a community; rather, the congregation is grounded in God's eternal self-determination which centers in the life, death, and resurrection of Jesus, and the effective working of God's Holy

---

1. In this regard, Hofmann's understanding of the Trinity is different from Jüngel's and closer to Pannenberg's and Moltmann's respective views which emphasize the historical fulfillment of the divine life only in the eschaton. See Moltmann, "The Unity of the Trinity," in *The Trinity and the Kingdom,* 177–78, and Pannenberg, "The World as the History of God and the Unity of the Divine Essence," in *Systematic Theology,* 1:327–36.

Spirit.[2] Likewise, the present rebirth experience of the individual Christian is not grounded in an immediate self-determination of the individual, but only in the effective working of the Spirit of Christ through the mediation of preaching and sacraments within the congregation (*ET* 87).[3] Both "the personal rebirth" experience and "the establishment of the congregation" are the real effects of the working of the Holy Spirit (*SBb* 2.2:27). Just as humanity is determined through a common human nature, so the Christian congregation is defined and determined through the Spirit of Christ who acts to transform human nature within the congregation (*DVL* 104).[4] Thus, for Hofmann, authentic Christian life is disposed to the kind of communal orientation which Hofmann holds so high, for it is a life that is ordered primarily to faith that is active in loving obedience, and such obedience always involves "others."

According to Hofmann, God sustains the life of the church through the mediation of God's grace in the written and proclaimed word of God and in the sacraments, but also through the extension of God's love through Christian service in the world. Thus, the seventh doctrinal part of Hofmann's doctrinal summary (*Lehrganze*) concerns the means of grace and church offices, but also the ethical responsibilities of Christians. In this seventh doctrinal section, Hofmann stresses that the church itself is the first, basic sacrament, from which all other sacraments are derived.[5] Through Christ's

---

2. See also *CF*, sec. 121–23. Here Schleiermacher writes, "All who are living in the state of sanctification feel an inward impulse to become more and more one in their common co-operative activity and reciprocal influence, and are conscious of this as the common Spirit of the new corporate life founded by Christ" (*CF* 560). "Only after the departure of Christ from earth was it possible for the Holy Spirit, as this common spirit, to be fully communicated and received" (ibid., 565). "The Holy Spirit is the union of the Divine Essence with human nature in the form of the common Spirit animating the life in common of believers" (ibid., 569).

3. See also Behr, *Politischer Liberalismus*, 105. According to Ritschl, the importance of Hofmann's renewed thinking about the atonement resides in the intimate connection he articulated between the faithfulness of Christ to establish reconciliation between God and humanity and the establishment of a new historical community that is grounded in this reconciliation. See Ritschl, *Rechtfertigung und Versöhnung*, 1:620.

4. "The fact that the church is formed and grows through the Spirit as its communal spirit is the central idea in the ecclesiology of Hofmann" (Behr, *Politischer Liberalismus*, 109). But, contrary to Behr's reading, Hofmann does not separate the Spirit's activity from the church's activities of preaching the word and administering the sacraments. The Spirit works through these means of grace to constitute and develop the church.

5. Hofmann's ecclesiology is in tension with most forms of Lutheran ecclesiology, which deny that the church is a basic sacrament from which all other sacraments derive. See Eberhard Jüngel, "The Church as Sacrament?" in Eberhard Jüngel, *Theological Essays* (ed. and trans. John Webster; Edinburgh: T & T Clark, 1989), 189–213. "By living from Jesus Christ as the one and really unique sacrament, the church celebrates the sacramentality of *his* being. And only insofar as it celebrates his sacramentality, that is, the history of Jesus Christ as the declaration and impartation of God's gracious presence, can the church be called, not a basic sacrament but rather the great *sacramental sign* which represents Jesus Christ. The church is the analogate which points to Jesus Christ as the analogue. As analogate, the church reveals that Jesus Christ

indwelling Spirit, the historical church becomes the means of Christ's activity in the world (*DVL* 104–5). This activity involves both the preaching of the gospel and the administration of the sacraments, as well as acts of mercy toward those in need. These "churchly activities" are the means by which "the salvific relationship in Christ becomes our personal experience..." (*DVW* 388). The goal of the activities of the church is the greater and greater indwelling of the Spirit within the church, i.e., bringing more and more people into gracious communion with God. The historical process of the expansion of the church is therefore the means of fulfilling the historical process of Christ's redemption: the history of the church fulfills itself in the transformation of all humanity into the humanity of God.

The principal activity of the church in the world is to proclaim the gospel, since this word of the gospel alone creates and sustains faith and brings people into communion with God in Christ's church. The "word is the means through which God creates faith" (*BH* 49).

> The effect of the triune God, through whom the human being becomes a participant in that salvation once and for all accomplished in Christ Jesus, happens by means of the word, which — as the community-forming sermon of the first witnesses to Christ, or as Scripture, which is intended to govern all self-expressions of the congregation that has come into being, or finally as a proclamation of the congregation determined and directed either according to the former or [according] to the latter — always has Jesus as the content and is always a work of the Holy Spirit. (*DVL* 104–5)

The church has its origin and continuing life on the basis of the preached word of the gospel, which announces the forgiveness of sins, life and salvation. So the church receives its life from the preaching of the gospel (*SKS* 186–87). This preaching is grounded in Scripture and yet it cannot be simply identified with Scripture, since the preaching of the gospel involves interpretation and application of Scripture. Hofmann defined the church's preaching of the gospel as nothing other than the preaching of the risen Christ through his Spirit in the words of human beings in his church. By the graceful activity of the Holy Spirit, human preaching in the church is the voice of the living Christ, whose voice cannot simply be identified with Scripture (ibid., 186). The criterion by which one is to judge whether the preaching of the church is the true preaching of Christ is the results of such preaching, i.e., whether

---

himself is the one who brings men and women into correspondence with himself as the church. And we may — with Schleiermacher — speak of a self-representation of Jesus Christ occurring in the actions of the church" (ibid., 206). Jüngel refers to Richard Rothe's ecclesiology, but does not mention Hofmann.

such preaching engenders faith, hope, and love.[6] If preaching leads to these, then one may say that that preaching is not the preaching of a human being but that of Christ (*TE* 66).

But the living Christ is not only mediated to human beings through the preaching of the gospel. The sacraments of the church also serve to ground Christian faith in the merciful promises of God (*DVL* 107–8).

> The effect of the triune God, through whom the human being be-comes a participant in that salvation once and for all available through Christ Jesus, happens by means of the two activities of the commu-nity, through which the individual gets to experience in his natural life communion with the redeemed human nature of Christ. (Ibid., 107)

"Although the human being has become a new person through the effect of the word," the individual Christian is still marked by "the presence of and power of sin" until death (ibid.). "Therefore, insofar as the Christian is still under the effect of evil and the world, he is in need of an op-posite effect within the natural" (ibid.). Hofmann believed this "opposite effect" is provided through the Spirit who works through the natural means of water baptism and the Lord's Supper. While these "two activities are not absolutely necessary for salvation — at least not in the way that the word is absolutely necessary — they are necessary, provided that one has become a person of Christ and wants to be a member of Christ's visible community on earth, ... the new human being in communion with Christ (*Menschengemeinschaft*)" (ibid., 108).[7]

Through baptism, antitype to Jewish circumcision and ritual washings, the divinely transfigured human nature of Christ is imparted to human be-ings who become members of his body, the church. "When a human being enters the community of Christ, the Spirit of this community, which is the Spirit of the transfigured Christ, will begin its effect as such" (*DVL* 108). The sacrament of baptism establishes the individual in relationship of faith to the risen Christ and to his church, but the Spirit of Christ continues to transform the earthly nature of the individual into the redeemed nature of Christ. Thus, the spiritual effects of baptism are faith, hope, and love. These effects work against the effects of the sinful nature and the effects of evil within the world. "The baptized thereby has a pledge of salvation, which he

---

6. J. v. Hofmann, "Dr. Kliefoth's acht Bücher von der Kirche," *ZPK* 31 (1856): 79. See also Hofmann, "Kliefoth's Theorie des Kultus der evangelischen Kirche," *Mecklenburger Kirchenblatt* 1 (1845): 116–39.

7. See also J. v. Hofmann, "Gegen eine irrige Verhältnisbestimmung von Wort und Taufe," *ZPK* (1863): 187–91; and idem, "Zur Schriftlehre von der Taufe," *ZPK* 48 (1864): 127–28.

needs only to affirm again and again in order to be certain of his salvation, which is valid not merely for his person but also for his nature" (ibid.).

Through participation in the Lord's Supper, antitype to the Jewish Passover meal, Christians experience a renewed indwelling of the risen Christ, who unites participants with the whole people of God on earth and in heaven. As is the case with the Passover, the Lord's Supper is a celebration of the spiritual communion, not merely a personal reception of the benefits of Christ. Nonetheless, the individual communicant receives the Lord's bodily presence "in, with, and under the bread and wine," humble, earthly elements that they are.[8] Hofmann stressed that people are formed into Christ's community by means of "the transfigured human nature of Christ" that is given in the sacrament. The "partaking of bread and wine is the means through which the glorified Christ is at work in his church" (*BH* 49). This transfigured human nature is that which the members of Christ's community have in common. This sacrament, too, serves to strengthen Christian faith, hope, and love.

Within the context of the preaching of the word and the administration of the sacraments, one needs also to note Hofmann's extensive attention to the problem of the office of holy ministry that emerges in Lutheranism in the nineteenth century.[9] For Hofmann there is no church without the office of the holy ministry, since "where there is common life, there is also office, not to be derived from the former but simultaneously along with it. So also in the community of Christ ... " (*KG* 17). The purpose of the office is to proclaim the word and administer the sacraments, since the "foundation of the congregation is word and sacraments" (ibid.). Nevertheless, the office of the holy ministry is nothing more than a means of making sure the gospel is proclaimed and the sacraments administered in accordance with the gospel (cf. Articles V and VII of the *Augsburg Confession*). "Bearers of the office of church administration, as [were] elders in the earliest church, are not to be differentiated as laity and clergy, but only as theologians and non-theologians."[10] Hofmann emphasized both the priesthood of all believers, but also a special office of preaching and sacramental administering into which certain believers are called by the congregation for the sake of preaching and church administration of the sacraments, which have as their

---

8. Hofmann, "Die rechte Verwaltung der Konfirmation, eine Grundvoraussetzung rechter Kirchenverfassung," *ZPK* 18 (1849): 13; See also *SBb* 2.2:257.

9. See especially, J v. Hofmann, "Über Löhes drei Bücher von der Kirche," *Mecklenburger Kirchenblatt* 1 (1845): 284–307; idem, "Das Amt und die Ämter in der apostolischen Kirche," *ZPK* 18 (1849): 129–53; and idem, "Wie Man das göttliche Recht des kirchlichen Amtes nicht verteidigen muss," *ZPK* 23 (1852): 174–91. On the problem of *"Kirche und Amt"* in Lutheranism, see Elert, *The Structure of Lutheranism*, 1:339–85.

10. Hofmann, "Die rechte Verwaltung," 15.

ends "the edification of the community" (*DVL* 109).[11] The "action of the triune God, through whom the human being becomes a participant in that salvation present once and for all through Christ, occurs by means of the entire ecclesial community," i.e., through the various gifts and abilities of its individual members, and within the context of their relationships, actions, and interactions among themselves and with non-Christians (*DVL* 108–9). This ecclesial activity not only recognizes and promotes the word and the sacraments, but also actually grows out of them as well. Real, living people form Christ's community. Thus, the church should not be understood to be "invisible," but the "visible community." This is due to the proclaimed and audible word, the visible sacraments, and living Christians who are marked by faith, hope, and love (ibid., 109).

The Goal of Word and Sacraments: Christian Faith and Rebirth

For Hofmann faith, hope, and love are that which characterizes the human response to God's restoration of human nature in the risen Christ and the communication of that restored human nature through the effective working of Christ's Spirit in the ecclesial word and sacraments.[12] Consequently, the divine-human relationship in Christ not only advances the being of God by including the restoration of humanity in communion with God, it also completes the being of humans with a power that is able to transform human existence in a way that humans on their own are unable to do. God's grace transforms human life by calling people to faith, hope, and love. As a result of the Spirit's working, human beings are called out of themselves to faith and love toward God, to hope toward the future of the world, and to love for others.

> The human being becomes a different person by entering into communion with the nature of Jesus which is offered through proclamation. This historically given human being, Jesus, is thus the actual mediator between God and humanity, and although he is a human being he is

---

11. See also *TE* 188, where Hofmann states that to be called into the office of the holy ministry is not a personal entitlement (*Berechtigung*), but the means whereby a community commits an individual to the service of spiritual self-sacrifice. Hofmann understands the office of the holy ministry to be the *heilsgeschichtliche* fulfillment of the Old Testament "type" of priesthood.

12. For Hofmann's theology of liturgy, see Hans Kretzel, *Die Liturgik der Erlanger Theologie. Ihre Geschichte und ihre Grundsätze* (2d ed.; Göttingen: Vandenhoeck und Ruprecht, 1948). See also Martin Peters, "J. Chr. K. v. Hofmann als praktischer Theologe," *NKZ* 30 (1919): 157–90.

essentially the object of God's love. ... From this experience it follows that the human being who has become the object of God's love in person will become in his nature as God wants humanity to be. (*DVW* 387)[13]

Hofmann understood this new humanity, the new creation, to be a new situation in which the individual acknowledges his sins and separation from God and recognizes that through Christ the individual has been forgiven and, through his Spirit, established within a new relationship to God. Hofmann called this new situation "the experience of rebirth." This experience includes the forgiveness of sins but also the reception of Christ's human nature as a gift that has been given through the Holy Spirit. "Christian faith" is therefore "the rebirth of the human individual" through repentance and the reception of the forgiveness of sins by faith and the indwelling of Christ in the believer. This transformation is the reign of God that is coming to dwell among all people.

Christian faith is not merely a belief that something is true, nor is it merely "remaining true or faithful to God." Rather, in relation to God, "faith means 'to trust in [and rely upon] God, to hold firmly to God.' God is the 'place' upon which an individual has been placed and established. Thus it becomes clear here how closely related the concept of faith is to the concepts of fidelity and perseverance in God" (*BH* 65).

While Hofmann did not often use the word "justification" (*Rechtfertigung*) in his writings, the important concept is present in his theology.[14] The justification of the sinner is not possible on the part of the sinner, but only possible because of the nature of God to be faithful and just, to forgive sinners their sins. God's "righteousness (δικαιοσύνη) consists in the fact that God follows the plan he has laid out. Therefore his deeds in holy history are called 'acts of righteousness' because in them he executes his divine plan" (*BH* 63–64). God's justification of the sinner (Rom 4:5) is the result of God's faithfulness to act in history to reconcile people to God's self through Christ. God declares the sinner just on the condition which he himself has

---

13. Hofmann's comments about faith as "a possession" (*Besitz*) need to be qualified by statements such as this one. Hamann, too, describes the Christian life as "a becoming" and not "a having." "This life is not piety, but becoming pious; not a state of health, but a process of becoming healthy; not a being, but a becoming. We are not yet, but we shall become. It has not yet been accomplished and it has not yet come to pass, but is in process and in motion. It is not the end, but the way. As yet, all does not glitter and glisten, but all is furbishing itself" (Hamann, as quoted in Leibrecht, *God and Man in the Thought of Hamann,* 186). See also Larry Vaughn, *Johann Georg Hamann: Metaphysics of Language and Vision of History* (New York: Peter Lang, 1989), 87–106.

14. Flechsenhaar points out the probable reason for this: Hofmann "had a certain aversion against overused dogmatic expressions" (Flechsenhaar, *Das Geschichtsproblem,* 71).

established, namely, on the basis of his own saving activity in the life and death of Christ (ibid., 64). The justification and reconciliation of the sinner to God lies solely in Christ (*BA* 190). Through baptism, however, and the reception of the gospel in faith, the individual believer participates in the reconciliation accomplished in Christ. So the rebirth experience is created by means of the Holy Spirit's actions in and through the church's sacraments. In baptism, the "Spirit takes the baptized from out of the context of the sinful world and places him in the context of the holy congregation, creates for him a beginning of life and a new community of life, in a word effects his rebirth."[15] Hofmann thought that the baptism of infants especially underscores the gracious, monergic action of God to justify and reconcile sinners to God and to place them into his new community of faith, hope, and love. Even "the justifying faith" which receives God's forgiveness is itself "a work of God in us."[16]

Since Hofmann understood the justification and reconciliation of the sinner to God ("the rebirth experience") to be the result of God's faithful action in history, this experience of rebirth also includes an awareness of one's relationship to God's *Heilsgeschichte*. The rebirth of the Christian is itself understood as a "fact" (*Tatsache*) in the process of *Heilsgeschichte*. This historical fact of the individual's rebirth experience means for the Christian that she is herself conscious of a total newness in her relationship to God, including also her thinking and acting in the world. This individual *Heilsgeschichte* therefore forms a necessary element in the Christian's self-understanding. All Christian self-understanding is subordinate to this rebirth experience: *Notione regenerationis sublata tollitur omnis theologia.*[17] Precisely because the individual believer is historically situated within the Christian congregation, the universal *Heilsgeschichte* has its relationship to the individual within history. "Indeed, this individual self has its uniquely individual *Heilsgeschichte* within the universal," since the Christian comprehends that she is living in the same historic and communal relationship between God and humanity that is witnessed to in Scripture.[18]

Christian Hope

Because the Christian rebirth experience is only the rebirth of the "person," and not yet the glorification of the person's "human nature," the Christian

---

15. J. v. Hofmann, "Wort und Sakrament," *ZPK* 15 (1848): 6.
16. J. v. Hofmann, "Ob der rechtfertigende Glaube allein selig macht," *ZPK* 38 (1859): 371.
17. Hofmann, "Thesis 1," *De Argumento Psalmi Centesimi Decimi*, 47.
18. Schellbach, *Theologie und Philosophie*, 75.

fully expects that the new life begun in the rebirth will be perfected in the glorification of his or her body in the resurrection from the dead on the last day (*SBb* 2.2:133). This hope is grounded in Christ's own resurrection which is the precondition of one's being in faithful relationship with God and is understood by Hofmann to be the principal or driving force of history itself. This means, in addition, that as an individual member of God's new community on its way to perfection in the *eschaton*, the individual Christian is situated "between the times." The individual Christian, as a participant in *Heilsgeschichte*, waits with the whole people of God for the end of history, which for Hofmann is tantamount to the glorification of human bodies through the resurrection into the perfect community of God's love. Thus, the rebirth experience is "a new birth into a living hope" (1 Pet 1:3).

But for Hofmann Christian hope is not merely oriented to the individual, since an aspect of Christian hope is also the expectation of the restoration (ἀποκατάστασις) of all things in Christ (cf. Acts 3:21; Matt 17:11). "Just as [the individual Christian] will become wholly and completely what he is, i.e., a person of God, so the church will become wholly and completely what it is, i.e., the humanity of God" (*SBb* 1:55). Christian hope is also trans-personal and includes the expectation that *Weltgeschichte* will become fulfilled in *Heilsgeschichte*. The Christian recognizes that his or her life is finite and coming to an end insofar as it derives from herself, but that it is approaching its consummation insofar as it derives from God. This means that only eschatological faith opens one's eyes to the reality of one's own being and to the reality of creation of which one is a part. The one who shares that eschatological faith will give up the folly of trying to glorify oneself and the world, but will instead live one's life in the expectation of the new creation. Hofmann thought that this is the true meaning of Jesus' announcement of God's coming kingdom which receives its focus in "the new creation," the resurrection of Jesus from the dead. The resurrection of Jesus is the meaning of history, understood as the development and expansion of the relationship between God and humanity in Jesus.[19]

So the gospel promise includes not only the hope of the transformation of individuals from the dead, but also of the whole of humanity. *Heilsgeschichte* is headed toward an inclusive whole, a goal of completeness, though this completeness has already begun in the resurrection of Jesus from the dead. For example, Hofmann held out hope that "Israel" would also become a member of the church, i.e., that "the history of God's people, both the Old Testament and the New Testament people, has found its conclusion in the

---

19. Schleiermacher also understood the church as "the locus of Christ's continuing influence and the historical means by which the Kingdom of God must be extended and the divine election consummated" (Gerrish, "Friedrich Schleiermacher," 144). See *CF* 546–81.

new Jerusalem" (*SBb* 2.2:728). Indeed, Hofmann believed that there will come a time wherein all of humanity will be found within the Christian church. Until that time, the church's mission is to proclaim the gospel, including the hope of the complete restoration of all things "in Christ" (*TE* 183–85). This message is a part of the church's "prophetic voice."

Furthermore, the church's fulfillment is bound to the historical self-fulfillment of the Trinity and is "guaranteed by the unconditionality of the community of the Son with the Father in the Spirit" (*SBb* 1:54). The reality of the church is not merely "immanent," but includes this transcendent fulfillment of the communion of the Son with the Father in the Holy Spirit, "when God will be all in all" (1 Cor 15:29). "The mediating activity of Jesus no less than the power which he exercises over all the non-divine forces including death will come to an end when its purpose has been fulfilled, namely, that God should be all in all; in other words, when there will be a world which is entirely God's and in which there is nothing found which is alien to him" (*BH* 209). Thus, Hofmann understood God to be the unity of all reality since God is both the source and the goal of all reality.[20] Hofmann took this to mean that the Trinitarian decision of love will realize itself in "the perfection of the church" (*SBb* 1:56). The transcendent Trinitarian fulfillment is the perfection of the church in the *eschaton*. But the world itself has its fulfillment in the perfection of the church. The Christian expects that at the end of the world all will recognize that the world is grounded in the eternal God (*DVL* 110).

Even though Hofmann's entire thought was oriented to "the eschatological new creation," he did not take a triumphalist stance with regard to the church's relation to the world. Though Hofmann stressed that the triune God exerts a decisive power on the life of humankind through the church and works against the influence of evil to extend God's consummate community of love throughout all creation, Hofmann specifically viewed the Spirit of God as the one who strives for the realization of the communion between God and humanity. Hofmann emphasized that the present world contains powers that are arrayed against the new creation and opposed to Christian faith, hope, and love. These powers are found even within the individual Christian's life and within the historical manifestations of communities claiming to belong to the church. These powers are to be resisted

---

20. Hofmann here anticipates Pannenberg's claim that "[s]peaking about God and speaking about the whole of reality are not two entirely different matters, but mutually condition each other. Presumably it is not even possible to speak of the whole of reality without in some way thinking of God. In any case, the converse is true: it is utter thoughtlessness to leave undecided or even to repudiate the idea of the whole of reality while at the same time speaking about God as the all-determining reality" (Pannenberg, "On Historical and Theological Hermeneutic," in *Basic Questions in Theology*, 1:156).

on the basis of faith, hope, and love, grounded in God's own activity in the world through God's Spirit. It is therefore incorrect to view Hofmann as a participant in the *Kulturprotestantismus* that marked much of liberal Protestantism in Germany in the second half of the nineteenth century.

> It is not the fulfillment of a continually progressing process of salvation for the world that the church has in prospect but rather the most extreme resistance of the world against the church, from which the church will be delivered through the second coming of its Lord and will be transfigured to the corresponding appearance [epiphany], whereby begins a new age of its involvement in the world.[21]

According to Hofmann, the Holy Spirit is the cause of that which participants in the community have in common, namely, the new "humanity of Christ." Insofar as the church remains under the power of sinful human nature, it is in need of redemption and perfection. Insofar as the Spirit of the living Christ dwells within the church and its members, and proclaims to the church and its members the forgiveness of their sins, the church is holy and perfect. Since the church's historical existence is quite different from the expectation of the church's fulfillment or perfection in the *eschaton* — due largely to heresies, the power of human sin, and cultural divisions within the empirical church — Christian hope also includes an ethical and an ecumenical orientation. In light of the expectation of the church's perfection in the *eschaton,* Hofmann thought that contemporary churches and theologians needed to be engaged in ecumenical dialogue in an effort to overcome theological differences and divisions. For Hofmann the eschatological unity of the church is the fundamental motivation for seeking ecumenical reconciliation.

Christian Obedience and Love

According to Hofmann, the Christian experience involves a two-fold orientation. First and foremost, the Christian experience is grounded in God's love for the individual in and through Christ. In Christ, the individual becomes an object of God's love.

> The other side of Christian experience is the joyous certainty that the Christian has love for God. One who loves God has, however, first become such a one through Christ; thus the more grounded he is in the community of faith which is in Christ, the more growth in the love

---

21. Hofmann, "Dr. Kliefoth's acht Bücher," 100.

for God. And this love is all the more complete, the more it is a love of God in Christ; and all the objects to which [this] love is able to direct itself are all the more worthy of it, the closer they are to the community that exists with God in Christ. (*DVW* 387)

For Hofmann the love of God in Christ leads immediately to the love of God in the individual Christian. This second dimension of "the Christian experience" leads decidedly in both an ecclesial/missional direction as well as an ethical direction. The eschatological unity of the church is the motivation for Christian obedience and love in the present. So, for Hofmann, the doctrine of Trinity is not only the result of God's self-emptying in history, but also the motivation for human action in the present.

In Christ the old way of life, marked by sin and the fear of death, has come to its end; yet for the moment only through faith and hope have people become participants in the new relationship with God established in Christ. Nonetheless, even though Christians live now by faith in a "personal" relationship with God, and while they also hope in their own glorification as well as the glorification of all creation in the *eschaton,* they also realize that they continue to live by "nature" in "the old creation" conditioned as it is by finitude, historical development, sin, and death (*WE* 1:37). The Christian life is not marked by a steady line of progress; rather, Christians slip again and again back into old patterns of living. Christians realize that they live in a world that includes forces that are opposed to the new creation, including even inclinations within themselves against God's will of love. The call to faith and hope must therefore include the call to love and obedience, which, in the power of the Holy Spirit, work against these inclinations and anti-godly forces (*TE* 89–91).

For Hofmann the personal experience of rebirth involves an ethical responsibility which mirrors God's own self-giving in history. Christian ethics, oriented to the present, is entirely grounded in the eschatological vision of God's fulfilled community of love. "The eschatological prophecies are never meant simply to provide knowledge of the future course of events. Rather they serve an ethical purpose" (*BH* 254; Hofmann cites Matt 25:31–46). For this reason, Hofmann did not think that Christian ethics is a theological discipline that is separate from Christian dogmatics. Like systematics, Christian ethics grows out of the understanding of "the new humanity" given in Christian existence, not out of the general question of "morality" or even out of supposed timeless and ahistorical principles (*LE* 251–56).[22] The task

---

22. See also Forde, *The Law-Gospel Debate,* 32–33.

of Christian ethics is to describe the new humanity in Christ and not to dictate what ought to be done in the Christian life according to a set of laws.[23] Hofmann explicitly rejected a so-called "third use of the law" in the life of the Christian (*LE* 253–56).[24] The new life of the reborn Christian is one that is free of the law and marked by faith active in love. If there is any "demand" within the Christian life, it is the apostolic injunction "to regard yourselves as dead to sin, but alive unto God." The Christian is called to live her life within the new humanity that has been given to her through Christ's Spirit.

> Neither a doctrine of duty nor a doctrine of virtue is apropos here. The virtue of the Christian is the new life in which he stands, and his duty is to show himself ever and again as one who stands in such a new life. But in the new life itself everything is already included towards which he must unfold. (*LE* 253–54)

In light of the vision of the archetypal goal of the world, the Christian is called to act within the concrete structures of one's finite and historical existence. This means for Hofmann that the Christian has distinct responsibilities within the several callings (*Berufe*) of one's life: faith, family, occupation, church, civic duty, nation, and world.[25] Through one's "placement in history"

---

23. Hofmann is here following the procedure set forth by Schleiermacher. See Friedrich Schleiermacher, *Christliche Sittenlehre Einleitung* (Stuttgart: Kohlhammer, 1983).

24. See also Paul Althaus, "Der deskriptive Charakter der Ethik bei Joh. Chr. K. v. Hofmann," *Theologische Blätter* 1 (1933): 308–9. One feature that runs through the Erlangen theological tradition from Hofmann to Althaus and Werner Elert (1885–1954) is the critique of a so-called "third use of the law." This critique is not limited to the Erlangen tradition, however, and includes theologians as diverse as Friedrich Gogarten (1887–1967), Bultmann, Ebeling, Helmut Thielicke (1908–1986), Aulèn, Robert Bertram, and Gerhard Forde. For the history of the idea of a "third use" of the law, see especially Gerhard Ebeling, "On the Doctrine of the Triplex Usus Legis in the Theology of the Reformation," in *Word and Faith* (trans. James Leitch; Philadelphia: Fortress, 1963), 62–78. "Most Lutheran theologians have limited law strictly to the old age; they stand, as I have contended, at the end of a line of development in which law has been increasingly generalized as that which characterizes man's existential predicament in the old age. They define law as 'that which accuses the sinner.' Since the gospel means the eschatological advent to faith of the new age, such accusation must 'end' when Christ is received in faith. Law must therefore emphatically and radically be excluded from the new age. The gospel is the end and *telos* of the law.... Law is the 'form' of this age. This explains the Lutheran tendency to limit law to the first two uses — civil and theological. The law gives form to this age and it accuses the sinner. As such it is an existential power which will continue to accuse as long as man remains in his sin. Only a living faith in Christ as the end of the law can hold the law in its proper perspective. Faith alone makes and keeps the law 'natural' " (Forde, *The Law-Gospel Debate,* 201, 211). For additional critiques of the so-called "third use of the law," see Werner Elert, *The Christian Ethos* (trans. Carl Schindler; Philadelphia: Muhlenberg Press, 1957), 49–76, 294–303; idem, *Law and Gospel* (trans. Edward Schroeder; Philadelphia: Fortress Press, 1967); and James Gustafson, *Christ and the Moral Life* (Chicago: The University of Chicago Press, 1968), 116–49.

25. For an excellent analysis of Hofmann's ethics, see especially Behr, *Politischer Liberalismus,* 133–70.

each human being has an individually conditioned nature, unique offerings, a particular occupation, etc. But one cannot prescribe duties and virtues for the Christian life, since the ethical life is to be an evolution or unfolding (*Entfaltung*) of what the new life in Christ truly is. Thus, for Hofmann, theological ethics cannot be based on the divine law, but only on a creative and historical description of the new life in Christ.

Despite his rejection of the law's prescriptive force in the life of the reborn Christian, Hofmann did think the preaching of the divine law is still necessary in the life of every Christian, since all Christians, insofar as their lives are determined by the power of sin, are still under the historical judgment of God. While the new life is present in Christ, who lives within the individual reborn Christian, that life is hidden. Such a new life is not yet perfectly present in the life of the Christian and will not be until the resurrection from the dead and the coming of the *eschaton* (*LE* 256).[26] Until then, each Christian has the responsibility to act by means of the Spirit according to the new relationship in which he or she stands (*TE* 78).

All of the individual's responsibilities and activities, however, occur within the hope of personal glorification and the glorification of all creation in eternity. Hofmann understood the kingdom of Jesus to be one in which all people from all nations are being brought together into a community of equality as children of God. The actions of the church — as the concrete self-representation of Christ in the world — insofar as they are truly actions of the living Christ, become the means for extending Christ's community of love to embrace all peoples. "The important fact is that one serves in the wider spheres of family, state, and humanity in general only from the center, from the starting point of the new life. The wider spheres, one might say, are a series of concentric circles extending out from the center in the new life."[27] "Through the historical-theological interpretation of Christology a political dimension is opened up in the church. It is the start of a new humanity in which the orders, which are rooted in sin and the fear of death, no longer are in force. The unity of spiritual life realized in the church itself on the basis of peace and equality of people and nations should more and more become the world-order of humanity with the expansion of the church."[28]

---

26. See ibid., 133–47.
27. Forde, *The Law-Gospel Debate,* 34. "In cases of conflict between spheres the rights and responsibilities of each are to be noted and respected. Were the state, for instance, so to enlarge itself as to threaten either family or church on the one hand, or on the other to attempt forcibly to subject humanity in general to itself in a universal kingdom, it would become despotic and one would be constrained to resist it" (ibid.). See also the discussion by Behr, *Politischer Liberalismus,* 172–231.
28. Sturm, "Die integrierende Funktion der Ekklesiologie," 318. "Ecclesiology has become the principle by which universal history is constructed" (ibid., 321).

Since Wendebourg's study has influenced at least one American study of Hofmann, one should point out that in this area of Christian ethics his study is incorrect to suggest that "both [Hegel and Hofmann] envision a total human passivity in relation to the course of history."[29] Not only is this judgment inaccurate with regard to Hegel, it fails to account for Hofmann's understanding that God works *through* contingent, historical agents to accomplish God's purposes.[30] The activity of human beings, culminating in the activity of *the* human being, Jesus, and his community of renewed human beings, *is* the activity of the triune God. Wendebourg is therefore not only unable to account for Hofmann's own personal involvement in liberal political activity and in several missionary and social-service societies, but he also overlooks Hofmann's own statements regarding human freedom and responsibility in his *Theologische Ethik*. These lectures affirm the responsibility of the faithful and hopeful Christian to use his or her life in freedom to serve the neighbor and society in love.

---

29. Wendebourg, *Die heilsgeschichtliche Theologie*, 131.
30. See Taylor, *Hegel*, 366–88; and Harris, *The Spirit of Hegel*, 177–94.

CHAPTER ELEVEN

The Future of God:
Heilsgeschichte and *Weltgeschichte*

Kirchengeschichte and *Heilsgeschichte*

While Hofmann avoided speaking of church history (*Kirchengeschichte*) as salvation history (*Heilsgeschichte*), because the definite working of God in the church cannot be recognized as such, he stressed that nevertheless God continues God's salvific activity in and for the world through the church.[1] Since the history of the church is not completed, and because its history is more ambiguous than the scriptural monument of *Heilsgeschichte*, Hofmann did not orient himself to questions about "the church-historical whole." The "whole" of that history is still in the process of development and so the recognition and understanding of that "whole" is more difficult (*SBb* 1:19; *ET* 310). It is not surprising, then, that in his *Encyclopedia of Theology* Hofmann devotes the least amount of space (pp. 255–310) to the discipline of church history.

Despite the ambiguities associated with the interpretation of church history, Hofmann maintained that the end of church history and the end of human history coincide (*ET* 73). God's historical actions (in Israel, but centering in Jesus and his redeemed community of love) are always aimed at the whole of humanity and the whole of history (ibid., 264–65, 271, 278). The end of *Heilsgeschichte* is not bound to biblical time but reaches forward to the end of time itself (*SBb* 1:55). The present time of the Christian church, therefore, is "the time between the times" (*Eine Zwischenheit zwischen Anfang und Ende*) (ibid., 1:50). This "time of the church" has "the *heilsgeschichtliche* self-revelation of God for its decisive presupposition," but it is also the goal of God's history with God's people since the church is

---

1. See J. v. Hofmann, "Zur neutestamentlichen Geschichte," *ZPK* 22 (1851): 114–20, 329–34; and *ZPK* 26 (1853): 260–72. See also Hofmann's unfinished commentary on the Gospel according to Luke, *HS* 8.1. In keeping with his *heilsgeschichtliche* perspective, Hofmann begins his commentary on the Gospels with Luke, whose view of history Hofmann takes as normative for the other Gospels, indeed, for the entire Bible. See also idem, "Das Geschichtswerk des Lukas," *ZPK* 59 (1870): 335–63.

the beginning of the new humanity in Jesus (ibid., 2.2:151). The history of the church stands "between the beginning and the completion of the New Testament *Heilsgeschichte*" (ibid., 2.2:97). The essential content of all history is the unfolding of the loving lordship of Christ throughout the whole world. Thus, the future perfected kingdom of God unlocks for Hofmann the nature of the present and the past.

Hofmann indicates that the faith of the individual Christian is a necessary precondition for theological understanding and is itself an important historical event in the *heilsgeschichtliche* whole, since Christian faith allows the individual to become a participant in God's continuing history.[2] This fact alone makes it possible for the theologian, in his or her correspondence to the will of God, to perceive the actions of God in history, at least indirectly. "Miracles on the one hand and faith on the other, that is the character of history" (*TE* 46).[3] Hofmann was quick to state, however, that this fact of God's salvation-historical revelation in Christ comes to consciousness as a fact in the believer. *Heilsgeschichte* itself is not the result of human effort, psychological or otherwise. This *Tatbestand,* which includes the rebirth of the Christian, is a gift of the grace of the God who reveals God's self historically, and as such is an important presupposition of Hofmann's assertion that the Trinity is relational and temporal.

In distinction from his teacher, Ranke, Hofmann believed, in light of his baptismal regeneration through the Holy Spirit, that God has revealed the end or goal of all history in the event of Jesus who enables the Christian to see its whole course before God (*coram deo*). This view of the "whole" does not come from splicing together individual facts of history; nor does it arise on the basis of historical research. Only the experience of rebirth, itself a historical fact, enables one to inquire into a deeper understanding of the biblical "whole," and by means of that to a deeper understanding

---

2. Hofmann understands the experience of rebirth as an historical event, "which is easily comprehensible if one considers that it represents the admission of the individual Christian into the process of the self-realization of the church" (Sturm, "Die integrierende Funktion der Ekklesiologie," 309).

3. Here "miracle" (*Wunder*) is understood to be God's effect on the human being, which effect is itself mediated to the human being through sensual perception in history. Indeed, the relationship between God and humanity occurs in the arena of sensually perceptible reality, i.e., history. This relationship presupposes that God has gone into history, that God desires to relate to human beings, and that such a relationship is possible because human beings are embodied personalities, created in the image of God. Consequently, all historical events that are recognized as being willed by God are viewed as "miracle" and "inspired." "Since Scripture is the document of *Heilsgeschichte,* its content too must be miracle. Since basically Christ is the content of this history, he is the absolute miracle. All miracles in the Bible, both those which point to him and those which he performs himself, must be understood and measured with reference to him.... A biblical miracle remains unintelligible and lacks true value for theological understanding when treated by itself and apart from its special place and significance for *Heilsgeschichte*" (*BH* 38–39).

of the whole process of history. While Hegel, for example, and Hofmann thought that the course of history is rational and intelligible, for Hofmann it is the historical-eschatological gift of spiritual rebirth which grants this possibility. For Hofmann the perception of universal history is grounded in the personal experience of *Heilsgeschichte,* and yet that perception leads the theologian to conclude that his personal experience of rebirth is itself grounded in a *heilsgeschichtliche Tatbestand* that is prior and external to himself. The Christian recognizes that she stands within the development of the entire *Heilsgeschichte* and that she cannot overstep her place in that development. Only God the transcendent Creator is "beyond history." All others, including the Christian, cannot go "outside of history." Thus, it is never possible for even the Christian to speak about history as though from a position "above" history. Such a possibility would be a contradiction of the historicity that constitutes an important aspect of the nature of human being and the nature of the Christian *Tatbestand* itself. Therefore, Hofmann stressed the historicality and temporality of the individual Christian as a corollary to the temporality and relationality of the triune God: "The point at which I enter is Christ himself, who has made me into a Christian, and this point is at the same time also the circle that encloses me and the whole world, visible and invisible, present and future" (*BD* 55).

But one must emphasize that even though Hofmann's theological method led him to ground Christian theology independently within the Christian *Tatbestand,* such a grounding did not mean for him that theology has nothing to learn from the extra-theological disciplines, including secular history. Hofmann's method, as we have seen in chapter three, is like those theological approaches that seek to relate the truth of Christian theology to those relevant truths from the extra-theological disciplines. Theology must do this since, as Hofmann often stated, the risen Christ is the Lord of all reality. Thus, insights from secular historians must be incorporated into the Christian theology of history.[4] Since the Christian theologian is most concerned with discerning the identity of God on the basis of historical events, those university disciplines that also address history (e.g., philosophy of history) are of utmost concern to the Christian theologian. For Hofmann the whole of world history thus becomes important for the discipline of theology.

---

4. Compare Hofmann's approach with Dalferth's summary of Barth's approach to "history:" "...what 'history' really means is shown by the one history of Jesus Christ which, when interpretively applied to our common understanding of history, shows this to be, at best, a preliminary, abstract, and inauthentic understanding of history" (Dalferth, "Karl Barth's Eschatological Realism," 38).

Heilsgeschichte and Weltgeschichte

At the intersection of theology and the other university disciplines, Hofmann was most concerned to relate a Christian understanding of God to world history (*Weltgeschichte*). Hofmann thought such a relation needed to be clarified in order to provide a true account of God's actions in the world. Since a number of interpreters of Hofmann's conception of salvation history (*Heilsgeschichte*) have accused Hofmann of separating a special, miraculous "history" from the rest of world history, it is important to examine his conception more closely.[5]

The typical interpretation is that for Hofmann world history is a more comprehensive category than salvation history, but that *Heilsgeschichte* is the only history that has any positive value. In this reading, *Heilsgeschichte* is a special stream of miraculous events that occurs in the middle of all other world events. This typical interpretation of Hofmann's conception accuses Hofmann of ultimately rejecting the contingency of historical events and the possibility of a truly open future.

Part of the difficulty with interpreting Hofmann's theology of history correctly is the fact that his conception of *Heilsgeschichte* appears to be ambiguous and open to misunderstanding. On the one hand, he sometimes did speak of *Heilsgeschichte* as if it is a "miraculous history" that is "completely different from profane history." "It is quite another history which the theologian investigates" (*ET* 24). This line of thinking is especially evident in the second edition of *Der Schriftbeweis,* where Hofmann attempted to distinguish *Heilsgeschichte* from world history so as to accentuate God's unique and central self-revelation in Jesus. Here the sense of divine *Wunder* in history (*Geschichte*) is important for Hofmann's conception of *Heilsgeschichte*. On the other hand, even when Hofmann spoke of the "miraculous character" of *Heilsgeschichte,* his concern was to attempt to provide a meaningful interpretation of *all* history on the basis of God's relationship with Israel and Jesus and the anticipation of the complete salvation of all humanity and creation at the end of time. In other words, Hofmann sought to comprehend

---

5. See, for example, Flechsenhaar, *Das Geschichtsproblem,* 22; Sturm, "Die integrierende Funktion der Ekklesiologie," 311; and Barth, *Protestant Theology,* 613–14. "This assumption of a suprahistorical kernel of history, which was actually present already in Hofmann's delimitation of a theology of redemptive history (*Heilsgeschichte*) over against ordinary history (*Historie*), and which still lives today especially in the form of Barth's interpretation of the Incarnation as 'pre-history' (*Urgeschichte*), necessarily deprecates real history just as does the reduction of history to historicity" (Pannenberg, "Redemptive Event and History," 15–16). Pannenberg describes Hofmann's theology of history as "a redemptive history severed from ordinary history" (ibid., 41). Pannenberg's understanding of Hofmann appears to be dependent upon Wendebourg's reading of Hofmann's theology of history.

the whole of history from the perspective of God's salvation revealed in Israel and Jesus: "The self-representation of Christ in the world is the essential content of all history" (*WE* 1:40). "The extension of the Lordship of this man [Jesus] is now the essential content of all world-history" (ibid., 2:299). Thus, " . . . [B]iblical history is something other than an errorless part of world-history" (*BH* 75–76). This line of thinking is especially evident in his early work on "prophecy and fulfillment," where he emphasized the organic relationship between salvation history (*Heilsgeschichte*) and history (*Geschichte*). The former is more comprehensive than the latter and as such is the key to the meaning of the latter. The history of Jesus Christ is the focus of all history. This idea of the organic relationship between *Heilsgeschichte* and *Geschichte* is also expressed in the first thesis of his philosophical dissertation: "There is no distinction between universal history and church history except the distinction between Gentiles being gathered into the church and the church extending out among the Gentiles" (*DBAE* 52). This second line of thinking emphasizes that history (*Geschichte*) is in the process of becoming salvation history (*Heilsgeschichte*).

If we take this second line of thinking as more central to Hofmann's theological concern, which is a universal concern, then despite his ambiguous comments to the contrary, Hofmann did not mean to suggest that *Heilsgeschichte* is inherently distinct from or even opposed to profane history. God is active in the whole of human history to disclose God's self and God's salvation in Christ: "If it is true, that all things, big and small, are used to bring about the unification of the world under the lordship of Christ, there is, then, nothing in all of world history in which something divine does not reside, nothing whatsoever that must remain foreign to prophecy" (*WE* 1:7).[6] Hofmann thought that such an understanding was inherent in the prophetic witness to the Lordship of the God of Israel over all the nations. The goal of *Heilsgeschichte* is "that all things shall be gathered into a unity under Christ" (*BH* 40).

> Altogether, Hofmann formulated a theological view of history that leaves the superficial, pragmatic view of history in the Enlightenment far behind. Hofmann formulated this view by returning to the roots of European ideas on history. In this interpretation of history, general world-history is necessarily also included, so that the truth of Christ is true not only in the church but also true with respect to universal

---

6. Though Hofmann does not cite Hamann, this statement is reminiscent of a similar view put forth by the latter: "If one assumes that God is the cause of all effects great and small, both in heaven and on earth, then every hair of our head is just as divine as the Behemoth, that beginning of God's ways" (Hamann, as cited in Leibrecht, *God and Man in the Thought of Hamann*, 75).

claims of validity. *Heilsgeschichte* is not a part of world-history (so the modern view) but rather world history is a part of salvation history (so already Augustine).[7]

Like Hegel and Ranke, Hofmann developed an idea of world history or universal history that served as a useful hermeneutical tool. Just as Ranke considered the history of the church in relation to universal history, so also Hofmann sought to interpret the history of the people of God (Israel and the church) in relation to world history. According to Hofmann, world history is to be structured on the basis of the development of Christianity. Already in his historical dissertation Hofmann gives evidence of the direction his later theological works would take: "History is falsely divided into ancient, medieval, and recent" (*DBAE* 52). In his textbook on world history for high school students, Hofmann took the position that world history is to be divided into two large parts: (1) the world before Christ; and (2) the world after Christ. This is not merely a convenient B.C./A.D. division, since the incarnation of Christ, the archetypal goal of world history, inaugurates the end of world history in the "middle of history." "Since the goal of world history is now nothing other than that everything be drawn up under a head, which is Christ, so individual [events] will be understood from Christ and in Christ who is their whole."[8] Christ's self-representation occurs in the history leading up to his incarnation, in the history of his earthly life and ministry, and in the history of his community. Each period of his "self-representation" (*Selbstdarstellung*) or "self-giving" points to all the others, backwards and forwards. So this self-representation of Christ is both prophecy and world history at the same time. Thus, universal history and church history coincide (*DVL* 110–11). The history of all people must be viewed in relation to the history of the mission of the church: "Thus it is true also about Jesus Christ, in whom the calling of humanity and Israel comes to its final completion, that his appearance and activity aimed not merely at the formation of a community of the Holy Spirit, but precisely thereby at the transformation of the entire world" (*SBb* 1:216).[9] History is a unified whole, the

---

7. Beyschlag, *Die Erlanger Theologie,* 65–66.

8. J. v. Hofmann, "Probestücke e. angeblich kirchlichen Geschichtsbetrachtung," *ZPK* (Alte Folge) 2 (1839): 14.

9. Especially in the early years of his professional life Hofmann's concern for the universal focus of God's mercy and grace gave him motivation for his deep involvement in several missionary societies and their activities throughout the world. See Sturm, "Die integrierende Funktion der Ekklesiologie," 310. Despite the universal and comprehensive focus of God's love and grace, Hofmann did not teach that in the end "all are saved." He was not a "universalist." He interpreted literally those biblical texts that speak of God's final judgment against those who persist against God's eternal will and election. " . . . [T]he end of history, the stage of which will be Israel according to God's election, will bring to non-Israelitic humanity both blessing and judgment. The Gentile world will be judged on account of its enmity against the people of the

progressing formation of the community between God and humankind mediated in Christ. Hofmann went so far as to assert that "universal history is church history."[10] In other words, Christ himself is a provisional conclusion of the human race from which the end of the same may be understood, and this is what gives history its typological or symbolic character. Thus, the meaning of history must be typological or symbolical because the meaning of history is grounded in its end which has been already disclosed "in the middle of history:" "People have remarked that the symbolic character of a narrative is characteristic of the mythical. But history, which has a center toward which it is aiming and from which it fulfills itself, must have symbolic force because it [i.e., history] points forwards and backwards. Its character manifests itself in its epoch-making events" (*BH* 39).

Just as Hegel sought to conceive the totality of reality as temporal development, so also Hofmann articulated a notion that the world of becoming is from the Creator of all that is, including time itself.[11] History itself is best explained and interpreted in light of the eternal presuppositions which clarify its eschatological orientation and meaning. The eternal God is therefore understood as the cause of all history, the center of all history, and the fulfillment or end of all history (*WE* 1:39–40; *SBb* 1:35). Because "the triune God does not merely establish historicality but actually proceeds into historicality," the continuity of all history is grounded in the eternal God (*ET* 61). *Heilsgeschichte* is "not a mere action of that acting Trinity, but a historical self-fulfillment of the same" (*SBb* 1:45). History as such is a "self-activity of the triune God" and therefore the meaning of *Weltgeschichte* is *Heilsgeschichte* (ibid., 1:54–55). *Heilsgeschichte* so understood is not something that only entails the history of Israel and the Christian church; *Heilsgeschichte* provides the interpretive key to the meaning of

---

true God, but all those will be blessed who were willing to be led to the knowledge of God (cf. Ps. 22:27). The promise given to Abraham stated that no generation on earth will receive a blessing except through him and his descendents. The psalmist knows that enmity against Israel can have no other end than the destruction of her enemies" (*BH* 91–92).

10. Sturm, "Die integrierende Funktion der Ekklesiologie," 312. " . . . Christianity is the basis for our life as a people and . . . our life as a people must be defined more and more clearly by the idea of Christ" (J. v. Hofmann, "Anmerkungen zur Geschichte," *ZPK* 23 [1852]: 357). This idea, too, was also expressed by Hamann. For Hamann "[a]ll of history relates to Christ, and consequently universal history proves to be essentially church history, or *Heilsgeschichte*, which can be interpreted only on the basis of the revelation of Christ. Even sin, the opposition to God, is impotent against the divine plan, which has already been executed and concluded in Christ, and is forced to serve that plan against its will" (Leibrecht, *God and Man in the Thought of Hamann*, 183).

11. Hofmann, however, criticizes Hegel for establishing "a unity of the divine and human Spirit." The personality of God and the personality of human beings are lost in the process. "No longer God and the human being, He the eternal, and he the temporal, but two neuters, the absolute Spirit and the finite Spirit, stand in relation to each other" (*WE* 1:10).

all history.[12] Thus, "Biblical history is something other than an error-free excerpt from world history"; biblical history *is* world history (*BH* 75–76).

Hofmann thought that such a notion is grounded in the Old Testament wherein, especially through the prophets, the God of Israel is identified as the God of all nations. The prophetic witness to God underscores that Israel's God is universal, but God will not be known by the nations as such until the end of history, on "the last day." According to Hofmann's reading of the prophets, including especially his study of Jeremiah and Daniel, all history is under the Lordship of God, in whom the whole world finds its fulfillment.[13] Until that fulfillment, however, the future is beyond human understanding. Even the fact that Jesus is "the end of history" will not be known until the last day; only then will it become clear to all that God has revealed God's self in Jesus.

In turn, this history points ahead to the eschatological perfection of God's revelation which will embrace all of humankind. The present, historic community of Christ, the whole Christian church on earth, awaits its perfection and glorification in the *eschaton*. This hope is grounded in the risen Christ who is not only head over the church but also over the historical process of all creation.[14] When the lordship of Christ struggles against nothing more,

---

12. Compare Hofmann's theology of history with that of von Rad: "What the Deuteronomist presents is really a history of the creative word of Jahweh. What fascinated him was, we might say, the functioning of the divine word in history.... The decisive factor for Israel does not lie in the things which ordinarily cause a stir in history, nor in the vast problems inherent in history, but it lies in applying a few very simple theological and prophetic fundamental axioms about the nature of the divine word. And so it is only this word of Jahweh which gives continuity and aspiration to the phenomenon of history, which unites the varied and individual phenomena to form a whole in the sight of God. Thus the Deuteronomist shows with exemplary validity what *Heilsgeschichte* is in the Old Testament: that is, a process of history which is formed by the word of Jahweh continually intervening in judgment and salvation and directed towards a fulfillment" (Gerhard von Rad, "The Deuteronomistic Theology of History," *Studies in Deuteronomy* [trans. David Stalker; London: SCM Press, 1953], 91). See also idem., *The Theology of the Old Testament* (trans. David Stalker; New York: Harper and Row, 1965), 2:80–125. For Hofmann's influence on von Rad, see Robert Dentan, *Preface to Old Testament Theology* (rev. ed.; New York: Seabury, 1963), 78–80.

13. See J. v. Hofmann, *Die Siebenzig Jahre des Propheten Jeremia und die Siebenzig Jahrwochen des Propheten Daniel: Zwei exegetisch-historische Untersuchungen* (Nürnberg: Theodor Otto, 1836). The essential prophecies of Jeremiah and Daniel disclose that the Lord is the Lord of all nations. Hofmann understood the number seven and its cognates in Jeremiah and Daniel to be both actual periods of time but also typological symbols whose meaning is grounded in the six days of creation followed by the seventh day of "a complete and perfect rest." So, for example, Hofmann interpreted the seventy weeks of years in Daniel to be both a prophecy of the destruction of the Babylonian kingdom through "God's servant, Cyrus," but also a typological prophecy of the coming messianic kingdom at the end of history.

14. "The faithful Christian is only comprehended in the context of the community and its historical place within the word of Scripture, but that place is only understood within *Heilsgeschichte* to which the word testifies. Because the community indeed is situated in the economic-organic-eschatological context of *Heilsgeschichte*, only in it is the goal of glorification certain" (Schellbach, *Theologie und Philosophie*, 88).

then it will have become fulfilled and Christ will give everything over to the Father (WE 2:299). On "that day" history will be fulfilled in *Heilsgeschichte* just as the dissimilarity within the historical Trinity will be fulfilled into an eternal similarity of perfect and complete peace.[15]

> The intra-Trinitarian activity [*Lebendigkeit*] turns back into itself in that it absorbs humanity into the intra-divine relationship. After the ground of its procession out of itself into the historical dissimilarity is transcended [*aufgehoben ist*] with the restoration of the naturally stable relationship between God and humanity, it comes to the rest of the always uniform peace.[16]

The Eschatological Orientation of *Weltgeschichte*

As we have seen, for Hofmann the orientation of *Heilsgeschichte* is eschatological since the meaning of history lies in its end. "The value and meaning of an individual fact resides in relation to its ultimate result" (*WE* 1:33). There can be no *Heilsgeschichte* without an eschatological end toward which all prophecy/history is proceeding. Furthermore, history cannot be understood as universal history apart from an eschatological orientation: "No one is able to narrate probingly the whole of past things without paying attention to biblical prophecies about future things" (*DBAE* 53). All history is prophecy of the *eschaton*, and thus history is only fully understandable from its end (*WE* 1:33).[17] "The outcome of all history becomes the cornerstone of the

---

15. See Schellbach, *Theologie und Philosophie*, 66.

16. Sturm, "Die integrierende Funktion der Ekklesiologie," 330.

17. This, of course, was Hegel's perspective as well, though in a very different form from Hofmann's. One should note here Althaus's critique of Hofmann's teleological-*heilsgeschichtliche* scheme. Althaus was especially critical of Hofmann's hope toward a supposed eschatological end of history. For Althaus, biblical eschatology must be thoroughly rethought to fit only within the category of "personal fulfillment." Althaus attempts to understand eschatology as a consequence of the doctrine of justification: faith and hope depend on God's forgiveness of the guilty sinner now, and this acquittal summons the guilty person to be responsible for his or her own life, which God will judge in the future. As a result of discussion, however, Althaus attempted to integrate a form of "teleological eschatology" in the fourth (1933) and subsequent editions of his book, *Die Letzten Dinge* (8th ed.; Gütersloh: C. Bertelsmann, 1981). Althaus's mature eschatology, though still beginning with a discussion of "personal fulfillment," now included discussion of the hope for an eschatological end of history, an end that is inclusive of all humanity and, indeed, all creation, not merely individuals. The eschatological theologians of the next generation (e.g., Moltmann and Pannenberg) have emphasized the latter concern and have thereby approached positions that are more similar to Hofmann than to the existentialist theologians (e.g., Althaus, Bultmann). See Moltmann, "Trends in Eschatology," in *The Future of Creation*, 20–23; and Pannenberg, *Systematic Theology*, 3:538–46, 586–95.

whole building. In the final result all developments summarize themselves and receive their illumination."[18]

For Hofmann this "end of history" is the appearance of Jesus Christ and his kingdom "in the midst of history." Universal history has its fulfillment in his reign. Jesus "is the essential content of all history," not merely the content of the history of the people of Israel and their religion. The deepest significance of all things resides in Christ, their true end. In his kingdom all things receive their complete fulfillment. So all historical events are truly oriented toward Christ and these become prophecies of "their end." In this way, for Hofmann, all of history is "the self-representation of Christ," not just the history leading up to Christ. This conception makes all history into prophecy, i.e., prophecy of the end of history. This orientation of Christ to the whole of history means that his redemption is as comprehensive as the whole of creation. The salvation that Christ brings is the establishment of perfect community with God, so all history is "the prophecy and history" of the developing communion with God: "history, namely the always progressing formation of the community of God and humanity; prophecy, namely the always certain indicator toward the final form of the community of God and humanity" (*WE* 1:40).

Christ as the "archetypal world-goal," precisely in his dissimilarity with God (in which he entered into the history of sinful humanity), is the means toward this final form. But he is also a type of this final form, since his birth, his life, his suffering, his death, and his resurrection and exaltation are a further prophecy of the perfection of this community with God (*WE* 2:248). His birth, life, and death are a prefiguring of the lowly and inconspicuous form of his revelation in the world, and yet just as his death was overcome in the resurrection, so also the lowly form of his revelation in the world will be overcome in the end of history. Now, as resurrected and ascended Lord, Jesus Christ calls people into his community of love (ibid., 2:259).

Since for Hofmann the growth of the lordship of Jesus over against all other world powers is the essential content of world history, the prophecy of the end is being fulfilled even now in the historical community of Christ which itself is a prophecy of the end of history. Hofmann defined this end as the consummation of the communion between God and humanity, when sinful and mortal human nature will be glorified in the general resurrection of the dead, Christ will hand over his kingdom to the Father, and "God will be all in all" (ibid., 2:299; cf. 1:34).

More than any other major theologian of the nineteenth century, Hofmann devoted himself to understanding the eschatological character of the

---

18. Procksch, "Hofmanns Geschichtsauffassung," 1034.

prophetic and eschatological biblical texts.[19] Already in his first theological work, *Die Siebenzig Jahre des Propheten Jeremias und die Siebenzig Jahrwochen des Propheten Daniel* (1836), Hofmann wrestled with the nature of apocalyptic literature and its eschatological witness. He found in apocalyptic both a problem and an answer. The difficulty for Hofmann was accounting for the disruption into history that apocalyptic literature expects if history is the purposeful (teleological) means for God's self-fulfillment. Apocalyptic seems to call into question a notion of historical development, so central to Hofmann's conception of *Heilsgeschichte*. The parousia of Christ, the eschatological perfection of all creation, is understood not as a sudden change that brings about the destruction of history but "as a growing island in the sea of history until the solid ground has completely replaced the sea."[20] History is an organic process of development whose driving force is Christ, the archetypal goal of all creation.

On the other hand, apocalyptic and eschatological biblical texts provided Hofmann an escape when the vitalities and complexities of world history did not coincide with his conception of historical development. Apocalyptic becomes helpful to the *heilsgeschichtliche* theologian who must acknowledge the uncertainty of real history and the unavailability of God's future.[21] Thus *Heilsgeschichte* must account also for apocalyptic disruption and historical ambiguities that give rise to apocalyptic visions.

While Hofmann refused to speculate as to when the *eschaton* will happen, his *heilsgeschichtliche* orientation led him to treat as literal-historical those statements in the book of Revelation that concern the millennial reign of Christ.[22] Hofmann was not beyond trying to break apocalyptic coding through gematria (the use of numbers to signify things). Like his forefather, Johann A. Bengel (1687–1752), Hofmann, too, was a millennialist and expected a literal thousand-year reign of Christ (Rev 20).[23] "Whoever doubts the millennial reign of Christ will likewise be suspicious of the newest things that agree with it."[24] These "newest things" included, for Hofmann, the advent of Zionism and the hope of a return of the Jewish people to Palestine:

---

19. Contra Wenz who states, " . . . Hofmann concedes only a marginal value to futurist eschatology . . . " (Wenz, *Geschichte*, 2:35 fn. 5]). Wenz does not consider Hofmann's dogmatics lectures or his exegetical writings.

20. Schellbach, *Theologie und Philosophie*, 64.

21. See Steck, "Die Idee Heilsgeschichte," 33.

22. See Hofmann, *Die Offenbarung St. Johannis, nach Vorlesungen des J. C. K. von Hofmann* (ed. E. von Lorenz; Leipzig: A. Deichert, 1896); but also Hofmann, "Antichiliastischer Fanatismus," *ZPK* 41 (1861): 124–25; idem, "Paulus, der Chiliast," *ZPK* 42 (1861): 338–41; and idem, "Die sieben Sendschriften der Offenbarung Johannis," *ZPK* 52 (1866): 74–82.

23. On Bengel's approach to the Bible, see William Baird, *History of New Testament Research*, 1:69–80.

24. Hofmann, "Thesis 5," *De Argumento Psalmi Centesimi Decimi*, 47.

"Prophets of the Old Testament predicted ahead of time that the people of Israel would return to the land of Canaan."[25]

While it would be tempting from a post-Enlightenment perspective, working with the hermeneutical principles that have resulted from the rise of historical criticism, to dismiss Hofmann's entire theological enterprise on the basis of his naïve interpretive decisions, one should resist this impulse for the sake of Hofmann's basic theological concern, the relation of the triune God to human beings in historical reality. Clearly, Hofmann worked with "a first naiveté" when he was interpreting the protological and eschatological scriptural material and so the symbol had not yet "given rise to thought" in every instance of his biblical and theological studies.[26] But this serious deficiency does not necessarily invalidate the potentially important theological positions he takes with regard to his doctrine of God, especially those which appear to have anticipated later theological developments.

One way that Hofmann attempted to reconcile *Heilsgeschichte* with eschatology was to assert that *Heilsgeschichte* always shows time itself as short, even if the beginning and the end appear to be far apart from each other. Thus, Hofmann acknowledged that teleology is not eschatology. Still, he could not help but state that all things now stand under the lordship of Christ, even though such lordship is "hidden." According to Hofmann, not until the *eschaton* will it become evident that all history was moving toward its fulfillment and completion in Christ.

Hofmann acknowledged that in the interim between now and the end, the meaning of history is ambiguous, even for people of Christian faith. The reality of evil in the world and the complexities accompanying the differing ways of construing past events complicate the Christian's perception of the hand of God at work in history. More than once Hofmann cites Paul's aphorism, "We see through a clouded glass."[27] "We had to give up the hope of forming a clear picture of the events which precede the actual termination of the present eon, and of the event itself, because the only way in which they can be described is by borrowing the means of expression from present events or the past" (*BH* 254). "...[T]he literary form has to be treated merely as a means of giving expression to things which transcend our imagination" (ibid., 258).

For both God's eternal being and his eternal decree are, to be sure, revealed in real events but in the events of a history which occurs on

---

25. Hofmann, "Thesis 6," *De Argumento Psalmi Centesimi Decimi*, 47.
26. See Ricoeur, *The Symbolism of Evil*, 347–57.
27. Hofmann expresses the ambiguities inherent in Christian knowledge in his remarks about 1 Cor 13:12. See *HS* 2.2:303–6.

the basis and ground of a world estranged from God; because of this, what he is and what is in him only mirrors itself in the way in which the world is thus constituted (ἐν ἐνίγματι) and because of this his self-revelation assumes a form which only lets him be known in his essential nature to the one who takes into account the conditionality of the world through the way in which the world is now constituted and only to the degree that he succeeds in accounting for its conditioned nature. This two-fold mediacy of the knowledge of God stands in contrast to the immediacy of the knowledge of God which then occurs when we behold God at the goal of his ways where nothing alien stands anymore between him and us (*HS* 2.2:303).[28]

In the meantime, Christian existence is defined by faith, hope, and love. If all of world history were figured out completely in advance, as if this were even possible, there would be no need for faith, hope, and love.

---

28. Hofmann is here providing commentary on 1 Cor 13:12. See also *BH* 254ff., where Hofmann acknowledges the ambiguous character of the eschatological events portrayed symbolically in Scripture.

CHAPTER TWELVE

Evaluation and Criticism of Hofmann's Doctrine of God

Trinitarian Historicality

While it is generally correct that the doctrine of the Trinity fell into disuse in Protestantism in the nineteenth century, one must take notice of the unique contribution that Hofmann made to Trinitarian theology two generations prior to Barth. Hofmann's Trinitarian reflections clearly anticipate theological emphases that became more popular some ninety years after Hofmann delivered his dogmatic lectures. Like the respective theological projects of Barth and Rahner, Hofmann's theological reflections are the outcome of his attempt to take seriously God's self-revelation in Jesus Christ through the Holy Spirit. The divine self-revelation is the all-encompassing circle that surrounds the Christian *Tatbestand*. The heart of Hofmann's theology is the development of the Trinity in history. He sought to express the divine self-revelation as the fulfillment of the divine love for all creation. In view of the above, it is surprising that none of the major contemporary Trinitarian theologians has deigned even to refer to Hofmann's Trinitarian thought.

Negative Features of Hofmann's Trinitarian Thought

Before attending to the positive contribution Hofmann has made to a Christian doctrine of God, we must first examine those elements in his Trinitarian thought that are problematic. While Hofmann's Trinitarian theology has many good intentions, he was not always able to carry them out successfully. Despite his important contribution, his Trinitarian theology is not persuasive in some respects.

First, Hofmann's naiveté about the genre of the biblical narratives often restricts his theological assertions about God's being-in-becoming. Although Hofmann was aware of historical criticism, he generally rejected it in favor of simply presupposing the historicity of certain "history-like" narratives that are not "history" in the proper sense of the term (e.g., Gen 1–11; the apocalyptic texts). A number of features of Hofmann's doctrine of God deal with biblical narratives at the edge of human experience: the protological narratives, eschatological texts, evil spirits, and so on. Hofmann wanted to justify the reliability of the creation narratives as historical truth, and this justification often gets in the way of potentially positive theological truth. In this regard, Hofmann's theology is timebound by his failure to relate his dogmatic understandings ("faith") to critical-historical investigation of the biblical texts.

Second, perhaps the sharpest criticism of Hofmann's doctrine of God concerns the method by which Hofmann articulates his knowledge of God. How is one able to proceed from the historicality of the Trinity to postulate eternal presuppositions? What justifies the conclusion of a Trinitarian dissimilarity on the basis of an eternal self-similarity and the identification of both? Breidert has argued that the "outcome of the historical from the eternal, the outcome of the historical dissimilarity out of the eternal self-similarity of the intra-divine relationship is not actually supportable. Consequently, Hofmann is not able to make understandable his theoretical limitation of knowledge to the historical, even as he still speaks of an eternal nature in Christ."[1]

In response to this criticism, one might argue on Hofmann's behalf that the historical knowledge of God is knowledge of the eternal *in* history. Hofmann attempted to maintain the classical distinction between the immanent and economic Trinity, holding that the economic is the key to the immanent. Contrary to his own assertion that the immanent Trinity is incomprehensible, Hofmann's concerns would have been better served if he had made clearer the intimate relation between the economic self-giving of God and the identity of God. While Hofmann is not Rahner or Barth (or Jüngel), his theological concerns are similar to these later theologians, whose identification of the economic and the immanent Trinity is clearer and stronger than in Hofmann's thought. Hofmann's doctrine of God is, however, *open* to corrective modification from these later developments.

Third, despite Hofmann's intentions to base his theology on the Christian *Tatbestand,* including the biblical witness to God's actions in history, Hofmann's doctrine of God is partly grounded in metaphysical speculation about the pretemporality of God and this, too, complicates his theological goals. While Hofmann asserted that the eternal is only comprehensible on the basis of the eternal's historical self-giving, Hofmann was not unwilling to

---

1. Breidert, *Die kenotische Christologie,* 184.

make metaphysical assertions about the eternal per se. Here Hofmann's theology shares significant traits with ideas put forth by those idealist thinkers he finds most helpful for his theological explication (e.g., Schelling, Spinoza, Böhme, and Hamann). It appears that Trinitarian speculation not directly arising from the Bible partially shaped his doctrine of creation and his kenotic Christology. Hofmann did not acknowledge that theosophical speculation had shaped his interpretation of the biblical texts. For example, although Hofmann rejected Spinoza's claim that God is dependent upon the world, Hofmann himself argued that the triune God comes to fulfillment through historical development. Even though one might be able to develop such an idea on the basis of the biblical witness, it clearly is an idea that had been shaped in relation to early nineteenth-century Idealism.

Fourth, in light of Hofmann's ambiguous relation to German Idealism, Hofmann appears to have been inconsistent with his affirmations about God's being. In rejecting the Spinozist view, Hofmann wanted to preserve the freedom of God over against the world, and yet on other occasions he also acknowledged that God's freedom is the basis for God's self-determination in history and that God's being is realized through an historical process of self-limiting development. Thus, God's freedom is the basis on which God's being is dependent upon the world of becoming. Hofmann would have been more consistent in his doctrine of God if he had paid more attention to the implications of his assertions that God's will of love is realized in history and that God's historical *kenosis* in Jesus truly creates change in God's being.

Fifth, another criticism of Hofmann's doctrine of God might center on the ambiguity that attends his discussion of the relation between divine freedom and human freedom. What are the implications of the divine freedom in Hofmann's doctrine of God in relation to modern understandings of human freedom? Does not the freedom of God undermine the freedom of human beings? In response to questions like these, Hofmann stressed that the end of history disclosed in the resurrection of Jesus is that which changes and motivates human beings in the present to live toward the future. The vision of the future perfection of the communion between God and humanity leads people to act on the basis of that vision in the present. Hofmann thus recognized that history is open to novel actions by people, though he held that ultimately even these actions will serve God's final purposes for humankind. Hofmann based his view on the biblical prophets who acknowledged that human beings were actors on the stage of human history (e.g., Nebuchadnezzar, Cyrus), but that the final cause of their actions was God. In this way Hofmann wanted to emphasize human responsibility to act freely in the present while at the same time hold on to the priority of God's freedom over all of human history. While God is necessarily acting and effective in all historical events, God is not the sole historical agent. Nonetheless, the agency of God to bring history to its "end" guarantees God's freedom vis-à-vis human freedom.

Finally, Hofmann was working with an Idealist notion which holds that for history to have any meaning it must have an absolute and literal "end." Only with an "end" can one speak of history as a meaningful "whole." But such a view of an absolute and literal "end" to history challenges both human freedom/contingency and the openness of history. Since God has predestined humanity in Christ to that communion with God established in and through Jesus and revealed in Jesus' resurrection from the dead, are human actions in any way truly contingent and free? Have not historical relativism and the experience of radical evil in the modern world forever called into question the traditional view that God is working in history to bring history to its predetermined "end?" Hofmann did not ask or answer this question. Perhaps if his biblical hermeneutic would have allowed him the freedom to interpret the apocalyptic texts less literally, he might have been in a position to read them as imaginative symbols that illuminate important theological truths and that serve as motivation for human beings to live toward true human community with God. While such a view of human actions would seem to put some limits on the freedom of God, something Hofmann did not wish to do, it seems to be more consistent with Hofmann's primary assertion that God's being is found in God's historical becoming, i.e., that God's being (including the freedom of God) is already limited within the world of historical contingency, historical relativity, and even a world of "evil powers" opposed to God's will of love. For Hofmann the limitation of God's being in history centers in God's *kenosis* in Jesus whereby God redeems that which is opposed to God.

Positive Features of Hofmann's Trinitarian Thought

Despite the limitations to Hofmann's doctrine of God, his Trinitarian thought is fruitful and promising for contemporary theology. We may note the following positive features of his theology:

First, Hofmann sought to situate the doctrine of the Trinity in the life of the church. For Hofmann the doctrine of the Trinity is grounded in God's self-giving, which gives rise to the Christian *Tatbestand* that is both historical and experiential. Hofmann was thus critical of the orthodox Lutheran understanding of the Trinity since it tended to divorce the doctrine of the Trinity from the life of the church. This scholastic approach failed to see the deep connection between the triune God, the Bible, and the actual life of ecclesial faith. The content of orthodox dogmatics was often regarded as so many intellectual statements extracted from the Bible. Hofmann showed that the content of dogmatics, centering in the self-giving of the triune God, must be that which is the possession of a living faith. There must be a central desire on the part of the theologian to unite systematic-biblical theology with the piety of Christian spirituality in a common witness to the self-giving of the triune God in the world. Thus the Bible cannot be appropriated simply by a systematic arrangement of its doctrines or by a retreat into the pietism of prayer and hymnody, but only when it is understood as the witness to the living God's actions in history, including the history of the biblical interpreter. The Trinity is the living God who causes the Christian *Tatbestand,* which "gives shape and form" to the Christian's life. "The total of the biblical history is referential to God's revelation in Jesus Christ and opens itself up from that."[2] An implication of this view is that the Christian theologian must take historical events seriously, as if God has something to do with them.

Second, contrary to Preus, who concludes that Hofmann "was in perfect agreement with the historic formulation of [the doctrine of the Trinity]," Hofmann's theological procedure for grounding his talk of God led to a new understanding of God's being.[3] Hofmann's theological method led him to break with the normative understanding of God as atemporal Being. God and history belong together and mutually condition each other. God's being is given through God's actions in history, and these actions in turn are the focus of the biblical witness to the God who is love. The self-giving of God in history for the sake of uniting God and humanity in a communion of love qualifies what can be said about God's eternal being. In this respect, Hofmann's Trinitarian ideas anticipate certain themes that will become important in the period after Barth and Rahner. For example, Hofmann anticipates both a "subject" paradigm as well as a "communal" paradigm, though he emphasized the former. Hofmann's attempt to articulate an adequate understanding of the implication of God's relationality to God's nature clearly establishes him as an important precursor to many theologians today.[4]

---

2. Swarat, "Die heilsgeschichtliche Konzeption," 235.

3. " ... [W]hile [Hofmann] was in perfect agreement with the historic formulation of this doctrine, he disapproved of the traditional means of establishing it" (Preus, "The Theology of Johann von Hofmann," 127). If Preus were correct, Thomasius would have had no reason for criticizing Hofmann's understanding of *kenosis* and Hofmann's rejection of the classical understanding of God's wrath.

4. For example, David Tracy states that "the central theological question of God's nature in our period" is "how, most adequately, to understand the divine relationality" (David Tracy,

Third, Hofmann's theology anticipates contemporary Trinitarian concerns because he gave primacy to divine love over God's power. The most true statement one can make about God, according to Hofmann, is that God is love. God's identity as love is the ground for God's being-in-becoming, i.e., that God gives God's self to the Other out of his eternal love in order to redeem the Other. Thus Hofmann criticized traditional metaphysics in favor of God's own self-determination and self-giving in history. Hofmann rejected the classical ontology which conceives God's power as absolute because it had obscured the soteriological orientation of God toward the world. This soteriological orientation is grounded in God's eternal love. If love is primary, then God's power is not absolute in an unqualified manner; rather, it is directed by love. Thus, Hofmann understood God as the God of history, and not as the eternal in the sense of steady and invariable being. God's being is understood properly only when it is understood as historical "self-giving" for the sake of humanity, that is, as grace.

Fourth, in keeping with the priority he gave to divine love Hofmann rejected Spinoza's view that seemed to make God dependent on the world. Hofmann believed that such a view undermined the nature of God's love for the world. Hofmann thought that the Spinozist view of the relationship of God to the world makes God need the world, and that such "needing" is contrary to God's love, which is "giving." In contrast to Spinoza, Hofmann asserted the freedom of the eternal and pretemporal God to enter freely into an historical relationship with the world for the sake of God's eternal love for the world. For Hofmann God's becoming historical is a free and unnecessary decision of God to be self-giving love in and for the world.

Hofmann thus emphasized that the biblical view of God centers on God's creative freedom to do new things in history. The actions of God in history surpass expectations and are thus unpredictable, non-necessary, and contingent. For Hofmann the event of Jesus' resurrection from the dead is the central divine act in history. As such, the resurrection of Jesus from the dead is the appearance of the "end" (*telos*) of human history in the "middle" of history. This means, for Hofmann, that the resurrection of Jesus is the ultimate meaning of the totality of history. God determines everything toward its fulfillment in the end of Jesus, which has already been disclosed in his resurrection. This is partly why Hofmann asserted that

---

"Approaching the Christian Understanding of God," in *Systematic Theology: Roman Catholic Perspectives* [ed. Francis Schüssler Fiorenza and John Galvin; Minneapolis: Fortress, 1991], 143). Tracy continues, "On the one hand, the recovery of the centrality of the Trinitarian understanding of God is the prime instance of the importance of the concept of relationality. This is especially the case in those theologians who have rethought the intrinsic unity of the 'economic' and 'immanent' Trinity (Karl Rahner, Walter Kasper, et al.)" (ibid., 143).

> Christianity as an eternal *Tatbestand* is based upon a three-fold *Tatbestand:* on the personality of God, on the inner relationship of the Trinity, and on the predestination of humankind. As personal God he is the one who is self-determining, his Trinity is his inward self-determination, and the predestination of humankind is his outward self-determination. (*ET* 60)

The "outward self-determination" of the triune God is the election of all humanity to salvation in Jesus. His resurrection from the dead is the end or goal of human history.

While the revelation of this "end" is hidden to the world outside of faith, it is "visible" to those who have faith. Faith trusts that God hidden in his revelation is working to accomplish his eschatological fulfillment. Thus, Hofmann did not understand God's actions in the present to be the actions of a God who is absent in the present and who only exists in the future, as in Pannenberg's notions that God is the power of the future, that the future has ontological priority to the present and thus "causes" the present, and that the kingdom of God is wholly a future reality. Rather, the freedom of God leads God to be present (though hidden) and active in the world as God seeks to move all creation to its established end in the communion of Christ. In this regard, Hofmann's doctrine of God is partly grounded in a temporal ontology that is like Hegel's.

Fifth, although Hofmann did not respond directly to Fichte's critique of "the personality of God," it appears that he had Fichte in mind when he argued that human personality is grounded in the divine "Self" and not the other way around. Hofmann undoubtedly would have thought that Fichte's grounding of "personality" in the human self is inadequate. For Hofmann the notion of God's "personality" is not tied directly to human finitude but to the freedom of God to give God's self as love to human beings. The "personality" of God thus is not inherently anthropomorphic but the result of God's freedom to be the God of love.[5]

Finally, Hofmann affirms that theology is about community with God and others. The grace of God that is grounded in God's being-in-becoming in history has implications for the history of all humanity. Christianity is not merely about the individual Christian's relation to God; rather, God's relation to the Christian necessarily involves the Christian in communion with other human beings. Trinitarian historicality led Hofmann in a comprehensive, humanitarian direction.

---

5. This line of argumentation would also serve Hofmann against the atheistic criticism of faith and theology leveled by Feuerbach.

Kenosis and Atonement

Just as Hofmann's Trinitarian ideas place him in the center of the most creative theologians between Hegel and Barth, so Hofmann's attempts at Christological reconstruction put him in the center of the most creative theologians between Schleiermacher and Ritschl. Nonetheless by the time of Ritschl kenotic understandings of Christ and the atonement, at least in Germany, were on the wane.[6] Ritschl's theology, with its critique of metaphysics, was not sympathetic to discussions about the person of Jesus, even those which attempted to emphasize the full and complete humanity of Jesus over against traditional understandings. While Ritschl at least wanted to take seriously the humanity of Jesus, the focus of his theology is upon the actions of Jesus and not his person. One could argue that, to the degree that Hofmann's Christology also emphasizes the work of Jesus as the real meaning of his person, Hofmann's theology merely anticipates Ritschl. Largely because of the criticism of Hofmann by Ritschlians (and also by Barth) and the criticism by the history-of-religions school (including also criticism by Bultmann), Hofmann's Trinitarian and kenotic theology was soon passed over for other alternatives. If he was appreciated, it was only as a transitional figure. As a result of this view, several positive features of Hofmann's Christology and atonement theory have been forgotten. This neglect is unfortunate, especially in light of renewed appreciation for *kenosis* among several contemporary theologians.[7]

Negative Features of Hofmann's Kenotic Christology

There are, to be sure, several features of his Christology that are problematic. First, Hofmann was not greatly concerned with the problem of the historicality of the Christ event. Even though Hofmann wanted to take seriously the whole "pattern" of Jesus' life as disclosed in the New Testament writings, including the witness to his resurrection, he was not generally interested in a "life of Jesus" (*Bild Jesu*) in the sense of critical historical investigation into the life of Jesus. The one exception to this is his lengthy review of the work of Strauss and Renan. For Hofmann Jesus is an historic human being, whose life is understood to be the consequence of the eternal will of God. In this regard, Hofmann anticipated the theological work of Kähler. While it is not correct to say that a "picture of Jesus" was superfluous to his Christology,

---

6. Breidert, *Die kenotische Christologie*, 14.
7. See, for example, Jon Sobrino, *Christology at the Crossroads* (Maryknoll, N.Y.: Orbis, 1978), and the works by Walter Kasper.

what really counted for him was the dogmatic judgment that this human life constitutes the center of God's life with the world. While Hofmann held that Jesus' earthly existence defines who God is as love, Hofmann had little interest in clarifying the conditions of that earthly life by means of critical historical investigation of the potential sources of that life (e.g., the Gospels).

Second, in spite of all his intentions to the contrary, does not Hofmann's Christology, which speaks of Christ's humanity so unremittingly in terms of self-renunciation, *kenosis,* suffering, and death, lead ineluctably to a docetic Christ?[8] Is this not the fate of all "high Christologies" that start "from above?" Is the human Jesus forced by his mission to become so utterly transparent to the eternal Self as to nearly vanish altogether, leaving only a created cipher? Does Jesus' historical existence, its contingency, get robbed of its significance and lead in the direction of Monophysitism? This seems to be the case especially when Hofmann speaks of "humanity" as a whole in Christ. In what sense is it correct or meaningful to say that "humanity" is in Jesus? Even if one could defend such a notion, does not this idea rob Jesus of his true, concrete, historical human existence? Related to these questions is the question about Hofmann's knowledge of God. Does not Hofmann's theology claim to know too much about the inner life of God, despite his intentions to base his theology strictly on the witness of Scripture to God's historical revelation that centers on the resurrection of Jesus from the dead? Has not Hofmann's theology drifted off in a mythological direction that leads toward a Gnostic understanding of God and a docetic understanding of Christ?

While a detailed response to these difficult questions cannot be made in Hofmann's defense, one could reply by saying, again, that Hofmann's *intentions* were to take Jesus' full and true humanity quite seriously as revealing the inner life of God. It is not that Hofmann began with speculative knowledge of God and then sought to apply that knowledge to Jesus. That would be to fall back into the very trap created by the traditional language of "two natures" in Christ. Rather, Hofmann's procedure was to work back from Jesus Christ, especially the witness to his resurrection, into the Trinitarian source of Christ's life. Furthermore, Hofmann's intentions were to focus on the work of Christ and to infer from the work about the person. Who must this person be for him to act this way, to be acted upon in the way of his resurrection from the dead? Thus, for Hofmann, the union between Jesus and the second person of the Trinity is at the level of Christ's human existence and the actions of Jesus, including also his resurrection from the dead. In other words, the divine and the human are conjoined in Christ in enacting

---

8. So Forde, *The Law-Gospel Debate,* 72.

that particular life of self-renunciation, self-emptying, obedient love which is the mode of existence of the second person of the Trinity. For a human being to live life according to this eternal will of love in no way prevents this particular human being from existing in every respect as a fully human person, but neither does it preclude that same human person from being identified as the person of the eternal *Logos* of God. This reflects well Hofmann's concern to emphasize Christ's deep immersion in the most realistic details of alienated human existence.

Positive Features of Hofmann's Kenotic Christology

Despite the above negative features of his Christology, a number of positive aspects, indispensable to his Trinitarian theology, are worth highlighting. First, a kenotic Christology, grounded in the Trinity, is the underlying structure of Hofmann's approach to the incarnation and atonement. Hofmann's understanding of the atonement is grounded in the concrete form of the triune God's self-giving, saving love in the man Jesus. While Hofmann did not hesitate to ground the life and ministry of Jesus in the eternal God, he criticized all Eutychian-like Christologies that de-emphasize the full and complete humanity of Jesus of Nazareth. For Hofmann the existence of the human being Jesus as the historical existence of the person of the *Logos* is a definitively complete *human* existence every human characteristic of which, including a human mind and will, is actually preserved and perfected, not circumvented or supplanted, by coming into existence. Indeed, Hofmann argued that the eternal Self that is the second person of the Trinity is enclosed in the humanity of Jesus.

While Hofmann sometimes gives the impression that he was still working within the traditional "two natures" paradigm, most often he wrote of the man Jesus as perfectly establishing the eternal love of God for the world, as obediently enacting the divine sonship in human form. By so transposing Christological understanding from essentialist to actualist and relational terms, Hofmann attempted to ease the kind of metaphysical discomfort with essentialist language in Christology which theologians have felt since Schleiermacher and Strauss.

For Hofmann the whole life of Jesus "actualizes" and "completes" the self-giving and self-emptying of the triune God. Thus, by conceiving the incarnation and life of Jesus in terms of a particular "divine Self-giving," Hofmann was ensuring that his Christology did not become separated from its Trinitarian basis. In other words, he wanted to emphasize that it is not undifferentiated divine self-communication which results in the incarnation and life of Jesus, but rather it is the particular mode of existence of the eternal person which Jesus lives out in his human existence as the Son of God. In addition to its Trinitarian strengths, Hofmann's approach has the advantage that it does not transmute Jesus into a quasi-divinity. The humanity of Christ is itself the living action of the self-giving, self-emptying of the *Logos* that is grounded in the Father's love.

Second, Hofmann stressed correctly that since history is the self-fulfillment of the triune God and since God loves humanity eternally in Christ, there is no other *ultimate* relation of God vis-à-vis humanity than that of love. God's love has priority over God's justice. Thus, Hofmann's Christology is inclusive and universal. The salvation that God wills eternally is oriented to humanity as a whole in Jesus Christ. Because God has assumed a Trinitarian form in history for the sake of redeeming sinful humanity, a form in which the second person of the Trinity has "emptied himself" into the man Jesus, the divine will of love is realized in history. Everything that occurs after this *kenosis* is only an extension and consequence of this basic "starting point" in the history of God's Trinitarian dissimilarity. In this context, the death of Jesus is understood as the moment of "greatest opposition" within the development of Trinitarian dissimilarity, but not as a "vicarious satisfaction" or "penal ransom" as in classic Lutheran theology following Anselm.

Thus, in contrast to classic Lutheran Orthodoxy, Hofmann took the whole revealed life of Jesus, not merely his death on the cross, as the revelation of God's love for humanity. The whole ministry of Jesus is the place of God's saving activity. The life of Jesus is the basis for the Christian's confidence in God's self-determination and relationality to be the God of love. The radical self-emptying of Jesus is not merely necessitated by the sins of a fallen world but also reflects the utterly kenotic reality of the eternal Trinitarian self-giving.

Third, it follows that Christ's active ministry cannot fit into the classic juridical framework wherein Christ suffered divine punishment instead of humanity. God emptied God's self in Jesus in order that Jesus might fulfill his own calling. Thus, the righteousness of Christ is something more than a mere fulfilling of God's divine law for the sake of appeasing divine wrath; the righteousness of Christ includes his free obedience to empty himself in love, to take the form of a slave within the conditions of humanity, to suffer, and to die for the sake of re-uniting fallen humanity with God. The whole ministry of Jesus is not, therefore, merely the fulfilling of the divine law in response to the divine justice; rather it is principally the historical fulfillment of the eternal will of love.

Fourth, Hofmann stressed that God is always a free and active subject and never a fixed object. The freedom of God is grounded in God's love for the world. The freedom of God also informed Hofmann's understanding of the person and work of Christ. Christ is the historical revelation of the eternal Self that is the triune God. As such, he is the revelation of the Father's love for all creation in the power of the Spirit. God's freedom to give God's self in the man Jesus is the corollary to the affirmation that God is love. But the freedom of God also means for Hofmann that Christology is more about the free obedience of Jesus to the Father than about the ontology of Jesus. Christ's humanity, while remaining perfectly human in its essence, is lived out according to the love that God has for the world, a mode of existence that is the perfect establishment in human terms of the divine love. Here, Hofmann's notion of "person" may prove helpful in comprehending the mission of Jesus, the Son of God, that is grounded in the Trinity. Jesus is definitively "person," and since all humanity is oriented toward fulfillment in him, each human being receives his or her own fulfilled personhood by participating in communion with Christ.

Finally, Hofmann attempted to take seriously the witness to the resurrection of Jesus as the key to the meaning of Jesus' life and death. Hofmann might respond to Ritschl's criticism of metaphysics by arguing that one can't help but involve oneself in metaphysical assertions when one seeks to describe the nature of God's *relation* to the world in Jesus Christ on the basis of the witness to his resurrection. In this regard, Hofmann anticipates such theologians as Wolfhart Pannenberg and Jürgen Moltmann, who understand the resurrection of Jesus to be the epistemological key to understanding God's relation to the world. God's relation to the world is given in God's relation to Jesus of Nazareth.

History and Eschatology

Since chapter six has already partially criticized Hofmann's understanding of *Heilsgeschichte,* the criticisms presented there do not need to be amplified here. However, several additional criticisms of Hofmann's theology of history need to be highlighted.

The Negative Features of Hofmann's Theology of History

First, a major criticism of Hofmann's theology of history concerns his naïve interpretation of the biblical symbols of "the beginning" and "the end."

Hofmann remained a precritical thinker when he failed to see that such symbols are nonliteral, analogical, and mythical. Hofmann did not attempt to work out a way to maintain a continuing role for revelation, universal history, and hope for the future without having to treat the eschatological symbols in strictly literal terms. Hofmann would have benefited from the language and insights of later thinkers, such as Gadamer and Ricoeur. These thinkers offer important correctives to Hofmann's literalistic interpretation of eschatological symbols while at the same time affirming Hofmann's basic intention to understand the meaning of historical events in light of an overarching "universal history."

> That transcendent source of the meaning of life is thus in such relation to all temporal process that a profound insight into any process or reality yields a glimpse of the reality which is beyond it. This reality can be revealed and expressed only in mythical terms. These mythical terms are the most adequate symbols of reality because the reality which we experience constantly suggests a center and source of reality, which not only transcends immediate experience, but also finally transcends the rational forms and categories by which we seek to apprehend and describe it.[9]

So, too, Ricoeur's understanding of "myth," as a means to a deeper comprehension of things, could help to unlock Hofmann's literalism and open the door to a critical-creative appropriation of the biblical symbols of "beginning" and "end."[10]

Second, in light of the ecological crisis and the threat of nuclear holocaust, the anthropocentric elements in Hofmann's teleology of history should be challenged as untenable and dangerous. In keeping with the spirit of his age, Hofmann did not develop an ecological understanding of nature even though his theology is oriented to God's relation to the whole of reality, and his literalistic reading of Gen 1–3 could actually lead in the direction of ecological disaster. According to Hofmann, the natural world serves human ends. The anthropocentric character of Hofmann's theology of history is also problematic in view of the established conclusions of post-Darwinian

---

9. Reinhold Niebuhr, "The Truth in Myths," in *The Nature of Religious Experience: Essays in Honor of Douglas Clyde Macintosh* (ed. J. S. Bixler; Freeport, N.Y.: Books for Libraries Press, 1937), 135.

10. See Ricoeur, *The Symbolism of Evil,* 330–57, esp. 353–57. "I wager that I shall have a better understanding of man and of the bond between the being of man and the being of all beings if I follow the *indication* of symbolic thought. That wager then becomes the task of *verifying* my wager and saturating it, so to speak, with intelligibility. In return, the task transforms my wager: in betting *on* the significance of the symbolic world, I bet at the same time *that* my wager will be restored to me in power of reflection, in the element of coherent discourse" (ibid., 355; italics original).

biological science. While one might find some justification for the theological assertion that humanity appears to be the goal of nature, an anthropic principle defended by some theologians and scientists today, this notion has done little to stem the rapid descent into environmental crisis.

In order to subordinate the anthropocentric features of Hofmann's theology of history and make viable other aspects of his theology, one would have to expand the comments he makes about the relationality of the triune God to all of creation. Such a development, fully consistent with Hofmann's primary theological emphases on the triune God, would transform his theology of (human) history into a more coherent Trinitarian theology of history and nature or a theology of the cosmos in relation to God. The idea is present in Hofmann's theology, particularly in his strong emphasis that "the self" is only truly "a self in relation to others" (e.g., God, nature, history, others), but one may easily lose sight of it if one examines only Hofmann's statements about humanity as the goal of creation. Hofmann did discern a fundamental relatedness of the triune God to the world of nature and history, a relatedness that bears important similarities to Hamann's and Schelling's ideas about nature. This relatedness of the triune God to all of reality does not lead to any sharp distinction between "history" and "nature." Indeed, at times Hofmann recognized that the cosmos is itself historical. So Hofmann was not strictly anthropocentric in a reductive sense since the center of his theology is the self-giving of the triune God for all of reality and that the individual self is always "a self in relation to others." The world as a whole is the object of the love of the triune God. Thus, while Hofmann did not explicitly develop the notion of God's relation to nature, his doctrine of God's relationality and temporality at least allows for a theology of nature/cosmos that includes ecological concern and praxis. In this regard one should also note that Hofmann's theological method also encourages correlation between articulations of Christian faith and the subject matters and methods of the other disciplines in modern universities, including the ecological sciences.

Third, Hofmann's theology of history appears to contain at least one major internal inconsistency: Hofmann seems to have viewed history sometimes as a teleological development that is oriented toward its *telos* in Christ and yet at other times Hofmann spoke of the fulfillment of creation in an *eschaton* that breaks into history. Hofmann connected both perspectives uncritically. He used eschatology when historical events did not seem to fit with his *heilsgeschichtliche* scheme and teleology when they did.

But may something which is right not perhaps lurk in the question [Hofmann] puts — first of all, that is, in his desire to understand as prophecy not the individual words of the Old Testament, but the history of which it tells us; and so his desire to interpret this history on the basis of Christ, its 'end,' as prophecy? Does his error not lie in his effort to reach this understanding with the aid of the philosophical idea of history as a process of development, in which tendencies originally active in whatever takes place attain their realization in the natural course of events? According to the New Testament, Christ is the end of *Heilsgeschichte* not in the sense that he signifies the goal of historical development, but because he is its eschatological end.[11]

The idea of a teleological development of the church, which appears as a proleptic representation of redeemed humankind, stands in contradiction to the eschatological approach. The unbalanced tension is definite in Hofmann's understanding of history.[12]

Hofmann's understanding of *Heilsgeschichte* seems to "obscure the eschatological newness of the gospel."[13] To the extent that Hofmann's notion of history is one of a teleological-organic development, Bultmann's and Forde's critiques are correct. However, Forde and others seem to minimize the radical disruption between "the old age" and "the new age," "the old Adam" and the "new Adam," that Hofmann himself, at least on occasion, allowed within his overall theology of history. While Hofmann wanted to maintain some kind of continuity between "Adam" and "Christ," his main theological assertion was that Jesus is "the *new* human being," whose incarnation and resurrection is the revelation of "the end of humanity" in the midst of history.

One way in which Hofmann could have resolved the apparent tension between a teleological development and an eschatological disjunctive view of history is through the category of "hope" that Hofmann often highlights. Parallel to this, one must note that the organic teleological view, from his perspective, is grounded in the Christian *Tatbestand*, which is a *faith* perspective and not an unambiguous metaphysical-idealist ahistorical construct.

---

11. Bultmann, "Prophecy and Fulfillment," 58.
12. Sturm, "Die integrierende Funktion der Ekklesiologie," 319.
13. Forde, *The Law-Gospel Debate,* 131. "Hofmann rightly challenged the orthodox concept of law and atonement. His main positive contribution to a more viable position was the idea that Christ's death should be understood as a victory over the forces which tyrannize man and that by this victory Christ established a new humanity. Hofmann's problem, however, was that because of his method he was led to understand this victory as part of a historical process of divine self-realization, and the newness of the victory was threatened. Law was made part of a historical dispensation. . . . Because of the scheme, law and wrath are no longer a real threat, love tends to become self-evident and sentimentalized, and the eschatological dimension loses its radical nature" (ibid., 132).

Hofmann did not dissolve the creaturely limitation of existence and time. He regarded any attempt to arrive at a knowledge of the universal unity of all things by means of a rational construct or mystical contemplation as an act of human pride, as a failure to remember that even Christians live by faith. Hofmann believed he was able to speak of the unity of all things in Christ as a hoped for reality that is nonetheless present to faith only because of the self-giving of the triune God to faith. Hofmann's understanding of typology also allows for ambiguity, discontinuity, and novelty in history. Finally, Hofmann's concrete participation in politics, mission societies, orphanages, and so on, qualifies a strictly idealist interpretation of Hofmann's notion of *Heilsgeschichte*. Hofmann's theology of history did acknowledge historical ambiguity, the need for praxis, and the presence of disjunctive events in history.

Fourth, despite Hofmann's best intentions to base his understanding of history solely on the scriptural witness within the Christian *Tatbestand*, his theology of history often rubs against the complexities and ambiguities inherent within the realities of history. To the degree that Hofmann allowed "universality" to take precedence over "contingency," his theology of history is problematic. For example, in several places he forces "history" to be understood on the basis of categories (e.g., "prophecy," "fulfillment") that most modern historians would find puzzling. Are such standards as "prophecy" and "fulfillment" inherent in history itself, as Hofmann maintained, or are they not rather constructs that Hofmann formulated to find meaning in historical events?[14] Could not someone else, looking at the same *heilsgeschichtliche* facts, arrange them into a different line of development, or even into no "development" at all? To the degree that Hofmann understood history as a teleological-organic development, he seems to have minimized the stark reality of evil, tragedy, and sin in all human situations. Hofmann's understanding of history would be more persuasive if it accounted better for radical ambiguity and "interruptions" in history.[15] His theological understanding would have been stronger had he given more weight to the categories of Christian hope and faith, which live with the

---

14. For similar criticism, see Flechsenhaar, *Das Geschichtsproblem*, 42, 50–52.

15. See especially Tracy, "Radical Ambiguity: The Question of History," in *Plurality and Ambiguity*, 66–81. "Historical ambiguity means that a once seemingly clear historical narrative of progressive Western enlightenment and emancipation has now become a montage of classics and newspeak, of startling beauty and revolting cruelty, of partial emancipation and ever-subtler forms of entrapment. Ambiguous is certainly one way to describe our history. At one time we may have believed realistic and even naturalistic narratives of the triumph of the West. But these traditional narratives are now overlaid not only with modernist narratives and their occasional epiphanies amidst the mass of historical confusion, but also by postmodernist antinarratives with their good-byes to all that" (ibid., 70).

ambiguities and discontinuities of life, under the cross.[16] These categories, which are present in Hofmann's theology, could surely be thematized with our post-Enlightenment spectacles, in "wiser though sadder" vision.

Fifth, what does Hofmann mean when he says that "Jesus is the end of history?" Does the claim that "Jesus is the end of history in the midst of history" mean that Hofmann has the future figured out in advance? If so, how does Hofmann preserve historical contingency? Does Hofmann's theology of history allow for an open future and contingent events, surely conditions that are demanded by contemporary understanding of history? "History is not only contingent; history is interruptive. Western history is, through and through, an interruptive narrative with no single theme and no controlling plot."[17] But more pointedly, how did Hofmann *know* that Jesus is God's final revelation, since one cannot demonstrate the absoluteness of Christianity historically — as Kierkegaard argued against Hegel and as Troeltsch also concluded?[18] Is Hofmann's theology of universal history as outdated as Hegel's philosophy of history? Is it really possible to discern and/or construe *any* kind of theology of history or eschatology today?[19] Does the Christian faith demand a (renewed) overarching conception of history?

A previous generation of Christian theologians, largely influenced by existentialist philosophy (e.g., Bultmann, Gogarten, Althaus) has criticized every *Heilsgeschichte* as theologically wrong-headed. The stark idolatries of the Nazi era were but a further example that Kierkegaard was correct to have rejected every *Heilsgeschichte,* especially those based on an idealist apotheosis of finite reality. For the theologians influenced by Kierkegaard, an overarching theology of history is too idealist and all eschatologies, theological as well as secular, are too mythological. For Bultmann the meaning

---

16. Perhaps here is the place to repeat Ignazio Silone's important aphorism: "In the sacred history of man on earth, it is still, alas, Good Friday" (Ignazio Silone, "To the Reader," in *And He Hid Himself* [trans. Darina Tranquilli; New York: Harper and Brothers, 1945], vi).

17. Tracy, "Radical Ambiguity," 68.

18. For a discussion of the problems this question creates, see Harvey, *The Historian and the Believer,* 3–37; and Stephen Crites, *In the Twilight of Christendom: Hegel vs. Kierkegaard on Faith and History* (Chambersburg, Pa.: American Academy of Religion, 1972). In Kierkegaard's writings especially, the individual *coram Deo* becomes isolated from the world of nature and history. The Christian's involvements in political affairs, in nature and history, are ultimately of little importance to the God-human relationship which establishes authentic existence. There is, for Kierkegaard, no meaning in history as such. Meaning is given only in the "moment." *Heilsgeschichte* becomes dissolved in the moment of "becoming a Christian" or of "becoming contemporary with Christ," which do not take place in "history." See especially James Collins, *The Mind of Kierkegaard* (Princeton: Princeton University Press, 1983), 137–240.

19. One thinks of the philosophical critique of all eschatologies as provided by Jean-François Lyotard. See Jean-François Lyotard, *The Postmodern Condition* (Manchester: Manchester University Press, 1984).

of history lies only, if anywhere, in the present decision of the believer.[20] The meaning lies only in the existential response of faith in the preached word.

> The "now" receives its eschatological character by the encounter with Christ and the word that preaches him, since in the encounter with him the world and its history come to their end and faith as the new creature is freed from the world.[21]

Christian faith is confidence in God by means of the preached word alone, often despite historical events. Thus Bultmann, the early Barth, and Althaus criticize Hofmann for thinking that faith is to be grounded in anything other than the preached word.[22]

Some of Hofmann's statements about *Heilsgeschichte* are problematic in their original form, because of their teleological-developmental elements. Such a view of history is nonpersuasive, not merely because of Nietzsche's and Marx's and Benjamin's critiques, but because history is not as neat and tidy as Hofmann's theology sometimes seems to suggest.[23] All such "meta-narratives," both theological and secular, have to be criticized because of their systemic distortions and their inability to account for radical ambiguity. One could argue that Hofmann's notion of *Heilsgeschichte* yokes together the modern sense of linear development with a theological understanding to create a teleological narrative of the progressive emergence of the communion between God and humanity. Such an understanding can lead to the uncritical acceptance of the present as an expression of the will of God (in

---

20. Bultmann's critique of Hofmann's theology of history is largely dependent upon Kierkegaard's theology of time and eternity. See especially Bultmann, "Die christliche Hoffnung und das Problem der Entmythologisierung," in *Glauben und Verstehen* (Tübingen: J. C. B. Mohr [Paul Siebeck], 1960), 3:81–90; idem, "The Eschatology of the Gospel of John," in *Faith and Understanding*, 165–83; idem, "Geschichte und Eschatologie im Neuen Testament," in *Glauben und Verstehen*, 3:91–106; idem, *History and Eschatology: The Presence of Eternity* (New York: Harper and Brothers, 1957); and idem, "History of Salvation and History," in *Existence and Faith: Shorter Writings of Rudolf Bultmann* (ed. and trans. Schubert Ogden; New York: Meridian, 1960), 226–40.

21. Bultmann, "Geschichte und Eschatologie im Neuen Testament," 105. See also Sauter, *What Dare We Hope?*, 80–90.

22. For similar criticism, see also Weth, *Die Heilsgeschichte*, 231–33; Schellbach, *Theologie und Philosophie*, 89ff.; and Keller-Hüschemenger, *Das Problem der Heilsgewissheit*, 46–49.

23. Walter Benjamin was particularly critical of the perception that time is a continuously flowing current, an idea that is basic to the Western ideology of "progress." Such an idea, according to Benjamin, is devastating: it sweeps past everybody that it doesn't carry along. Left behind are the forgotten ones, the sufferers, the weak, etc. See especially Benjamin, "Theses on the Philosophy of History," in *Illuminations*, 253–64. See also Johann Baptist Metz, "Hope as Imminent Expectation of the Struggle for Forgotten Time: Noncontemporaneous Theses on the Apocalyptic View," in *Faith in History and Society: Towards a Practical Fundamental Theology* (trans. David Smith; New York: Seabury Press, 1980), 169–79; and Josef Wohlmuth, "Zur Bedeutung der 'Geschichtsthesen' Walter Benjamins für die christliche Eschatologie," *Evangelische Theologie* 50 (1990): 2–20.

which case history is a history of the victors), but such a view is also contrary to authentic Christian hope, since it avoids dependence on God and lacks "openness for the advent of the unexpected."[24]

Hofmann's primary response to this criticism of his theology of history would surely center on the apostolic witness to Jesus' resurrection from the dead, which Hofmann received in faith and which he took to be an actual historical event that discloses the meaning of history in the midst of history. Hofmann's contention was that history as a universal whole becomes comprehensible on the basis of the Trinitarian self-fulfillment of God in history that centers in "the man of God who is becoming." Hofmann argued that the resurrection of Jesus reveals God's will of love for all humanity. Such a disclosure confirms the apocalyptic expectation of "the end of history" and that the end of humanity is disclosed in the risen Jesus. The key, for Hofmann, is "the end" *in the middle* (*Mitte*), not merely "the End," as if the future were already worked out (as Hofmann thought Hegel had claimed; see *BH* 38–39).[25] Thus Hofmann criticized people who "harp on 'development' and fail to come to terms with the decisive turning-points, want to make history comprehensible and cannot address its fundamental questions . . . " (*HS* 11:12–13). And though Hofmann wanted to address history's fundamental questions, he did not claim to comprehend and explain an end that has already been reached, as Hegel did, and upon which he could only now look backwards. Hofmann was aware that history runs in all sorts of directions and creates confusion (see, for example, his comments about the hiddenness of God's actions in history, *WE* 1:33ff.). *Heilsgeschichte* should not be thought of as a continuous line of development, but must be viewed as including "breaks" and "interruptions." Hofmann acknowledged that the fulfillment of prophecy is much more an *un*expected fulfillment than an expected one. Hence, the need for a focal point, a "center," the *Mitte*, which in faith provides a perspective on the whole of reality.

This faith perspective is the key to Hofmann's understanding of history. Even though his horizon was not and could not be our horizon, it is remarkable that he articulated these few but powerful wedges to demarcate his position from that of those who operate with a thorough-going organic view of history's "development."

Hofmann's theology of history, in its broad contours, is actually quite like Pannenberg's, apart from the latter's unique understanding of divine action.

---

24. Sauter, *What Dare We Hope?*, 91.
25. Compare with Hamann: "I found the unity of divine will in Jesus Christ's work of redemption: all of history, all miracles, all commandments and all works of God converge in this central point" (Hamann, as quoted in Leibrecht, *God and Man in the Thought of Hamann*, 182).

Pannenberg, too, speaks of "the end of history in the midst of history," though he does not attribute this expression to Hofmann.

> We have said that the anticipated coming of the end of history in the midst of history, far from doing away with history, actually forms the basis from which history as a whole becomes understandable. This does not make possible, however, an oversight over the drama of world history as from a stage box. Second Corinthians 5:7 applies here: "We walk by faith and not by sight." Jesus Christ, the end of history, is not available to us as the principle of a "Christologically" grounded total view of world history. Christ's Resurrection, the daybreak of the eschaton, is for our understanding a light which blinds as Paul was blinded on the Damascus road. Even the New Testament witnesses, however powerfully they attempted to express as clearly as possible the reality of this event, could only stammer of it, each in his own way, all of them together in a right contradictory way. Also our participation in this event, the hope of our own resurrection, is still hidden under the experience of the cross.[26]

For Hofmann, as well as for Pannenberg, the meaning of history is grounded in Christian faith and hope on the basis of the risen Christ, though Pannenberg understands "faith" to be more a "cognition" than an attitude or perspective. For Hofmann faith is the existential base from which to view the problems and ambiguities of history in light of history's *Mitte*. "In faith the Christian is certain that *the history between God and humanity* has come to its *provisional* conclusion in Jesus" (*WE* 1:33, italics added).[27] For Hofmann one can speak of God only within the framework of faith and universal history, and vice versa, since all of reality is in relation to the triune God. Hofmann held that to speak of God this way is not due to an identity of God that is inherent to the human being but solely because the triune God has given God's self to be known by faith in the life of Jesus.

---

26. Pannenberg, "Redemptive Event and History," 37.
27. Similarly, Pannenberg adumbrates, "It is one thing to renounce from the very beginning every universal conception of history. It is something quite different if the total view of reality as history which moves from promise to fulfillment is broken open as it were from within. This happens first of all through the unexpected way in which God fulfills his promise, but then through the fact that this fulfillment, the end of history in Jesus Christ, had provisionally already come — and yet precisely thereby is deprived of all comprehension. We can say what such an outbreak of the incomprehensibility of the eschaton in history means only in the framework of a universal historical understanding of the reality in which this outbreak occurs, just because through it the universal historical scheme itself is forced open. Also the sending and history of the eschatological community in the world can be understood only from this point of view" (Pannenberg, "Redemptive Event and History," 37–38).

Perhaps it would be impossible today to attempt such a "universal history" in the sense that Hofmann used the term, but if one were to make that attempt one would need to clarify, much more carefully than Hofmann did, the "historical" nature of Jesus' resurrection and its import for identifying who God is.[28] Hofmann's theological method would be deficient today since he, unlike Pannenberg (at least in principle), is incapable of operating with an empirical historical-critical method that carefully considers the contingent, immanent causation of historical events and which follows critical principles of historical verification.[29] Of course, such principles highlight a problem for those who wish to affirm the historical actuality of the resurrection of Jesus.

> It is only too easy to sacrifice the contingency of events in favor of a conception of the unity of history. The justifiable fears of Kierkegaard about an obliteration of individual existence by the "universal," and of Gogarten about a threatening blanketing of the openness of man for the future by a philosophy of history that anticipates it, are aroused at this point. It is in the face of the question raised by these thinkers that every projection of the unity of history will have to prove that it has not betrayed the peculiar contingency of historical events.[30]

In Hofmann's theology, universality regularly takes precedence over contingency.

Hofmann's Positive Contribution to a Christian Theology of History

Despite the above criticisms against Hofmann's theology of history, perhaps there are elements that are still worth retrieving. If one were to attempt to

---

28. For an example of contemporary discussion on the resurrection of Jesus, see the essays in *The Resurrection* (ed. Stephen Davis, Daniel Kendall, and Gerald O'Collins; Oxford: Oxford University Press, 1997).

29. "Theology must take a burning interest in this side of historical work. It is characteristic of the activity of the transcendent God, whose essence is not adequately expressed in any cosmic order but remains free from every such order, that it constantly gives rise to something new in reality, something never before present. For this reason, theology is interested primarily in the individual, particular, contingent. In the revelatory history, the theological stress falls not least upon the new, upon that which is peculiar to the particular event within the contexts of the history and the promises to which it belongs..." (Pannenberg, "Redemptive Event and History," 48). "...[A] projection of the course of events must be so construed that it does not exclude the contingency of the historical. This demand sounds almost self-evident. Contingency and individuality are indeed fundamental characteristics of the historical. Still, it has proven extremely difficult to uphold the unity of history in acknowledging this demand" (ibid., 72). For an argument that Pannenberg himself has been unable to maintain a legitimate contingency to historical events, see especially Kolden, "Pannenberg's Attempt to Base Theology on History," 247–83.

30. Pannenberg, "Redemptive Event and History," 72.

retrieve Hofmann as a valuable voice in current theological conversation, one would have to make certain (perhaps especially hermeneutical) moves within his thought. Moreover, in fairness to Hofmann, the existentialist criticism of Bultmann and others may well be criticized by a perspective that is informed by the central concerns of Hofmann's theology of history.

First, one could argue on Hofmann's behalf that Christian theology must be about the Christian *Tatbestand,* including the "historical facts" that shape that *Tatbestand,* if it is to be true to its *historical* object and if it is to avoid metaphysical speculation. Similar to Pannenberg's efforts, Hofmann's theology of history directly confronts the claims of Bultmann and Harvey that "history" is of little importance to Christian faith. Contrary to Bultmann's agnostic historicism and existentialist anthropology, Hofmann's theology argues that "historical realism" is only possible when God is understood to be freely active in history. For Hofmann history matters, and the interpretation of historical events is really the result of history and not merely the expression of a unique self-understanding. Solipsistic introversion, for Hofmann, is always the necessary result of an artificial separation of the individual from reality, from history, and ultimately from God.

In contrast to an existentialist position, Hofmann argued that the meaning of history involves "promise and fulfillment," "faith and historical facts," and not merely the preaching of the word. The reason is that the God who is revealed in Christian preaching is precisely a God who gives God's self as self-emptying love in history. When Hofmann speaks of the Christ-event, his emphasis is not on the paradoxical breaking in of the infinite into the finite. The emphasis is on the self-giving of the love of the triune God who, through *kenosis* and humiliation, identifies with the human situation of suffering, despair, and joy, and who acts to overcome the alienation between human beings and God. The incarnation of Jesus for Hofmann means that the eternal and living God is creatively and redemptively present and freely active in all of reality, in nature, and in history. Thus Hofmann would be dissatisfied with the sharp transcendentalism of Bultmann and the early Barth.[31] If Christian theology is to be true to its object, it must also

---

31. The criticism of Bultmann's rejection of apocalyptic by Ernst Käsemann (1906–1998) is consistent with Hofmann's central affirmation that biblical apocalyptic articulates the hope for the redemption of all creation from its bondage to sin and death. See Ernst Käsemann, "The Beginnings of Christian Theology," in *New Testament Questions of Today* (trans. W. J. Mantague; London: SCM Press, 1969), 82–107; and idem, "On the Subject of Primitive Christian Apocalyptic," in *New Testament Questions of Today,* 108–37. See also the critique of Bultmann's theology of history by Pannenberg, "Redemptive Event and History," 22–28. Pannenberg criticizes Bultmann for not considering "the connection between the apocalyptic picture of history and the Old Testament scheme of promise-fulfillment. On the basis of this connection, he could have understood the end of history as the goal of fulfillment belonging to history..." (ibid., 23).

speak of "the whole" of reality, which Hofmann understood is by nature "historical" and related to the eternal God who is love. But to speak of the whole, it must be stressed, is to speak in faith from within the Christian *Tatbestand,* which is historical and personal, and thus always provisional.

Second, Hofmann's theology of history is grounded in the biblical vision of God's "beginning" and "end" and is thus comprehensive and inclusive.[32] Unlike Bultmann, Hofmann held that apocalyptic texts exhort the faithful to hope for the redemption and liberation of creation itself (e.g., Rom 8:22–23). Thus, Hofmann sought to take seriously the claim that the central message of salvation given through the man Jesus is a part of a much larger context of God's relation to humanity as a whole and to all of creation. God's actions are not confined to the present moment of decision or to a narrow stream of wondrous events in the midst of secular history; rather, God's redemptive actions extend to the whole of creation and thus involve universal history. *Heilsgeschichte* is more comprehensive than *Weltgeschichte,* so the former gives meaning to the latter.

A feature of the comprehensive character of Hofmann's theology of history is his effort to disclose the organic-historical continuity between the two Testaments. Here Hofmann's theology of history anticipates later concerns, notably the efforts of Gerhard von Rad (1901–1971) and more recently Brevard Childs and Francis Watson. Though Hofmann admitted that there is tension and even polarization between the two Testaments (e.g., Hofmann held that Christ is the end of the whole law, not merely of the purity laws), his intention was to maintain a fundamental unity that discloses the coherence of the total biblical witness to God.

One could also argue that even Nietzsche and post-structuralist historians involve themselves in "totalizing" discourse and the formation of metanarratives. Recent criticism of so-called "new historicism" is like Hofmann's criticism of old historicism: the historian or biblical interpreter always operates out of an inescapable, totalizing framework that is constantly in need of revision. Furthermore, just as Schelling left room for the irrational and evil in history, so too did Hofmann. Hofmann did not always speak of *Heilsgeschichte* as a simple and progressive development; sometimes he speaks of history as marked by evil, sin, conflict and by opposition between God and creation and between church and world as well as church and church. Hofmann was neither an optimist nor a pessimist when it came to talking of the future. His language is grounded in Christian faith, hope, and love. This

---

32. Compare with Claus Westermann, *Beginning and End in the Bible* (trans. Keith Crim; Philadelphia: Fortress, 1972), esp. 37–39.

is in keeping with his understanding of the triune and kenotic God who is self-giving love for all of reality.

Third, Hofmann's theology of history is grounded in the free actions of the triune God who is love. This means that God the creator intends to bring God's creation to its fulfilled goal that is grounded in God's love. Within this concrete goal, humankind has a purpose and a meaning that cannot be frustrated by any non-divine reality. While Hofmann articulated a confidence about the future and believed that the broadest contours of history had already been disclosed in the life, death, and resurrection of Jesus of Nazareth, he acknowledged that the specific details of the future are ambiguous. Thus, Hofmann's theology cannot properly be understood to be strictly a pure model of "progress unable and unwilling to face the tragedy and suffering in human existence."[33] Hofmann would agree with the vision of Robert Benne:

> Considering the intractability of human sin and evil, the end will not come smoothly or without judgment. Nevertheless, God's kingdom will come. God's sovereignty will finally be completely realized in a kingdom that has been anticipated in the coming of Jesus as the Christ. History, then, is an interim in which God struggles with the forces of darkness. Hints and parables of the future kingdom of God may appear in history, but they will not triumph completely until God brings in his future. The kingdom has come and it will come.[34]

So Hofmann's theology of history is ultimately grounded in a vision that is as wide as God's mercy and as inclusive as the new creation that comes with the resurrected Christ.

Finally, Hofmann's theology of history highlights the ethical responsibilities of those called to live in light of this universal, biblical vision of God's eschatological love.[35] This ethical responsibility involves the Christian in concrete ethical and political action within the actual ethical and political spheres of one's individual life (family, congregation, community, nation, world). Such action grows out of the Christian's calling to faith, hope, and love. Hope appears as the motivating power behind action. It is also important that it be the right kind of hope, as David Tracy summarizes:

---

33. David Tracy, "Cosmology and Christian Hope," in *On Naming the Present: God, Hermeneutics, and Church* (Maryknoll, N.Y.: Orbis, 1994), 76.

34. Robert Benne, *The Paradoxical Vision: A Public Theology for the Twenty-first Century* (Philadelphia: Fortress, 1995), 119.

35. Hofmann's concern to articulate the ethical consequences of a Christian eschatology anticipates that of Moltmann. See especially Jürgen Moltmann, *Theology of Hope: On the Ground and Consequences of a Christian Eschatology* (trans. James Leitch; New York: Harper and Row, 1967).

Neither optimism nor pessimism but hope is at the heart of the Christian vision of both nature and history. That hope not merely allows but demands both theoretical reflection and concrete praxis. Christian hope is grounded in the always/already/not-yet reality of Jesus Christ as a primary theological clue for our new cosmological and historical situation. Insofar as that situation now demands a theology of history *and* nature, a theology of redemption *and* creation, it suggests that all theologians would do well to focus again on that central category of hope.... Then we may begin to see more fully — in critical conversation with modern science, history, philosophy and praxis — some fuller reasons for "the hope that lies in us" and the beginnings of a new Christian construal of God, self, and world.[36]

Hofmann himself exemplified "the humanistic Christian" life that does not avoid engaging the various areas of responsibility in the world. Hofmann's theology thus emphasizes the important Christian category of hope for all of reality. Christian hope provides Hofmann with a legitimate basis for ethical and political action in the world. Such hope is grounded in the concrete form of the triune God's self-giving, saving love in Jesus.

---

36. Tracy, "Cosmology and Christian Hope," 81.

Selected Bibliography

Primary Sources by
Johannes Christian Konrad Von Hofmann*

Principal Writings

De bellis ab Antiocho Epiphane adversus Ptolemäos gestis dissertationem auctoritate ordinis philosophorum amphissimi pro capessendis honoribus licentiati philosophiae. Ph.D. diss., University of Erlangen, 1835.

Die Siebenzig Jahre des Propheten Jeremia und die Siebenzig Jahrwochen des Propheten Daniel: Zwei exegetisch-historische Untersuchungen. Nuremberg: Theodor Otto, 1836.

Die Geschichte des Aufruhrs in den Cevennen unter Ludwig XIV nach den Quellen erzählt. Nördlingen: C. H. Beck, 1837.

De argumento psalmi centesimi decimi dissertationem auctoritate ordinis theologorum summe reverendi pro capessendis honoribus licentiati theologiae. Th.D. diss., University of Erlangen, 1838.

Lehrbuch der Weltgeschichte für Gymnasien. 2 vols. Nördlingen: C. H. Beck, 1839, 1842. 2d ed. 1843–1844.

Weissagung und Erfüllung im Alten und im Neuen Testamente. Ein theologischer Versuch. 2 vols. Nördlingen: C. H. Beck, 1841, 1844.

Aegyptische und israelitische Zeitrechnung: Ein sendschreiben an den Herrn Geheimerath Dr. Böckh. Nördlingen: C. H. Beck, 1847.

Der Schriftbeweis: Ein theologischer Versuch. 2 vols. Nördlingen: C. H. Beck, 1852–1855. 2d ed. 1857–1860.

Schutzschriften für eine neue Weise alte Wahrheit zu lehren. 4 parts. Nördlingen: C. H. Beck, 1856–1859.

Beleuchtung des über Dr. Baumgartens Lehrabweichungen abgegebenen Consistorial-Erachtens. Nördlingen: C. H. Beck, 1858.

Die Aufgabe: Ausgangspunkt der Untersuchung: Der erste und zweite Brief Pauli an die Thessalonischer. Vol. 1 of *Die heilige Schrift Neuen Testaments zusammenhängend untersucht.* Nördlingen: C. H. Beck, 1862. 2d ed. 1869.

Der Brief Pauli an die Galater. Vol. 2, book 1 of *Die heilige Schrift Neuen Testaments zusammenhängend untersucht.* Nördlingen: C. H. Beck, 1863. 2d ed. 1872.

An die protestantische Geistlichkeit des diesseitigen Bayern: Ein Wort zur Verständigung im Hinblick auf die bevorstehenden Landtagswahlen. Nördlingen: C. H. Beck, 1864.

---

*In this bibliography, I am arranging works by Hofmann in chronological order of publication.

259

Der erste Brief Pauli an die Korinther. Vol. 2, book 2 of *Die heilige Schrift Neuen Testaments zusammenhängend untersucht.* Nördlingen: C. H. Beck, 1864. 2d ed. 1874.

Der zweite Brief Pauli an die Korinther. Vol. 2, book 3 of *Die heilige Schrift Neuen Testaments zusammenhängend untersucht.* Nördlingen: C. H. Beck, 1866. 2d ed. 1877.

"Aus der lutherischen Kirche der neupreussischen Lande. 2 Teile. Erlangen, 1867." Pages 71–85 in *Neulutherische Kirchenpolitik im Zeitalter Bismarcks.* Edited by Gerhard Besier. Gütersloh: Gerd Mohn, 1982.

Der Brief Pauli an die Römer. Vol. 3 of *Die heilige Schrift Neuen Testaments zusammenhängend untersucht.* Nördlingen: C. H. Beck, 1868.

Der Brief Pauli an die Epheser. Vol. 4, book 1 of *Die heilige Schrift Neuen Testaments zusammenhängend untersucht.* Nördlingen: C. H. Beck, 1870.

Der Briefe Pauli an die Kolosser und an Philemon. Vol. 4, book 2 of *Die heilige Schrift Neuen Testaments zusammenhängend untersucht.* Nördlingen: C. H. Beck, 1870.

Der Brief Pauli an die Philipper. Vol. 4, book 3 of *Die heilige Schrift Neuen Testaments zusammenhängend untersucht.* Nördlingen: C. H. Beck, 1871.

Ausserbibliches über des Paulus lezte Lebenszeit: Geschichtliche Bezeugung der paulinischen Briefe: Der Brief an die Hebräer. Vol. 5 of *Die heilige Schrift Neuen Testaments zusammenhängend untersucht.* Nördlingen: C. H. Beck, 1873.

Das Nahende Ende der Dinge und die Hoffnung Israels nach der Schrift. Erlangen: by the author, 1873.

Die Augsburger Rechtfertigung der Augsburger Adresse. Nördlingen: C. H. Beck, 1874.

Die Briefe Pauli an Titus und Timotheus. Vol. 6 of *Die heilige Schrift Neuen Testaments zusammenhängend untersucht.* Nördlingen: C. H. Beck, 1874.

Der erste Brief Petri. Vol. 7, book 1 of *Die heilige Schrift Neuen Testaments zusammenhängend untersucht.* Nördlingen: C. H. Beck, 1875.

Der zweite Brief Petri und der Brief Judä. Vol. 7, book 2 of *Die heilige Schrift Neuen Testaments zusammenhängend untersucht.* Nördlingen: C. H. Beck, 1875.

Der Brief Jakobi: Geschichtliche Bezeugung der Briefe Petri, Judä und Jakobi. Vol. 7, book 3 of *Die heilige Schrift Neuen Testaments zusammenhängend untersucht.* Nördlingen: C. H. Beck, 1876.

Das Geschichtswerk des Lukas. Vol. 8, book 1 of *Die heilige Schrift Neuen Testaments zusammenhängend untersucht.* Nördlingen: C. H. Beck, 1878.

Journal Articles

"Die Polemik der Münchner historisch-politischen Blätter." *Zeitschrift für Protestantismus und Kirche* (Alte Folge) 1 (1838): 125–31.

"Probestücke e. angeblich kirchlichen Geschichtsbetrachtung." *Zeitschrift für Protestantismus und Kirche* (Alte Folge) 2 (1839): 2–17.

"Stimme aus der Propaganda über das göttliche Recht der Könige." *Zeitschrift für Protestantismus und Kirche* (Alte Folge) 2 (1839): 19–20.

"Deutsche Geschichte im Zeitalter der Reformation von Leopold Ranke." (1839) Pages 272–85 in *Vermischte Aufsätze von Professor von Hofmann: Eine Auswahl aus der Zeitschrift für Protestantismus und Kirche.* Edited by Heinrich Schmid. Erlangen: A. Deichert, 1878.

"Das Hohepriestertum Jesu Christi und das Messopfer der römischen Kirchen." (1839) Pages 285–325 in *Vermischte Aufsätze von Professor von Hofmann: Eine Auswahl aus der Zeitschrift für Protestantismus und Kirche.* Edited by Heinrich Schmid. Erlangen: A. Deichert, 1878.

"Bekenntnissschriften der lutherischen Kirche und die theologische Wissenschaft." *Zeitschrift für Protestantismus und Kirche* (Alte Folge) 4 (1840): 35–36.

"Das Prinzip unserer Kirche nach dem innern Verhältniss seiner zwei Seiten betrachtet von Dr. I. A. Dorner, Kiel 1841." *Zeitschrift für Protestantismus und Kirche* (Neue Folge) 4 (1842): 133–55.

"Das Buch 'Weissagung und Erfüllung im Alten und Neuen Testamente' in seinem Verhältnisse zur gegenwärtigen Aufgabe der Theologie." *Mecklenburger Kirchenblatt* 1 (1844): 54–82. Reprinted as pages 1–29 in *Grundlinien der Theologie Joh. Christ. K. v. Hofmanns in seiner eigenen Darstellung.* Edited by J. Haussleiter. Leipzig: A. Deichert, 1910.

"Kliefoths Theorie des Kultus der evangelischen Kirche." *Mecklenburger Kirchenblatt* 1 (1845): 116–39.

"Der Streit der Kirchen." *Mecklenburger Kirchenblatt* 1 (1845): 255–83.

"Über Löhe's drei Bücher von der Kirche." *Mecklenburger Kirchenblatt* 1 (1845): 284–307.

"Schellings kirchlicher Standpunkt." *Zeitschrift für Protestantismus und Kirche* (Neue Folge) 12 (1846): 157–70.

"Die preussische Generalsynode und die Union." *Zeitschrift für Protestantismus und Kirche* (Neue Folge) 13 (1847): 1–24.

"Die Kirche und die Gnadenmittel." *Zeitschrift für Protestantismus und Kirche* (Neue Folge) 14 (1847): 1–22.

"Wort und Sakrament." *Zeitschrift für Protestantismus und Kirche* (Neue Folge) 15 (1848): 1–17.

"Pfarrer Franz von Ingenheim, der ehrliche Schriftausleger." *Zeitschrift für Protestantismus und Kirche* (Neue Folge) 15 (1848): 89–97.

"Was Lehrt die Heilige Schrift von der Kirchenverfassung?" *Zeitschrift für Protestantismus und Kirche* (Neue Folge) 17 (1849): 137–51.

"Notgedrungene Kundgebung." *Zeitschrift für Protestantismus und Kirche* (Neue Folge) 17 (1849): 205–6.

"Die rechte Verwaltung der Konfirmation, eine Grundvoraussetzung rechter Kirchenverfassung." *Zeitschrift für Protestantismus und Kirche* (Neue Folge) 18 (1849): 1–18.

"Das Amt und die Ämter in der apostolischen Kirchen." *Zeitschrift für Protestantismus und Kirche* (Neue Folge) 18 (1849): 129–53.

"Wesen und Gesetz des Schriftbeweises." *Zeitschrift für Protestantismus und Kirche* (Neue Folge) 18 (1849): 195–226.

"Die schleswig-holsteinische Geistlichkeit und die evangelische Kirchenzeitung: ein Wort zu Schutz und Trutz." *Zeitschrift für Protestantismus und Kirche* (Neue Folge) 20 (1850): 65–89.

"An den Verfasser der Schrift: 'Die Kirche und ihre zeitgemässe Reorganisation' (gegen Karsten)." *Zeitschrift für Protestantismus und Kirche* (Neue Folge) 20 (1850): 183–90.

"Paulus, eine Döllingerische Skizze." *Zeitschrift für Protestantismus und Kirche* (Neue Folge) 21 (1851): 273–304.

"Zur neutestamentlichen Geschichte." *Zeitschrift für Protestantismus und Kirche* (Neue Folge) 22 (1851): 114–20, 329–34; 26 (1853): 260–72.

"Bitte um Unterstützung der vertriebenen schleswigschen Geistlichen." *Zeitschrift für Protestantismus und Kirche* (Neue Folge) 22 (1851): 197–98.

"Die gegenwärtige Stellung Löhes und seiner Freunde zur lutherischen Landeskirche Bayerns." *Zeitschrift für Protestantismus und Kirche* (Neue Folge) 22 (1851): 282–90.

"Gegen Rudelbachs dänische Parteischrift." *Zeitschrift für Protestantismus und Kirche* (Neue Folge) 22 (1851): 355–58.

"Wie Man das göttliche Recht des kirchlichen Amtes nicht verteidigen muss." *Zeitschrift für Protestantismus und Kirche* (Neue Folge) 23 (1852): 174–91.

"Anmerkungen zur Geschichte." *Zeitschrift für Protestantismus und Kirche* (Neue Folge) 23 (1852): 356–72.

"Und Auch." *Zeitschrift für Protestantismus und Kirche* (Neue Folge) 26 (1853): 337–38.

Von Hofmann, Johannes Christian Konrad, Gottfried Thomasius, et al. "Das Bekenntniss der lutherischen Kirche gegen das Bekenntniss des berliner Kirchentags gewahrt von ntlichen Lehrern der Theologie und des Kirchenrechts." *Zeitschrift für Protestantismus und Kirche* (Neue Folge) 26 (1853): 273–79.

"Was sich die gelben Blätter erzählen." *Zeitschrift für Protestantismus und Kirche* (Neue Folge) 27 (1854): 81–84.

"Herr Dr. Ebrard III." *Zeitschrift für Protestantismus und Kirche* (Neue Folge) 27 (1854): 338–40.

Von Hofmann, Johannes Christian Konrad, and Gottfried Thomasius. "Wider eine Entgegung, die doch keine Antwort ist." *Zeitschrift für Protestantismus und Kirche* (Neue Folge) 27 (1854): 341–57.

"Zur Entstehungsgeschichte der Heiligen Schrift." *Zeitschrift für Protestantismus und Kirche* (Neue Folge) 28 (1854): 85–95; 31 (1856): 1–23, 329–50; 34 (1857): 266–326; 37 (1859): 37–59, 337–45; 39 (1860): 65–103; 40 (1860): 331–45.

"Fragezeichen zu Dr. Kliefoths Lehre vom Gnadenmittelamt." *Zeitschrift für Protestantismus und Kirche* (Neue Folge) 29 (1855): 77–81.

"Dr. Kliefoth's acht Bücher von der Kirche." *Zeitschrift für Protestantismus und Kirche* (Neue Folge) 31 (1856): 69–100, 197–226; 32 (1856): 52–68, 227–46.

"Begründete Abweisung eines nicht begründeten Vorwurfs." *Zeitschrift für Protestantismus und Kirche* (Neue Folge) 31 (1856): 175–92.

"Deuterokanonisch." *Zeitschrift für Protestantismus und Kirche* (Neue Folge) 33 (1857): 397–400.

"Dr. K. Lechler's neutestamentliche Lehre vom heiligen Amte." *Zeitschrift für Protestantismus und Kirche* (Neue Folge) 36 (1858): 230–51.

"Höfling und Jesabel." *Zeitschrift für Protestantismus und Kirche* (Neue Folge) 36 (1858): 321–22.

"Was die heilige Schrift über Ehescheidung sagt." *Zeitschrift für Protestantismus und Kirche* (Neue Folge) 37 (1859): 1–18.

"Fragen der christlichen Hoffnung." *Zeitschrift für Protestantismus und Kirche* (Neue Folge) 38 (1859): 140–50.

"Ob der rechtfertigende Glaube allein selig macht." *Zeitschrift für Protestantismus und Kirche* (Neue Folge) 38 (1859): 368–74.

"Paulinische Theosophie." *Zeitschrift für Protestantismus und Kirche* (Neue Folge) 39 (1860): 195–98.

"Ob Dr. Huschke das Schriftwort über Ehescheidung recht versteht." *Zeitschrift für Protestantismus und Kirche* (Neue Folge) 39 (1860): 350–65.

"Ein antichiliastischer Synodalbeschluss." *Zeitschrift für Protestantismus und Kirche* (Neue Folge) 41 (1861): 1–7.

"Wie wir zur Bedrängnis des Pabstthums stehen." *Zeitschrift für Protestantismus und Kirche* (Neue Folge) 41 (1861): 30–39.

"Antichiliastischer Fanatismus." *Zeitschrift für Protestantismus und Kirche* (Neue Folge) 41 (1861): 124–25.

"R. Rothe's Lehre von der heiligen Schrift." *Zeitschrift für Protestantismus und Kirche* (Neue Folge) 41 (1861): 129–43.

"Anmerkungen zu Dr. v. Döllinger's Christenthum und Kirche in der Zeit der Grundlegung." *Zeitschrift für Protestantismus und Kirche* (Neue Folge) 41 (1861): 265–80, 329–49.

"Zur neutestamentlichen Lehre von der Erwählung." *Zeitschrift für Protestantismus und Kirche* (Neue Folge) 41 (1861): 318–28.

"Paulus, der Chiliast." *Zeitschrift für Protestantismus und Kirche* (Neue Folge) 42 (1861): 338–41.

"Dr. v. Döllinger's Kirchengeschichtliche Aussichten." *Zeitschrift für Protestantismus und Kirche* (Neue Folge) 43 (1862): 33–61.

"Geschichtlicher Ausgangspunkt für die wissenschaftliche Selbstrechtfertigung des Christentums." *Zeitschrift für Protestantismus und Kirche* (Neue Folge) 43 (1862): 259–68.

"Für die Leser des Kliefoth'schen Buchs über Sacharja." *Zeitschrift für Protestantismus und Kirche* (Neue Folge) 44 (1862): 57–59.

"Für Höfling gegen Stahl." *Zeitschrift für Protestantismus und Kirche* (Neue Folge) 44 (1862): 103–27.

"Die Aufgabe der biblischen Hermeneutik." *Zeitschrift für Protestantismus und Kirche* (Neue Folge) 45 (1863): 34–44.

"Gegen eine irrige Verhältnisbestimmung von Wort und Taufe." *Zeitschrift für Protestantismus und Kirche* (Neue Folge) 45 (1863): 187–91.

"Lutherische Ethik." *Zeitschrift für Protestantismus und Kirche* (Neue Folge) 45 (1863): 251–56.

"Gedanken über Theologie." *Zeitschrift für Protestantismus und Kirche* (Neue Folge) 46 (1863): 229–38.

"Ist eine von der ersten Kommunion getrennte Konfirmation berechtigt?" *Zeitschrift für Protestantismus und Kirche* (Neue Folge) 46 (1863): 91–100.

"Renan, Strauss, Schenkel." *Zeitschrift für Protestantismus und Kirche* (Neue Folge) 48 (1864): 81–122.

"Zur Schriftlehre von der Taufe." *Zeitschrift für Protestantismus und Kirche* (Neue Folge) 48 (1864): 127–28.

"Die menschliche Entwicklung Jesu." *Zeitschrift für Protestantismus und Kirche* (Neue Folge) 49 (1865): 1–40.

"Liberalismus." *Wochenschrift der Fortschrittspartei in Bayern* (August 1865): 275–76.

"Was Herr Lic. Hausrath von Apostel Paulus weiss und nicht weiss." *Zeitschrift für Protestantismus und Kirche* (Neue Folge) 51 (1866): 309–16.

"Über die religiöse Bedeutung der Grundthatsachen des Lebens Jesu." *Zeitschrift für Protestantismus und Kirche* (Neue Folge) 52 (1866): 1–29.

"Die sieben Sendschriften der Offenbarung Johannis." *Zeitschrift für Protestantismus und Kirche* (Neue Folge) 52 (1866): 74–82.

"Ein organischer Fehler der Herren Apologeten." *Zeitschrift für Protestantismus und Kirche* (Neue Folge) 54 (1867): 391–94.

"Einer von den Vornehmen." *Zeitschrift für Protestantismus und Kirche* (Neue Folge) 56 (1868): 341–66.

"Die Kirche." *Wochenschrift der Fortschrittspartei in Bayern* (November 1868): 379–81.

"Das Verhältnis von Staat und Kirche." *Zeitschrift für Protestantismus und Kirche* (Neue Folge) 57 (1869): 259–73.

"An die protestantische Geistlichkeit des diesseitigen Bayern." *Wochenschrift der Fortschrittspartei in Bayern* (October 1869): 338–40.

"Das Geschichtswerk des Lukas." *Zeitschrift für Protestantismus und Kirche* (Neue Folge) 59 (1870): 335–63.

"Eine vielleicht abgewendete Gefahr." *Zeitschrift für Protestantismus und Kirche* (Neue Folge) 60 (1870): 133–37.

"Das Ergebnis der Berliner Oktoberversammlung." *Zeitschrift für Protestantismus und Kirche* (Neue Folge) 62 (1871): 319–22.

"Dr. Fabris Kritik der Bismarck'schen Kirchenpolitik." *Wochenschrift der Fortschrittspartei in Bayern* (March 1872): 89–92.

"Eine Probe theologischer Geschichtsforschung." *Zeitschrift für Protestantismus und Kirche* (Neue Folge) 67 (1874): 57–64; 68 (1874): 115–35.

"Dr. Pfleiderers Paulinismus." *Zeitschrift für Protestantismus und Kirche* (Neue Folge) 68 (1874): 275–86.

"Die Kirche im Staat." *Zeitschrift für Protestantismus und Kirche* (Neue Folge) 69 (1875): 119–26.

"Aussichten." *Zeitschrift für Protestantismus und Kirche* (Neue Folge) 69 (1875): 169–74.

"Des Apostels Paulus christliche Freiheit." *Zeitschrift für Protestantismus und Kirche* (Neue Folge) 69 (1875): 262–68.

"Bemerkungen zu vorstehender Entgegung." *Zeitschrift für Protestantismus und Kirche* (Neue Folge) 69 (1875): 322–26.

"Ephesians 3:10." *Zeitschrift für Protestantismus und Kirche* (Neue Folge) 71 (1876): 233–45.

"Der Zustand der Seele nach dem Tode." *Zeitschrift für Protestantismus und Kirche* (Neue Folge) 71 (1876): 285–99.

"Vom Gehorsam gegen die Obrigkeit." (1876). Pages 206–15 in *Vermischte Aufsätze von Professor von Hofmann: Eine Auswahl aus der Zeitschrift für Protestantismus und Kirche*. Edited by Heinrich Schmid. Erlangen: A. Deichert, 1878.

"Die Weltgeschichtliche Bedeutung des modernen Socialismus." *Zeitschrift für Protestantismus und Kirche* (Neue Folge) 72 (1876): 269–75.

University Speeches

"Die neuen Aufgaben der Universitäten in der neuen Zeit." Rede beim Antritte des Prorektorats der Königlich bayrischen Friedrich-Alexanders-Universität Erlangen am 4. November 1848 gehalten. Erlangen: University of Erlangen, 1848.

"Der sittliche Beruf der Universitäten." Rede beim Antritte des Prorektorats der Königlich bayrischen Friedrich-Alexanders-Universität Erlangen am 4. November 1853 gehalten. Erlangen: University of Erlangen, 1853.

"Das unterscheidende Wesen der Universitäten." Rede beim Antritte des Prorektorats der Königlich bayrischen Friedrich-Alexanders-Universität Erlangen am 4. November 1856 gehalten. Erlangen: University of Erlangen, 1856.

"Die Universitäten im neuen deutschen Reich." Rede beim Antritte des Prorektorats der Königlich bayrischen Friedrich-Alexanders-Universität Erlangen am 4. November 1871 gehalten. Erlangen: University of Erlangen, 1871.

"Über die Berechtigung der theologischen Fakultäten." Rede beim Antritte des Prorektorats der Königlich bayrischen Friedrich-Alexanders-Universität Erlangen am 4. November 1875 gehalten. Erlangen: University of Erlangen, 1875. [Reprint: Erlangen: Deichert, 1875].

Correspondence

Briefe von J. Chr. K. v. Hofmann an Heinrich Schmid. Edited by Charlotte Schmid. Leipzig: A. Deichert, 1910.

Von Hofmann, Johannes Christian Konrad, and Franz Delitzsch. *Theologische Briefe der Professoren Delitzsch und v. Hofmann (1859–1861)*. Edited by D. Wilhelm Volck. Leipzig: J. C. Hinrichs, 1891. 2d ed., 1894.

Posthumous Writings

Dogmatik-Vorlesung Sommersemester 1842. Manuscript 1998 in the University Library, Friedrich-Alexander University, Erlangen, is a 236–page hand-written transcript of these lectures. The lectures began on April 21, 1842 and ended on August 23 of that same year. This transcript was made by a Pastor Schneider. A portion of Hofmann's lectures are reprinted in *Johannes von Hofmann* by Paul Wapler, 379–96. Leipzig: A. Deichert, 1914. A more complete summary was published by Christoph Luthardt as "Aus J. Chr. K. Hofmanns Vorlesung über Dogmatik." *Zeitschrift für kirchliche Wissenschaft und kirchliches Leben* 10 (1889): 39–53, 99–111.

Theologische Ethik: Abdruck einer im Sommer 1874 von Professor Dr. J. Chr. K. v. Hofmann gehaltenen Vorlesung. Edited by H. Rutz. Nördlingen: C. H. Beck, 1878.

Vermischte Aufsätze von Professor von Hofmann: Eine Auswahl aus der Zeitschrift für Protestantismus und Kirche. Edited by Heinrich Schmid. Erlangen: A. Deichert, 1878.

Encyklopädie der Theologie, nach Vorlesungen und Manuscripten. Edited by H. J. Bestmann. Nördlingen: C. H. Beck, 1879.

Biblische Hermeneutik, nach Vorlesungen und Manuscripten. Edited by W. Volck. Nördlingen: C. H. Beck, 1880. Most of this work has been translated by Christian Preus as *Interpreting the Bible.* Minneapolis: Augsburg, 1959.

Zusammenfassende Untersuchung der einzelnen neutestamentlichen Schriften, nach Manuscripten und Vorlesungen. Vol. 9 of *Die heilige Schrift Neuen Testaments zusammenhängend untersucht.* Edited by W. Volck. Nördlingen: C. H. Beck, 1881. Pages 160–181 of this volume were translated as "Hofmann on the Epistle to the Hebrews." *London Quarterly Review* 59 [1883]: 74–95.

Die biblische Geschichte neuen Testaments, nach Manuscripten und Vorlesungen. Vol. 10 of *Die heilige Schrift Neuen Testaments zusammenhängend untersucht.* Edited by W. Volck. Nördlingen: C. H. Beck, 1883.

Die biblische Theologie des neuen Testaments, nach Manuscripten und Vorlesungen. Vol. 11 of *Die heilige Schrift Neuen Testaments zusammenhängend untersucht.* Edited by W. Volck. Nördlingen: C. H. Beck, 1886.

Die Offenbarung St. Johannis, nach den Vorlesungen des J. C. K. von Hofmann. Edited by E. von Lorenz. Leipzig: A. Deichert, 1896.

Die heilige Schrift Neuen Testaments zusammenhängend untersucht. 11 vols. 2d ed. Edited by W. Volck. Nördlingen: C. H. Beck, 1896.

Secondary Sources

Althaus, Paul. "Der deskriptive Charakter der Ethik bei Joh. Chr. K. v. Hofmann." *Theologische Blätter* 1 (1933): 308–9.

Auberlen, K. A. "Besprechung von Hofmanns Schriftbeweis." *Theologische Studien und Kritiken* 26 (1853): 103–33.

Bachmann, Philipp. "J. C. K. von Hofmann." *Neue kirchliche Zeitschrift* 21 (1910): 909–62.

———. *J. Chr. K. v. Hofmanns Versöhnungslehre und der über sie geführte Streit: Ein Beitrag zur Geschichte der neueren Theologie.* Gütersloh: C. Bertelsmann, 1910.

———. "Die Stellung und Eigenart der sogenannten Erlanger Theologie." Pages 1–17 in *Festgabe für Theodor Zahn.* Leipzig: A. Deichert, 1928.

———. "Subjektivismus und Realismus als Grundzüge der Frankschen Theologie." *Neue kirchliche Zeitschrift* 28 (1927): 202–35.

———. "Wapler über v. Hofmann." *Beiträge zur Bayern Kirchengeschichte* 21 (1915): 42–44.

Baepler, Richard. "The Hermeneutics of Johann Christian Konrad von Hofmann with Special Reference to His Influence on Georg Stoeckhardt." B.D. thesis, Concordia Seminary, St. Louis, 1954.

Barth, Karl. "Evangelical Theology in the 19th Century." Pages 11–33 in *The Humanity of God*. Translated by John Newton Thomas and Thomas Wieser. Richmond, Virginia: John Knox Press, 1960.

———. *Die protestantische Theologie im 19. Jahrhundert: Ihre Vorgeschichte und ihre Geschichte*. 3d ed. Zürich: Evangelischer Verlag, 1960. ET *Protestant Theology in the Nineteenth Century: Its Background and History*. Translated by Brian Cozens and John Bowden. Valley Forge, Pa.: Judson Press, 1973.

Baumgärtel, Friedrich. *Verheissung zur Frage des evangelischen Verständnisses des Alten Testaments*. Gütersloh: C. Bertelsmann, 1952.

Baur, Ferdinand Christian. *Kirchengeschichte des neunzehnten Jahrhunderts*. Edited by Eduard Zeller. Tübingen: Fues, 1862.

Becker, Matthew L. "Appreciating the Life and Work of Johannes v. Hofmann," *Lutheran Quarterly* 17 (Summer 2003): 177–98.

———. "Hofmann as Ich-Theologe? The Object of Theology in Johann von Hofmann's *Werke*." *Concordia Journal* 29 (July 2003): 265–93.

———. "Hofmann's Revisionist Christology." *Lutheran Quarterly* 17 (Fall 2003): 288–328.

———. "The Self-Giving God: Trinitarian Historicality and Kenosis in the Theology of Johann von Hofmann." Ph.D. diss., University of Chicago, 2001.

———. "The Self-Giving God: The Trinity in Hofmann's Theology." *Pro Ecclesia* 12 (Fall 2003): 417–46.

Behm, D. Johannes. *Heilsgeschichtliche und religionsgeschichtliche Betrachtung des Neuen Testaments*. Berlin: Runge, 1922.

Behr, Wilfried. *Politischer Liberalismus und kirchliches Christentum: Studien zum Zusammenhang von Theologie und Politik bei Johann Christian Konrad von Hofmann (1810–1877)*. Stuttgart: Calwer Verlag, 1995.

Betz, Otto. "History of Biblical Theology." Pages 432–37 in vol. 1 of *The Interpreter's Dictionary of the Bible*. Edited by George A. Buttrick et al. New York: Abingdon, 1962.

Beyschlag, Karlmann. *Die Erlanger Theologie*. Erlangen: Martin-Luther Verlag, 1993.

Biener, H. "Die 'Zeitschrift für Protestantismus und Kirche' (1838–1876) in ihrer Entwicklung." *Zeitschrift für bayerische Kirchengeschichte* 55 (1986): 113–57.

Breidert, Martin. *Die kenotische Christologie des 19. Jahrhunderts*. Gütersloh: Mohn, 1977.

Broemel, A. *Herr Professor Dr. von Hofmann und die Actenstücke die Amts-Entlassung des Professors der Theologie, Dr. Baumgarten in Rostock betreffend*. Berlin: Schlawitz, 1858.

Bultmann, Rudolf. "Weissagung und Erfüllung." *Zeitschrift für Theologie und Kirche* 47, 3 (1950): 360–83. ET "Prophecy and Fulfillment." Pages 50–75 in *Old Testament Hermeneutics*. Edited by Claus Westermann. Translated by James C. G. Greig. Richmond: John Knox Press, 1963.

Clements, R. E. "The Study of the Old Testament." Pages 109–41 in vol. 3 of *Nineteenth Century Religious Thought in the West.* Edited by Ninian Smart et al. Cambridge: Cambridge University Press, 1985.

Delitzsch, Franz. *Kommentar zum Briefe an die Hebräer: Mit archäologischen und dogmatischen Excursen über das Opfer und die Versöhnung.* Leipzig: 1857. ET *Commentary on the Epistle to the Hebrews.* Translated by Thomas Kingsbury. Edinburgh: T & T Clark, 1868.

———. "Prolegomena über den bisherigen Entwicklungsgang der Grundbegriffe der Versöhnungslehre." Pages 5–46 in *Vom Zorne Gottes: Ein biblisch-theologischer Versuch.* Edited by Ferdinand Weber. Erlangen: T. Bläsing, 1862.

Dieckhoff, A. W. "Die evangelisch-lutherische Lehre von der heiligen Schrift gegen Dr. von Hofmann's Lehre von der heiligen Schrift und vom kirchlichen Worte Gottes vertheidigt." *Kirchliche Zeitschrift* 5 (1858): 711–873.

———. "System und Schrift. Noch einmal wider von Hofmann." *Theologische Zeitschrift* 1 (1860): 189–413.

Ebrard, Johannes H. A. *Die Lehre von der Stellvertretenden Genugthuung…Mit besonderer Rücksicht auf Dr. v. Hofmanns Versöhnungslehre.* Königsberg: A. W. Unzer, 1857.

Edelmann, H. "Subjektivität und Erfahrung: Der Ansatz der theologischen System-bildung von Franz Hermann Reinhold v. Frank in Zusammenhang des 'Erlanger Kreises.' " Th.D. diss., University of Munich, 1980.

Elert, Werner. *Der Kampf um das Christentum: Geschichte der Beziehungen zwischen dem evangelischen Christentum in Deutschland und dem allgemeinen Denken seit Schleiermacher und Hegel.* Munich: C. H. Beck, 1921.

Fagerberg, Holsten. *Bekenntnis, Kirche, und Amt in der deutschen konfessionellen Theologie des 19. Jahrhunderts.* Wiesbaden: Otto Harrassowitz, 1952.

Flechsenhaar, Günther. *Das Geschichtsproblem in der Theologie Johannes von Hofmanns.* Giessen: O. Kindt, 1935.

Forde, Gerhard. *The Law-Gospel Debate.* Minneapolis: Augsburg, 1969.

Frank, D. Gustav. *Geschichte der Protestantischen Theologie.* 4 vols. Leipzig: Breitkopf und Härtel, 1863–1905.

Frank, Franz Hermann Reinhold von. *Geschichte und Kritik der neueren Theologie, insbesondere der systematischen, seit Schleiermacher.* 4th ed. Edited by R. H. Grützmacher. Leipzig: A. Deichert, 1908.

Fritsch, Charles. "Biblical Typology: Part II." *Bibliotheca Sacra* 103 (1946): 418–30.

Fuerbringer, Ludwig. *Eighty Eventful Years.* St. Louis: Concordia Publishing House, 1944.

Gadamer, Hans-Georg. *Truth and Method.* 2d rev. ed. Translated by Joel Weinscheimer and Donald Marshall. New York: Continuum, 1998.

Graf, F. W. "Konservatives Kulturluthertum. Ein theologiegeschichtlicher Prospekt." *Zeitschrift für Theologie und Kirche* 85 (1988): 31–76.

Grass, Hans. "Erlanger Schule." Pages 566–68 in vol. 2 of *Die Religion in Geschichte und Gegenwart.* Edited by Kurt Galling. 3d ed. Tübingen: J. C. B. Mohr (Paul Siebeck), 1962.

Grau, Rudolf F. *August Erd. Chr. Vilmar und J. Chr. K. von Hofmann.* Gütersloh: C. Bertelsmann, 1879.

Grützmacher, R. H. "Der ethische Typus der Erlanger Theologie." *Neue kirchliche Zeitschrift* 28 (1917): 441–53.

Harless, Adolf von. "Briefe an Höfling 1833–1852." Edited by E. Dorn. *Beiträge zur Bayrischen Kirchengeschichte* 22 (1915): 195–203.

Harnack, Theodosius. *Luthers Theologie mit besonderer Beziehung auf seine Versöhnungs- und Erlösungslehre.* 2 vols. Erlangen: Theodor Bläsing, 1862, 1886. Repr., Munich: Chr. Kaiser Verlag, 1927.

Harrisville, Roy A., and Walter Sundberg. "Johann Christian Konrad von Hofmann: The Bible as Salvation History." Pages 131–54 in *The Bible in Modern Culture.* Grand Rapids: Eerdmans, 1995.

Hauck, Albert. "Hofmann, Johann Chr. K." Pages 234–41 in vol. 8 of *Realenzyklopädie für protestantische Theologie und Kirche.* Edited by Albert Hauck. 3d ed. Leipzig: Hinrichs, 1908.

Haussleiter, Johannes. "Vorwort." Pages v–xii in *Grundlinien der Theologie Joh. Christ. K. v. Hofmanns in seiner eigenen Darstellung.* Edited by J. Haussleiter. Leipzig: A. Deichert, 1910.

Heick, Otto W. "In Memory of Konrad von Hofmann, 1810–1877." *Consensus* 6 (1980): 119–25.

Hein, Martin. "Erlangen Universität." Pages 159–64 in vol. 10 of *Theologische Realenzyklopädie.* Edited by Gerhard Krause and Gerhard Müller. Berlin: Walter de Gruyter, 1982.

———. *Lutherisches Bekenntnis und Erlanger Theologie im 19. Jahrhundert.* Die Lutherische Kirche, Geschichte und Gestalten. Vol. 7. Gütersloh: Gerd Mohn, 1984.

Herrmann, Wilhelm. *Christlich-protestantische Dogmatik.* Pages 298–361 in vol. 1 of *Schriften zur Grundlegung der Theologie.* Edited by Peter Fischer-Appelt. 2d ed. Munich: Chr. Kaiser, 1966–1967.

Hirsch, Emanuel. *Geschichte der neueren evangelischen Theologie im Zusammenhang mit den allgemeinen Bewegungen des europäischen Denkens.* 5 vols. 5th ed. Gütersloh: Gerd Mohn, 1975.

Hodge, C. W. "Hofmann's Prophesy and Fulfillment." *Biblical Repertory and Princeton Review* (1858): 189–225.

Höfling, Johann. "Bemerkung zu Hofmanns Aufsatz: Die rechte Verwaltung der Konfirmation eine Grundvoraussetzung rechter Kirchenverfassung." *Zeitschrift für Protestantismus und Kirche* 18 (1849): 18–21.

Hübner, Eberhard. "Hofmann, Johann Christian Konrad v." Pages 420–22 in vol. 3 of *Die Religion in Geschichte und Gegenwart.* Edited by Kurt Galling. 3d ed. Tübingen: J. C. B. Mohr (Paul Siebeck), 1962.

———. *Schrift und Theologie: Eine Untersuchung zur Theologie Joh. Chr. K. v. Hofmanns.* Munich: Chr. Kaiser, 1956.

Jelke, Robert. "Die Eigenart der Erlanger Theologie." *Neue kirchliche Zeitschrift* 41 (1930): 19–63.

Joest, Wilfried. "Erfahrung als theologisches Prinzip in der älteren Erlanger Schule." Pages 165–76 in *Glaube und Gesellschaft: Festschrift für W. F. Kasch.* Edited by K. D. Wolff. Bayreuth: Fehr, 1981.

Johnston, Paul I. "An Assessment of the Educational Philosophy of Johann Michael Reu, Using the Hermeneutical Paradigms of J. F. Herbart and J. C. K. von Hofmann and the Erlangen School." Ed.D. diss., University of Illinois, 1989.

————. "Reu Reconsidered: The Concept of *Heilsgeschichte* in the Hermeneutic of J. M. Reu and J. C. K. von Hofmann." *Concordia Journal* 18 (1992): 339–60.

Jordan, Hermann. "Beiträge zur Hofmannbiographie." *Beiträge zur Bayern Kirchengeschichte* 28 (1922): 129–53.

Kaftan, Theodor. "Hofmanns Exegese." *Neue kirchliche Zeitschrift* 30 (1919): 637–44.

Kähler, Martin. *Geschichte der protestantischen Dogmatik im 19. Jahrhundert.* Edited by E. Kähler. Munich: Chr. Kaiser, 1962.

Kantzenbach, Friedrich Wilhelm. "Das Bekenntnisproblem in der lutherischen Theologie des 19. Jahrhunderts." *Neue Zeitschrift für Systematische Theologie* 4 (1962): 243–317.

————. *Die Erlanger Theologie: Grundlinien ihrer Entwicklung im Rahmen der Geschichte der theologischen Fakultät, 1743–1877.* Munich: Evang. Presseverband für Bayern, 1960.

————. *Gestalten und Typen des Neuluthertums: Beiträge zur Erforschung des Neokonfessionalismus im 19. Jahrhundert.* Gütersloh: Gerd Mohn, 1968.

————. "Johannes von Hofmann und der politische Liberalismus." *Lutherische-monatshefte* 4 (1965): 587–93.

————. "Modelle konfessioneller Hermeneutik und die Funktion der Konkordienformel im Neuluthertum." Pages 277–96 in *Widerspruch, Dialog und Einigung: Studien zur Konkordienformel der Lutherischen Reformation.* Edited by Wenzel Lohff and Lewis Spitz. Stuttgart: Calwer Verlag, 1977.

————. "Schelling und das bayerische Luthertum." *Zeitschrift für bayerische Landesgeschichte* 36 (1973): 115–45.

Kattenbusch, Ferdinand. *Die deutsche evangelische Theologie seit Schleiermacher: Ihre Leistungen und ihre Schäden.* 5th ed. Giessen: Alfred Töpelmann, 1926.

Keller-Hüschemenger, Max. "Das Problem der Gewissheit bei J. Chr. K. von Hofmann in Rahmen der Erlanger Schule." Pages 288–95 in *Gedenkschrift für D. Werner Elert.* Edited by F. Hübner. Berlin: Lutherisches Verlagshaus, 1955.

————. *Das Problem der Heilsgewissheit in der Erlanger Theologie im 19. und 20. Jahrhundert: Ein Beitrag zur Frage des theologischen Subjektivismus in der gegenwärtigen evangelischen Theologie.* Berlin: Lutherisches Verlagshaus, 1963.

Kliefoth, Theodor F. D. "Der 'Schriftbeweis' des Dr. J. Chr. K. von Hofmann." *Kirchliche Zeitschrift* 5 (1858): 635–710. Repr. with five additional parts as *Der Schriftbeweis des Dr. J. Chr. K. von Hofmann.* Schwerin: Otto, 1860.

————. "Zwei politische Theologen. Dr. Daniel Schenkel in Heidelberg und Dr. J. Chr. K. von Hofmann in Erlangen." *Theologische Zeitschrift* 5 (1864): 651–778. Repr., Schwerin: Otto, 1865.

Kolbe, A. "Die Bedeutung Hofmanns für die Kirche und die kirchliche Wissenschaft." *Neue kirchliche Zeitschrift* 2 (1891): 394–407, 675–86.

Kolde, Theodor. *Die Universität Erlangen unter dem Hause Wittelsbach 1810–1910.* Erlangen: A. Deichert, 1910.

Kraus, Hans-Joachim. *Geschichte der historisch-kritischen Erforschung des Alten Testaments von der Reformation bis zur Gegenwart.* 2d ed. Neukirchen: Neukirchener Verlag, 1969.

Kretzel, Hans. *Die Liturgik der Erlanger Theologie: Ihre Geschichte und ihre Grundsätze.* 2d ed. Göttingen: Vandenhoeck and Ruprecht, 1948.

Kühn, Ulrich. "Das Bekenntnis als Grundlage der Kirche. Nachdenkenswerte und problematische Aspekte der Rückbesinnung auf das Bekenntnis in der lutherischen Theologie des 19. Jahrhunderts." Pages 393–413 in *Bekenntnis und Einheit der Kirche: Studien zum Konkordienbuch.* Edited by Martin Brecht and Reinhard Schwarz. Stuttgart: Calwer, 1980.

Kunze, J. "Frank und Hofmann." Pages 235–72 in *Festschrift zum fünfzigjährigen Stiftungsfest des theologischen Studentenvereins Erlangen.* Edited by J. Kunze. Erlangen: Junge & Sohn, 1910.

Leo, Paul. "Revelation and History in J. C. K. von Hofmann." *Lutheran Quarterly* 10 (August 1958): 195–216.

Lindbeck, George A. "The Confessions as Ideology and Witness in the History of Lutheranism." *Lutheran World* 7 (1961): 388–401.

Loewenich, Walther von. "Johannes Christian Konrad von Hofmann: Leben und Werk." Rede anlässlich einer akademischen Gedenkfeier des theologischen Fachbereichs zum 100. Todestag von Hofmanns am 20. Dezember 1977. *Erlanger Universitätsrede* 3,1. Erlangen: University of Erlangen, 1978.

———. "Zur neueren Beurteilung der Theologie Johann Christian Konrad von Hofmanns." *Zeitschrift für Bayerische Kirchengeschichte* 32 (1963): 315–31.

Luthardt, Christoph. "Sendschreiben Dr. Luthardts an Dr. v. Hofmann, das letzte Vierteljahrsheft des fünften Jahrgangs der Kirchlichen Zeitschrift betreffend." *Zeitschrift für Protestantismus und Kirche* 37 (1859): 224–72.

Merz, Georg. *Das bayerische Luthertum.* Munich: Evangelischen Presseverbandes für Bayern, 1955.

Mildenberger, Friedrich. *Geschichte der deutschen evangelischen Theologie im 19. und 20. Jahrhundert.* Stuttgart: W. Kohlhammer, 1981.

———. "Hofmann, Johann Christian Konrad v. (1810–1877)." Pages 477–79 in vol. 15 of *Theologische Realenzyklopädie.* Edited by Gerhard Müller. Berlin: Walter de Gruyter, 1986.

Müller, Gerhard. "Die Erlanger Theologische Fakultät und Wilhelm Löhe im Jahr 1849." Pages 242–54 in *Dem Wort Gehorsam: Landesbischof d. Hermann Dietzfelbinger DD. Zum 65 Geburtstag.* Edited by Gerhard Müller. Munich: Claudius Verlag, 1973.

Oman, John. *The Problem of Faith and Freedom in the Last Two Centuries.* London: Hodder and Stoughton, 1906.

Ott, Heinrich. "Heilsgeschichte." Pages 187–89 in vol. 3 of *Die Religion in Geschichte und Gegenwart.* Edited by Kurt Galling. 3d ed. Tübingen: J. C. B. Mohr (Paul Siebeck), 1962.

Pannenberg, Wolfhart. "Heilsgeschehen und Geschichte." *Kerygma und Dogma* 5 (1959): 218–37, 259–88. ET "Redemptive Event and History." Pages 15–80 in vol. 1 of *Basic Questions in Theology.* Translated by George Kehm. Philadelphia: Westminster, 1970.

Perriraz, Louis. *Historie de la théologie protestante au XIX Siècle surtout en Allemagne.* Neuchatel: Editions Henri Messeiller, 1949.

Peters, Martin. "J. Chr. K. v. Hofmann als praktischer Theologe." *Neue kirchliche Zeitschrift* 30 (1919): 157–90.

Pfleiderer, Otto. *The Development of Theology in Germany since Kant, and Its Progress in Great Britain since 1825.* Translated by J. Frederick Smith. London: Swan Sonnenschein, 1890.

Philippi, Friedrich A. *Dr. v. Hofmann gegenüber lutherischer Versöhnungs- und Rechtfertigungslehre.* Erlangen: T. Bläsing, 1856.

Planck, Adolph. "Schellings nachgelassene Werke und ihre Bedeutung für Philosophie und Theologie: Ein Beitrag zum Verständniss und zur Beurteilung." *Zeitschrift für Protestantismus und Kirche* 39 (1860): 1–42.

Pöhlmann, Hans. "Die Erlanger Theologie: Ihre Geschichte und ihre Bedeutung." *Theologische Studien und Kritiken* 80 (1907): 390–433, 535–563.

Powell, Samuel Morgan. "The Doctrine of the Trinity in Nineteenth-Century German Protestant Theology: Philipp Marheineke, Isaak Dorner, Johann von Hofmann, and Alexander Schweizer." Ph.D. diss., Claremont, 1987.

Preus, Christian K. "The Contemporary Relevance of von Hofmann's Hermeneutical Principles." *Interpretation* 4 (July 1950): 311–21.

——. "The Theology of Johan [sic] Christian Konrad von Hofmann with Special Reference to His Hermeneutical Principles." Th.D. diss., Princeton Theological Seminary, 1948.

Procksch, Otto. "Hofmanns Geschichtsauffassung." *Allgemeine evangelische-lutherische Kirchenzeitung* 43 (4 Nov 1910): 1034–38; 1058–63.

Pünger, B. "J. Chr. K. v. Hofmann." *Protestantische Kirchenzeitung* (1878): 213–22.

Ritschl, Albrecht. *Die christliche Lehre von der Rechtfertigung und Versöhnung.* 3 vols. 3d ed. Bonn: Adolph Marcus, 1888–1889. Repr., Hildesheim: George Olms, 1978. ET of vol. 3, *The Christian Doctrine of Justification and Reconciliation.* Translated by H. R. Mackintosh and A. B. Macaulay. Edinburgh: T & T Clark, 1900. Repr., Clifton, N.J.: Reference Book Publishers, 1966.

——. *Gesammelte Aufsätze.* Edited by Otto Ritschl. Leipzig: A. Deichert, 1896.

——. "Review of *Theologische Ethik* by J. C. K. v. Hofmann." *Theologische Literaturzeitung* 3 (1878): 514–17.

——. "Über das Verhältniss des Bekenntnisses zur Kirche." Pages 1–24 in *Gesammelte Aufsätze.* Edited by Otto Ritschl. Leipzig: Deichert, 1896.

——. "Über die Methodischen Prinzipien der Theologie des Herrn v. Hofmanns." *Allgemeine evangelische-lutherische Kirchenzeitung* 1, 12 (1858): 353–64.

Ritschl, Otto. *Albrecht Ritschls Leben.* 2 vols. Freiburg: J. C. B. Mohr (Paul Siebeck), 1892, 1896.

Rogerson, John. *Old Testament Criticism in the 19th Century: England and Germany.* London: Fortress, 1984.

——. "Geschichte und Altes Testament im 19. Jahrhundert." *Biblische Notizen* 22 (1983): 126–38.

Rutz, H. "Zum Ehrengedächtnis Hofmanns." *Die Volkskirche* 2 (1878): 91–93.

Schaeder, Erich. *Theozentrische Theologie: Eine Untersuchung zur dogmatischen Prinzipienlehre.* 2d ed. 2 vols. Leipzig: A. Deichert, 1914–1916.

Schellbach, Martin. *Theologie und Philosophie bei v. Hofmann. Beiträge zur Förderung christlicher Theologie.* Gütersloh: C. Bertelsmann, 1935.

Schmid, Heinrich. *Dr. v. Hofmanns Lehre von der Versöhnung in ihrem Verhältnis zum kirchlichen Bekenntnis und zur kirchlichen Dogmatik.* Nördlingen: C. H. Beck, 1856.

———. "Zum Gedächtnis an Hofmann." Pages v–xxiii in *Vermischte Aufsätze von Professor v. Hofmann: Eine Auswahl aus der Zeitschrift für Protestantismus und Kirche.* Edited by Heinrich Schmid. Erlangen: A. Deichert, 1878.

Schröer, Henning. "Hermeneutik III: Neues Testament." Pages 144–56 in vol. 15 of *Theologische Realenzyklopädie.* Edited by Gerhard Müller. Berlin: Walter de Gruyter, 1986.

Schultz, Robert C. *Gesetz und Evangelium in der Lutherischen Theologie des 19. Jahrhunderts.* Arbeiten zur Geschichte und Theologie des Luthertums. Vol. 4. Berlin: Lutherisches Verlagshaus, 1958.

Seeberg, Reinhold. *Die Kirche Deutschlands im 19. Jahrhundert. Eine Einführung in die religiösen, theologischen und kirchlichen Fragen der Gegenwart.* 2d ed. Leipzig: A. Deichert, 1904.

Seiler, Christoph von. *Die theologische Entwicklung Martin Kählers bis 1869.* Gütersloh: Gerd Mohn, 1966.

Senft, Christoph. *Wahrhaftigkeit und Wahrheit: Die Theologie des 19. Jahrhunderts zwischen Orthodoxie und Aufklärung.* Tübingen: J. C. B. Mohr (Paul Siebeck), 1956.

Simon, Matthias. "Die konfessionelle Entwicklung Bayerns im 19. Jahrhundert." *Zeitschrift für bayerische Kirchengeschichte* 28 (1959): 206–19.

Spitta, Friedrich. "Zum hundertjährigen Geburtstage J. Chr. K. von Hofmanns." *Monatschrift für Gottesdienst und kirchliche Kunst* 15 (1910): 355–61.

Stählin, L. "J. Chr. K. v. Hofmann." *Allgemeine evangelisch-lutherische Kirchenzeitung* 11 (1878): 937–42; 961–66.

Staats, R. "Der theologiegeschichtliche Hintergrund des Begriffes 'Tatsache.'" *Zeitschrift für Theologie und Kirche* 70 (1973): 316–45.

Steck, Karl Gerhard. "Der Erlanger Hofmann als Politischer Theologe." Pages 419–31 in *Richte unsere Füsse auf den Weg des Friedens. Festschrift für Helmut Gollwitzer.* Edited by A. Bandis. Munich: Kaiser, 1970.

———. "Die Idee der Heilsgeschichte: Hofmann, Schlatter, Cullmann." *Theologische Studien und Kritiken.* Vol. 56. Edited by Karl Barth and Max Geiger. Zollikon: Evangelischer Verlag, 1959.

———. "Johann Christian Konrad von Hofmann (1810–1877)." Pages 99–112 in *Theologen des Protestantismus im 19. und 20. Jahrhundert.* Edited by Martin Greschat. Berlin: W. Kohlhammer, 1978.

Steffen, Bernhard. *Hofmanns und Ritschls Lehren über die Heilsbedeutung des Todes Jesu.* Gütersloh: C. Bertelsmann, 1910.

Stephan, Horst, and Martin Schmidt. *Geschichte der deutschen evangelischen Theologie seit dem deutschen Idealismus.* 3d ed. Berlin: Walter de Gruyter, 1973.

Sturm, Klaus. "Die integrierende Funktion der Ekklesiologie in der lutherisch-konfessionellen Dogmatik des Erlangen Kreises." Th.D. diss., University of Erlangen, 1976.

Swarat, Uwe. "Die Heilsgeschichtliche Konzeption Johannes Chr. K. von Hofmanns." Pages 211–39 in *Glaube und Geschichte: Heilsgeschichte als Thema der Theologie.* Edited by Helge Stadelmann. Giessen: Brunnen, 1986.

Thielicke, Helmut. *Modern Faith and Thought.* Translated by Geoffrey Bromiley. Grand Rapids: Eerdmans, 1990.

Thomasius, Gottfried. *Das Bekenntnis der lutherischen Kirche von der Versöhnung und die Versöhnungslehre D. Chr. K. v. Hofmanns.* Erlangen: T. Bläsing, 1857.

———. *Christi Person und Werk. Darstellung der evangelisch-lutherischen Dogmatik vom Mittelpunkte der Christologie aus.* 3 vols. Erlangen: T. Bläsing, 1853–1861.

Trillhaas, W. "Bemerkungen zum Begriff der Geschichte bei J. Chr. K. v. Hofmann." *Theologische Blätter* 8 (1929): 54–57.

Volck, Wilhelm. *Zur Erinnerung an Johann Christian Konrad von Hofmann.* Erlangen: A. Deichert, 1878.

———. "Zur Versöhnungslehre v. Hofmanns." *Neue kirchliche Zeitschrift* 2 (1891): 845–50.

Wach, Joachim. *Die theologische Hermeneutik von Schleiermacher bis Hofmann.* Vol. 2, *Das Verstehen.* Tübingen: J. C. B. Mohr (Paul Siebeck), 1929. Repr., Hildesheim: Olms, 1966.

Wagner, Siegfried. *Franz Delitzsch: Leben und Werk.* 2d ed. Giessen: Brunnen, 1991.

Wapler, Paul. "Die Genesis der Versöhnungslehre Hofmanns." *Neue kirchliche Zeitschrift* 25 (1914): 167–205.

———. *Johannes v. Hofmann: Ein Beitrag zur Geschichte der theologischen Grundprobleme, der kirchlichen und der politischen Bewegungen im 19. Jahrhundert.* Leipzig: A. Deichert, 1914.

———. "Die Theologie Hofmanns in ihrem Verhältnis zu Schellings positiver Philosophie." *Neue kirchliche Zeitschrift* 16 (1905): 699–718.

Welch, Claude. *Protestant Thought in the Nineteenth Century.* 2 vols. New Haven: Yale University Press, 1972, 1985.

Wendebourg, Ernst-Wilhelm. "Die heilsgeschichtliche Theologie J. Chr. K. v. Hofmanns in ihrem Verhältnis zur romantischen Weltanschauung." *Zeitschrift für Theologie und Kirche* 52 (1955): 64–104.

———. *Die heilsgeschichtliche Theologie J. Chr. K. v. Hofmanns kritisch untersucht, als Beitrag zur Klärung des Problems der Heilsgeschichte.* Göttingen: Vandenhoeck & Ruprecht, 1953.

Wenz, Gunther. *Geschichte der Versöhnungslehre in der evangelischen Theologie der Neuzeit.* 2 vols. Munich: Chr. Kaiser, 1984, 1986.

Weth, Gustav. *Die Heilsgeschichte. Ihr universeller und ihr individueller Sinn in der offenbarungsgeschichtlichen Theologie des 19. Jahrhunderts.* Vol. 2 of series 4 of *Forschungen zur Geschichte und Lehre des Protestantismus.* Edited by Paul Althaus, Karl Barth, and Karl Heim. Munich: Chr. Kaiser, 1931.

Winter, Friedrich Wilhelm. *Die Erlanger Theologie und die Lutherforschung im 19. Jahrhundert.* Gütersloh: Gütersloher Verlagshaus, 1995.

Wittern, Renate, et al., eds. *Die Professoren und Dozenten der Friedrich-Alexander-Universität, Erlangen (1743–1960).* Vol. 1. Erlangen: University of Erlangen, 1993.

Wolf, Karl. *Ursprung und Verwendung des religiösen Erfahrungsbegriffes in der Theologie des 19. Jahrhunderts.* Gütersloh: C. Bertelsmann, 1906.

Wolff, Otto. *Die Haupttypen der neueren Lutherdeutung.* Stuttgart: W. Kohlhammer, 1938.

Woudstra, Sierd. "Old Testament and Holy History: An Analysis and Evaluation of the Views of Johann Christian Konrad von Hofmann." Th.D. diss., Westminster Theological Seminary, 1963.

Zahn, Theodor von. *Johann Chr. K. von Hofmann: Rede zur Feier seines hundertsten Geburtstags in der Aula der Friederico-Alexandrina am 16. Dezember 1910 gehalten.* Leipzig: A. Deichert, 1911.

———. "Lebenserinnerungen Theodor Zahns, 1838–1868." Edited by Friedrich Hauck. *Zeitschrift für bayerische Kirchengeschichte* 20 (1951): 92–93.

Index

Abraham, 168, 204

Adam

first or old (*see also* human beings),
127, 161, 169–70, 189–90, 192,
202, 247

second or new (*see* Jesus Christ, as
new Adam)

allegory, 78

Althaus, Paul, 22n. 17, 37n. 15,
217n. 24, 228n. 17

ambiguity, 231–32, 248–49

anhypostasis (*see* Jesus Christ)

Anselm, 186, 202

apocalyptic, 230–32, 236, 254n. 31,
255

Arianism, 181

atonement

controversy about, 26n. 29, 88,
194–203

as forgiveness of sins, 211

Hofmann's understanding of, 25–28,
187–203, 240–44

as justification, 196–203, 211–12

as reconciliation, xix, xxi, 23, 28,
172, 184, 196

as vicarious satisfaction, xiii, 26n. 30,
27–28, 85–88, 149, 186–87,
195–203

as victory over anti-godly forces,
192–93, 200–201

Auberlen, Karl, 18n. 8, 69n. 25

Augustine, 8, 124n. 8, 137n. 11, 149,
225

Aulèn, Gustav, 200n. 54

Awakening, Religious, xiv, 3–4, 112

Baader, Franz von, 112

Bachmann, Philipp, 3n. 1, 8n. 22,
26n. 29, 102n. 55, 173n. 1

baptism (*see also* experience; means
of grace, sacraments as), xix, 20,
38–39, 41, 52, 54, 208–9, 212

Barrett, William, 130n. 19

Barth, Karl

Church Dogmatics of, 16

on history, 24, 161n. 3, 222n. 4

on Hofmann, xvii–xviii, 19, 23n. 20,
55n. 47, 64, 124–27, 129n. 18,
223n. 5

on "humanity of God," 185n. 23

on method in theology, 50n. 37

on revelation, 46n. 30, 170n. 16

on Trinity, 135–38, 143n. 27, 158,
233–34

Baur, Christian, 16n. 1

Bavaria, 4, 13n. 35,

Beck, Johann, 69n. 25

Behr, Wilfried, 14n. 38, 36n. 14,
39n. 17, 52n. 41, 147n. 34,
159n. 1, 183n. 21, 206nn. 3, 4,
217n. 25

Bengel, Johann, 230

Benjamin, Walter, 131

Benne, Robert, 256

Berlin, university of, 5, 91, 102–3

Bernstein, Richard, 121n. 2

Beyschlag, Karlmann, 8n. 21, 18n. 7,
25n. 25, 42n. 24, 57nn. 50, 51,
62n. 8, 103n. 60, 113n. 86, 174n. 2,
225n. 7

277